D1559405

Did Jesus Exist?

Did Jesus Exist?

G.A.WELLS
Professor of German, Birkbeck College London

Elek/Pemberton London

Published in Great Britain in 1975 by
Elek Books Ltd
54-58 Caledonian Road, London N1 9RN

in association with Pemberton Publishing Co Ltd.

ISBN 0 236 31001 1

Typeset in Great Britain by
Preface Limited, Salisbury, Wilts
in IBM Press Roman
and Printed by
Unwin Brothers Limited, Old Woking, Surrey

To my teacher
F. R. H. ENGLEFIELD
in friendship and gratitude

Bienheureux donc aujourd'hui ceux à qui un Christ pourrait
dire: 'Hommes de peu de foi'!

Guyau

Contents

Acknowledgements and Note on Quotations and Abbreviations

This book is a sequel to my *The Jesus of the Early Christians*, London, 1971 (which I shall call JEC), but will be perfectly intelligible to readers unacquainted with it. To ease the reading of my text I have referred to the works of other authors by the numbers which these works are given in my bibliography below (p 208ff). Abbreviations used only in the bibliography are listed at its head.

The Scripture quotations are (except when otherwise indicated) from the RSV – the Revised Standard Version Bible, copyright 1946, 1952 © 1971 by the Division of Christian Education, National Council of the Churches of Christ in the USA, and used by permission. The NEB or *New English Bible*, (2nd edition, copyright 1970) is used by permission of the Oxford and Cambridge University Presses.

The Old and New Testaments are designated OT and NT.

I follow the usual terminology in calling the first three of the four canonical gospels 'the synoptics'. They are called synoptic because they frequently agree in the subjects treated, and in the order and language of the treatment. And while they thus take, to some extent at any rate, a common view, they all diverge markedly from the fourth gospel.

As a concise means of distinguishing a gospel from the person who wrote it, I refer to the four *gospels* as Mt., Mk., Lk. and Jn., and to their respective *authors* as Matthew, Mark, Luke and John.

For conciseness I have used abbreviations in referring to other books of the New Testament (except where this would give a harsh reading). A statement such as 'the second epistle to the Thessalonians, chapter two', would be wasteful of print and would weary the reader; and I ask him to accept '2 Thess. 2' as a rational alternative, to which the list on page xi supplies the key.

I obtained much of the literature I consulted from Dr Williams's Library in Gordon Square, founded by an eighteenth-century Christian minister for readers of any faith or of none. I am glad to record my debt to the impartiality of the founder and of the library trustees, and to the kindness and helpfulness of the present library staff. I only wish I could say anything remotely comparable about the reading room of the British Museum.

I compiled the indexes at some of the numerous boring committee meetings with which universities and colleges today contrive to waste the time of their staffs.

My secretary, Mrs Evelyn Stone, has shown unfailing patience and care in typing many revisions of my manuscript. I am also grateful to my friends Dr D. Banthorpe, Dr C. Lofmark and Dr D. Oppenheimer for their constructive criticism.

Abbreviations (In Alphabetical Order) for Books of the New Testament

Acts	The Acts of the Apostles
Coloss.	Paul's epistle to the Colossians
1 and 2 Cor.	Paul's first and second epistles to the Corinthians
Ephes.	Epistle to the Ephesians (ascribed to Paul in the canon)
Gal.	Paul's epistle to the Galatians
Hebrews	Epistle to the Hebrews
James	The general epistle of James
Jn.	The gospel according to John
1, 2 and 3 Jn.	The three epistles ascribed in the canon to John
Jude	The general epistle of Jude
Mk.	The gospel according to Mark
Mt.	The gospel according to Matthew
Lk.	The gospel according to Luke
1 and 2 Peter	The two epistles ascribed in the canon to Peter
Phil.	Paul's epistle to the Philippians
Rev.	The Revelation of John (The New Testament Apocalypse)
Rom.	Paul's epistle to the Romans
1 and 2 Thess.	Paul's first and second epistles to the Thessalonians
1 and 2 Tim. / Titus	known as 'Pastoral epistles' — The first and second epistles to Timothy (ascribed in the canon to Paul); the epistle to Titus (ascribed in the canon to Paul)

Introduction

Now that uncritical acceptance of the NT is much less common than was formerly the case, theories are multiplying as to how it came to be written and to what extent the persons and events referred to in it have any historical basis. It is not surprising that some of these theories are not much less extravagant than the one they seek to replace. A good example is Allegro's (4), on which I have commented elsewhere (406). Most of these theories, however, do not impugn the historicity of Jesus, and there is a widespread belief that his teaching and character, as given in the gospels, could not have been invented. But in fact the teaching did not need to be invented, as it is widely admitted to be totally unoriginal. As for his character, it is a mixture of violence, intolerance, pity, pride, patience – in fact it varies according to the context. About as much invention would have been required as was needed by the authors of the Arabian Nights. Furthermore, Jesus' miraculous powers, if true, make any attempt to describe his character in human terms inappropriate. A man who can raise the dead, walk on water and turn it into wine, and be resurrected after three days of death is obviously not describable in terms of human character, any more than Samson, Hercules or Venus.

It is also commonly supposed that a historical Jesus was a necessary starting-point for Christianity. But when called upon to explain Jesus' rôle in Christian origins, the various apologists all give different accounts. Professor Barclay, for instance, surrenders (17) the virgin birth, the bodily resurrection, and the claim that Jesus set up a new standard of morality. Other theologians have made him into a freedom-fighter; yet others admit that very little is known of him at all. Professor Trilling concedes that 'not a single date in his life' can be determined with certainty, and that it is indeed 'strange that, with modern scientific methods and enormous labour and ingenuity, so little has been established' (393, p 64). During the past thirty years theologians have come increasingly to admit that it is no longer possible to write a biography of him, since documents earlier than the gospels tell us next to nothing of his life, while the gospels present the 'kerygma' or proclamation of faith, not the Jesus of history. Many contemporary theologians therefore regard the quest of the historical Jesus as both hopeless and religiously irrelevant – in that the few things which can, allegedly, be known of his life are unedifying and do not make him an appropriate object for worship. (See the recent surveys by Downing, 136, and McArthur, 291). Bultmann and his school go so far as to say that

Christianity began only 'after Easter', which the more conservative Jeremias finds an astounding thesis, comparable to the suggestion that Islam began only after the death of Mahommed (332, p 17). Kahl even holds that nothing at all is known of Jesus beyond the bare fact that he 'existed at a date and place which can be established approximately' (242, p 103). On this view, both his teaching and his manner of death remain unknown, so that 'the name of Jesus is bound to remain cryptic and meaningless, indistinguishable from a myth'. But why, then, insist on his historicity? To put my point another way: William Tell is a myth. Everything about the origin of the Swiss Confederation that can be explained at all can be explained without supposing his existence. But there are many things difficult to explain if we do not assume the existence in the sixteenth century of Martin Luther. To which of these two cases is a Jesus who is no more than a name parallel? The question has only to be asked in this form to make it apparent that an unknown Jesus is not helpful as an explicans. An explanation must be given in terms of something understood, not in terms of an enigma.

The tenacity with which apologists cling to the name of Jesus as the founder of Christianity – however vaguely the person with that name is conceived – is readily explicable; for the name is firmly associated in most minds with the biography, as portrayed in the gospels, of the person so named. And so if it be admitted that Christianity originated from one Jesus, then it is impossible to prevent the tacit assumption that it originated broadly in the manner described in the gospels.

In my earlier book, *The Jesus of the Early Christians* (which I shall call JEC), my purpose was to show the difficulties and problems which arise when the gospels are interpreted as historical records, and how Christianity could have arisen even had there been no historical Jesus. Some theological reviewers (e.g. Professors Grayston and Simon, 183 and 372) admitted that I had stated serious 'difficulties' to which a satisfactory solution has not yet been found. Others, however, took the view that only trained theologians and not an outsider such as myself can contribute to the discussion. I would reply that in the past orthodox theologians have repeatedly been caused to revise their views by amateurs not committed to orthodox premises. In Germany the whole debate about the historical Jesus was initiated in 1778 by Reimarus, who was not a theologian. In the mid-nineteenth century, Colenso, a practical missionary bishop, was led to his important work on the Pentateuch not by the scholarship of expert theologians, but by awkward questions from his Zulu converts. And Kuenen, the spokesman of the experts, admitted that Colenso's book had forced him to view the Pentateuch differently. Sometimes the work of the amateur critic has survived the oblivion which has overtaken the experts he criticized. Voltaire, for instance, is more widely read today than are the theologians who were his contemporaries. Outsiders, then, have made a significant contribution to the debate and I am glad to find a theologian expressing uneasiness because today 'most serious research into the teaching of Jesus is carried on by historians who are also Christians, and who, therefore, by definition have some concept of the risen Lord of their faith and experience, and of his teaching to them' (320, p 50). What Jesus taught, indeed whether he led a human life at all, is a historical problem, to be examined by those who are prepared to use the ordinary tools of historical enquiry. It is not to be settled by enthusiastic believers or disbelievers, whose approach is sentimental rather than scientific, nor by people who allow their profession to influence the conclusion they reach.

In the present book I discuss (in chapters 3–7) more fully than in JEC the gospel evidence for Jesus' existence. I try to answer such questions as: do the 'twelve apostles' prove his historicity? Were the James and the Cephas whom Paul says he met in Jerusalem companions of a historical Jesus? If Jesus is a fiction, how are we to explain the gospel accounts of his connection with Nazareth and of his relations with John the Baptist and Pilate, who certainly existed? And how could incidents so discreditable as his betrayal by one of his closest associates ever have been invented? Reviewers of JEC complained that I gave little indication of how gospel stories, if they are not true, came to be told and collected. In this present book, I try to indicate more fully what motives led to their composition.

Before these chapters on the gospels comes chapter 2, on the early Christian epistles – the longest chapter in the book, and of crucial importance to the argument. The NT epistles deal with a later period (post AD 30) than the gospels purport to portray, and are printed in Bibles after the gospels. It is therefore easy for the lay reader to assume that any account of Christian origins must begin with the gospels. In fact, however, nearly all the epistles were written *earlier* than the gospels and therefore provide the most important clues as to how the early Christians conceived Jesus. I give evidence that these epistles are not merely astoundingly silent about the historical Jesus, but also that the Jesus of Paul's letters (the earliest of the NT epistles and hence the earliest extant Christian documents) is in some respects incompatible with the Jesus of the gospels; that neither Paul, nor those of his Christian predecessors whose views he assimilates into his letters, nor the Christian teachers he attacks in them, are concerned with such a person; and that the same is true of the other NT epistles written before the end of the first century. The facts are admitted but not explained in some current theological scholarship, and my purpose has been both to account for them, and to suggest how it came about that, by the time the epistles of the early second century and the gospels were written, Jesus had come to be regarded so differently, and as a contemporary of Pilate. Chapter 3 gives evidence that all four gospels even Mk., which theologians date at about AD 70 – may well have been written only near the end of the first century. These dates are important, since any theory of how Christian thinking developed depends on establishing what documents and what stock of ideas were already available to each particular apologist.

There is little basis for the oft-repeated assertion that Paul's 'Christ crucified' was an embarrassment to him and to early Christians generally, and would therefore not have been invented. This issue is discussed both in chapter 4 and chapter 8, which takes up the theme of the second part of JEC, where I specified elements in the pagan and Jewish thinking of the first century AD from which the Christian idea of a god who came to earth to suffer, die and rise again, could have been derived. I try to come to terms with recent criticisms of the view that a resurrected saviour god was widely worshipped by pre-Christian pagans. I also draw on recent discussion concerning the evidence for a pre-Christian gnosticism; and I argue that the social and intellectual conditions in the Roman Empire at the beginning of our era favoured the amalgamation of existing religious ideas. My readers can judge for themselves whether I have surmounted what Professor Trocmé takes to be two 'insurmountable difficulties' which denial of Jesus' historicity entails: namely (i) the absence of any such denial in antiquity, 'even amongst the adversaries of Christianity and the heretics who were most inclined to deny the humanity of Christ'; and (ii) 'the Jewish and more particularly Palestinian features which abound in the synoptic gospels and make it impossible to regard them as the later creation of an almost entirely Hellenized Church' (396, p 8).

In JEC I stressed the work of the nineteenth and early twentieth century theologians, especially the Germans, for the tradition of candid discussion has been longer and better established there than here. Some reviewers charged me with ignoring later scholarship altogether and implied that the whole idea of Jesus not being a historical personage can be supported only by such oversight. On the other hand, some theologians concede that it is important not to lose sight of older scholarship. My discussion of the story of Jesus' birth, as given in Lk., drew extensively on the evidence marshalled by Schürer, and it has recently been admitted that 'most of the recent attempts to rescue the historical reliability of Luke have failed to throw any fresh light on the matter' and 'rest more on the hope that the reader may not have access to the material in Schürer than on new evidence or fresh ideas' (10, p 146). Another old book to which I referred Bousset's *Kyrios Christos* of 1913 – has recently (1970) been translated into English and welcomed by a theologian on the ground that later writers on NT Christology have 'almost invariably' failed to face squarely the issues raised by Bousset (50, p 450). I also drew on Dibelius' 1909 study of the prominence in Paul's thinking of angels and other supernatural entities. Caird complained in 1956 that the majority of later works on Paul's theology, 'especially those written in English', have 'evaded this aspect of his teaching' or given it but 'niggardly acknowledgement' (94, p viii). Such examples illustrate why I placed reliance on the older commentators. When these older writers are more conservative than their modern successors, then they are sometimes, even today, preferred. Neil, for instance, commenting on recent work on Lk. and on Acts which has shown how untrustworthy these books are as history, complains that it

4

pays 'too little attention to the established findings of a past generation which point in the opposite direction' (308, p 19).

In the present volume I have drawn extensively on recent theological work, and my readers will be able to see whether I have thereby weakened my case. My references are not meant as a display of learning (of which some critics of JEC accused me) but serve the purpose of acquainting my readers with the radical arguments advanced by many theologians today in books and articles that are seldom consulted except by other theologians. The nineteenth century theologians thought that they were serving Christianity by clearing away an encrusting layer of myth and misconception, after which the central truth would shine forth more brightly. Their modern successors do not find it easy to retain this confidence. Many of them proceed with valuable detailed investigations without asking how their findings affect the faith. But when this question is faced, uneasiness is sometimes apparent. Braun, for instance, concedes that the NT is, for us, an alien book: 'Its statements are to a great extent legendary in character; it shares the ancient belief in demoniacal possession; it reckons on the world coming to a speedy end; and it draws the path of Jesus in the colours of the gnostic redeemer myth'. He nevertheless claims that we can often discern what historical truth underlies the NT legends; that, for instance, Jesus was born in Nazareth, not Bethlehem; and there was 'a stage of Christian tradition which did not regard Mary as a virgin mother' (72, pp 285, 288). But, as other theologians have rightly insisted, early tradition and historical truth are not synonymous. An early tradition is still a tradition, not necessarily a reliable record. Fawcett has recently claimed that 'no known mythological pattern appears in the gospels without being twisted into an entirely new shape by the stubborn facts of history' (153, p 33). This means either that we have independent means (not specified by Fawcett) of settling what is fact and what is fiction in the gospels; or that any deviation from a 'known mythological pattern' is itself proof of fact. But apart from the difficulty of establishing what constitutes a 'mythological pattern', it ought to be obvious that the gospel writers were to some extent constrained by earlier traditions about Jesus – not necessarily historically reliable ones, but too well established to be totally rejected. It will be important to my purpose to show how the Christian writers of the late first and early second centuries reworked the traditions that reached them; and such reworking itself suffices to explain deviation from *a priori* mythological schemes.

It is with contemporary theologians as it was with Strauss: they are at their weakest when defending the creed which their own critical work has done so much to destroy. As I shall not have occasion to comment on their more philosophical apologetics in the body of this book, a brief account of how they defend those gospel stories which they admit to be unhistorical will be appropriate in this introduction. Now that the mythical character of much of the Bible has become too obvious to be denied, the

5

idea has become popular that myth is 'an important form of religious truth' (336, p 33). According to Fawcett, the most recent apologist, we should not make the 'arbitrary judgement' of calling myth fiction and history fact, but should rather 'accept that myth is a means whereby the meaning and spiritual reality of the world can be expressed' (153, pp 22, 24). The man of science, the philosopher, the prophet, the preacher all claim to reveal the truth; but as they do not all reach the same conclusions, either some of them must be mistaken, or there is more than one kind of truth. Since it is impossible that there should be agreement as to who is mistaken, it is good tactics to claim that there is a special kind of truth for each investigator. Myth and science, Fawcett insists, represent different kinds of truth (p 39). The obvious corollary is that scientific evidence is irrelevant to beliefs based on myth.

I will conclude this introduction with a criticism of Dr Robinson's discussion of this matter. Other apologists of course come forward with other arguments, but I propose to discuss his because he is particularly well-known as an NT scholar.

Dr Robinson's discussion of this question of myth includes the claim that:

'Myth relates to what is deepest in human experience, to something much more primal and archetypal and potent than the intellect. Psychologically and sociologically myth has been the binding force holding individuals and societies together. The loosening of it has had a disintegrative effect on our culture . . . . ' (338, p 20)

There is here, first, a mystification: myth is declared to be 'something much more primal and archetypal and potent' than intellect. In truth, a myth, or a narrative of any kind, can either convey some ideas, or stimulate some emotions, or have both of these effects. Psychology knows of nothing else in the mind to which appeal can be made. The truth underlying what Robinson says is that myths often convey ideas and emotions linked with social instincts. The belief, for instance, among Hitler's Germans that they were all men of the same 'blood' had a cohesive effect on the society which accepted it. And the same may be true of many other beliefs which a community has in common. The purpose of Robinson's argument is fairly clear. He is implying that, now that there is no longer universal acceptance of such Christian myths as the resurrection, society has become hopelessly divided into conflicting factions. What he overlooks is that myth is cohesive in its effects only when there is no rival, competing myth. In an isolated community such uniformity of outlook may well obtain, for all animals are conservative in a static environment. It is only when conditions change that new forms of behaviour arise. When, however, there is interchange of ideas, then rival ideas and rival myths compete for supremacy. If the ideas in question are verifiable (as in the case of scientific ideas and hypotheses), experience and experiment will in time discredit one view and establish another. In the case of myths,

6

however, where no practical tests can settle their truth or falsehood, rival systems may divide a community. The cohesive effects which Robinson stresses will only be possible if there exists a strong central authority to suppress any deviation from the myths which this authority approves – as in mediaeval Europe, in Nazi Germany, and in Eastern Europe today. In sum, in order to discourage us from rejecting Christian myths as fiction, Robinson (i) posits a fantastic psychological apparatus, and (ii) alleges cohesive effects which, in truth, are produced by myths only in specialized circumstances.

Robinson refers (336, p 24) with approval to what he calls Bultmann's 'critique of mythology', that is, the view that the gospel myths are a kind of 'language' in which the evangelists tried to express the 'depth, dimension and significance' of 'the historical event of Jesus of Nazareth'. But this theory of Bultmann-Robinson leaves us faced with the questions: what *was* the historical event, and who were the men who were able to judge of its depth, dimension and significance? And what other means have we for answering these questions except inferences from the gospels themselves, for we know nothing about their authors and have no independent knowledge of the 'historical event'? We cannot possibly know whether these unknown persons were capable of estimating correctly the depth, dimension and significance of the unknown historical event, and if they were capable, how they would set about 'expressing' it in the 'language' of myth. It is obvious that he who undertakes to 'interpret' this mythological language may give completely free reign to his imagination. We have no means of testing what he claims, and the apologists are not even agreed as to what constitutes an appropriate method of interpretation.

The stories of Jesus' birth and infancy in Mt. and in Lk. have recently been much discussed apropos of gospel myths and their significance. In JEC I dwelt on these birth narratives because they illustrate so well the type of difficulty and problem present everywhere in the gospels: namely that the silence of the earliest documents (in this case the NT epistles and Mk.) is superseded by later narratives which contradict each other, are sometimes self-stultifying, are uncorroborated by external testimony, and also display the writers' obvious desire to invent incidents as fulfilment of prophecy. Nevertheless, the birth narratives are, even today, used as a basis for inferences about Jesus' biography. Professor Yamauchi, for instance, claims that 'it is now certain that Jesus was born before 4 BC' – because of Mt.'s story that the magi inquired of him from Herod, who died in that year (416, p 97)! Some apologists deny that the gospels allege a virgin birth at all. Professor Barclay maintains (17) that they represent Jesus' origin as 'a quite ordinary birth' and that 'the holy one' or Holy Ghost did no more than bless the intercourse of the parents. This seems a strange interpretation to put upon the following passages:

(i) 'Now the birth of Jesus Christ took place in this way. When his mother Mary had been betrothed to Joseph, before they came

7

together she was found to be with child of the Holy Spirit.' (Mt.
1:18)

(ii)   'Joseph . . . took his wife, but knew her not until she had borne a
son.' (Mt. 1:24—5)

(iii) 'And Mary said to the angel, "How shall this be, since I have no
husband?" And the angel said to her, "The Holy Spirit will come
upon you".' (Lk. 1:34—5)

Dr Robinson likewise believes that 'human intercourse' is in no wise ruled
out by such passages (338, p 50). He admits that Matthew states clearly
enough that Joseph was not the father of Jesus and had no intercourse
with Mary until after Jesus' birth. But he holds that this does not exclude
prior intercourse between Mary and some unknown male which Joseph
subsequently condoned on the basis of the angel's statement to him that
the foetus was 'of the Holy Ghost' — a statement which, in Robinson's
view, does not exclude normal conception, but may simply affirm 'the
initiative of God in and through it all' (338, p 46). In other words, the
Holy Ghost did no more than bless the intercourse of the parents, and did
not make superfluous the role of the father. In the case of Luke's
narrative, harmonization of the evidence is more difficult, and Robinson
admits (p 45n) that the first three chapters of that gospel may represent a
combination of conflicting traditions (cf. pp 159f below).

The reason why Dr Robinson is so anxious to leave open the possibility
that Jesus originated in the same way as any other human being is that,
unless this is the case, he could not have been what we understand by
human; in which case Robinson would have failed in his purpose of solving
'the problem of Christology', namely to show 'how Jesus can be fully God
and fully man, and yet genuinely one person' (336, pp 64—5). The simple
answer is, of course, that the whole thing is an absurdity and that nobody
in his senses should try to solve such a pseudo-problem. The real problem
is, how did such a contradictory conception ever get into the minds of
rational beings, and this is a problem for the psychologist and the
historian. We cannot, in any case, understand how Jesus can be 'truly God'
unless we know what is meant by God; and Robinson is not here very
helpful. The mystery of *theos*, he declares, is 'the mystery of what lies
ultimately at the heart of being' (338, p 5). But how can 'being' be said to
have a 'heart' 'at' which something 'ultimately' lies? These must be
metaphors and they do not help out the description, but conceal an
absence of coherent ideas. He adds that this mystery 'points to the
ultimate, incommunicable ineffable mystery of reality'. In this type of
writing one thing is commonly said to 'point to' another when the author
wishes to posit some connection between the two, but has no intelligible
relationship in mind. And what are we to make of the entities so linked? Is
there any difference between 'being' and 'reality'? The plausibility of
much of Robinson's book depends on the very dubious assumption that
such phrases do mean something.

Robinson does not wish to offend older-type Christians by categorically denying e.g. either that the evangelists allege a virgin birth, or that this allegation may be true (338, p 138). But he realizes (336, p 43) that such traditional views are great obstacles to 'intelligent faith'; so he tries to show that the evangelists are not unequivocally committed to them. We must therefore have two interpretations of the gospel. We must allow virgin birth, physical resurrection, or any other proposition of traditional Christianity, together with 'rational' alternatives. In the case of the resurrection, the alternative he proposes is that the disciples experienced hallucinations which made them love one another (338, pp 130–1). He even argues – on the basis of his doctrine that myth is a form of truth – that the mutual incompatibility of the traditional and the new interpretations is only apparent. They are 'simply different ways of expressing reality' and 'we must choose whatever means most to us' (p 195).

Some people think that these matters are better not discussed at all. After the publication of JEC I received a number of letters arguing (1) that, if such a book is widely read, people will lose the religious consolation they need in times of distress; and (2) that religious belief is necessary to make people behave themselves decently. I would reply that (1) if my arguments are wrong, they will in time be disposed of; and that if they are correct, then it is not worth-while suppressing them to benefit the deluded. Can it still seriously be argued that one should encourage people to believe what suits them rather than what is true? Furthermore, (2) if we are to be truthful and unselfish because Jesus died on the cross for us (as is implied by Titus 2:14), then it may seem natural that we should cease to regard these virtues if we come to think that he never existed. But we find them respected all over the world, and centuries before the Christian era. They have their real foundation in human social instincts, which prompt all normal men to consider the interests of their fellows, and in human experience of life in a community.

I have also been asked whether the non-existence of Jesus need make any difference to anyone's religious ideas. This is a matter on which theologians are divided. Bultmann's view is that if the Jesus of faith is religiously satisfying, his historicity need not be insisted on. Nineham has replied that such a standpoint reduces the gospel to a senseless paradox; that he cannot believe that God would 'proclaim salvation through a series of false statements about the life of a man who either never lived or was in fact *toto caelo* different from the statements about him' (313, p 13). With this I can sympathize. If Jesus is the revelation of God in human form, then clearly, if there was no human form, there was no revelation of God. If however the believer is prepared to disregard questions of mere historical fact, and concentrate on some kind of 'higher' truth which is embodied in the gospels, then my views need not concern him, any more than his concern me.

1 Jewish and Pagan Testimony to Jesus

There is widespread belief that Jewish and pagan testimony establishes Jesus' existence beyond all reasonable doubt, and makes any further discussion of the matter unnecessary. The principal Jewish witness is the historian Josephus (d. ca. AD 100). He makes no mention of Christians, who presumably existed only as an obscure sect during the period about which he was writing (which extended up to AD 73), and not as followers of a historical Jesus of renown. His works do indeed contain two passages about Jesus the Christ. But the longer of these has been shown fairly conclusively to be wholly a Christian interpolation. It is a glowing description which no orthodox Jew could have written. If Josephus had really believed what he is here represented as saying, he would not have restricted his remarks to a paragraph of ten lines. Furthermore, the passage occurs in a context concerning the misfortunes of the Jews, with which it has no connection, except from the standpoint of a Christian, who would naturally regard Jesus' condemnation by Pilate at the demand of the Jewish leaders as the very worst misfortune ever to have befallen the Jews. That the passage thus divides the responsibility for Jesus' death between Romans and Jews suggests an acquaintance with the gospels (see below, p 63). Other aspects of the passage, as Conzelmann has recently pointed out (103, p 622), view Jesus not merely in a Christian manner, but specifically in the manner propounded in Lk.-Acts — works which were certainly not available to Josephus. Attempts are still made to defend some of the statements in the passage by regarding it as a Christian reworking of something much less complimentary that Josephus wrote about Jesus at this point. (This is the view argued by the late Paul Winter in the revised English edition of Schürer, 360, pp 432ff). But this defence does not do justice to the fact that, if the passage is excised, the argument runs on in proper sequence.

These objections also apply to a more plausible version of this passage about Jesus which is quoted from Josephus in Arabic translation by the tenth century bishop Agapius of Hierapolis in his Arabic *World History*. This version, because less complimentary to Jesus, has been taken by Professor Pines (324) to represent what Josephus actually wrote (with perhaps just a minimum of Christian retouching). On this view, the familiar Greek text of the passage is a much more radical Christian reworking of the original. But even Agapius makes Josephus say that Jesus 'was perhaps the Messiah' — a statement which is still too friendly to have been made by one who was, on his own declaration, a follower of the Pharisees (see Morton Smith's review of Pines' book, 375). Bammel has shown (15) that the features characteristic of Agapius' version could well have been designed to promote Christian interests in the three-cornered fight between Christianity, Judaism and Islam; and that the version is therefore more likely to have 'originated in an Islamic environment than in an earlier one'.

The second passage in Josephus which mentions Jesus consists of half a dozen words in a paragraph about an intemperate Sadducean high priest who in AD 62 brought a number of men before the Sanhedrin as 'breakers of the law' and 'delivered them to be stoned'. The victims are described as 'James and certain others', and James is further specified as 'the brother of Jesus, him called Christ'. Now it is unlikely that Josephus would have mentioned Jesus here simply — as it were — in passing, when he mentions him nowhere else. Nor can his silence be defended by alleging that he habitually suppresses mention of leaders of Messianic proportions. O'Neill gives details of his mention of 'perhaps ten leaders who gathered followings and might have been considered Messiahs by a people who were looking for the Messiah'. None of these men actually called themselves Messiah, but neither — according to O'Neill and other theologians — did Jesus (317, pp 158, 165). In Josephus' entire work the term 'Christ' occurs only in the two passages about Jesus and his brother James. This hardly strengthens the case for their authenticity. Schürer, Zahn, von Dobschütz and Juster are among the scholars who have regarded the words 'the brother of Jesus, him called Christ' as interpolated. The words have the character of a brief marginal gloss, later incorporated innocently into the text. Josephus probably wrote of the death of a *Jewish* Jerusalem leader called James, and a Christian reader thought the reference must be to James the brother of the Lord who, according to Christian tradition, led the Jerusalem Church about the time in question. This reader accordingly noted in the margin: 'James = the brother of Jesus, him called Christ' (cf. the wording of Mt. 1:16: 'Jesus, him called Christ') and a later copyist took this note as belonging to the text and incorporated it. Other interpolations are known to have originated in precisely such a way. And it is also of interest that even a second century Christian account of 'James the brother of the Lord' (that of Hegesippus, preserved as a quotation in Eusebius) represents him as in some respects a Jewish rather than a Christian saint. This lends some force to my suggestion that the James of whom Josephus wrote was within Judaism.

In another passage Josephus mentions John the Baptist. Barrett has shown that it differs significantly from the gospels in the vocabulary with which it refers to him; and it is on other grounds almost certainly genuine (see below, p 152). But it also qualifies John with the phrase 'him with the byname the Baptist', and Barrett thinks that this may be 'a Christian explanatory insertion' (23, p 26). If interpolation is admitted as a possibility here, it can be urged in the phrase qualifying James.

11

The other principal Jewish source is the Talmud, and Klausner's very full survey of the relevant material in it led him to the conclusion that the earliest references to Jesus in rabbinical literature occur not earlier than about the beginning of the second century, and that the Talmud thus informs us 'what the "Sages of Israel" thought of his origin and teaching some seventy years after he was crucified' (251, p 20). If there had been a historical Jesus who had anything like the career ascribed to him in the gospels, the absence of earlier references becomes very hard to explain. When Rabbis do begin to mention him, they are so vague in their chronology that they differ by as much as 200 years in the dates they assign to him (see below, pp 198f). It is clear from this that they never thought of testing whether he had existed, but took for granted that the name stood for a real person. And according to Professor Barclay, we are uncritically to follow their example; for he contends that Jesus must be historical because no Jew (as far as we know) ever denied his historicity.

Dr Stockwood finds it significant (379) that modern Rabbis believe Jesus existed, even though they have no motive for wishing that he did. One could also, in this connection, point to the relevant writings of psycho-analysts and Marxists, who also have accepted a historical Jesus whom their own teachings do not require.[1] But let us at least see what modern Jewish scholarship, as represented by Sandmel and Goldstein, has to say about Jesus' historicity. Sandmel concedes that what knowledge we have of him 'comes only from the NT', 'since he went unknown in the surviving Jewish and pagan literature of his time'; and that passages about him in the ancient rabbinic literature reflect NT material and give no information that is independent of Christian tradition. Goldstein, he says, takes the contrary view, but 'what he ends up with is so little material as to make it useless', except 'to refute those who deny that there ever was a Jesus' (345, pp 17, 28). But this is to claim for Goldstein's evidence more than he himself does. He admits that the five 'authentic passages' about Jesus in the 'vast' rabbinic literature of the first two and a quarter centuries AD do not conclusively establish his historicity, as none of them can be shown to be sufficiently early.[2] That the Talmud is useless as a source of reliable information about Jesus is conceded by most Christian scholars. Bornkamm declares that it 'betrays no independent knowledge whatsoever and is nothing but a polemical and tendentious misrepresentation of the Christian tradition. It makes Jesus into a magician, seducer and political agitator, and tries to justify his condemnation' (55, p 28). Thus it is clear that Jewish traditions, though rich and detailed, contain no independent reference to a historical Jesus, though Jews in the second century adopted uncritically the Christian assumption that he had really lived.

The pagan references to Jesus in the first 150 years of our era are no more helpful, and a well-known classical scholar has declared that pagan and Jewish texts alike 'contribute nothing' (157, p 189). Professor Martin has censured me (289) for not mentioning the testimony of Thallus. But articles on the sources for Jesus' life in Christian religious encyclopaedias either make no reference to him at all, or mention him only in order to say that he cannot be included among the witnesses to Jesus' historicity. His *History* has not survived, and only a few references to it in Christian writers are extant. Of these the one that Martin has in mind is the statement of Julius Africanus (d. ca. 240) who, while discussing the three hour darkness from noon which covered the earth at Jesus' crucifixion (Mk. 15:33), said: 'Thallus says — wrongly it seems to me — that this darkness was an eclipse of the sun'. Now of course it was not an eclipse: according to the gospels, Jesus died at the passover, when an eclipse of the sun is impossible, as the full moon cannot lie between the sun and the earth. Schweizer has noted that 'Mark is thinking of ... Amos 8:9, according to which the sun will set at noon and darkness will cover the earth at midday on the Day of the Lord, i.e. the Day of Judgement ... Mark is therefore trying to say that ... what the prophets had been expecting on the day of God's fulfilment of his purpose has taken place' (367, p 10). Clearly, disappointment at Jesus' failure to come in his glory to judge and end the world led believers to concentrate their attention on what had already been achieved by his first coming, and in this way to invent such a tradition as this one recorded in Mk. But let us return to Thallus. He may have made no mention at all of Jesus or Jewish history, but simply have recorded (as did Phlegon and presumably other chroniclers) the eclipse of the sun in the reign of Tiberius for which astronomers have calculated the date 24 November, AD 29. It may have been Africanus who brought Jesus into the argument by retorting — from his knowledge of Mk. — that this was no eclipse but a supernatural event. If, however, Thallus did mention the death of Jesus, then his testimony would be important if it antedated the gospel traditions. But in fact all we know of him is that he may well have written earlier than Phlegon (a freedman of Hadrian, who reigned AD 117—38), from whom Eusebius supposes he took his information about the eclipse.[3] If he wrote in the second century (as Jacoby suggests, 220, p 835) and if he mentioned Jesus' crucifixion at all, he probably derived his information from what Christians were then alleging, and is therefore not an independent witness.

The one pagan reference to which appeal is still commonly made is the statement of Tacitus that Christians 'derived their name and origin from Christ, who, in the reign of Tiberius, had suffered death by the sentence of the procurator Pontius Pilate'. Tacitus wrote this about AD 120, and by then Christians had themselves come to believe that Jesus had died in this way. I tried to show (JEC, pp 187—8) that there are good reasons for supposing that Tacitus was simply repeating what was then the Christian view, and that he is therefore not an independent witness. I did not (as I have been accused of doing) *assume* that Tacitus was repeating what contemporary Christians believed. I gave reasons for thinking this to be probable, which is quite a different thing. Trilling, even though an orthodox apologist, goes so far as to state that 'what Tacitus actually says

13

could have reached him from any educated contemporary' and is 'no more than what could be learned anywhere in Rome' (393, pp 58–9). But in thus conceding the main point at issue Trilling has obscured the fact that Tacitus obviously considered it necessary to explain to his educated readers what manner of persons Christians are. He evidently did not expect the educated public of his own day to know, even though, in the same context, he implies that as early as Nero's reign (fifty years earlier) the common people of Rome knew and hated them. This is valuable evidence that Christianity had made little headway among the educated Romans of Tacitus' day. How came it, then, that he himself knew something of them? As governor of Asia about AD 112 he may well have had the same kind of trouble with them that Pliny experienced as governor of Bithynia at that very time (see below, p 42). The cities of Asia included some of the earliest Christian congregations (Rev. 1:4) and may well have been the foci for active disturbance between pagan and Christian: for some of these cities were 'centres of a strong national Roman feeling . . . The emperor-cult was especially vigorous in that region, and the older deities also had not lost their hold on the enthusiastic devotion of the populace' (Merrill, 296, p 97). Merrill adds wryly that 'it is altogether likely that Tacitus returned to Rome from his province with no favourable opinion indeed of Christianity, but with some knowledge of it that he might not have acquired without his period of official service in the particular province, and that his fellow-citizens of his own class at Rome would hardly be expected to possess'.

The only supposition which would make Tacitus' testimony independent of Christian tradition, and therefore of great value, would be that he derived his information from a Roman record of the crucifixion. But that his statement was not based on any such close inquiry into the matter is suggested by the fact that he gives Pilate an incorrect title. An inscription found in 1961 records the dedication by Pilate of a building in honour of Tiberius, and shows that he was 'prefect', not procurator, of Judaea (391, p 224 gives a photograph). Dodd (133, p 96n) thinks that the title used by Tacitus is an anachronism; for provincial governors of equestrian status bore the title 'procurator Augusti' only from the time of Claudius (i.e. from AD 41). That Tacitus used the term current in his own lifetime suggests, then, that he did not obtain his information from records or archives. The same conclusion is also supported by his failure to name the executed man. He says nothing of 'Jesus' and uses the title 'Christ' as if it were a proper name.

The Rev. Dr Bouquet insists that an 'undisputed record' of the execution of Jesus by Pilate is extant. But his only evidence is this Tacitus passage and the gospels; this late material does not suffice to nullify earlier Christian traditions about his death which (as I shall show in the next chapter) view it quite differently. A comparison with the evidence concerning William Tell is relevant here. Tell was long believed to have founded the Swiss Confederation. Evidence for this from the time of his supposed existence is nil, but within two hundred years of this time every reference to him assumes that he did so. Similarly, with Jesus, the view that he died under Pilate is taken for granted from about AD 110, and it long escaped notice that this is not alleged of him in any document — Christian, Jewish or pagan — that can confidently be dated earlier than Mk. (the date of origin of which is therefore of crucial importance to my inquiry). How little Dr Bouquet understands the problem becomes clear when he puts up the Platonist Celsus, who wrote an attack on Christianity about AD 178, as a witness to Jesus' historicity (58, p 73 and note). One could as well establish the historicity of Osiris by citing the acquiescence of Christian writers. Dr. Witt too has noted that Celsus, although 'shockingly rude' about Jesus, nevertheless 'accepted as a fact that he had lived in Egypt and had there acquired thaumaturgic powers'; and that he was the illegitimate child of 'a soldier named Panthera' (414, p 224). All these details are alleged of Jesus in the Talmud, and it is clear that Celsus made no independent inquiry, but drew his weapons against Christianity from Jewish traditions which, we have just seen, are today admitted to be worthless.[4]

Today Christianity has been so important for so long that one is apt to assume that it must have appeared important to educated pagans who lived AD 50–150; and that if they fail to discuss Jesus' historicity or the pretensions of his worshippers, their silence must be attributed to their consciousness that they were unable to deny the truth of the Christian case. In fact, however, there is no reason why the pagan writers of this period should have thought Christianity any more important than other enthusiastic religions of the Empire. Dio Cassius, who wrote a history of the realm as late as ca. AD 229, makes no mention at all of Christians or of Christianity, and alludes but once to its then great rival, Mithraism. Because Christianity so long remained insignificant, except among the lower classes, its major pagan critics — Lucian (d. ca. 200), Celsus, Porphyry (d. 303) and the Emperor Julian (d. 363) — all wrote long after the gospels had become established, and gathered from these gospels that Jesus was a teacher and wonder-worker of a kind perfectly familiar to them. As they could thus assign him to a familiar category, they had no reason to doubt his historicity. Porphyry seems to have been close to the standpoint of those modern writers who hold that, although Jesus existed, we can know nothing of him; from the contradictions between the gospel passion narratives he infers that the evangelists are in general unreliable, and he calls them 'inventors, not narrators' of events (309, pp 62, 69).

Notes to Chapter One

1 Marxists claim impartiality on the ground that Engels did not give his opinion as to whether Jesus existed, and so they are free to take any view on this matter of so little importance for 'Marxist science' (390, p 609). For the psycho-analysts Lloyd argues (278, p 3) that Jesus was crucified probably 'while suffering from a

15

psychosis', and that evidence that he 'became psychotic' is his extraordinary behaviour in cursing a fig tree for not bearing fruit out of season and in clearing the temple of traders. Lloyd considers Jesus to have been of very high intelligence because he was capable of making so 'beautifully perceptive' a statement as 'consider the lilies of the field . . .'. Psycho-analysis is tentative enough when performed on patients who can be interrogated. It is likely to be fantasy when the subject is someone known only from written records (as Medawar has recently shown (294) apropos of analyses of Darwin), and it is ridiculous when he is someone most of whose biography – if indeed he existed at all – is unrecorded.

2 The material is as follows: (1) Yeshu was stoned and hanged on the eve of passover because he practised sorcery and led Israel astray. For forty days before the execution, a herald unsuccessfully urged people who knew anything in his favour to come forward. Of the date of this material, Goldstein says, 'we know only that it originated prior to 220 AD'; (2) Yeshu had five disciples – Matthai, Nakkai, Netzer, Buni and Todah. Goldstein comments weakly that 'conjecture identifies Buni as John or Nicodemus, Nakkai as Luke, Netzer as Andrew'; and he admits that this tradition may be as late as 'just beyond the second century'; (3) Rabbi Ishmael refused to allow a healing to be performed in the name of Yeshu ben Pantera. This 'might have occurred in 116 AD'; (4) Rabbi Eliezer is reminded of a conversation he once had with one of the disciples of Yeshu the Nazarene which 'might have occurred in 109 or 95 AD'; (5) an obscure passage involving Rabbi Gamaliel II in which 'Jesus is not mentioned specifically', and which tells of a judge quoting 'a teaching like that given by Jesus in Mt. 5:17 and which may well have been taken from the Logia, or Testimonia, or Christian Gospel'. If so, it would not be independent of Christian tradition. Goldstein says that, if the incident took place at all, it must have occurred before the death of Gamaliel in AD 110 (175, pp 29, 31–3, 39–40, 52, 55, 94–6, 101).

3 Some have emended the ms of a passage in Josephus' *Antiquities* so as to make it name a wealthy freedman of Tiberius as Thallus, and have inferred that this was the chronicler Thallus, who therefore wrote in the reign of Tiberius. Windisch admits that this is not a plausible conjecture, and he himself assigns Thallus to the second half of the first century (409, p 286).

4 One would suppose, from what Witt says, that Celsus represents these views as his own, whereas in fact he puts them into the mouth of an imaginary Jewish interlocutor of Jesus (318, 1:28 and 32). When he speaks on his own account, he affirms the historicity of the Dioscuri, Hercules, Asklepios, Dionysus and Orpheus (3:22 and 42; 7:52). Does Witt regard his testimony as here decisive? That Celsus confuses 'the tenets of orthodox Christianity with beliefs held by gnostic sects' (Chadwick, 318, p 29) does not suggest that he was well informed about historical details.

2 Early Christian Epistles

(i) Paul

(a) The Dates of the Letters Ascribed to Paul

If Jesus was alive about AD 30, we should expect the earliest Christian writings of ca. AD 60 – the principal Pauline letters – to indicate this. I may be told that Paul's mystical view of Jesus is an aberration from the earliest Christianity. If we approach Christian origins by assuming the truth of the gospels with their man Jesus, born in Herod's reign and killed in Pilate's prefecture, then Paul's mystical Christ is indeed an aberration. But if we are to understand the development of Christianity aright, we must start with the conceptions embodied in the earliest documents. Mk., the first of the gospels, cannot reasonably be dated earlier than the destruction of Jerusalem in AD 70 (see below, pp 79ff), whereas Paul had such contacts with the Christian community there (Rom. 15: 25–8 and 1 Cor. 16: 1–4) as imply that this catastrophe had not yet occurred. His conversion must be dated before the death of King Aretas of the Nabataeans in AD 40, since, while cataloguing the maltreatment he has suffered because of his Christianity, he mentions (2 Cor. 11:32) that Aretas' commissioner watched for him in Damascus to have him arrested. All his surviving letters were written late in his career as a Christian[1], and are therefore dated AD 55–60 – which correlates with the evidence of Acts[2], although this is of doubtful reliability, as almost everything Acts says about Paul is tendentious.[3]

Most critics regard 2 Cor. as a collection of different letters (or parts of letters) written by Paul at various stages of his trouble with the Corinthians about the middle of the century, but assembled only at the end of it by an editor who wished to transmit them to other Churches. Schmithals has given evidence that all the principal Pauline letters (apart from the one to the Galatians) are likewise composite – a fact which would account for striking unevenness and even contradictions within each one. (I gave examples from 1 Cor. in JEC, pp 143–4).

The authenticity of the second letter to the Thessalonians, and of the letters to the Colossians and Ephesians is 'debatable' (268, p 178). The latter is the most suspect, for it evidences ecclesiastical organization of a more developed kind than existed in Paul's day; the faithful are said (2: 20–1) to be dependent not directly on Christ but on officers of the Church (in clear contradiction to 1 Cor. 3:11). That letters were written in

17

Paul's name is clear from the exhortation not to be misled 'by some letter purporting to be from us' (2 Thess. 2:2), and from the fact that the author of this same epistle finds it necessary (3:17) to authenticate himself with his signature. All these letters, even the spurious ones, are dated not later than AD 90.

The Pastoral epistles – the two to Timothy and the one to Titus – purport to be from Paul, but are very widely agreed to be works of an unknown Paulinist writing early in the second century to refute, in Paul's own name, certain agnostic views (cf. below, p 45). In 2 Tim, and Titus he included (if Harrison is right) some genuine notes by Paul (see 200, p 10) but 1 Tim. is entirely his own, and it is significantly in this composition of the early second century that Jesus is said (6:13) to have been a contemporary of Pontius Pilate.

(b) The Jesus of Paul

This reference to Pilate sharply distinguishes 1 Tim. from all the other epistles so far mentioned, none of which assigns Jesus' life to any historical period, nor suggests that he lived on earth in the recent past. Paul characteristically applies to him titles such as Lord and Son of God – titles which already existed within Judaism and also in pagan religions (see 71, pp 350–1) – although Jewish monotheistic influence prevents the earliest Christian writers from calling him God. Paul supposes that he existed as a supernatural personage before God 'sent' him into the world to redeem it. (Such pre-existence on the part of the agents of God's activities on earth – such as Wisdom and the Logos – was part of the Judaic background).[4] He assumed human flesh sometime after the reign of David, from whom, Paul says, Jesus (as man) was descended (Rom. 1:3) – a Jew 'according to the flesh' (9:5), the scion of Jesse to govern the gentiles (15:12) predicted by Isaiah. There are many centuries between David and Paul, and Paul gives no indication in which of them Jesus' earthly life fell. The common argument (stated by Michaelis, 332, p 322) that Rom. 1:3 constitutes a clear affirmation of Jesus' Davidic descent within a few decades of his death, and so – for fear of contradiction by properly informed persons – would never have been asserted unless true, pre-supposes the very point I am challenging, namely his existence in Palestine in the first decades of our era – a presupposition for which there is very little evidence in Paul.

The Pauline epistles are hard to read, as one cannot easily relate them to the circumstances under which they were written. But the dilemma they pose is clear: if the gospels were based on reliable historical tradition, how is it that Paul and other Christian writers of the first century make no reference to it? Bornkamm records the 'astonishing' fact that Paul 'nowhere speaks of the Rabbi from Nazareth, the prophet and miracle-worker who ate with tax collectors and sinners, or of his Sermon on the Mount, his parables of the Kingdom of God, and his encounters with Pharisees and scribes. His letters do not even mention the Lord's Prayer'

(56, p 110). Indeed, his statement that 'we do not even know how to pray as we ought' (Rom. 8:26) implies his ignorance of this prayer which the gospel Jesus introduces with the words: 'Pray then like this'. Paul, then, says nothing about clashes between Jesus and Jewish—nor indeed Roman — authorities. He does not mention any of the miracles Jesus is supposed to have worked, nor does he ascribe to Jesus any of the ethical teachings which the gospels represent him as delivering. These two omissions are particularly significant, for ethical teachings are prominent in Paul's epistles, and Jesus' biography, as we know it from the gospels, consists almost exclusively of miracles and teachings. The Jews certainly expected that miracles would characterize the Messianic age — this is clear from the apocalypse of Ezra, 13:50 — and they probably also expected the Messiah himself to perform them.[5] Paul, however, not only fails to record miracles of Jesus, but even seems to deny that he in fact had worked any such 'signs': 'Jews demand signs and Greeks seek wisdom, but we preach Christ crucified, a stumbling-block to Jews and folly to gentiles' (1 Cor. 1:22). Nor could Paul have known anything of Jesus' instruction to baptize men everywhere (Mt. 28:19); otherwise he could not have declared that 'Christ did not send me to baptize' (1 Cor. 1:17). As to ethical teachings, Paul gives a whole list which includes doctrines familiar to us from the gospels, such as 'bless those who persecute you'. But he gives them on his own authority (Rom. 12:3), with no indication that Jesus had inculcated the very same precepts. To support his teachings Paul characteristically appeals not to any words of Jesus, but to passages from the OT. He insists that Christ (by his manner of death) has put an end to the Jewish law, but makes no appeal to words of Jesus which, in the gospels, do precisely this. Indeed, Rom. 15:8 implies that Jesus lived in accordance with the law, as Paul would naturally assume a Jew to have done. Paul also fails to support his protracted plea for celibacy (1 Cor. 7) by any reference to Jesus' praise of those who renounce marriage for the sake of the kingdom of heaven (Mt. 19:12). And when he explains that at the resurrection man's body will be changed from flesh and blood into an imperishable form (1 Cor. 15:35—54), he does not mention Jesus' statement that 'when they rise from the dead, they neither marry nor are given in marriage, but are like angels in heaven' (Mk. 12:25) — even though this dictum would have been a good deal more to the point than the 'scripture' (Isaiah and Hosea) to which he does appeal. In such cases critical theologians are often prepared to set aside as unhistorical the relevant gospel details (see e.g. 95, pp 93—5; 191, p 411).

It will be clear from these examples that Paul is silent about teachings and other supposedly biographical details of Jesus which — if they were truly historical — would have helped him to establish the very case he was arguing. Even when he writes of Jesus' death he says nothing of Pilate, nor of Jerusalem, but declares that Jesus was crucified at the instigation of wicked angels — 'the rulers of this age' (1 Cor. 2:8). That angels or demons, and not human rulers are meant is admitted by commentators, who explain that, by the beginning of our era, the Jews were so conscious of undeniable evil in the world that they could no longer accept that God ruled it; and so they repudiated the view, held in the OT, that Satan and other angels were obedient instruments of God's will, and supposed instead that these demonic powers had rebelled and seized control of the world. Paul's idea is presumably that these angelic governors had stirred men up to crucify Jesus. But Paul's concern is with these angels, not with their human agents.

The Jews naturally hoped that the angelic governors would eventually be routed, and Paul certainly believed that, in crucifying Jesus (in ignorance of his true identity) they had forfeited their influence over the world. He thus declares that on the cross Jesus 'disarmed the principalities and powers and made a public example of them, triumphing over them' (Coloss. 2:15). Brandon has admitted that Paul gives this crucifixion 'no historical context, so that nothing is known of when or where this Jesus had lived ... or where he had been buried and the mode of his resurrection' (62, p 159). And Käsemann finds that 'the scantiness of Paul's Jesus' tradition is surprising in general, but his silence here [i.e. concerning the concrete circumstances of the crucifixion], where he is so deeply engaged, is positively shocking' (240, p 49).

Critics of JEC have deplored the significance I attached to Paul's silence. G.M. Lee, for instance, complained that I assume that 'any person or thing germane to [the] subject and left unmentioned is non-existent' (272, p 45). He then applies this principle to my own silences, and finds that it would justify the inference that 'Dodd and Sherwin-White are non-existent' and that I had 'never heard of Proto-Luke'. But to discuss Jesus' historicity without mentioning Sherwin-White's work on his trial is not the same as failure to mention the trial at all. It was the latter kind of silence which I found significant in Paul. Any modern book on Jesus must leave unmentioned a large number of serious works already existing on the same subject, and the exclusion is often justified (because what one writer provides is obtainable equally well from another) or excusable (because the enormous volume of relevant literature makes oversights – even of important works – inevitable). As to Proto-Luke, I did not mention this hypothesis (which includes the view that the material in Lk. 1 and 2 was not placed at the beginning of this gospel until its final redaction) because I did not consider it sufficiently well founded to support any argument, and because it was not directly relevant to my argument (not even to my discussion of the virgin birth, where the Lucan material presents a problem largely because of contradictions *within* the first two chapters (cf. below, pp 159f). The same cannot be the ground of Paul's silence about the whole substance of the gospels, and not a few theologians regard this silence as a matter of serious concern.[6] Schmithals has candidly acknowledged it as a 'problem to which no satisfactory solution has been given during two hundred years of historical and critical research, and to the solution of which great theologians have sometimes not even attempted to contribute' (349, p 156). And Kümmel, who is sharply critical of Schmithals, admits the reality of the problem (267, p 177). It of course remains a problem only for those who insist that there was a historical Jesus to be silent about.

Brandon explains Paul's indifference to Jesus' biography by assuming that the post-resurrection community of Christians at Jerusalem (whose writings have not survived) based its faith on the historical Jesus of Nazareth, and that Paul had to seek a quite different basis if he was successfully to maintain his independence of the Jerusalem leaders (63, p 283: 65, pp 150ff). In support Brandon argues that they may be equated with the rival teachers whom Paul attacks, particularly in his two letters to Corinth. I shall later give evidence against this equation, and against the supposition that Paul's Christian rivals (whether at Jerusalem or elsewhere) were any more concerned than he was with the historical Jesus.

The only statements Paul makes which are commonly held to imply that the Jesus of his faith was a recently deceased human being are (i) his single mention (1 Cor. 15:5) of a Christian group he terms 'the twelve'. I shall show below that some theologians have recently taken up the suggestion of Wellhausen (404, p 112) that this group is not to be uncritically identified with the twelve companions of Jesus of the gospels; (ii) his references to 'Cephas' (which will also be discussed below), and (iii) his mention of 'James the Lord's brother' (Gal. 1:19) – this being taken to mean blood brother of a historical Jesus. I argued in JEC (pp 141–2) that James is given this title because he belongs to a Jerusalem group which Paul calls the brethren of the Lord (1 Cor. 9:5), a term which is perfectly intelligible as the title of a religious fraternity. Paul complains (1 Cor. 1:11–13) of Christian factions which bore the titles 'of Paul', 'of Apollos', 'of Cephas' and – most significant of all – 'of Christ'. If there was a group at Corinth called 'those of the Christ', there may well have been one at Jerusalem called the brethren of the Lord, who would have had no more personal experience of Jesus than Paul himself. The vizier of the Nabataean kings regularly bore the title 'brother of the king' and this accords well with my suggestion that the Lord's brothers were a group of those eminent and zealous in his service, rather than his kinsmen. In the pagan world, the term 'brethren' was certainly used at the time to denote members of the same religious community. (Examples from papyri are given in 305, p 9; and there is the obvious case of the fratres arvales in pre-Christian Rome). Paul habitually addresses his fellow Christians as 'brethren'.

Furthermore, there is no correlation between the brethren of the Lord mentioned in two of Paul's epistles as leaders of the Jerusalem Church, and the family of Jesus mentioned in the gospels (which are of later date). This family, so far from supporting Jesus, seems to have had little time for him (see below, pp 148ff). Some theologians have dealt with this difficulty by supposing that the James named in 1 Cor. 15:7 as a personage who had, like Paul, experienced an appearance of the risen Jesus, was the brother of Jesus, and that this experience converted him to the faith.

Mk. 6:3 does name one James as a brother of Jesus, and this is repeated in Mt. but not in the corresponding passage in Lk., even though both evangelists knew Mk. and used it as one of their sources. Luke's suppression of the information is very striking. Lk. and Acts are universally agreed to be the work of the same author, and if the James the Lord's brother whom Paul says he saw in Jerusalem had been a brother of Jesus, one would expect the author of Lk.-Acts to say so, especially since he gives (in Acts) a full account of this Jerusalem meeting between Paul and James. But none of the various Jameses mentioned in Lk.-Acts is called the brother of Jesus, nor even the brother of the Lord. In Acts 12:17 there is (for the first time) mention of a group called 'James and the brethren' (NEB 'members of the church'). This cannot be James the son of Zebedee (one of the twelve), whose execution is reported earlier (12:2). Whoever this new James is, by ch. 15 he functions as the leader of the Jerusalem community.

I shall no doubt be accused of trying to explain away the passages in Paul that do not fit my theory. But my point is that, apart from 2 Cor. 5:16, which I discuss below (p 98), the few passages I have mentioned are really the only ones which even remotely suggest that Paul was close in time to Jesus' life on earth, and that, by themselves, they are not sufficient to establish this inference.

Martin has adduced, additionally, 1 Thess. 2:15 as 'a tacit appeal to Jesus' death as of recent memory' (289). The passage in fact merely alleges that he was killed by the Jews. Brandon sets it aside as an interpolation on the ground that Paul 'elsewhere consistently shows himself proud of his Jewish origin' (62, p 174n); and Harvey concedes a 'marked contrast' between the anti-Semitism here and Paul's lengthy discussion of the Jews in Rom. 9–11 (201, p 652). Paul never accuses them of killing Jesus except in this passage from 1 Thess.; and in 1 Cor. 2:8 he attributes the death not to the Jews but to wicked angels (see above, p 19). Furthermore, 1 Thess. continues with the statement that, because the Jews murdered Jesus, 'retribution has now overtaken them for good and all' (NEB). Notwithstanding Kümmel's demurrer (266, p 221) this can hardly be other than an allusion to the destruction of Jerusalem in AD 70, and therefore an interpolation, since the epistle is of earlier date.

The difficulty commentators have in finding statements of Paul which suggest any knowledge of Jesus' life is clear from the quite inconclusive nature of the passages which they have quoted in criticism of my argument as set out in JEC. Barclay, for instance, thinks that Paul's reference to the 'meekness and gentleness of Christ' (2 Cor. 10:1) betrays that he was writing for people already acquainted in detail with the biography of a historical Jesus. But the ascription of particular qualities of character to a god does not establish his historicity. That the worshippers of Ares regarded him as pugnacious and irascible does not prove that he displayed these qualities in a recent historical existence. Paul probably means that Jesus' meekness and gentleness (NEB magnanimity) consisted in his condescending to come to earth in human form at all – the doctrine of other Pauline passages.[7]

James Dunn (139) has adduced the following passages:

(i) The faithful will not 'give themselves up to licentiousness' because they 'did not so learn Christ' (Ephes. 4:19–20). Dunn obviously supposes that they 'learned' of a recent historical personage who led a pure and blameless life. But the context shows the meaning to be that the act of accepting Christ as Lord involves laying aside our old sinful nature and putting on 'the new nature, created after the likeness of God' (verse 24; cf. Rom. 6:6 where the sinful tendencies of the believer are said to have been killed by a kind of mystical assimilation to the death of Christ). Even ignoring the context, no more is implied than that devotion to Christ inspired purity of conduct, and such purity is by no means unique in the religious life of the time. Some of the pagan mystery brotherhoods seem to have attracted members to their secret meetings by the encouragement of sexual licence (for which there was abundant authority in some of the older traditional rituals), while others put the stress on restraint and even asceticism. In the one case the worshippers would think of their deity as indulgent, in the other as ascetic. Both tendencies could be linked with the name of one and the same deity. Isis, for instance, was for some the chaste virgin, for others the universal mother (413, p 85). In either case her example could be appealed to as a model for conduct, without involving any belief that she had recently been leading a blameless (or lascivious) life on earth.

(ii) Christians have 'received the word in much affliction' and are thus imitators of Christ (1 Thess. 1:6). The implication is that Jesus is known to have suffered affliction, and again I must note that other divinities have likewise been regarded as suffering, and as examples to be imitated in this respect.[8]

In sum, when Paul refers to ethical qualities displayed by Jesus in his lifetime, the reference is either to his incarnation or to his death,[9] neither of which is given a historical context.

(iii) The faithful 'received Christ Jesus' in that they have 'the knowledge of God's mystery, of Christ, in whom are hid all the treasures of wisdom and knowledge' (Coloss. 2:2 and 6). This is the purest mysticism, and the 'knowledge' of Christ mentioned here and in other epistles is acquired from communion with hidden powers or higher spirits. 1 Tim. 6:20 and James 3:15 contrast the true wisdom 'from above' with false knowledge from demons. Witt observes that the importance of Hellenistic mystery religions for Christianity appears from such passages, and from Paul's designation of himself and his fellows as 'stewards of the mysteries of God' (1 Cor 4:1) – the technical name for the stewards at the temples of Serapis.

What Paul proclaims is the mystery of God's will, namely the divine plan for man's redemption through Christ, which will 'unite all things in him, things in heaven and things on earth' (Ephes. 1:7–10). The reference to 'things in heaven' which need to be reconciled to God is taken up in Ephes. 3:10, where we learn that, as a result of Paul's preaching, 'the manifold wisdom of God' is to be 'made known to the principalities and powers in the heavenly places', i.e. to evil angels. (Harvey betrays the usual embarrassment of the commentators when he designates this a 'startling thought').[10] Paul sees his function as that of making 'the word of God fully known, the mystery hidden for ages and generations but now made manifest to his saints' (Coloss. 1:25–6). The 'saints' who know the mystery are the Christian equivalents of the initiates of the pagan mysteries of the day. Paul repeatedly refers to Jesus in the language of mysticism, of which the use of prepositions is symptomatic: in Christ, unto Christ, through Christ, to Christ – suggesting some indescribable relation between Christ and himself. The Greek original sometimes has a simple dative instead of a preposition. My point is that the preposition or the case suggests a relationship of some kind which the context fails to explain. Nor can commentators elucidate it. Barclay, for instance, attempts to do so, but says little more than that it is a 'spiritual relationship' not to be understood with reference to the pagan mystery religions of the day (16, pp 93, 97–8).

A number of recent writers who have reacted sharply against attempts to link Paul with pagan mystery religions nevertheless concede that 'the mysteries quite definitely formed part of the milieu into which be brought his gospel'; that he 'undoubtedly would therefore be open to their influence'; and that 'many of the terms he used would have an undertone of meaning which would strengthen the appeal of the gospel to the Hellenistic world' (Davies, 123, p 98). Father Rahner allows that Paul lived in a world 'filled with the "mystery" atmosphere', and that we cannot deny that he and such later writers as Ignatius 'adapted a subdued sort of mystery language to their own needs'. Rahner's own summary of the NT 'mysterion' is that it is:

'the free decision of God, taken in eternity and hidden in the depths of the godhead, to save man, who in his sinfulness has been separated from God; this hidden decision is revealed in Christ the man-God, who by his death gives "life" to all men, that is, calls them to participate in his own divine life, which through the ethical will is comprehended in faith and sacrament and transcends earthly death in the beatific vision of perfect union with God.' (328, pp 353, 356)

The keynote is reconciliation – as, according to William James, is true of mysticism generally: 'It is as if the opposites of the world, whose contradictoriness and conflict make all our difficulties and troubles, were melted into a unity' (222, p 350). The mystic has silenced doubt and fear by conceiving the world and his own self in such a way that there appears to be no antagonism between them. He feels deeply secure because he has identified the whole power of the universe with that being on whom he relies and from whom he expects protection. His quaint ideas are merely elaborate methods of achieving this harmony with a show of logic which appears cogent largely because the thinking involved is so abstract, and the ideas so attenuated, that conflict between the vague entities posited is almost impossible. It is obvious that a religion of this kind does not need to be based on the historical career of a redeemer-god, even though the chief difference between Christianity and pagan mystery religions is invariably alleged to be 'the historical basis of the former and the mythological character of the latter' (298, p 12). It did indeed matter to Paul that Jesus had *a* human history; but as the details of that history were unimportant to him, his 'Christ' would have seemed, to a newcomer familiar with the mystery religions, merely another cult Lord. Downing concedes that 'it is at least arguable that Paul's and other early Christianity may have been strongly moulded by the presence of such quite a-historical devotion', and that this type of influence cannot be discounted just because the NT includes later books (particularly the gospels and Acts) of a more 'historical' kind (136, p 89).

(c) Words of the Lord Quoted by Paul

The only occasion when Paul quotes a saying of Jesus which is ascribed to him in the gospels is when he reports (1 Cor. 11:23–5) words very similar to those which are, in the synoptics, represented as instituting the Lord's Supper or eucharist. Paul records what, he alleges, Jesus said 'on the night when he was betrayed' (NEB 'on the night of his arrest'). The Greek verb signifies that he was 'handed over' or 'delivered up', and to translate this as 'betrayed' or 'arrested' is to interpret Paul from the gospels (see JEC, pp 271–2). Kramer has given evidence that, in early Christian usage, this verb 'to deliver up' referred to the coming of the Son of God into the life of the world. Thus 'God did not spare his own Son but gave him up for us all' (Rom. 8:32). Here 'gave him up' means much the same as 'sending' his own Son (verse 3; cf. Gal. 4:4: 'God sent forth his Son'). Kramer does not dispute that, even in the earliest usage, all the implications of the coming into the world, including the death, are present in this being 'delivered up': but his point is that only at a later stage was the idea narrowed down so that it came to refer exclusively to the sufferings and death (265, p 117), as in Rom. 4:25: Jesus was 'delivered up [RSV put to death] for our trespasses and raised for our justification'. That Paul uses this vague and general term in his eucharistic narrative suggests that he did not have any knowledge of the supposedly historical circumstances of an arrest. Jeremias thinks it indisputable that Paul is here echoing the Septuagint of Isaiah 53, where the suffering servant of Yahweh is repeatedly said to have been 'delivered up' for our sins. The idea is that he was delivered by the Father as a sacrifice for sinners, and this is what Paul seems to have in mind when he talks about Jesus being 'delivered' (see JEC, p 272). 1 Cor. 11:23 thus means no more than 'on the night when the Passion began' (see Perrin, 321, p 208). Popkes comments, in his very detailed study, that we cannot now tell what Paul had in mind, and that he was perhaps deliberately vague, since his interest in Jesus' person was 'kerygmatic, not biographical' (326, p 208). What is, however, clear is that, in placing the origin of the eucharist on the night when Jesus was delivered up, he means to link the rite with Jesus' death. Achtemeier has recently argued that Paul is not here indulging in historical reminiscence, but trying to discredit a type of Christian eucharist which linked it with the resurrection instead of with the death (1, p 217; cf. the more detailed discussion below, p 186).

Paul claims that his knowledge of what Jesus said on the night in question came to him directly from the Lord:

'For I received from the Lord what I also delivered to you, that the Lord Jesus took bread . . . broke it, and said, "This is my body which is for you. Do this in remembrance of me". In the same way also the cup, after supper saying, "This cup is the new covenant in my blood. Do this as often as you drink it, in remembrance of me".'

Paul could not have received this information from the earthly Jesus who, on any account, had died before Paul acknowledged him as Lord. What seems to be implied is that the risen Jesus made the disclosure in a supernatural appearance to Paul. On the other hand, the many unpauline words in the passage (listed by Jeremias, 226, p 104) suggest that it is a formula which existed before him in the Christian community, and which he 'delivered' or passed on as standard Christian teaching. One can perhaps resolve this contradiction by supposing that the formula is pre-Pauline, and reached Paul from tradition, but that it was ratified by the risen Jesus in an appearance to him. An obvious question is: do the words of Jesus in this formula represent what he actually said at the 'Last Supper' on the night of his arrest? A number of theologians (see 154) have denied this, and some (e.g. Nagel, 332) regard the formula as liturgical, recited at the cultic celebration of the eucharist in Paul's day. Once a eucharistic meal had become established among early Christians, it would be natural for them to suppose that Jesus had ordained it (although the words of institution could hardly have been recited in a *Corinthian* liturgy – otherwise Paul would not have needed to give them in full, but only to have briefly reminded his readers of them). For the Corinthians who read Paul's epistle, the eucharist was an already existing rite, and they will have understood his account as an explanation of its origin. Bultmann and Braun regards the passage as a 'cult-legend' (a story which aims at accounting for the origin of a rite practised by a religious community) – a legend formed in Hellenistic circles (83, pp 285–6; 73, p 50). Higgins observes that the clause 'which is for you' (qualifying the words 'this is my body') is obviously Hellenistic, for it cannot be 'retranslated' from the Greek into Aramaic (205, p 29). He and others (e.g. Davies, 123, p 251) think that the expression 'new covenant' was also put into Jesus' mouth by Paul because the Hebraic conception of a covenant in blood (Exodus 24:8) was central to the latter's theology. (He says, for instance, alluding to Jeremiah 31:31, that God 'has qualified us to be ministers of a new covenant', 2 Cor. 3:6).

The view that the passage is a cult-legend is supported by the fact that the version of it recorded in the earliest gospel (Mk. 14:22—5) does not fit the context the evangelist has given it, and is therefore, as Taylor admits, probably 'an isolated unit of tradition' (384, p 542). Jesus here actually equates the wine with his blood, saying 'this is my blood of the covenant, which is poured out for many'. Paul's version avoids this express equation, and makes Jesus say: 'This cup is the new covenant in my blood'. Mark has obviously rephrased the words about the wine so as to make them exactly parallel to those about the bread; so that he makes Jesus say not only 'this is my body' (as did Paul) but also 'this is my blood'. This change in phrasing shifts the emphasis away from the Jewish idea of a covenant, and has been seen as the beginning of a Hellenistic modification whereby ideas of sacrifice came ultimately to replace all covenant ideas in the Christian Mass (129, pp 108—9). The 'pouring out' of Jesus' blood clearly implies sacrificial death, for his blood is not 'poured out' at the Last Supper. Had a historical Jesus said anything like this, his Jewish audience could hardly have understood — let alone accepted — this suggestion that they should drink his blood. The drinking of blood is foreign to Palestinian thinking, and the Levitical law (17:10—11) expressly prohibits even non-Jews resident in Israel from doing so. In earlier gospel episodes Jesus' disciples have been repeatedly represented as incapable of understanding him, and as particularly obtuse (Mk. 9:32) when he tried to explain to them that it was necessary for him to die. But on this occasion they make no demur and show no sign of bewilderment. The fair inference is that these words in which he predicts the atoning power of his death are creations of the Christian community.

Finally, the command 'do this in remembrance of me' is recorded in Paul's version (which is of course earlier than that of the synoptics) but not in the gospels (except in some manuscripts of Lk.). To suggest that an ordinance of such importance was made by Jesus, but forgotten by all the evangelists (Jn. does not even record the context in which it was allegedly made) is tantamount to abandoning all confidence in the gospels. It is reasonable to infer that it was originally absent not only, as now, from the synoptics, but also from Paul's epistle. At a later date it was interpolated both into the epistle and into some Lucan manuscripts. It is easier to explain how such a command could come to be inserted than how it could have been omitted. The expanded text of Lk. (i.e. the text which includes the command) is clearly a conflation; for it agrees with Paul, against Mark, in calling the cup 'the new covenant in my bood' (and thus does not equate wine with blood); yet it adds to Paul's text two Marcan clauses — 'gave to them' and 'is poured out for you' (Lk. 22:19—20).

On four other occasions Paul represents certain of his views as having the authority of the Lord. First, he gives as the Lord's word (1 Cor. 7:10) a strict doctrine on divorce which is in harmony with what Jesus says in Mk. 10:11 (although not with the more liberal doctrine which Matthew, in adapting this passage, ascribes to Jesus). Paul, however, goes on to allow an exception, not mentioned by Jesus in any gospel, to the total prohibition of divorce. He is clearly adapting what he regards as the Lord's ruling to the circumstances of his own times, and his readiness to do this enables us to understand how, later, Matthew came to change Mark's wording ('whoever divorces his wife and marries another commits adultery against her') by interpolating the saving clause 'except for unchastity' (Mt. 19:9). Even the Marcan wording can hardly be accepted as that of a historical Jesus, for it stipulates (10:12) that a woman likewise commits adultery by divorcing her husband and remarrying. Such an utterance would have been meaningless in Palestine, where only men could obtain divorce (see Harvey, 201, p 163) and must therefore be understood as a ruling for the gentile Christian readers of Mk. which the evangelist put into Jesus' mouth.

Second, according to Paul, 'the lord commanded' that Christian preachers are entitled to financial support (1 Cor. 9:14). There is a tenuous connection with a saying of the gospel Jesus (see JEC, p 134), but, as Bultmann has said, this ruling on finance and the one on divorce were regulations which were becoming established in Christian communities in Paul's day, and which were secured by anchoring them to the authority of Jesus (81, p 222). It was the risen (not the earthly) Jesus who proclaimed these rules to his community by appearing supernaturally to Paul and to other Christian leaders of that time, or by speaking through Christian prophets. Just as OT prophets introduced their directives with 'thus saith the Lord', so the early Christian ones — 'appointed', Paul says, in the Church by God (1 Cor. 12:28) — would have spoken in the name of the risen Lord. The seven letters of Christ to the seven Churches in Asia Minor (Rev. 2–3) and other sayings of the Lord (e.g. Rev. 1:17–20; 16:15; 22:12ff) show that early Christian prophets 'addressed congregations in words of encouragement, admonition, censure and promise, using the name of Christ in the first person' (Jeremias, 228, p 2). At a later stage such prophets, and their audiences, would naturally suppose that Jesus must have spoken during his lifetime in the manner they thought his spirit spoke to them. And so the earthly Jesus was made to say things which the risen Christ could appropriately have said. For instance the statement that 'where two or three are gathered together in my name' (Mt. 18:20) clearly presupposes a Jesus who is not limited by time or space.[11]

Third, to Thessalonian Christians who inquired how deceased brethren would fare at Christ's second coming, Paul gives the assurance that 'with the archangel's call and with the sound of the trumpet of God, the Lord himself will descend from heaven . . . And the dead in Christ will rise first; then we who are alive who are left, shall be caught up together with them in the clouds to meet the Lord in the air' (1 Thess. 4:15–17). There is nothing in the gospels which corresponds to this, even though Jesus there expatiates on the subject of his second coming. Köster notes (264, p 240) that a tradition similar to this 'word of the Lord' is called a 'mystery' in 1 Cor. 15:51ff, 'the same term that is the technical designation of apocalyptic secrets in Daniel and in the Qumran literature'. The question the Thessalonians addressed to Paul implies that they lacked the idea of a general resurrection. They believed that Christ had power to save those who were still alive at his final coming, but they grieved as men who had no hope (verse 13) for those who would not survive until then. Bornkamm thinks that the 'word' with which Paul answers the question was never spoken by Jesus, but was 'coined and put into the mouth of an inspired prophet' to settle the doctrinal point at issue; and that Paul then had recourse to it in order to comfort the Church (56, p 222). Later, as in the synoptic gospels, some of these messages are ascribed to the earthly Jesus, who is represented as delivering long apocalyptic discourses.

Finally, Paul stipulates (1 Cor. 14:34–7) as 'a command of the Lord' that women are to 'keep silence in the churches; for they are not permitted to speak'. This again is a rule of a Christian community – a rule to which nothing in the gospels corresponds, and which contradicts the doctrine of 1 Cor. 11:5 that women may 'prophesy' at meetings. Harvey acknowledges the difficulty and says that 'either Paul is being inconsistent, or else there is a distinction between "prophesying" and "addressing the meeting", which we cannot now understand' (201, p 564).[12]

Paul obviously thought it important to have a 'word of the Lord' to settle a debatable matter of discipline in the community, or of doctrine. 'This', says Bultmann, 'makes it the more certain that when he does not cite such a word where it would be expected, he knows of none' (81, p 222).

(d) The Basis of Paul's Knowledge of Jesus
One source of Paul's knowledge of Jesus was the OT, the whole of which he regards as 'prophetic writings', 'written down for our instruction' because they elucidate facts about Jesus (Rom. 15:3–4; 16:25–6) and about the Christian life (1 Cor. 10:11). He also affirms that 'the mystery was made known to me by relevation' (Ephes. 3:3) and that

> *'The gospel* which was *preached* by me is not man's gospel. For I did not receive it from man, nor was I taught it, but it came through a revelation of Jesus Christ.' (Gal. 1:11–12. On my italics, see below, p 30).

'Revelation' here seems to mean two things: first, his visions of the risen Jesus. He expressly claims that the risen one had 'appeared' to him (1 Cor. 15:8), and he records that he and other early Christians were prone to supernatural visions (Coloss. 2:18; 2 Cor. 12:1–4). This is quite in accordance with normal religious psychology.[13] Second, 'revelation' refers to the 'spiritual gifts' operative in Christian communities. These included ability to state profound truths, to prophesy, and to make and to interpret ecstatic utterances (1 Cor. 12: 8–11). He himself claims to be gifted in ecstatic utterance (1 Cor. 14:18) and to possess 'insight into the mystery of Christ' (Ephes. 3:4). He also declares that God has revealed such things to him through the spirit; and he adds that, as a result of possessing the spirit, 'we have the mind of Christ' (1 Cor. 2:9–16). He feels entitled to give ethical advice because he has 'the Spirit of God' (1 Cor. 7:40). Such passages, says Nineham (314, p 21), show that Christians 'took it for granted that the heavenly Christ was continually revealing further truth about himself to his followers'. Teeple has pointed out that early Christianity as a whole agrees with Paul in basing its preaching not on historical traditions about Jesus, but on the promptings of the spirit (386, p 66). The gospel is preached through the holy spirit (1 Peter 1:12); the author of 1 Clement tells (ch. 63) that he wrote his epistle to Corinth through revelation from the spirit. When Christians are arrested and brought to trial, the holy spirit, not an oral tradition from the teaching of the historical Jesus, will tell them what to say (Mk. 13:11).

A further source of information about Jesus was what was being said about him in the Christian communities which already existed when Paul was converted. Naturally, some of these traditions were passed on to and accepted by him. He does, it is true, expressly deny (in a passage I have just quoted from Gal.) that the 'gospel' which he 'preached' reached him in this way. And in 1 Cor. 15:1–8 he reminds the brethren

> 'in what terms I *preached* to you *the gospel* which you received . . . For I delivered to you as of first importance what I also received, that Christ died for our sins in accordance with the scriptures, that he was buried, that he was raised on the third day in accordance with the scriptures, and that he appeared to Cephas, then to the twelve. Then he appeared to more than five hundred brethren at one time, most of whom are still alive, though some have fallen asleep. Then he appeared to James, then to all the apostles. Last of all, as to one untimely born, he appeared also to me.'

The words I have italicized show that the same 'gospel' is meant in both passages; in any case there is, for Paul, only one gospel (see below, p 36). Both passages use the terms 'receiving' and 'delivering', which were the technical terms at the time for the receiving and transmitting of tradition. In the passage I have quoted from Gal., however, Paul uses 'receiving' in order to *deny* that he has received his gospel from human tradition. In the present passage from 1 Cor. he does not say whence he 'received' his gospel, and so the assumption must be that he means to reaffirm what he had said both in Gal. and a few chapters earlier in 1 Cor., namely that he received it directly 'from the Lord' (1 Cor. 11:23; cf. above, p 26). Norden points in this connection to Jesus' statement that 'all things have been delivered to me by my Father' (Mt. 11:27). This knowledge, although 'delivered', comes directly from God; and in the same way the words 'deliver' and 'receive' often have, for Paul, mystical connotations because of the special nature of the information delivered (315, p 289).

Nevertheless both passages from 1 Cor. are full of unpauline words and phrases which show them to be, at least in part, formulas passed on to Paul by others (see Conzelmann's discussion, 104). Paul, then, obviously knew of Jesus both from tradition and revelation, and is capable of drawing from both sources. Conservative critics identify Paul's human informants, implied in the passage I have quoted from 1 Cor. 15, as the Jerusalem Christians (who, so it is further supposed, knew Jesus personally) and point to Semitisms in the passage for support. These could at most prove that the formula arose in a Palestinian community. But in fact the Semitisms may well be merely what theologians call 'Septuagintalisms' (echoes of the phraseology of the Greek OT), and the phrase 'according to the scriptures' appears to have no Semitic equivalent and to be possible only in Greek (see Fuller, 167, pp 10–11). A strong Jewish orientation is obvious from the reference to sacrificial death constituting redemption from sin. But the originators of the tradition may as well have been Greek-speaking as Aramaic-speaking Jewish Christians and any connection between them and the historical Jesus is pure speculation. Nor does mention of 'the third day' constitute a precise historical allusion. As the other indications of time in the passage ('then', 'after that') are vague, and as it supplies no time reference for the death of Christ from which to reckon the three days, the preciseness of this one reference in it cannot be attributed to any general interest in chronology, but is (as Evans concedes) more likely intended as 'a theological statement' (151, p 48). Pagan gods, whom no one now believes to have existed, were resurrected on the third day.[14] Metzger has observed that 'in the East, three days constitute a temporary habitation, while the fourth day implies a permanent residence'; hence the purpose of Paul's formula may be to 'convey the assurance that Jesus would be but a visitor in the house of the dead and not a permanent resident therein' (299, p 123). The influence of pagan parallels could have been strengthened by the rabbinical idea that the general resurrection – presaged according to Rom. 8:29 and Coloss. 1:18 by Christ's resurrection – will occur three days after the end of the world. 'In these conditions', says Goguel, 'it is natural that the resurrection of the Christ was placed in a chronological rapport with his death similar to that which was thought would occur between the end of the world and the general resurrection'. If so, then 'on the third day' is 'not a chronological datum, but a dogmatic assertion: Christ's resurrection marked the dawn of the end-time, the beginning of the cosmic eschatological process of resurrection' (Fuller, 167, pp 26–7, with references to Goguel; cf. Vermes, 398, pp 234–5 for other saving events occurring, in Jewish lore, 'on the third day').

Paul's words occur in a context where he is concerned to refute Corinthian Christians who denied 'resurrection of the dead' (1 Cor. 15:21). They may have denied immortality, or believed that their faith in the risen Jesus had launched them on an immortal resurrection life, and that they therefore would not experience death. If they took this latter view then their opinions would resemble those of the Christians mentioned in 2 Tim. 2:18 and 2 Thess. 2:2 who thought that 'the resurrection is past already', and that 'the day of the Lord [i.e. of judgement] has come'. A relatively minor reinterpretation of Paul's views would lead to such a position; for although he lived in anticipation of a coming judgement which would bring complete salvation to the faithful, he also held that the earthly mission and resurrection of Christ had already inaugurated the epoch of salvation, and so to some extent he, like his opponents, looked back to the past, and not exclusively forward to the future.[15] In the passage quoted above he answers the Corinthians by pointing out that Jesus himself entered upon his resurrection life only after death and burial; and that faith in, and even visions of, the risen one do not exempt from death, since some of the five hundred who saw him have since died.

The appearances of the risen Jesus which Paul lists must also be understood as part of his refutation of those who denied 'resurrection of the dead'. All the appearances were, for Paul, recent — they were made to persons who were his contemporaries. But he does not say that the crucifixion and resurrection were also recent. (It is our familiarity with the gospels which leads us to assume that the appearances followed rapidly after the resurrection.) If (as I believe) he did not regard the resurrection as a recent event, then the significance of the appearances would have been to show that the general resurrection of the dead, and the final judgement of both living and dead, were to occur very soon. Christ was risen: that meant that all would rise. But now that he was not only risen, but had begun to appear to men, the final events which would bring the world to an end could not be long delayed.

We shall later see more fully that Paul's Christian opponents were religious enthusiasts as little interested in the historical Jesus as was he. But what concerns us here is that he refutes them by reciting facts he had 'received'. Such 'facts' need not be historically reliable. Stories about William Tell purport to be facts, but are not on that account uncritically accepted. It is noteworthy that the tradition Paul here quotes has nothing to say of the time or place of the resurrection appearances it posits, and that later Christian documents which are explicit as to the place completely contradict each other, in that Mt. sites the appearances to the disciples exclusively in Galilee, whereas Lk. confines them to Jerusalem.[16] Further, among Paul's 'facts' are appearances to Cephas, to 'the twelve', to five hundred brethren and to James. The rest of the NT knows nothing of the two latter appearances. In the gospel resurrection stories Peter, who according to Paul was the first to see the risen Jesus, plays a very minor role;[17] and the appearances are made to eleven, not to twelve (see below, p 124). There was, then, little uniformity in the primitive traditions concerning resurrection appearances which were of the greatest importance as a basis to early Christianity. Allen writes in this connection of a 'serious break in continuity' in the tradition between Paul and the evangelists. 'Paul handed on to his churches what he had received from those who were in the faith before him. But this tradition did not come to the men who wrote the gospels . . . . The process of transmission was one in which fidelity did not exclude selection and interpretation, or even fresh creation' (5, p 353). This latter is evident from the fact that the discrepancies between Paul and the evangelists extend to the very nature of the appearances; for Paul never suggests that Jesus tarried on earth after his resurrection. In summarizing the relevant events he links Jesus' rising from the dead directly with his being at the right hand of God (Rom. 8:34; cf. 1 Thess. 1:10; Coloss. 3:1). He seems to have taken for granted that Jesus ascended to heaven immediately, and with a body of heavenly radiance (cf. 1 Cor. 15:43, where he writes of the dead being raised 'in glory'), and that his post-resurrection appearances were therefore made from heaven. Later Christian writers, however, show an increasing tendency to represent the risen Lord as returning to the conditions of earthly life before ascending to heaven. The empty tomb stories of the gospels are designed to stress the physical reality of his resurrection (whereas Paul knows nothing of a place of burial);[18] and in the gospels and in Acts his resurrection body is not a body of glory. (Not until the post-ascension appearance recorded in Acts 9 is there any suggestion that he has a body of heavenly radiance.) Clearly, the evangelists' motive was to establish the identity of the risen Jesus with the Jesus the disciples had known before the crucifixion; and Mt. 28:17 (which records that they saw the risen one 'and worshipped him, but some doubted') may be understood as showing awareness that the identity could be questioned (276, p 93n). The gospels, then, here diverge from Paul because they are influenced by a motive of which he could have known nothing.

Finally, that the earliest extant mention of the resurrection occurs in a formula handed down from even earlier Christians is what one would expect. The earliest Christians simply asserted that Christ is risen — just as the worshippers of other deities affirmed the same of them. Fuller's study of the development of the narratives shows that 'the earliest Church did not narrate resurrection appearances, but proclaimed the resurrection' (167, p 68). The first stage, then, was the simple declaration that the event had occurred. And the declaration was made in a preaching formula which consisted essentially of two statements: 'Christ died for us', and 'God raised him from the dead'. According to 1 Cor. 15:12 to 'preach Christ' means to preach the saving events summarized in such words, which recur in the NT epistles in stereotype form, and so obviously represent a standard affirmation of the faith. Next, Christians supported this affirmation by alleging that some had actually seen the risen Lord. His appearances were, in the first instance, simply listed, not narrated nor described in any way. Thus Paul adds to the proclamation of the resurrection a list of appearances. Christian leaders who believed that such appearances had occurred would not unnaturally expect to receive them themselves. Hence Paul's claim to such an experience. But he makes no attempt to describe or narrate even his own encounter with the risen one. Descriptions of resurrection appearances represent a yet later layer in the traditions, and are not found in documents earlier than the gospels and Acts. The sequence, then, was: (1) affirmation of the resurrection; (2) listing of appearances; (3) claim by an affirmer of appearances that he had himself been vouchsafed one; (4) description of appearances. (Description of the actual resurrection occurs as yet a further supplement in the apocryphal Gospel of Peter.) The first stage is appropriately represented in the records by what Paul himself describes if not as tradition, at any rate as information he 'received' from elsewhere. The *stories* of appearances did not form the basis for the resurrection faith, but resulted from it (403, p 165). Faith in Christ's resurrection was able to become a cardinal tenet of the early Christians for the reason that it guaranteed the resurrection of all believers. Christ raised from the dead is 'the first fruits of those who have fallen asleep' (1 Cor. 15:20), and will thus necessarily be followed by the resurrection of all who belong to him. And the idea that the Messiah would die and be resurrected is understandable as a synthesis of originally independent Jewish ideas about the end-time (see below, p 113).

Paul uses this phrase 'first fruits' not only apropos of Christ's resurrection, but also of the gift of the spirit to the Christian community (Rom. 8:23). It is not in dispute that both Jews and early Christians expected the end of the world to come quickly, and thought it would be presaged by a general resurrection and by the gift of the spirit. In these circumstances, it is hardly surprising that some men should come forward with 'gifts of the spirit' and make ecstatic utterances. But if the presence of the spirit was a sign that the first-fruits of the harvest of the end-time had already been gathered, then the resurrection must also be nigh. It may well have been partly on this basis that early Christians came to believe that Christ is risen, that the resurrection had, to this extent, already begun; and that a pledge had thus been given that a general resurrection of mankind would shortly follow.

(ii) Paul's Christian Predecessors and Contemporaries

Paul's writings are the earliest extant Christian documents, but there were still earlier Christians whom he persecuted prior to his conversion. It is commonly assumed, on the evidence of Acts, that these his victims were Jerusalem Christians, and that they were led by men who had known the historical Jesus personally. But Paul says nothing that would necessitate either of these assumptions, and the relevant narratives in Acts are tendentious in that they serve to underpin one of the author's cardinal beliefs, namely that Jerusalem was the centre from which Christianity developed.

Acts 8:1 represents Paul as conniving at the martyrdom of Stephen in Jerusalem and then (9:1) applying to the high priest for letters to the synagogues at Damascus authorizing him to arrest and bring to Jerusalem any members with Christian leanings. Commentators are baffled by this suggestion that the high priest had authority to order arrests in a Roman city 200 miles away, when the jurisdiction even of the Sanhedrin did not extend beyond Judaea. Paul's own (much earlier) statement affirms his connection with Damascus and denies one with Jerusalem (Gal. 1:17), where, he says, he was unknown to the Christian community even long after his conversion.[19] The letters of extradition alleged in Acts enabled the author of this work to assimilate this primitive tradition of an association with Damascus, while subordinating it to his thesis that Jerusalem was the real centre of Paul's activity. Paul also declares that he was moved to persecute by zeal for his native traditions (Gal. 1:14 and 22; Phil. 3:6). This implies that his victims were lax in their observation of the Jewish law and cult requirements, whereas the Jerusalem Christians — so he complained after his conversion — were too strict in these matters. From this evidence, a number of theologians have inferred that he persecuted Hellenists — Jewish Christians whose mother tongue was Greek and who were liberal enough in their interpretation of the law to sit at table with pagans who had turned Christian (cf. Gal. 2:11ff). Such permissiveness is unlikely to have originated in Jerusalem (although Acts alleges that there were some Hellenists in the city). Paul's vision of Jesus, which terminated his persecution of these Hellenists, naturally led him to adopt their liberal attitude to the law, and so brought him, in time, into conflict with the Jerusalem Christians.

The only un-Jewish element in the faith of Paul's Hellenist victims may well have been the belief that salvation comes from Jesus, not from the law. This would have sufficed to provoke the hostility of a Paul zealous for his native traditions, whether the Jesus in question was clearly conceived as a historical personage or as a mystic sacrifice. Paul, who became a convert to the faith he had persecuted, does not suggest that it entertained the former of these two views of Jesus.

There was, of course, a community of Christians in Jerusalem in Paul's day, and he repeatedly alleges his independence of them and of their leaders, whom he names as James, John and Cephas. It is normal to assume, not only that they had been companions of the historical Jesus, but also that when, three years after his conversion, Paul visited Cephas for a fortnight, his purpose was to inform himself about Jesus' life on earth. But if Paul had regarded this topic as of any importance, and Cephas as in a position to inform him concerning it, he would hardly have operated independently of Cephas for the first three years of his Christian life (as he stresses that he did, Gal. 1:16—18). In any case, to suppose that the historical Jesus was the subject of the conversation between the two men during their fortnight together is, as Klein has noted (254, p 289n), 'absolutely impossible, in view of the almost total lack of anything in the nature of Jesus' traditions in the Pauline writings'. Whatever they talked about, they seemed to have been in agreement, for Paul had no conflict with the Jerusalem Church until fourteen years later. Furthermore, the very fact that the Jewish and Roman authorities permitted Christians to practise their religion at Jerusalem at this early date is itself evidence against the view that the founder of the faith had a few years earlier been executed as a result of Jewish or Roman hostility.

In this letter to the Galatians Paul argues with opponents who insisted on circumcision (but not, he implies (6:13; cf. 5:3), on keeping the whole of the Jewish law). They had obviously accused him of having received his gospel from man, not from God; for he rebuts them by declaring that he received it by a direct divine revelation (cf. above, p 29). It has often been assumed that they had reproached him for dependence on the Jerusalem apostles. But recent scholarship has increasingly acknowledged that opponents who insisted on circumcision could not have *criticized* Paul on the ground that he was dependent on the Jerusalem Christianity which upheld circumcision with all other provisions of the Jewish law. Furthermore, these opponents must themselves have been independent of Jerusalem, for Paul does not dispute their view that the true apostle must be called directly to his office by God, but argues only that he himself enjoys this distinction as much as they. They also insisted on the keeping of special 'days and months and seasons and years' (Gal. 4:10), and this links them with the people who are criticized in Coloss. 2:16–18 because of their observation of 'festival, new moon or sabbath' – behaviour which is there said to characterize those who practise 'self-abasement' and angel-worship, and who take their stand on visions. The link between observation of particular 'seasons' and angel-worship is that the demonic powers embodied in the stars and planets are ascendant at certain times and then constitute a danger to man (349, p 49). Schmithals thinks that these people held views akin to those of second century gnostics, for whom angels were evil demons located between man and the realm of light, and making his ascent to it difficult and dangerous. On this view, the 'self-abasement' would be an attitude of humility towards such powers – unnecessary in Paul's view, because Christ has caused them to abandon their evil ways (1: 15–20), and has disarmed and humiliated them (2:15). Schenke thinks that the author of this epistle – whether Paul or (as he supposes) a pupil of Paul writing about AD 70 – controverts a radical gnosticism with a milder gnosticism of his own (346, pp 396, 399).

There is really little basis for assuming that Paul's Christology was very different from that of the Jerusalem leaders. He accepts their right to preach Christianity to Jews (while he is to take it to gentiles, Gal. 2:9), and also insists that there is only one true gospel of Christ (Gal. 1:7–8). If, then, he 'shook hands' over this agreement with James and Cephas, the inference is that they preached the same view of Christ to the Jews as he did to the gentiles. (This would still be the case even if it were true that in Gal. he is answering the charge that he had received his gospel from them; for if this gospel had not been substantially identical with theirs, the charge would have been meaningless.) What divided them was the question of keeping the Jewish religious law. They agreed that salvation comes from faith in Jesus, not from keeping the law; but James – indeed Judaean Christianity generally – could not openly disregard the law, still less preach against it, without inviting persecution from the Jewish authorities; whereas Paul, whose appeal was to gentiles, had nothing to fear from the Jews if he persuaded pagans, who had never kept the law, to embrace a kind of Christianity that dispensed with it. Schmithals, having argued on these lines for a considerable degree of harmony between Paul and James, records with some surprise that 'no one has yet given consideration to the fact that the Jerusalem Christians might be equally ignorant as was Paul of the historical Jesus'. His view (reiterated recently by Marshall, 286, p 284n) is that 'in primitive Christianity Paul's attitude to the historical Jesus seems to have been by no means peculiar but was much more likely to have been typical' (351, p 104n). Paul's attitude is, we shall see (below, pp 40ff), shared by other Christian letter-writers. And we have already seen that when his attacks on rival Christian teachers give plain indication of their theology, it is no more based on traditions about the historical Jesus than is his own. The danger facing him was that the Christian communities he fostered would 'dissolve into mystery cliques and mystic circles' (172, p 39). Such danger is hard to explain if Christianity originated from clearly defined teaching of a historical Jesus, but is perfectly intelligible if the early Christians were – in the words of Köster – 'a syncretistic group which emerged in the Hellenistic-Roman world'. The heresies Paul fought – if we may speak of heresies at all at a time when there was scarcely an organized Church-at-large – were not organized sects but 'ad hoc attempts, arising within the Christian movement, to solve the unavoidable internal problems of such a syncretistic group' (262, p 332).

In addition to attacks on rival Christian doctrines, Paul's letters contain passages which are agreed to be formula-like summaries of Christian beliefs current in his day, his acceptance of which he signifies by incorporating them. They include, as a creed already in use, the statement (quoted above, p 30) about Jesus' death, burial, resurrection and subsequent appearances to Cephas, James and others which Paul surely 'received' as tradition. In some cases he did not merely reproduce such creeds, but adapted or added to their wording in order to bring them into line with his own particular views. We saw, for instance (above, p. 26), that the words with which Jesus, according to Paul, instituted the eucharist, constitute a pre-Pauline formula which may have been adapted (either by Paul himself or by an earlier Christian) in order to link the eucharist with the death of Jesus. Adaptation of the texts in order to introduce allusions to Jesus' death by crucifixion has been discerned in Paul's version of two hymns which he did not himself compose (Phil. 2:5–11 and Coloss. 1:15–20). There is very wide agreement that both these passages are pre-Pauline – they are full of unpauline phrases – except for the references to the cross, which break the metrical structure (however this be analysed) and are usually regarded as Paul's own additions. They are italicized in the following quotations of part of the relevant texts from the RV:

'Christ Jesus ... , being in the form of God, ... emptied himself ... being made in the likeness of men, and ... humbled himself, becoming obedient unto death, *yea, the death of the cross.* Wherefore God also highly exalted him . . . .'

'It was the good pleasure (of the Father) that in him should all the fulness dwell; and through him to reconcile all things unto himself, *having made peace through the blood of his cross*; through him, (I say), whether things upon the earth, or things in the heavens.'

It is clear that, without the additional phrases supplied by Paul, the two hymns tell of the descent and ascent of a divine personage, Jesus, in the manner of the stories told of 'Wisdom' in the Jewish literature of the time. The figure of Wisdom as a personified being, existing before the creation, had arisen early in Jewish thought, probably under the influence of a foreign goddess (Astarte or Isis), rival to Yahweh. The Wisdom of Solomon, in the OT apocrypha, represents Wisdom as 'a breath of the power of God, a clear effluence of the Almighty', who comes forth to dwell among men and bestow her gifts on them (7: 25–7), but most of them reject her. The opening chapters of the book depict the fate of the 'just man', Wisdom's ideal representative. His humiliations are said to include suffering and death, which serve to show his perfect obedience, which in turn is the ground of his exaltation after death. Other Jewish Wisdom literature (sec 193) tells that, after being thus humiliated on earth, Wisdom returned to heaven. It is thus obvious that the humiliation and exaltation of Jesus in Phil. 2: 5–11 derives from ideas well represented in the Jewish background. The figure of the Messiah had not been equated with that of Wisdom, but there were points of connection (see below, p 116) which made it easy for the early Christians to merge the two. Furthermore, apart from ideas concerning Wisdom and the Messiah, it is clear from the Assumption of Moses, written in opposition to militant Messianism of a political kind by a Pharisaic quietist early in the first century, that 'the idea of obedience unto death, a passive acceptance of death out of loyalty to the revealed will of God as the crown of loyalty to the Torah, was in the air in first-century Judaism' (123, p 265). All these elements belonged, then, to the background of early Christian ideas on Jesus.

Paul himself was strongly influenced by the Wisdom traditions, and regards Wisdom as incarnate in Christ, whom he calls 'the wisdom of God' (1 Cor. 1:24), 'in whom are hid all the treasures of wisdom and knowledge' (Coloss. 2:3). Schweizer has shown (364) that statements made about Wisdom in Jewish literature (e.g. that all things came to be through her) are made of Jesus in the Pauline letters. Paul, then, found Jesus portrayed in terms of Wisdom in some already existing Christ hymns, and assimilated them because they accorded well with his own thinking. What these pre-Pauline Christian traditions did not seem to have contained was the idea that Jesus suffered death *by crucifixion*. In the two Christ hymns, this has been added by Paul: and the pre-Pauline formula in 1 Cor. about Jesus' death, resurrection and appearances says nothing about the *manner* of his death. Furthermore, in another passage agreed to be a pre-Pauline hymn, the statement that Christ reconciled things 'through the cross' (Ephes. 2:16) is also regarded as a Pauline addition. There is, then, evidence that some Christians before Paul did not share his view that Jesus was crucified. And that even afterwards some did not accept his crucifixion is suggested by the absence of any clear allusion to it in Rev. (where 11:8 is but an editor's gloss; see JEC, pp 284–5), and also in the hypothetical document known as Q (on which see below, p 84), recent study of which has shown that the cross-resurrection kerygma of Paul can no longer be taken for granted as having been, from the beginning, the basis of all Christian theology (142, p 249).

A crucified Messiah is normally regarded as so unlikely as an invention that the only basis for the view must be the historicity of Jesus' crucifixion. But the Wisdom literature to which Paul is so deeply indebted may have suggested the idea. This literature, which portrays the wise man as persecuted and rejected on earth and vindicated after his death – phases which correspond exactly to Paul's view of how Jesus fared on earth and afterwards – includes the suggestion that his persecution included a 'shameful death' (Wisdom of Solomon 2:12–20). It may well have been musing on such a passage that led Paul (or a precursor) to the idea, so characteristic of his theology, that Christ suffered the most shameful death of all.

That ideas among Jews and early Christians originated as a result of such musing on sacred texts is today admitted, even stressed, partly as a result of the Qumran discoveries. Lindars, in what has been described as 'a most important book' (320, p 23), has shown that, like the Qumran scribes, the earliest Christians developed major aspects of their beliefs and expectations from OT texts, interpreting the texts in the light of their experience and their experience in the light of the texts (277). I illustrated the methods of exegesis practised at Qumran in JEC (pp 248–9), and later in this present book I shall show that Paul's 'experience' is likely to have included knowledge of the crucifixion of holy men one and two centuries before his time – knowledge which could have influenced his interpretation of the 'shameful death' alleged in a text he probably knew well. (The majority of critics explain the undoubted resemblances to the book of the Wisdom of Solomon in the Pauline epistles as due to direct use of it made by Paul: 111, p 1461.)

Finally, none of the passages in Paul's epistles which are regarded as pre-Pauline shows any more knowledge of the historical Jesus than Paul himself does. Heitsch makes the following comment on them:

'Never is it said in these most ancient confessions of faith: because

Jesus of Nazareth has, by his words, opened my eyes to my true nature as man, it follows that he is the Christ. What is affirmed is: the risen one is the Son of God . . . Thus even these oldest formulas . . . are Christological . . . And Paul identifies himself completely with this oldest tradition, and is in full agreement in this respect with Peter, James and the other visionaries of the most primitive Christian community.' (332, p 75)

It is, then, clear that neither Paul's Christian foes nor his Christian friends were better acquainted with Jesus than he was.

(iii) The Post-Pauline Letters and Persecution in the Roman Empire

(a) Dates and Authorship
The silence of Paul is the more significant because it is shared by other NT epistles. Käsemann mentions as an 'astounding thing about the NT' that 'except in the gospels, the earthly Jesus has such small significance in it'; that, outside them, only his cross is of theological relevance, and that even his cross is 'smothered (rather than made historically intelligible) by mythology and hortatory applications of the story' (238, pp 51−2).

Unlike the canonical gospels, which are anonymous and whose titles (ascribing them to named authors) are later additions to the original manuscripts, the post-Pauline letters of the NT are nearly all pseudonymous. They purport to be written by persons whom Christian tradition then regarded as having been of authority − for instance Paul himself, Christian leaders mentioned in his letters (such as Peter or James), or figures known from other Christian tradition (e.g. 'the elder' who says he is the author of 2 and 3 Jn.). The author of the letter of James introduces himself as 'James, a servant of God and of the Lord Jesus Christ'. It is obvious from Paul and from traditions preserved in Acts that a person known as James was an influential leader in Jerusalem. Only 1 Jn. and Hebrews include no indication of authorship. (The ascription to 'John' occurs only in the title of the former.) Nearly all these letters were written in opposition to heretical ideas, and representing them as works of an 'apostle' or of an 'elder' of the early Church was an obvious way of recommending the views expressed in them.[20] Insincerity was not necessarily involved in this process. The real author could well have believed that the spirit of some important Christian of the past was upon him and using him as a mouthpiece (see JEC, pp 309−10). Some of these letters took a very long time to establish themselves as part of the canon of scripture − the epistle of James, for instance does not seem to have been so accepted until the middle of the third century.

The dates of composition of the post-Pauline letters of the NT can be inferred only very indirectly. Inferences are commonly based on references in them to persecution, and so we must look briefly at the evidence for persecution of Christianity up to about AD 120.

Persecution of Christians has been held to have occurred in Nero's Rome in AD 64, under Domitian (AD 81—96) and Trajan (AD 98—117). Tacitus, in an undoubtedly genuine passage, accuses Nero of having executed in savage fashion a 'great multitude' of Christians at Rome as scapegoats for arson for which he was himself rumoured responsible. Suetonius, in a single sentence, mentions Nero's execution of Christians, but says there nothing of the fire (which he does mention elsewhere) nor of any of the attendant circumstances. The sentence, placed in a context with which it ill accords, looks suspiciously like an interpolation (see JEC, pp 186—7). Dio Cassius, writing a century later, describes the fire, but says nothing of any subsequent persecution of alleged incendiaries, whether Christian or other; and the earliest unambiguous Christian reference to persecution under Nero is a statement made by Melito, bishop of Sardis, about AD 170. It would be surprising if a 'great multitude' of Christians lived at Rome as early as AD 64, and in JEC I supposed that Nero's victims were in fact Jews rather than Christians. But I now realize that this is excluded by Josephus' silence; for he promises to catalogue whatever calamities befell the Jews under Nero. In the same passage he also declares his intention to touch but lightly on matters that do not closely concern them (233, 20:8, 3). Thus, if Nero's victims had been Christians, Josephus' silence about the fire and its aftermath is perfectly intelligible. Neither he nor Dio Cassius make any mention of Christians in any of their works — doubtless because they regarded them as too insignificant to be worth attention. Apropos of the silence of Dio Cassius, Merrill has noted that there is no reason to suppose that a pagan historian, living in the first or second century, 'even if he perchance found a notice in some of his sources that Christians had suffered death as alleged malefactors, would see any especial cause on account of the prominence of the sect or the peculiarity of the cases for including any mention of them in his general history of the realm' (296, p 93). Dio Cassius was furthermore a compiler from other people's work. Tacitus, however, as governor of Asia under Trajan in AD 112, had probably had some first-hand experience of Christians which had caused him to dislike them (cf above, p 14); and Merrill has plausibly argued (p 101) that his reference to a 'great multitude' of them who had fallen victim to Nero is rhetorical exaggeration; for his purpose was to paint the Emperor as black as possible, and to show that his behaviour towards these admittedly contemptible persons was unreasonably severe and brought him just opprobrium. Again, the silence of Christians before Melito does not mean that the persecution never occurred; it means rather that it was local and quickly terminated, and also that Christian communities of the day did not keep full and accurate records or archives, nor inform other Christian communities of what had befallen them.

The evidence for persecution under Domitian is admitted to be very slight indeed.[21] There is no testimony earlier than the statement of Melito (made some seventy years after Domitian's death) that 'alone of all the emperors, Nero and Domitian . . . saw fit to slander our faith'. Barnard, who accepts this testimony as accurate, nevertheless admits that it is 'clearly influenced' by Melito's theory that the bad emperors were persecutors and the good ones favourable to Christianity. Barnard adds that 'tradition, after all, does not arise out of nothing' (18, pp 7–8, 13). Indeed it does not, but often from the kind of bias that he himself has ascribed to Melito!

Trajan, on the other hand, is known from the younger Pliny's letter to him of AD 112 to have persecuted Christians in the province of Pontus-Bithynia (along the southern coast of the Black Sea). Pliny was sent to keep order in this unsettled province. The cities there, as everywhere in the Graeco-Roman world, were full of clubs or private associations for various ostensibly non-political purposes, and it was the Roman practice in times of unrest to order the immediate dissolution of all such societies in case they became the foci of intrigue and conspiracy (see Merrill, 296, pp 175–6). Trajan followed this time-honoured precedent, and under his direction Pliny ordered the disbanding of all *collegia* in Bithynia. It is on the basis of this instruction that, in writing to Trajan, he takes it for granted that the profession of the Christian faith (involving as it did assembly for prayer and ritual) is illegal and liable to the penalty of death. His letter also reveals that, in the course of the trials he conducted, his assistants convinced him that the best way of ascertaining whether a person is really a Christian is to require him to invoke the gods, do reverence with incense and wine to their statues and to the Emperor's image, and to curse Christ; for – so it was explained to him – true Christians would always refuse to comply. This shows that Pliny's informants were familiar with action that had been taken by Roman authorities elsewhere against Christians, and that such persecution was not at that time a complete novelty. Nevertheless, the persecution could have been only local and sporadic. The questions that Pliny addressed to Trajan reveal that he 'evidently found nothing in the judicial records of his own predecessors in Bithynia to guide him, and his own by no means limited experience had never brought him into contact with the trial of Christians in other parts of the Empire' (Beare, 31, pp 14–15). That even this persecution was local and shortlived is obvious from the fact that the Christian Melito, in the none too distant Sardis, had clearly not heard of it when he declared about AD 170 that the Church had enjoyed unbroken prosperity under all emperors except Nero and Domitian.

Every Roman subject who was not a Jew was bound to at least nominal conformity to the state religion as much as to its political system; and every Christian, however politically loyal, would refuse if required to show his loyalty by making sacrifice to the state gods. Hence persecution of Christians was bound to occur from time to time almost anywhere in the Empire. Although the evidence that Domitian was responsible for such persecution is very slight indeed, it does seem to be true that 'it was under Domitian that the practices of taking an oath by the Emperor's genius, of offering libation and incense before his statue, and addressing him as *Dominus* grew up. These were retained by Trajan and later emperors' (164, pp 213–14). In other words, from about AD 90 practices to which no Christian could submit were coming increasingly to be demanded of Roman subjects, and refusal to comply meant death – not for any obvious crime, such as conspiracy, but, as it seemed to Christians, for the mere 'name' of being a Christian.

The resilience of Christianity under Roman persecution has often been adduced as an argument in favour of its tenets, even of its claim that there was a historical Jesus who died under Pilate. P. Gardner-Smith, in a long and generous review of JEC, has pressed this point upon me; he doubts 'whether the Christian martyrs would have gone cheerfully to the lion rather than deny their faith in a mythical deity' (170, p 565). In fact, readiness to die for beliefs without inquiry into the evidence supporting them is by no means uncommon; it has been evidenced by orthodox Jews and by Christian heretics as much as by orthodox Christians (all of whom regarded belief as in itself a virtue, and as the key to salvation), and is not even restricted to devotees of religious creeds. It raises the wider question of how behaviour is affected by ideas and emotions and, if one tries to generalize about this, one may say that an individual may be influenced by fear of punishment (in this world or the next), by the example, precept or command of a leader, and by general example and contagion when certain beliefs have become widespread. Fascism, Nazism and Communism, as well as religious beliefs of many kinds, have influenced their adherents in all these ways, not infrequently to the extreme extent of leading them to the supreme self-sacrifice. As Glover concedes – in a book which Gardner-Smith in his review urges me to read – 'men will die for anything that touches their imagination or their sympathy' (174, p 152).

Let us now turn to the problem of dating the post-Pauline letters. I shall use the non-canonical letters of Ignatius, bishop of Antioch, and the letter of Polycarp, bishop of Smyrna, as documents whose dates are already established. Ignatius' letters are generally agreed to have been written shortly before his martyrdom, ca. AD 110. (I have set out the arguments for this view in JEC, pp 164–5.) Polycarp's letter to the Philippians refers to Ignatius' epistles, and was written not much earlier than AD 120, and perhaps as late as AD 135 (see Barnard, 18, pp 33–7).

I Peter

This epistle makes use of Paul's letters and of the deutero-Pauline epistle to the Ephesians, and is therefore later than they. On the other hand it is itself used in (and therefore earlier than) Polycarp's letter. A more precise date for 1 Peter can be inferred from its references to a contemporary persecution of Christians which included those of Asia Minor to whom the epistle is addressed (1:1; 4:12–19; 5:9). The persecution conducted by Nero was (according to the few ancient authorities who are witnesses to the event) limited to the city of Rome, and so was not responsible for the ordeals of Christians in Bithynia and other provinces with which 1 Peter is concerned. On the other hand, Pliny's letter of AD 112 shows that Christians were persecuted in the very region specified in 1 Peter; and 'Pliny's description of his experience and methods could not conceivably correspond more closely to the words of 1 Peter 4:12–16' (Beare, 31, p 14). Most theologians nevertheless date the epistle in Domitian's reign – Kümmel, for instance, suggests AD 90–95 – although Best (who also prefers this earlier date) admits that there is 'a strong case' for a date within Trajan's time.[22]

Hebrews and 1 Clement

There are even fewer clues as to the date of the letter to the Hebrews. The Christians addressed in it are not under persecution: 'In your struggle against sin you have not yet resisted to the point of shedding your blood' (12:4). It is quoted in, and so earlier than, the document known as 1 Clement, an anonymous epistle written in the name of the Christian community in Rome to the Church in Corinth, and traditionally (from ca. AD 170) ascribed to the Clement who is supposed (on very dubious evidence) to have been the head of the Roman Church from AD 88 to 97 (see Merrill's searching discussion, 296, ch. 9). Modern scholars support their contention that 1 Clement was written about AD 96 by taking its opening words as a reference to persecution (although they probably represent merely the author's apology for not having written earlier because all sorts of 'bothering things' have prevented him from doing so) and by identifying this 'persecution' with the supposed persecution of Christians under Domitian. The author of 1 Clement (whom I shall call Clement of Rome) certainly says (ch. 6) that Christians have been persecuted in the past – it is not clear how long past – and some commentators believe that he expresses uneasiness in ch. 7 as to how they will fare in the immediate future (although he here refers to distress which, he feels, will result from 'jealousy and strife' rather than from persecution). Such statements point to no particular period. Internal evidence, however, suggests that Clement of Rome wrote late in the first or early in the second century. He speaks as though the office of 'presbyter' were of long standing, but still knows nothing of monarchical episcopacy (see JEC, pp 164–5); he was familiar with traditions about the deaths (possibly by martyrdom) of Peter and Paul; Christianity was, for him, old enough to be viewed as 'tradition'; and he states that some Roman Christians had lived in the Christian community ('among us') 'from youth to old age' (chs. 5, 7, 63). If, then, 1 Clement can be assigned approximately to the turn of the century, then Hebrews could have been written (as Kümmel supposes) about AD 80–90.[23]

James and 1, 2 and 3 Jn.

Kümmel also assigns the letter of James to the end of the century and 1, 2 and 3 Jn. to AD 90–110. Only a few conservatives still insist on an earlier date.[24]

The canonical post-Pauline letters so far mentioned can be distinguished from those where a date of composition later than AD 100 is much more widely agreed, namely the three Pastoral epistles to Timothy and Titus (ascribed to Paul in the NT), and 2 Peter, the latest book in the canon, later even than the gospels. It is, on internal and external grounds, dated as late as AD 130 (see JEC, pp 159—60). The Pastorals — so-called because they give advice on how to run the Church — contain evidence of a developed Church organization (there is mention of an episcopate), and Harrison has shown that linguistically they 'have more in common with the writings of the eighty-eight years AD 90—178 than with the vastly larger body of Greek literature from Homer downwards till AD 90' (200, p 10). He dates them twenty years later than Ephesians, which he shows is post-Pauline (ca. AD 90), so that the Pastorals were written late in Trajan's life. Hanson puts them at AD 105 (196, p 9). Both these scholars agree that the Pastorals were known to Polycarp and therefore existed in AD 135. Some of these arguments have been challenged by Conzelmann, who nevertheless does not dispute the basic contention of a second century date. He finds that 'judgement concerning the Pastoral Epistles depends less on a single argument than on the convergence of a whole series of arguments' (126, p 1); and they are set out in full in his commentary.

The three Pastorals then are probably, and 2 Peter certainly, of later date than the other canonical post-Pauline letters. Pilate and other gospel tradition about Jesus are mentioned only in these four latest of the NT epistles. And even they are by no means replete with references to such traditions. 2 Peter does indeed refer to the gospel transfiguration story, and has occasion to do so;[2.5] but the Pastoral epistles, although hortatory in character, fail to appeal to words of Jesus even in contexts which, as Davies has noted, clearly invite a reference to his teaching as recorded in the synoptics (121, p 378. He gives examples). What the Pastoral 1 Tim. does unambiguously affirm is that Jesus was a contemporary of Pilate. And that the Pastorals represent a transition to a heightened interest in Jesus' life as an event of the historical past is betrayed by the fact that reminiscence (quite apart from specific historical references) has become important in them in a way unknown in earlier Christian writings. For Paul, 'Christ risen from the dead' is something to be 'believed', something in which the Christian has 'faith' (Rom. 10:9; Coloss. 2:12). In the Pastoral 2 Tim., however, the injunction to 'remember Jesus Christ risen from the dead' (2:8) shows (as Kramer notes, 265, p 23) that the proposition is 'no longer the object of "believing" but of "remembering".'

Paul had said (Rom. 13:3—4) that only evil-doers need fear punishment from the authorities; and 1 Peter 2:13—14 urges submission 'to the emperor as supreme, or to governors as sent by him to punish those who do wrong'. The author of this latter statement surely knew of no tradition which made Pilate responsible for Jesus' death! The Pastoral 1 Tim. (which does link Jesus with Pilate) significantly does not state that governors punish evil-doers and urges rather that intercessions 'be made . . . for . . .

all in high positions, that we may lead a quiet and peaceable life' (2:1–2). A similar doctrine is found in 1 Clement 60–61. Although some of these epistles were written from experience of state persecution, they nevertheless counsel obedience as 'any other attitude would have been almost impossible; rebellion would have been completely crushed' (Best, 39, p 179). Thus Titus 3:1 urges submission 'to rulers and authorities'. Emperor-worship is, of course, not inculcated. 1 Peter 2:17 makes the distinction: 'Fear God. Honour the emperor'. Rev. 13 (of the late first century) does indeed regard the state as satanic, but says so only by means of obscure allusions.

The table opposite sums up what it is reasonable to assert about the dates of the post-Pauline epistles we have been discussing. Each document or group of documents was written within the time limits indicated by the ends of the arrows. Only the four latest (Ignatius, Pastorals, 2 Peter and Polycarp) mention Pilate or show knowledge of some of the four canonical gospels. We shall see later in this chapter that 1 Peter (following Hebrews) assigns Jesus to the recent past, and that the link with Pilate is intelligible as an inference from this tradition.

(b) The Johannine Writings and Docetism

Five NT books have titles ascribing them to someone named 'John' – a gospel (the fourth in the canon), three epistles and an apocalypse. The only one of these five in which the author's name is said, within the book itself, to be John is the apocalypse, and there is very wide agreement that it was not written by the author or authors of the other four. (For the evidence see JEC, p 279.) Of these four, the gospel and the first epistle are anonymous and the second and third epistles purport to be written by a person who calls himself 'the elder'.

Many phrases which occur as words of the author in the three epistles appear as words of Jesus in the fourth gospel. Both epistles and gospel are much concerned to posit a close relationship between the 'Father' and the 'Son'; both insist on the sinlessness of Christ and make much play with the words 'light', 'life' and 'love'. The three epistles and the gospel thus undoubtedly have to some extent a common background, and it is the more remarkable that nonetheless the epistles show no knowledge of the historical situation in which the gospel places Jesus, nor of the biographical details of his life as recorded there. For instance, the first of the epistles (1 Jn.) gives only the following information about him: God sent him as his Son into the world that we might live through him. He is our advocate with the Father, and is also the Christ, and has come in the flesh, sinless, to destroy the works of the devil. He has promised us eternal life and given us the message that God is light; and he (or God) commanded us to love one another. He came by water and blood, laid down his life for us, and his blood cleanses us from all sin.

2 and 3 Jn. (each consisting of but a single chapter) repeat some of these ideas, but add nothing further to the picture. It seems, then, that the

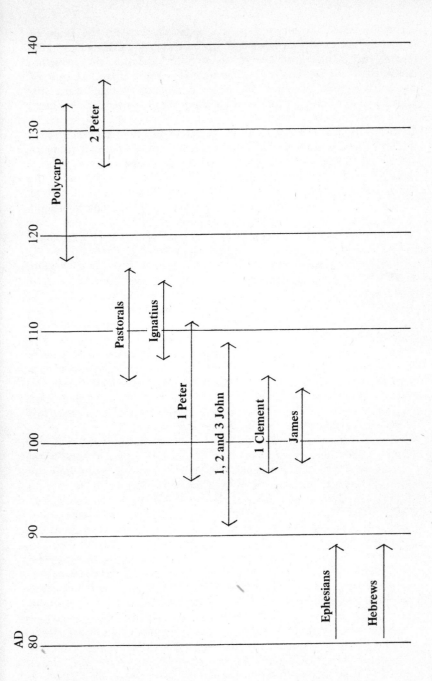

47

'school' of thought from which the gospel and the three epistles derive was broad enough to include Christians who had more and Christians who had less precise and detailed views about the historical Jesus. This is what one would expect if the details of his earthly life began to establish themselves in Christian tradition only at the end of the first century, and if the three epistles were written just prior to, and the gospel just after this time in the same environment.

In addition to the resemblances, there are sufficient linguistic differences to justify the view of those theologians who deny a common authorship for epistles and gospel. And the clear differences in theology between them do seem to indicate that the epistles are earlier. 1 Jn., for instance, still maintains the early Christian doctrine that the world is about to end, whereas in the fourth gospel this eschatology has been dropped (cf. below, p 90). Again, in 1 Jn. Jesus is twice said to be 'the expiation for our sins' (2:2 and 4:10), and this comes nearer than anything in the gospel to the older, Pauline view of the atoning character of his death.

2 and 3 Jn. were obviously composed for a Christian community which felt that it could survive only by strictly excluding all heretics; for 2 Jn. 10f. stipulates that those who do not bring the true doctrine should not be received into one's house, nor even greeted. Houlden concedes that 'this passage has, on any showing, an ugly look', and is distressingly severe in view of the fact that 'the early Church seems to have relied, for such internal cohesion as it possessed, largely upon frequent visits between congregations' (212, pp 146—7). Ignatius, writing probably some years later, likewise insists that the faithful must 'keep away' from heretics 'as from a pack of savage animals'. Christians who wrote on these lines evidently knew nothing of any Jesuine injunction to greet and even to love one's enemies (Mt. 5:44—8).

The author of 1 Jn. is likewise worried by the prevalence of false Christian doctrine. He declares that 'it is the last hour' because the Antichrist, who is to come immediately before the end, has arrived in the form of heretical teachers within the Church who deny that 'Jesus is the Christ' and 'the Son of God', and also that 'Jesus Christ has come in the flesh' (4:2). They were nevertheless Christians, and their views can be understood as a protest against Paul's idea that the heavenly Jesus had assumed a body of flesh — and had thus placed himself open to sinfulness — in order to redeem us by his suffering (2 Cor. 5:21; Coloss. 1:22). This exposure to sin came in time to be regarded as compromising his divine status, and so the so-called Docetists (i.e. 'seemers') insisted that he only *seemed* to have a real body of flesh but in fact had lived on earth as a phantom. They and other heretics took this view also because they regarded suffering (which implies change and imperfection) as foreign to the divine nature. An alternative method of exempting him from suffering was to suppose (as did Cerinthus, a gnostic heretic of the early second century) that the supernatural Christ abandoned the body of the man Jesus before his crucifixion.

The Docetism combated in 1 Jn. arose only late in the first century. Jerome does indeed say that it originated 'when the blood of Christ was still fresh in Judaea'. But he wrote at the end of the fourth century, and he took this view not because he was well-informed about the Judaea of AD 30, but because he was convinced that 1 Jn. was written by John the son of Zebedee and companion of Jesus. The really early Christian documents do not bear Jerome out. Paul unequivocally affirms that Jesus had been a Jew 'according to the flesh' (Rom. 1:3 and 9:5) and writes of Jesus' death 'in his body of flesh' (Coloss. 1:22); and there is no sign of Docetism either in the earlier Christian views he assimilates into his letters, or in the views of the rival Christians he attacks. He does, it is true, seem to equivocate when he declares that God 'sent his own son in the *likeness* of sinful flesh' (Rom. 8:3), and that Christ bore the human *likeness* (Phil. 2:7—8). The word he here uses (*homoioma*) also means 'form'; if there is any ambiguity, it arises from his concern to show that Jesus in his earthly career was similar to sinful men and yet sinless. But whatever Paul intended, his words could readily have been interpreted by a later generation as a compromise formula — and furthermore as one that did not go far enough in the direction of denying flesh to Jesus.

The 'false prophets' attacked in 1 Jn. obviously believed that, because they were in close spiritual contact with the supernatural Christ of their faith, they were themselves above the level of bodily flesh and were incapable of sin. Against their claim to be sinless (1:8; cf. 3:7) the epistle argues that we need Jesus' blood sacrifice to cleanse us (1:7), and that he therefore came 'not with the water only, but with the water and the blood' (5:6) and 'laid down his life for us' (3:16). Commentators see in the water a reference to his baptism. But the writer may be referring to a practice of salvation by baptism which, it was believed, Jesus had himself enjoined. If, however, we grant that he is alluding to Jesus' baptism while on earth, we shall see (below, pp 156f) that there is reason why such an incident should early have been added to the meagre Pauline record of his biography. Furthermore, the writer of the epistle could not have taken a reference to Jesus' baptism from the fourth gospel, in which this event is not recorded. If, then, the epistle refers to the baptism (and even bases an important argument on it), this is strong evidence against the commonly held view that the epistle is later than, and dependent on, the fourth gospel. Again, it is striking that the author of the epistle does not defend his allegation that 'Jesus is the Christ' by mentioning biographical incidents that would establish this, but by arguing that he is intimately linked with the Father: 'No one who denies the Son has the Father' (2:23). The same argument is offered for the same purpose in 2 Jn.

This most significant difference between the Johannine epistles and gospel is again illustrated when we find the statement of 1 Jn. that Jesus 'came with the water and the blood' appearing in the gospel as a specific incident in his human biography. We are there told (in a narrative unknown to the synoptic gospels) that the soldiers did not break his legs on the cross, but that one of their number pierced his side, 'and at once there came out blood and water' (Jn. 19:34). This is not only directed against the Docetic theory that his body was a mere phantom, but has — as Dodd concedes (134, p 428) — even further theological implications: the water is the spirit given to believers (7:38—9) which if a man drink he will never thirst again (4:14). (The reference is to Christian baptism, at which a man is reborn from water and spirit, 3:3—6); and the blood is the 'true drink' of which we must partake if Christ is to abide in us (6:55). For the evangelist, as for Paul (see below, pp 184, 186), the efficacy of both sacraments depends on the death and resurrection of Jesus. (The bestowal of the spirit and the forgiveness of sins acquired in baptism is, for instance, in virtue of Christ's death: for the spirit is said (7:39) to presuppose his 'glorification' in the Johannine sense of his death.) Cullmann is obviously right to say that the evangelist reports the issue of blood and water from Jesus' side 'because it is a very striking sign of the connexion between the death of Christ and the two sacraments' (114, p 114).

When the author of 1 Jn. insists — against the teaching of heretics — that Jesus 'came not with the water only but with the water and the blood', it is clear that the heretics found it harder to accept whatever is meant in this context by blood than whatever is meant by water. The meaning here cannot, therefore, be the issue of the two substances from Jesus' side, as reported in the gospel; for we cannot suppose that the heretics held that only water issued from his body on the cross! Rather must we seek a significance for the two terms which will allow them to be meaningfully distinguished. Houlden suggests that Jesus' baptism and death are meant; and that the heretics, like Cerinthus, believed that 'the divine spiritual redeemer entered the man Jesus at the moment of his baptism, but, being impassible, and belonging to the realm of immunity from death, he departed from him before the crucifixion' (212, p 126).

In the fourth gospel, the issue of blood and water from Jesus' side during the crucifixion is said to have occurred in order that two 'scriptures' might be fulfilled, namely the direction in Exodus 12:46 for the preparation of the paschal lamb ('Not a bone of him shall be broken'), and Zechariah 12:10 ('They shall look on him whom they have pierced'). Such concern with the OT is another of the features which distinguishes the Johannine gospel from the three epistles, which are unique in the NT for their paucity of reference to the OT. It has long been clear that all the evangelists recount Jesus' life and death 'in the context of the OT scriptures' — to use the disarming phrase with which Hoskyns and Davey explain the many gospel details which are so closely paralleled in the OT that we must suspect that they were deliberately inserted to give the appearance of fulfilment of prophecy. The fourth evangelist obviously feared that he would be accused of concocting these crucifixion details 'in the context of the OT' for the edification of believers; for he safeguarded himself by adding: 'He who saw it has borne witness — his testimony is true, and he knows that he tells the truth — that you also may believe.'

This solemn attempt to designate the spear thrust and its consequences as a historical fact reported by a reliable witness of the event suggests that he was aware that this interpretation of the manner in which Jesus 'came with water and blood' was something of a novelty to the community for which he wrote. Only the most conservative theologians (such as Professor Bruce) continue to insist that the evangelist's affirmation is to be taken entirely at its face value as based on an eye-witness report. Bruce even uses this text as a ground for the generalization that 'as in other details of the passion story, it is the event that has suggested the OT *testimonium*, not the other way round' (77, p 350)!

The whole story (Jn. 19:31–7) of the breaking of the legs of Jesus' fellow sufferers and of the spear thrust into his own body is clearly a tradition which the fourth evangelist was not able to work into complete consistency with the next section of his narrative. For the story begins with the statement that 'the Jews', anxious that the bodies should not remain exposed during the sabbath, requested Pilate to have the sufferers killed and their bodies taken down. But after the breaking of the legs and the spear thrust, and the explanation of their scriptural significance, we read that Pilate was approached by Joseph of Arimathea, who asked to be allowed to take Jesus' body down; 'and Pilate gave him leave' (verse 38). If we are to believe verse 31, Joseph came to Pilate too late, for 'the Jews' had already persuaded the governor to have the victims killed and their bodies removed. Haenchen notes (191, p 544n) that the repetition of the verb 'to take' (from the cross) in these two verses shows that verses 31–7 represent an insertion. In Mk.'s version of Joseph's approach to Pilate, the governor is surprised to learn from him that Jesus is already dead (Mk. 15:44). This is certainly irreconcilable with Jn. 19:31–7, according to which Pilate had himself earlier agreed to expedite the death of the sufferers so that their bodies could be removed quickly. In sum, the story of the leg-breaking and the spear thrust is not only absent from the synoptics but also includes a detail which is excluded by Mk. and which does not harmonize well even with the pericope that follows in Jn. Furthermore — contrary to what has often been affirmed — modern medicine is unable to explain the issue of water from Jesus' wound. Blinzler, having discussed a comprehensive survey of this subject which appeared in a Berlin medical journal in 1963, concedes that the issue of water is either to be understood symbolically or as a miracle (49, p 384).

(c) 1 Peter and Hebrews: Jesus Assigned to the Recent Past
1 Peter, the letter to the Hebrews, and the letter ascribed to James likewise do not refer to Jesus' life in the way one would expect. 1 Peter, for instance, 'contains no kind of hint of an acquaintance with the earthly Jesus, his life, teaching and death, but refers only to the "suffering" of Christ' (268, p 298) and obtains its information on this subject not from traditions about Jesus' life on earth, but from the description of the sufferings of the 'servant of Yahweh' in Isaiah 53 (see 211, p 57 and JEC,

51

p 154). All these writers, like Paul, stress the merit of belief in Christ, yet neither they nor Paul suggest that Jesus himself demanded such belief, although, according to the gospels, this inculcation is one of the most prominent and oft-repeated elements in his teaching. In Rom. 1:17 Paul quotes Habakkuk, but not Jesus, to establish that 'he who through faith is righteous shall live'. Hebrews 11 consists of a eulogy of faith; many OT characters and their deeds are mentioned as examples, but none of the instances familiar to us from the gospels. The epistle of James follows the same technique; the author 'does not point to Jesus as an example, but rather to the OT prophets, Job and Elijah' (268, p 288). The significance of such silence is recognized even by some theologians. Teeple says: 'If an oral tradition of Jesus' teaching was circulating in the churches, it is incredible that Christian writers did not quote it when they were *discussing the same subject*' (386, p 63. Teeple's italics).

I will not repeat the analysis given of these epistles in JEC (pp 151–60) but will confine further comments to the letter to the Hebrews, which has often been held to give more information about Jesus than any other first century epistle. It certainly uses the plain name 'Jesus' – with no added title of 'Lord' or 'Christ' – more frequently, and this has been interpreted as expressive of an interest in the earthly Jesus. But the real reason for the usage seems to be the concern of the writer to hint at a parallel between Jesus and Joshua (4:8). The two names are identical in Greek, and both mean 'Yahweh is salvation'.[26] It is surprising that so few NT passages exploit this identity. Jesus seems to owe his name to its links with 'salvation' rather than to its connection with the OT Joshua: Mt. 1:21 expressly says that his name is Jesus because 'he will save his people'. Early Christian writers tend to link him with Moses rather than with Joshua, for it was Moses whom the Jews of the first century AD regarded as the prototype of the Messiah.[27] Nevertheless, Joshua had not been lost completely from sight in the Messianic thinking of the time.[28]

For the author of Hebrews, as for Paul, Jesus is a pre-existent son of God. He existed before the world was created; indeed God 'created the world through him' (1:2; cf. Paul's affirmation that there is 'one Lord, Jesus Christ, through whom are all things', 1 Cor. 8:5–6). Like Paul, the author finds it necessary to attack Christians who worshipped angels, and insists that Jesus is superior to them. But how can Jesus, who suffered humiliation and death, be represented as superior to angels who transcend this earthly condition? The author seems to be trying to answer this objection when he affirms (i) that Jesus shared our flesh and blood only for a short time (2:7) as a Jew of the tribe of Judah (7:14) – the origin which many Jews expected the Messiah to have – and (ii) that he had to become like us 'in every respect' (2:17) in order to make proper expiation for human sin. Thus, as with some of his pagan predecessors (see below, p 66), his very appeal depends on his having participated in human suffering (2:18). His worshippers can look up to him as an ideal of fortitude, believing that if they stand firm under duress, they will finally be delivered as he was. Because of his likeness to us, he has been 'tempted' in every way, 'yet without sinning', and is therefore able to sympathize with our weaknesses (4:15–16). This is the only NT writing outside the synoptics which clearly states that Jesus was tempted; but the reference is not to the temptation in the desert which the synoptics place between his baptism and the beginning of his public ministry, but rather to his suffering and death. He 'learned obedience through what he suffered', and by this faithfulness under temptation he was 'made perfect' and thus made competent to save men (5:8–9). The 'hostility he endured from sinners' (12:3) designates not altercations with the scribes and Pharisees, nor an arrest and trial, but again his submission to a shameful death on the cross, after which he took his seat at the right hand of God (12:2). There is no mention of his baptism, discourses or miracles. This almost exclusive emphasis on his passion constitutes a notable development. In the pre-Pauline hymn of Phil. 2, Jesus is depicted, following Jewish traditions, as the just one whose obedience involves submission to suffering, and his death represents but the culmination of this obedience. Paul himself added the idea that the death was by crucifixion (cf. above, p 39) and was of overriding significance. In Hebrews these Pauline views have become so important that the death on the cross, and the suffering attending it, have come to represent the whole of the 'obedience' of which the earthly life was a manifestation (cf. Schweizer, 363, pp 52, 59).

A writer who thus stresses the passion would surely record such details of it as he knew. One passage (5:7) is sometimes interpreted as an allusion to the agony in Gethsemane; but it is not in accord with the gospel story and could easily have been constructed from material in the Psalms (see JEC, p 159). Throughout the epistle Jesus' humble submission to pain is not authenticated by reference to historical details, but is simply asserted as a theological postulate. One detail that looks like historical reminiscence is the statement that Jesus was executed 'outside the gate'. The expression occurs nowhere else in the NT, but has often been taken as an allusion to Golgotha. Grässer however points out that any writer who believed that Jesus was executed would naturally locate the execution outside a town, for this was eastern and Roman practice in cases of capital punishment (177, p 82). This crucifixion outside the gate provides the writer with proof that Jesus fulfilled the stipulations of the Jewish religious law concerning the sin offering on the day of Atonement.[29] It really does not look as though first century Christians found the crucifixion an embarrassing or compromising fact!

One of the main points of the epistle is to show the superiority of Jesus' single and unique sacrifice over that of the annually repeated Jewish atonement ritual. To demonstrate this superiority the author regards heaven as an ideal counterpart to the sanctuary in which the Levitical ritual takes place. Christ is said to have entered into a holy of holies 'not made with hands, that is, not of this creation' (9:11). The implication seems to be that, just as the high priest took into the innermost sanctuary the blood of animals killed outside it and sprinkled this blood there as atonement for sin, so Jesus, killed on earth, took his own blood into heaven and offered it to the Father. Furthermore, he did this but once (10:12). He has not 'entered into heaven itself . . . repeatedly, as the high priest enters the Holy Place yearly' but has appeared on earth 'one and for all at the end of the age' (9:24—6) and, having entered heaven after his death, has remained there. This 'once and for all' seems to mean that, while his suffering on the cross occurred but once, his priestly work in the heavenly sphere after his death is eternal (5:6) and has brought about a permanent atonement (cf. Brooks, 75, p 212).

It is, then, in the course of this complicated argument that the author uses phrases which imply the historical uniqueness of Jesus' life on earth: he offered up himself 'once for all' (7:27); he 'appeared once for all at the end of the age' (9:26—8; 10:10). Theologians have seen in this insistence that he came to earth at one definite time conscious opposition to the timeless redeemer myth of gnosticism (cf. Grässer, 177, pp 70—1); for the author does write with an eye to heretics — he instructs the faithful not to be 'led away by diverse and strange teachings' (13:8—9) — and he also stresses that Jesus did assume human flesh (a view unacceptable to gnostics). He does not say when it was that Jesus came to earth, but indicates that it was in the relatively recent past: 'in these last days' (1:2), 'at the end of the age' (9:26). This constitutes the really important difference between Paul's epistles on the one hand and such documents as Hebrews and 1 Peter on the other. Paul's epistles fill one hundred pages of the NEB and include many references to Jesus' death without once indicating when it occurred. But Hebrews, although a mere fifteen pages in length, and the even shorter 1 Peter assign it not to a vague, completely indeterminate past, but to the last times.

Paul does indeed come quite close to this idea when he says (Gal. 4:4) that God sent his Son to earth 'when the time had fully come' and when he implies (2 Cor. 5:17) that the Christian lives in a new era: 'If anyone is in Christ, he is a new creation; the old has passed away, behold, the new has come'. The lateness of Jesus' visit to earth is also suggested by the contrast Paul draws between Jesus and Adam. Jesus is the 'last Adam' or 'second man' (Rom. 5:14; 1 Cor. 15:45, 47) who restored mankind to the state of righteousness which had been lost by the first Adam. Whereas the first man disobeyed and fell, the second or last man obeys and is vindicated. Hence the emphasis on Jesus' obedience unto death characteristic both of Paul and of the Christ hymns before him (cf. above, p 38). Speculation on Adam was rife in gnostic thinking (see below, p 191) which may well have been known to Paul and which combined traditions about an Adam-like redeemer with traditions from the Wisdom literature. Particularly interesting in this connection is the thought of Paul's Jewish contemporary Philo of Alexandria. Philo, interpreting Genesis in the light of his Platonism, posited not only a human Adam made of clay, but an ideal heavenly counterpart to him, an archetypal 'first' or 'heavenly' man, whom he identified with 'Wisdom' or 'Logos' (see Fuller, 166, pp 96–7, 211, 236; Hamerton-Kelly, 193, pp 141–2, 163). Paul seems to be combining such thinking with Jewish apocalyptic ideas. According to him, the heavenly man will come at the end of time to bring the world to an end, as the apocalypses state, and has not come at the beginning, as Philo and other mystics held. But in so far as he has already been on earth, then this visit – by contrast with the life of the earthly Adam – would be assigned to the end, not to the beginning. The Wisdom literature tells of a whole series of emissaries who are rejected on earth as her spokesmen, and the early Christians could well have thought of Jesus as the last of these.

However, all that Paul says on the timing of Jesus' visit to earth falls short of the quite explicit statement of 1 Peter 1:20 that Christ, 'destined before the foundation of the world', was 'made manifest *at the end of the times* for your sake'. This may originally have meant no more than that his coming inaugurated the final epoch (however long) of man's history – the epoch which would culminate in his return to end the world and to judge mankind. But it could easily have come to mean that he was on earth in the recent past; and this is what the author of Hebrews had come to assume of Jesus. But it seems that this idea did not find immediate and universal acceptance, for it is not stated in the three Johannine epistles, nor in Clement of Rome's letter (all written about the end of the century: cf. the chart on p 47 above). Clement's silence is very striking as he obviously knew the letter to the Hebrews well. He does indeed mention 'apostles' who preached what they had 'received' from Jesus Christ. But the suggestion is not that they had been pupils of a historical Jesus, but rather that the Holy Spirit informed their preaching (1 Clement 42). It was surely in this sense that they 'were given to understand by our Lord Jesus Christ that the office of the bishop [or of 'overseer' in the Church – Clement knows nothing of monarchical episcopacy] would give rise to intrigues' (ch. 44); for, apart from the fact that Jesus' teaching in the gospels says nothing of bishops, such a statement would not have been intelligible to members of the nascent Church as it was before AD 70. Like the apostles of whom he writes, Clement himself speaks 'through the Holy Spirit' with Jesus' voice and must therefore be obeyed (chs. 59, 63). It may well be that this emphasis on the power of the risen Jesus to convey instruction through the spirit made Clement indifferent to when the earthly Jesus shed his blood for our salvation. (*That* he did so is clearly stated in ch. 7 of the epistle.) 1 Peter, on the other hand, is much less concerned with the spirit and dwells on the sufferings of the earthly Jesus in order to stiffen Christian resistance to the persecution then being directed at the Church.

In sum, the idea, adumbrated in Hebrews, that Jesus died recently, is ignored in the slightly later 1 Clement and in the Johannine letters, but is picked up in 1 Peter. The next stage was to pin-point the recent past in which Jesus had allegedly lived in such a way as to specify a precise historical context; and this is what we find in a number of documents which can with confidence be assigned to the early second century – the letters of Ignatius and the Pastoral epistle 1 Tim., which link Jesus with Pilate – as do Tacitus (ca. AD 120) and the authors of the gospels.

(d) Conclusion Concerning the First Century Evidence

This long account of the first century epistles has been a necessary prelude to later chapters on the gospels in that it provides the justification for viewing sceptically gospel claims of what Jesus said and did. Critical theologians themselves take a sceptical view of the gospels, but I need to make clear my basis for accepting their scepticism instead of the standpoint of their more orthodox colleagues. The problem can be illustrated from recent comments on Mk. Nineham points out that Mark represents Jesus as adopting in his miracles of healing the techniques of the pagan and Christian wonder-workers of the evangelist's own day, and that it is therefore not necessary to suppose that he drew his information from reliable traditions about the historical Jesus (314, p 217). To this Hanson has objected that Jesus may well have done what Mark's contemporaries also did, and that it is arbitrary to proceed from the assumption that what the evangelist says cannot be historically true and must be explained on some other basis (195, p 76). Hanson's objection can be answered by showing that the gospels are relatively late compositions – the task of my next chapter – and that, as shown in this present chapter, earlier Christian literature does not corroborate their statements. It is not merely a question of such details as healing miracles (which are incompatible with Paul's view of Jesus). My argument is that the Christian epistles of the first century do not support the historical setting which is fundamental to the whole gospel narrative of Jesus' life.

Theologians often attribute what Christian first century writers say and fail to say about Jesus to the dominance of 'the Easter events' even in the gospels, which devote a disproportionate amount of space to the final few days of his life. On this view, writers who are silent about his life and doctrines knew of them, but neglected them because they regarded the passion and resurrection as so much more important. This does not explain why the neglect extends to occasions when his life and doctrines would have supported the view which these writers were trying to establish (nor why even the 'Easter events' were so long in acquiring a historical context), and the facts are better explained if we assume that, for the earliest Christians, Jesus was a dying and rising god of whose human biography nothing was known. Grässer concedes that the importance of the resurrection to the NT epistle writers of the first century explains only their unwillingness to write of his life as detached historiographers, not their almost total silence about it; he candidly admits that this silence is an unexplained riddle (177; pp 64n, 89).

I am aware that one cannot always infer a writer's ignorance of something relevant to his interests from his silence about it. Two NT epistles (James and Jude) say next to nothing about Jesus, and James does not even mention his death and resurrection, which figure so prominently in Paul's writings. What I find significant are not occasional silences of this kind, but a silence which is persistent and repeated in all the documents of a period – documents written by different authors under different conditions – on matters to which they could not have been indifferent. One can try to account for the silence of an individual writer by ascribing to him a specialized theological standpoint, as Brandon does to Paul. But such hypotheses are built on questionable assumptions, and they entirely fail to explain why this silence is common to all writers of the period. Hahn (192) has recently been able to represent early Christian thinking as orientated primarily towards the historical Jesus only by taking the gospels as his point of departure, and by practically ignoring – as a theological reviewer (400, pp 196–7) has justly complained – the earlier evidence which betrays so clearly that Christology developed from reflection on the *risen* Lord.

Such reflection was stimulated by controversy. The Christology of an apologist was not completely fixed, but what he affirmed about Christ would to some extent depend on the kind of rival doctrines he was concerned to discredit. Sometimes deductions were made from premises about Jesus' nature. The view that he was the agent of creation (cf. above, p 52) is simply an inference from the belief that he was redeemer; for if he was, then there can be no place or force beyond his redemptive power. Stories of his descent into the nether regions can be similarly understood as inferences from the same fundamental belief. The nether world has often been regarded as beyond the reach of salvation. But 'a lord who is truly Lord can tolerate no dark corners in the universe unreached by his power' (Craddock, 109, p 112). And so it was confidently affirmed that he 'descended into the lower parts of the earth' (Ephes. 4:9; 1 Peter 3:19–20). That such deductive reasoning has never ceased to be a fertile source of biographical information about him is clear from present-day contentions that, because he must surely have led a full life, he may well have been married.

(e) Ignatius and 1 Timothy: Jesus linked with Pilate
Jesus is not linked with a recognizable historical situation in any document so far studied (Christian, Jewish, or pagan) that is likely to have been written in the first century. The utmost that is affirmed of him in the late first century epistles is that he lived in a past which is recent, but still unspecified. If, then, the view that he died under Pilate originated only about the very end of the century, few who had been alive in AD 30 were still alive to come forward and contradict it. Thus I am not supposing that this view became established under circumstances which ought immediately to have discredited it.

One factor which led Christians to specify in this way the time when Jesus had lived was the rival Christologies of early Christian communities. We shall study these in detail in chapter 4 below, but I must briefly anticipate one aspect of the discussion there that is relevant to the problem in hand here. A number of hymns included in the Pauline letters represent Christ as a supernatural personage who descended to earth, lived there in humility and obscurity, and then reascended to heaven. Somehow, however, Christians came in time to think of him as a prominent teacher and a worker of prodigious miracles, as a man whose life was the reverse of obscure. And so we find that the hymns included in the epistles of the very late first or very early second century represent his life on earth as a manifestation, not a concealment, of his divine glory. 1 Peter 1:20 declares that he was 'made manifest at the end of the times'; and the Pastoral 1 Tim. 3:16 that 'he was manifested in the flesh; . . . [was] preached among the nations, believed on in the world'. Now once Christians had come to believe not only that he had been on earth recently, but also that he had lived in eminence instead of obscurity, then a tradition bringing him into conflict with a recent ruler of the country could naturally arise.

Another factor leading to this result was the struggle against Docetism. We saw that 1 and 2 Jn. complain of Christians who denied that Jesus had 'come in the flesh'; and that these heretics − since they regarded flesh as sinful − probably thought that he had lived on earth, but with only a phantom body, which could of course not have experienced pain. These two epistles were written late in the first century, when − as we have just seen − the idea that Jesus had been on earth recently was beginning to take root (although they do not themselves express it); and so the obvious way to establish, against the Docetists, that Christ had come in the flesh would be to specify details of his recent birth from a human mother, and of recent activities which had involved his flesh in real suffering. Since the author of 1 and 2 Jn. does not do this, it seems that no such details were available to him. But the need to confute heretics of the type he mentions must have led fairly rapidly to the invention of the necessary biographical tradition; for Ignatius was able to draw on it ca. AD 110 in order to crush them. He considered salvation dependent on sacramental eating of the saviour's 'flesh'. If Jesus' body were a mere phantom, there could be no salvation, and so Ignatius insisted that 'Jesus Christ, David's scion and Mary's, was really born of a virgin and baptized by John, really persecuted by Pilate and nailed to the cross in the flesh'. And then the fourth gospel unambiguously affirmed that 'the word became flesh', thus 'correcting' the Pauline formula 'in the likeness of flesh'.[30]

Ignatius is most emphatic that Jesus suffered under Pilate, and, in three of the letters he wrote to Christian communities in Asia Minor as he passed through this region on his way to martyrdom in Rome, he presses this view upon the faithful. He assures the Trallians that Jesus was 'really persecuted by Pilate', and urges the Magnesians 'not to yield to the bait of false doctrine, but to believe most steadfastly in the birth, the passion and the resurrection, which took place during the governorship of Pontius Pilate'. That he needed to emphasize in this way when these events took place suggests that not all Christians were agreed on the matter − particularly as he specifies the time when as an integral part of the correct doctrine which, he admits, is in competition with other doctrine.

What, then, would cause a Christian of the late first or early second century, who had already come to believe that Jesus had been on earth in the recent past, to assign his life to Pilate's Palestine, rather than to some other recent period? Now the belief that Christ had died by crucifixion was firmly established as early as Paul — before the death had been given a date or even a period. It would therefore be natural for Christians of ca. AD 100, who were familiar with crucifixion as a Roman punishment, to think that he had been killed by the Romans. Such Christians would have known that 'Christ' or 'Messiah' was a royal title, and that anyone who made pretensions to it would immediately be charged with sedition by the Roman authorities, whether he understood the title in a political sense or not. There had been rebellion enough since AD 6 to justify nervousness on the part of the Romans, and hundreds of patriots had been crucified. Indeed, little is known of some procurators of Judaea except their severity in the face of rebellion. 'The one fact of importance' recorded of the procurator of AD 46—8 is that he ordered the crucifixion of two sons of a well-known rebel of the previous generation (Schürer, 360, p 457). The procurator of AD 48—52 captured some Samaritan rebels, and the governor of Syria had them crucified. The crucifixions ordered by Felix, procurator AD 52—60, were according to Josephus 'innumerable'. In AD 66 Gessius Florus had even Jews who were Roman citizens crucified at Jerusalem; and in AD 70 Titus, besieging the city, crucified whoever he captured. Jewish resistance did not cease after the crushing defeat of AD 70, as the revolt of Bar Cochba (AD 132—5) illustrates. If, then, Jesus had recently lived a conspicuous life on earth as son of David and as Christ, he would surely have been killed by the Romans. To the patriotically minded Jews or Jewish Christians such a fate would have appeared as a heroic and honourable death. The less militant would have regarded his murder as the inevitable Roman reaction to one who came forward as Christ. Hegesippus, a Church historian who wrote ca. AD 150—80, alleged that Jews were executed under Vespasian, Titus and Domitian simply on the ground that they were believed to be descendants of King David, so determined were the Romans to eliminate Messianic claimants (149, Bk. 3:12 and 19—20). The story may be mere legend (see Schürer, 360, p 528), but it shows what Christians were capable of assuming the Romans to have done to members of the house of David; and Jesus was regarded very early in Christian thinking as 'descended from David' (Rom. 1:3). Hence there is no difficulty in understanding the origin of the tradition, recorded in Mk. 15:26, that 'the inscription of the charge against him read, "The King of the Jews" '. Braun and Haenchen agree that this formulation is Christian, not Jewish, and represents the claim of the victim rather than the charge against him (73, p 50; 191, p 536). Admittedly, Paul was also familiar with Roman crucifixion. But his Jesus had lived a life of complete obscurity, and that not necessarily recently. Hence Paul did not have the motives of

Christians of AD 100 (for whom Jesus' life had been both prominent and recent) for supposing that he had been confronted with Pilate, nor even that his crucifixion had occurred during the Roman rule (cf. below, p 198).

These Christians of AD 100 were doubtless struck by the fact that, although Jesus had lived recently, there were nevertheless very few who could offer plausible reminiscences of him. It was therefore inferred that he could not have died very recently (e.g. in the war of AD 66 to 70), and must have come at an earlier date. This earlier date, to be nevertheless recent, would have to be during the Roman rule of Judaea (i.e. after AD 6); and from this premiss Pilate would naturally come to mind as his murderer; for Pilate was particularly detested by the Jews, and is indeed the only one of the prefects who governed Judaea between AD 6 and 41 who attracted sufficient attention to be discussed by Philo and Josephus. Philo describes him as 'naturally inflexible and stubbornly relentless', and accuses him of 'acts of corruption, insults, rapine, outrages on the people, arrogance, repeated murders of innocent victims, and constant and most galling savagery' (quoted by Brandon, 66, p 68). It also appears from this testimony that he was quite capable of murdering the innocent, so the supposition that Jesus was his victim would not necessarily imply that he was a rebel against Rome. Furthermore, a Christian writer who stamped Pilate as his murderer would not need to fear that such allegation would incur Roman displeasure. Both Philo and Josephus criticized Pilate harshly, yet were perfectly loyal to Rome, where Pilate does not seem to have been highly esteemed. (The legate of Syria sent him to Rome in AD 36 to answer to Tiberius for a massacre; the Emperor, however, died before he arrived, and nothing is known of his subsequent fate.)

I would stress that I am not imputing fraud to the Christians of the early second century. Those who lack understanding of the mythological process are apt to argue that, either a tradition is true, or else it must have been maliciously invented by cynics who knew the facts to be otherwise. The train of reasoning that I am envisaging as having occurred in the minds of these second century Christians can be summarized as follows: If Jesus is the god of the 'last times' who is soon to bring the world to an end, then his first coming, as well as his second, is surely to be allocated to the 'last times', i.e. is of recent occurrence. But if it had occurred very recently, there would be hundreds who could report in detail on it. As this does not seem to be the case, the occurrence cannot be quite so recent, and therefore probably occurred during Pilate's administration; for he was just the type of person to have murdered Jesus, and was also active sufficiently recently for a few contemporaries still to be (or to have recently been) alive.

Alfaric has pointed out that there is also scriptural basis for placing Jesus' lifetime in the early part of the first century. Genesis 49:10 reads:

'The sceptre shall not depart from Judah, nor the ruler's staff from between his feet, until Shiloh comes.

[The Septuagint here reads:
'Until there come the things stored up for him.'] And to him shall be the obedience of the peoples.'

The original sense seems to have been that Judah, the son of Jacob, will retain his command until he has achieved all that is his due, in particular the submission of the neighbouring peoples who disputed his authority. But 'Judah' was later understood as the tribe, or, more generally, as the inhabitants of Judaea, and the enigmatic phrase 'Shiloh' as the Messiah. Christians of the second half of the second century, such as Justin and Irenaeus, interpreted the oracle in this sense, and as implying that the Messiah would come before Judaea lost its independence.[31] This loss could be regarded has having occurred either in AD 6, when Augustus deposed Archelaus and annexed his territory, or in AD 44, when Herod Agrippa I (grandson of Herod the Great) died. With the connivance of the Emperor Caligula, he had ruled Judaea, as its last king, from AD 37. Justin and Irenaeus, both of whom were well acquainted with the synoptics, of course both believed, quite independently of the Genesis oracle, that Jesus was alive in the first century. But if the oracle was regarded Messianically earlier in the second century, then it may have helped to establish this view.

The earliest NT references to Pilate are in Mk. and in the Pastoral 1 Tim. The date of Mk. I have yet to discuss; but we have seen already that the Pastoral epistles are roughly contemporaneous with the (non-canonical) writings of Ignatius. By this time, looking back to Jesus' life on earth had become important in a way unknown in earlier Christian writings (cf. above, p 45). And it is, therefore, appropriate that in 1 Tim. 6:13 Jesus is said 'in his testimony *before* (Greek 'epi') Pontius Pilate' to have 'made the good confession'. This may well refer to the oral testimony which, according to the gospels, he gave, although the Greek can equally well mean that his 'testimony' or 'witness' was his martyrdom *in the time of* Pilate. Kelly has noted that Pilate has 'no place in the earliest summaries of the kerygma', but that the formula given in 1 Tim. rapidly became 'almost routine', and is found in Ignatius, Justin, Irenaeus and Tertullian. The passage occurs in a context of six verses which are widely regarded as an intrusion, as a unit inserted here by the author; and Kelly believes that it echoes a baptismal creed which mentioned Pilate in order to specify the historical setting of the crucifixion. 'A date was called for so as to bring out that these events did not happen anywhere at any time, and that the Gospel is not simply a system of ideas' (246, pp 149–50; 247, p 143). He of course accepts the historicity of the crucifixion, and argues only that specific mention of the governor in the creed became in due course expedient for the reason given. But I would argue that this reason was itself sufficient to originate a formula mentioning Pilate without any historical basis.

Another reason why Jesus' fate came to be linked with Pilate emerges if we take the Greek 'epi' to mean his confession *in the presence of* Pilate.

The earliest Christian documents mentioning Pilate were written when Christians were anticipating persecution for refusing to offer sacrifice to the Emperor as a token of their loyalty to Rome. The Pastoral 2 Tim. declares (3:12) that 'all who desire to live a godly life in Christ Jesus will be persecuted'. That the purpose of Mark was to give members of the Christian fellowship fortitude to face persecution is suggested by the form of his gospel. It is not a story of Jesus' life, and deals but sketchily even with his ministry. What it does show is 'Jesus suffering and victorious, as God's Anointed'; and that 'he expected his followers to suffer and be victorious also' (Beach, 29, pp 32–3). Mk. 13:13 implies a situation in which the 'name' of Christian, i.e. merely professing to be a Christian, is a capital offence (cf. below, p 83). Now a confession of the faith would be appropriate not only at a Christian's baptism, but also when he was being persecuted and required to renounce the 'name'. Cullmann considers that the reference to Pilate in the Pastoral 1 Tim. derives not from a baptismal confession formula, but rather from a summary of the affirmation which the Church expected of a Christian under persecution. The context, he says, proves that we are here concerned with a judicial action, and that Timothy had appeared already for the first time before a court, and had 'made the good confession in the presence of many witnesses' (6:12). He is instructed to continue the 'good fight', i.e. to confess his faith before the authorities. In this situation he could strengthen his courage by recalling that Christ had fearlessly proclaimed his Messianic kingship before Pilate. Hence 'Pilate probably owes the honour of being named in the Credo to the fact that Christians of the early period were summoned to confess their faith before the representatives of the Roman government' (113, pp 25–6). Conzelmann prefers to think of the 'witnesses' as those present at an ordination ceremony, and the 'confession' as the summary of the faith recited on this occasion by the candidate. He denies that there is 'any emphasis on confrontation with the Roman empire' (126, p 88). Nevertheless, an ordination address from a time when Christians were liable to persecution could well include a reminder that Jesus had stood up to Pilate. Both these theologians of course believe that the 'confession' recalled what had really been the historical facts of Jesus' behaviour. But it is equally possible to argue that the situation of Christians from the late first century was conducive to the formation of a legend that Jesus himself had been haled before a Roman authority and had behaved in the unflinching manner expected of Christians under similar duress. It is not in dispute that many legends have originated as tales of encouragement to the oppressed.

The author of the Pastorals does not write as an original theologian. He is a purveyor of other men's theology and tried (not altogether successfully) to make a consistent whole of what he collected from disparate sources – in accordance with his declared principle that the sacred tradition is to be guarded carefully and handed on intact. His greatest objection to the teachers he condemns is that they were original (see Hanson 197, pp 110–12). And nearly all his doctrinal statements seem to be quotations. Hence he is not likely to have himself originated the guess which linked Jesus with Pilate, but will have taken it over from earlier tradition. (This will obviously be the case if his reference to Pilate is a quotation from a creed, baptismal or other.) There is no reason why such a guess should have been seriously challenged, provided it was made as late as the latter part of the first century. Our study of the early Christian epistles has shown that their authors were very much concerned with correct doctrine (with what constitutes the proper Christian faith) and with Church order (the machinery for the conservation and propagation of the faith). The concern with order had become particularly strong by the beginning of the second century. Clement of Rome insists that presbyters be respected, Ignatius that bishops be obeyed. Any new tenet which conflicted with established faith or order would certainly have been resisted. But a linkage between Jesus and Pilate was, from any point of view except that of the Docetists, merely historical clarification of the established doctrine of 'Christ crucified'; and the specification of the circumstances under which he had suffered was additionally useful as a weapon against Docetist 'heretics' who denied that Jesus had suffered at all. Furthermore, it was published to people who, as Merrill has noted of the early Christians generally, knew 'nothing of the need or nature of criticism of sources, or of the interrelations of sources'. The non-existence of a competitive assertion, and the consecutive repetition of a given assertion, are 'no evidence whatever that the nucleus of the whole was not an invention, guess or unwarrantable inference'. Again:

'It should be remembered that neither these writers nor their public had developed any critical historical sense. Whatever was anywhere or anyhow mentioned or recorded that fitted into the general scheme of their convictions, or at least did not conflict with it, was unhesitatingly accepted by them. In this respect they did not differ essentially from very many intelligent people of the present day ... An inference, however vague, however slightly founded, was quite as good to them as a fact'. (296, pp 7, 25)

I have so far distinguished – taking Paul's views as the point of departure – three stages in Christian thinking about Jesus: that he was crucified (1) in some unspecified past, (2) in 'the last times', i.e. recently, and (3) under Pilate. A fourth stage transfers the responsibility for his death from Pilate to the Jews, and it is this stage that we see represented in the canonical gospels. That a tradition which blamed Pilate should soon have been modified in this way is quite intelligible. By the time our gospels were written, Christians were hated by Jews, and it was natural for the former to assume that this Jewish hatred existed not only in their own day, but in earlier times, and was thus responsible for Jesus' death. Furthermore, blaming the Jews was more satisfying theologically; for if his death was a divine act of salvation, then it was best attributed to those who would not accept his divinity. This, as Brandon says (66, p 8) 'might be deemed more spiritually fitting for one regarded as the Son of God'. It would have the added advantage of demonstrating to the Romans that second-century Christians were not Jews, and shared none of the Jews' rebellious aspirations. Scholars do not dispute that one of the motives underlying gospel stories is – in the words of Grant (178, p 35) – the desire 'to set Christianity in the right light in the eyes of the governing class and Roman officialdom generally'. And so Mark represents Pilate as doing his best to have Jesus acquitted, but as nevertheless forced into ordering his execution by the malice of the Jewish leaders. To make the governor's behaviour plausible, the evangelist could not allow Jesus to give a positive answer to the question 'Are you the King of the Jews?' (15:2); for this would have forced Pilate to return an immediate verdict of guilty, would have terminated the scene and thus eliminated any opportunity of introducing Jewish malice as the decisive factor in securing his connivance at the prisoner's execution. Nor, on the other hand, was a negative answer acceptable to the evangelist; for 'a forthright rejection of the royal title by Jesus could easily have been construed as subverting the assessment of him that prevailed in the apostolic churches' (Burkill, 88, p 326n). And so Jesus had to be made to return an indefinite answer, namely 'You have said so', implying that not he himself but Pilate had used the royal title. For the evangelist Jesus is, of course, the Jews' true Messianic king, but they are theologically blind. Mark conveys both these points by making them return a negative answer to Pilate's question 'Do you want me to release for you the King of the Jews?' (15:9). In this one verse Pilate is thus even represented as accepting Jesus' Messianic kingship in order that the reader may understand that the Jews denied it! In the fourth gospel any attempt to keep Pilate's references to Jesus within the bounds of plausibility has been abandoned. He repeatedly calls Jesus 'the King of the Jews' in order to show that they have rejected their true king and thus forfeited their status as the chosen people. For instance, when they demand his crucifixion, Pilate counters with: 'Shall I crucify your King?' (Jn. 19:15). From Mk. 15:26 we learn that the words 'the King of the Jews' were inscribed upon the cross to indicate the 'charge' against Jesus. This title really expresses not his guilt but the claims of early Christian communities concerning his true status. The fourth evangelist evidently realized that it was inappropriate as a statement of his guilt, and so made Pilate, as his advocate against the Jews, insist on writing the title onto the cross *against* the protests of the chief priests (Jn. 19:19–22). In this gospel Pilate even writes it in three languages – Hebrew, Latin and Greek – in order, as Haenchen says, to announce Jesus' true dignity *urbi et orbi*.

In order to blame the Jews instead of Pilate for Jesus' death the evangelists have to introduce further implausibilities – e.g. the betrayal by Judas, the Barabbas incident (both of which will occupy us below), and the incongruities of the Sanhedrin trial (which I discussed in JEC). Cohn is perfectly right to say (102, p 189) that all these features are 'so unrealistic

64

and unhistorical as to verge on the ridiculous'.[32] We shall see below that the attempt to exculpate Pilate is even more pronounced in Mt. and Lk. than in Mk. In Jn., the latest of the four, the accused gives the governor a short-course in Johannine theology, to which the perplexed Pilate replies: 'What is truth?'. To this the best answer is perhaps that of Anatole France's M. Bergeret: truth (unlike error) is but one; that is its great disadvantage.

(iv) Summary

If Jesus is a myth, how did he come to be regarded as a contemporary of Pilate? My explanation has been based on an attempt to distinguish chronologically four layers of Christian thinking, beginning with the Pauline letters of ca. AD 60, which preach 'Christ crucified', with no indication of where or when. What basis Paul had for his indifference to the where and the when will occupy us in later chapters. The second layer consists of the post-Pauline epistles of the late first century. None of these mentions Pilate, any more than does Paul; but some of them differ from him by assigning Jesus' life not to a vague, unspecified past but to 'the last times', to a past that, still unspecified, is nevertheless comparatively recent; and by regarding him as having been conspicuous, not obscure, on earth. The third layer consists of the letters of Ignatius and the Pastoral epistles of the NT — all ca. AD 110 — where Jesus' death is placed in Pilate's prefecture and represented as his responsibility. The fourth is the passion narratives of the gospels, which transfer the responsibility to the Jews. I shall argue in the next chapter that even the earliest of these gospels could have been written as late as AD 90–100. Earlier than any of these layers there is, possibly, a pre-Pauline tradition according to which Christ was rejected on earth, but not crucified.

Some overlap in date between these four strata is to be expected: for on the one hand a given tradition often arises somewhat earlier than the oldest of the extant documents in which it is recorded; and on the other it does not disappear as soon as a later tradition, which in due course is to supplant it, has arisen. But although the strata are not to be kept rigidly and completely apart, they can be clearly distinguished. The view that 'Jesus Christ is the same yesterday and today and for ever' (Hebrews 13:8) is the reverse of the truth; he is an idea gradually constructed and modified over a considerable period of time.

Notes to Chapter Two

1 Gal. 1:16–2:1 mentions more than fourteen years of his Christian activity, and in Rom. 15:19 he declares that he has completed his missionary work 'from Jerusalem as far round as Illyricum'.

2 In Gal. 2:1 Paul mentions a conference he had with James, Cephas and John in Jerusalem, fourteen or more years after his conversion. Acts 15 places this conference before his journey to Greece, where, after eighteen months in Corinth, he was brought before Gallio, the proconsul (18: 11–12). The year of Gallio's proconsulship of Achaia is known from a pagan inscription to be AD 51 or 52.

3 In order to stamp Christianity as politically innocuous, Acts has Paul haled before Roman officials, who invariably find him guiltless. If the author knew of Gallio's proconsulship, he had all he needed to produce his story of Paul's appearance in court before him (cf. Knox, 258, pp 81–2). The author also wishes to show that there was no necessity for the break between Christians and Jews (which had occurred by the time he wrote), and that the latter are entirely to blame for it. Hence he represents Paul as primarily a missionary to Jews, and as turning to gentiles only when Jews reject him (which they are represented as doing in one locality after another). The highly critical attitude to the Jewish law which Paul had expressed in his own letters is suppressed in Acts, which even makes him come forward as a Pharisee (23:6) and deny that his doctrine goes against this law (25:8); whereas Paul himself had said (Phil. 3:5ff) that on becoming Christian he ceased to be a Pharisee. Acts also represents Christians as clashing not so much with Jews generally as with the sectarian Sadducees (who deny 'that there is resurrection, angels or spirit') whereas the Pharisees take Paul's side (23:8–9) – as if their belief in resurrection meant that they would support a man who proclaimed that Jesus had risen and was the Messiah! This is intelligible not as history but as an expression of the author's aim to set Christianity in the right light to Roman observers by representing it as so close to Judaism as to deserve the special toleration granted by Rome to that ancient religion.

4 For instance, 'pre-existent Wisdom had functioned as the friend and guide of men from Adam to Moses: ... Philo's Logos was present to OT men and women. It could be identified with the angel of Exodus 23:20' – just as for Paul (1 Cor. 10:4) Christ was with 'our fathers' in their wilderness journeying (52, p 393).

5 That the Messiah was expected to perform miracles is suggested by Jn. 7:31, where the people say of Jesus: 'When the Christ appears, will he do more signs than this man has done?'. Furthermore, Moses was widely regarded as the prototype of the Messiah (see below, pp 68–9), and first century Jewish writers such as Philo of Alexandria and Josephus dwell on the miracles worked by Moses (see Meeks, 295).

6 The considerable literature on this subject is reviewed by Dungan, 138.

7 E.g. Phil. 2:5–8 and 2 Cor. 8:9, where Jesus is said to have 'emptied himself', 'humbled himself', and 'become poor' by assuming human form. Most commentators (e.g. Bruce, 76, p 102) concede that Paul is merely reiterating this same idea in two passages which James Dunn (139) has quoted against me, namely 1 Cor. 11:1, where the faithful are urged to imitate Paul in seeking not their own advantage, but the salvation of the many, even as he in this respect imitates Christ; and Rom. 15:3, where a Psalm is quoted to show that Jesus considered the interests of other people, not his own.

8 Mithra, like Hercules, accomplished 'miraculous deeds, though this not without labour', and 'in this way his earthly life serves as an example to his devotees' (391, p 253). Plutarch tells (325, § 27) that the mysteries of Isis – one of early Christianity's most powerful rivals – portrayed the trials and tribulations she had herself endured, both as a lesson in godliness and as 'an encouragement to men and women overtaken by similar misfortune'. And the Osiris worshippers of ancient Egypt believed, as did the early Christians (Hebrews 4:14–15) that 'man cannot be saved by a remote omnipotent deity but by one who has shared the experience of human suffering and death' (68, pp 44–5).

9 Braun makes this point (71, p 364n) when he observes that Jesus' 'generosity' (2 Cor. 8:9, NEB) and his 'serving' mankind (Rom. 15:8) refer to the mission to earth of this supernatural personage; and that his suffering, his 'obedience' and his 'act of righteousness' (Rom. 5:18–19; cf. Phil. 2:8) are allusions to his death. Cf. also Craddock, 108.

10 201, p 623. In Ephesians the word 'mystery' has connotations additional to those it bears in the undoubtedly genuine Pauline letters (see Kümmel, 268, pp 253–4). It nonetheless typifies Christian thinking of the late first century.

11 See 386, p 218; 35, p 127; 54, p 504. Mk. 3:28–9 (the subject-matter of which has no connection with what precedes or follows) has been interpreted (54, p 510

and refs.) as the pronouncement of a Christian prophet: 'Truly I say to you, all sins will be forgiven the sons of men . . . but whoever blasphemes against the Holy Spirit never has forgiveness'. The prophet, who spoke by the 'spirit', would naturally wish to insulate it from criticism. The oldest extant interpretation of this passage (in the manual of instruction known as the *Didache*) takes it to mean that prophets are to be accepted without challenge.

12 Conzelmann accounts for the contradiction by supposing that the harsh view of ch. 14, given on the authority of the Lord, is in fact an addition made to the text at the time of the composition of the Pastoral epistles (i.e. early in the second century), which are markedly anti-feminist (as is clear from 1 Tim. 2:11–12). Crouch, however, accepts the command that women be silent in church as genuinely Pauline and occasioned – as were later the similar statements in the Pastoral epistles – by the proclivity of women to unsettle the community with ecstatic utterances and enthusiastic excesses (112, pp 130–41).

13 Isaiah (6:1ff) was called to God's service by a vision of the Lord, and Amos (7:1, etc.) was vouchsafed visions in which God showed him Israel's doom. Initiation into the pagan mystery religions involved a 'personal meeting with the god', and Isis afforded 'comfort through visions' (413, pp 153, 189).

14 See JEC, pp 47n, 231. Betz concedes (41, pp 126–8) that the NT account may here be 'connected directly or indirectly with the Adonis cult'; and he notes that Plutarch reports the legend of Osiris' resurrection on the third day.

15 That the faithful will attain salvation at the future judgement is implied by 1 Thess. 4: 15ff, 1 Cor. 15: 51ff, and Phil. 3: 20f; that Christ has already inaugurated their salvation by Gal. 4: 4, 1 Cor. 15: 20 and Coloss. 1: 13; cf. Bartsch, 26, pp 267–73 and Köster, 262, p 324.

16 For details see JEC, p 41, and Steinseifer, 378. Matthew locates the appearance of the risen one to the eleven on an unspecified Galilean 'mountain' where 'Jesus had told them to meet him' (28: 16 NEB); but the evangelist has not recorded any such instruction, and – as Harvey says (201, p 109) – his 'phrase does not help us to locate the scene', and he was possibly 'more interested in the symbolic significance of the setting'. Important divine manifestations were traditionally sited on mountains, and such tradition obviously influenced the stories of the transfiguration on 'a high mountain' (Mk. 9:2) and of the Sermon on the Mount. The latter is 'an obvious attempt to parallel Jesus with Moses at Sinai by placing Jesus on a mount when he gives his "new" understanding of the Law' (Kallas, 243, p 9); it 'can only be understood as the trump to the law-giving on Sinai' (Haenchen, 191, p 36).

17 The gospels contain no *account* of an appearance of the risen Jesus to Peter. In Mk. 16: 7 an appearance to the 'disciples and Peter' is promised by the angel in the empty tomb; and Lk. 24:34 mentions – in what Kirsopp Lake has called an 'incredibly casual manner' (269, p 95) – that an appearance to Peter has occurred, without making it clear whether this was the first the risen Jesus made. The other two gospels are completely silent on the subject of an appearance specifically to Peter.

18 Mt. 28:1–10 and Jn. 20:1–18 even go so far as to posit appearances of the risen Jesus at his tomb, in contrast to Mk. 16:1–8 and Lk. 24:1–11. The final sentence of the genuine Mk., which states that the women fled from the empty tomb and 'said nothing to anyone' (16:8) is designed to account for the fact that, before the composition of this legend about the tomb, no one had heard of it. Dibelius thinks that Mark deleted a narrative about a resurrection appearance to Peter (implied by Mk. 14:28) in order to accommodate this tomb legend; and that the next stage in the development of the tradition was to insert an account of Jesus' burial into the passion narrative. This account, by alleging that the women 'saw where he was laid' (15:47), establishes that the women who later found the tomb empty had not gone to the wrong tomb.

19 After his conversion, the Christians in Judaea 'heard it said' (Gal. 1:23) that 'our former persecutor' is now a Christian. Haenchen (188, p 248) points to the significance of the phrase 'heard it said': the Judaean Christians did not

themselves say that Paul had been converted, but heard those whom he had persecuted (i.e. non-Judaean Christians) say so.

20 See 72, p 311; 159, p 411. Kilpatrick notes that such documents as 2 Peter, the epistle of Barnabas, and the apocryphal gospel and apocalypse of Peter 'show by their ascriptions that the value of an apostolic name was realised' (249, pp 5, 65). Their 'fictitious authors are primarily the custodians of an authoritative doctrinal tradition, particularly in the battle against false teaching and for the securing of the church's faith and order' (56, p 242). Rist (10, p 89) allows that about two-thirds of the twenty-seven books in the NT canon are pseudonymous.

21 Milburn (301) and Merrill (296, ch.6) show that there is no real evidence that Domitian persecuted Christians. Even Frend, who has been criticized for all too ready acceptance of Christian tradition alleging persecution, admits that the evidence concerning Domitian is far from decisive, and expresses himself with great caution on the matter (164, pp 212, 217).

22 Concerning the dependence of 1 Peter on Rom. and on Ephes., see Best, 39, p 35. Leaney tentatively agrees with Beare's dating when he says that 1 Peter is 'pseudonymous' and probably 'of the early second century' (271, p 72). Totally misleading is the statement of Toynbee and Perkins that the epistle is 'generally agreed' to have been written AD 62–4, and that 'the majority' even of Protestant scholars ascribe it to St. Peter (392, pp 128, 132). Toynbee and Perkins refer for support to Cullmann who, they say, while leaving the authorship open, accepts the letter as 'a very early document'. What Cullmann actually says is that 1 Peter is early in comparison with 2 Peter, which he dates at AD 150 'at the very earliest'. He places 1 Peter in 'approximately the same period' as Rev., 4 Ezra and the apocalypse of Baruch (116, pp 84–5) – documents which most scholars assign to the end of the first century. The conservative position of Selwyn (369) that 1 Peter was written by an 'eye-witness' of Jesus' life ca. AD 62 has been rebutted by Best (39, pp 51–4, 64) and Kümmel (268, pp 297–8). Nineham says that few scholars now hold this view (314, p 40).

23 Some theologians date Hebrews after the Pauline letters but before AD 70, since the author, who argues that God has set aside the outmoded Jewish sacrificial system (cf. above, p 53), would certainly have alluded to the destruction of the temple (and the cessation of the Jewish sacrifices there offered) had he known of it (so Robinson, 338, p 78n). Theologians, then, are quite prepared to argue from silence if they are thereby led to desirable conclusions! In this case, however, the silence is hardly decisive, as the author discusses the Jewish sacrificial system solely on the basis of OT scripture and the wilderness 'tent' or tabernacle. He is thus not concerned with the Herodian temple, and there is no reason why he should mention it or indicate whether it is still standing (cf. 156, p 11). Furthermore, there is considerable evidence (summarized by Clark, 101) that sacrifices continued to be made (on a reduced scale) at the temple after AD 70 until Hadrian razed it to the ground and excluded Jews from the site.

24 Some claim that the author of 1 Jn. poses as an eye-witness of Jesus' ministry; but Harvey rightly denies (201, p 760) that there is in fact any 'claim to have actually seen Jesus'. Cf. JEC, p 156, and Houlden, 212, p 52.

25 The author mentions Jesus' transfiguration (i) in order to authenticate himself as Simon Peter (1:1), a witness to this event (1:16–18); and (ii) as evidence of Jesus' 'power' and of his 'coming' in order to discredit heretics who had abandoned all hope that he would come again (3:3–4).

26 'Jesus' is the Greek form of the Hebrew name Jehoshua (or Joshua in its abbreviated form), so that in the Septuagint (the Greek translation of the OT) Joshua is rendered as 'Jesus'.

27 The Dead Sea Scrolls have shown that some Jews certainly thought of the coming age of salvation as a new Exodus, resembling that under Moses. And for Paul the redemption from Egypt was likewise 'the prototype of the greater redemption from sin wrought by Christ for the New Israel' (Davies, 121, p 349). Harvey

concedes (201, pp 20, 70) that some features in Mt. which are peculiar to this gospel (e.g. details in the narrative of Jesus' infancy which are incompatible with the parallel account in Lk.) obviously owe their origin to the evangelist's desire to model Jesus, the second deliverer, on Moses, the first.

28 Josephus tells of a fanatic named Theudas who promised to lead a multitude dryshod over the Jordan. He may have intended to duplicate Moses' miracle at the Red Sea, or his model may have been Elijah (2 Kings 2:4) or the achievement of Joshua before Jericho. Another fanatic, an Egyptian Jew, clearly posed as a new Joshua when he proposed to command the walls of Jerusalem to fall down so that his followers could slaughter the Roman garrison. That Josephus refers to these men as 'prophets' does not mean that they claimed to be mere forerunners of the Messiah: for prophecy was expected to return in the Messianic period, often in the person of the Messiah (cf. 418, pp 296–8). On the Samaritan Messiah as *Joshua redivivus*, see Merz, 297, p 43. The Sibylline oracles (5:256–59) say that a certain exalted man shall come down from the sky and cause the sun to stand still (as Joshua had done). Jeremias thinks that, even if this is Christian insertion, there may be a Jewish tradition underlying it (227, p 861 and note). The epistle of Barnabas (12:8) also links Jesus with Joshua.

29 The writer's purpose is to discredit some religious practice (the reference is obscure) involving the use of 'foods'. He argues that Christians have an altar (Jesus' place of execution) where sacrifice was made for sin, but that they draw no food from it; and he is at pains to show that this is in accordance with the ritual prescribed (Leviticus 16:27) for the day of Atonement, when the sacrifice slaughtered on the altar was – by way of exception – not to be eaten, but burnt 'outside the camp' after its blood had been brought into the holy of holies. 'So Jesus also suffered outside the gate, in order to sanctify the people through his own blood' (13:12). The writer is not disturbed by the imperfection of the analogy. In the atonement ritual the animals are slaughtered inside the camp and only burned outside it, whereas Jesus was killed 'outside the gate' and not burned at all.

30 Cf. Grant, 178, p 162; Köster, 260, p 61. It is true that Polycarp (the bishop of Smyrna who wrote not later than AD 135) knew Mt. and Lk. (see Harrison, 199, p 286) but does not refer to gospel incidents in order to establish his contention that Jesus has 'come in the flesh', and simply quotes 1 Jn. (without acknowledgement) for this purpose.

31 Alfaric, 3, pp 66, 80, 117; Justin, 235, ch. 33; 236, ch. 120; Irenaeus, 217, Bk. 4, ch. 10, § 2. '

32 The contrary view of Sherwin-White (371) has been adequately met by Burkill (88).

3 The Origin and Nature of the Gospels

(i) Form-Criticism

Critics who treat the books of the NT as historical documents must accept some criterion of their trustworthiness. They must try to determine *when* the books were written, for what *purpose*, and by *whom*. When they have ascertained these facts they can judge what knowledge the writer would be likely to have, how far he might be able to distinguish true from false reports, and how far he would be influenced by religious preconceptions or dogmatic purposes.

The form-critics give a theoretical answer to each of these questions by analysing gospels and epistles into short passages ('pericopes') of distinctive literary form (e.g. creeds, short sermons, etc.). Dibelius, one of the best-known exponents, believed that the gospels were written towards the end of the first century; that their purpose was edification and their authors compilers who pieced together the statements of apostles and missionaries. Their evidence is therefore at best secondhand. In fact he seems to suppose that the statements on which the evangelists relied were seldom, if ever, derived from the original disciples of Jesus, but belonged to a tradition handed on from preacher to preacher. As a result of this mode of transmission the data were reduced to stereotyped formulae and confined to points deemed of fundamental doctrinal importance. It must have been when the disciples who had known Jesus were all dead, and when their followers carried on their work, that the phraseology began to be stereotyped, since the new generation of teachers had to rely on what the first disciples had told them, and could not supplement it with recollections of their own.

The preachers would, according to Dibelius, be primarily concerned to convince their audience of the following broad facts: Jesus of Nazareth, a descendant of David, having been appointed by God the promised Messiah who should judge the world and bring salvation to the righteous, had been crucified under Pontius Pilate at the instigation of the Jews. His *bona fides* was established by his 'mighty works', in particular by his resurrection, which was vouched for by numerous persons. Some of these points are found in stereotyped form in the Pauline letters and others in the discourses of Peter and Paul in Acts.

Dibelius further argues that the purpose of the missionary preachers would not lead them to refer to the biographical details of Jesus' earthly career, and for that reason one would not expect them to record the miracles and discourses which form such an important part of the gospels. Such events were no longer of any importance in comparison with the great fact of his death and resurrection. If the preachers mentioned miracles and discourses at all, it would only be by way of illustration, and usually without any attention to time and place. The evangelists, in editing the material provided by these preachers, might try to arrange these few facts and fit them into a plausible biographical sequence. As they had little but their own imagination to go on, it is not surprising that they did not all arrange them in the same way. Only when they come to the doctrinally important death and resurrection do they show any considerable degree of harmony.

By means, then, of this theory, Dibelius undertakes to explain the lack of allusion in the epistles to the teaching and wonder-working of Jesus, the numerous discrepancies in the gospels, and also the lack of coherence in the gospel discourses, where Jesus passes with apparent arbitrariness from one topic to another. A good example is Mk. 9:35—50, where the individual items are linked only by what theologians call 'catchword connections' — a word or phrase in one seems to have reminded the evangelist of a similar word or phrase in another, independent saying, and this led him to put them together as successive utterances in a single speech. Form-critics are doubtless right in their insistence that such passages show that Jesus' sayings originally circulated independently of any connected narrative — a view which also gained support from the discovery, early this century, of three papyri at Oxyrhynchus in the Nile valley, containing a few sayings of Jesus in Greek, and of the Gospel of Thomas near Nag Hammadi in Upper Egypt in 1945. This apocryphal work consists of about 114 sayings of Jesus (including those that had been found at Oxyrhynchus), with no indication of where or under what circumstances they were pronounced. Many sayings which in the canonical gospels appear in a definite situation are here simply stated without it. Although some scholars have argued that the Gospel of Thomas is dependent on canonical gospels, the contrary view — that it is neither compiled from them, nor constitutes one of their sources, but is an ancient independent tradition — is also strongly held (358, pp 10—21).

It is also accepted today that not only Jesus' speeches but also the sequence of the events of his life familiar from the synoptics is no part of the primary material but a creation of Mark (whose order of events is, on the whole, preserved by Matthew and Luke). For instance, Mk. 1:16 reads: 'And passing along by the sea of Galilee he saw Simon and Andrew . . .'. Almost all commentators agree that the words 'by the sea of Galilee' were added by Mark. They are placed quite ungrammatically in the Greek syntax (for the verb 'passing along' is not normally used with the preposition 'by'). Mark, then, has interpolated a reference to *place* into a report which lacked it, and he also added a reference to *time* by placing this story of the call of Simon and Andrew at the beginning of Jesus' ministry. Both place and time are, as Professor Nineham says in his valuable commentary 'entirely St. Mark's doing' (314, 70). The evangelist has thus created a fictitious chronology and an apparent itinerary. The very vagueness of much of it does not inspire confidence. Jesus appears in *the* wilderness, on *the* mountain, in *the* house. In 2:15 he is at table in 'his house'. Commentators are not sure whether Jesus' house is meant, or where the house is. In 2:1 and 9:33 he is 'at home' and 'in the house' at Capernaum, as if he resided there. When the evangelist is more definite and precise, this is sometimes in the interests of a theological thesis, not from historical accuracy. I shall later give evidence that this is true of his repeated references to Galilee (below, p 144). If the gospels were compiled from relatively short pericopes, originally independent of each other, it follows that each gospel incident must to some extent be viewed in itself and not forced into harmony with others.

It seems to be the stereotyped nature of the references to Jesus in the epistles (and to some extent even in Acts) that has suggested the form-critics' theory. But the references in the epistles are in fact not all characterized by their verbal uniformity, but rather by a general absence of any details about the man Jesus. This is what is so hard to explain if the Jesus of the gospels was a real historical character and the original of the Jesus Christ of Pauline doctrine. The same objection can be made to the form-critics' view of the resurrection, which, on their hypothesis, would seem to be one of the best attested facts in the life of Jesus! For, together with the passion, it is one of the few details which the preachers always mentioned, and — according to Dibelius — with considerable agreement as to the essentials. But this is acceptable only on a narrow view of the essentials, for the gospels agree only in that they all allege an execution under Pilate and subsequent appearances,[1] and earlier accounts of the crucifixion and resurrection do not even link these events with Pilate, or indeed with any historical setting. Another point is that, whether the form-critics are right or not, their theory does not provide a very reliable criterion of trustworthiness. Dibelius admits that the preachers may have adapted their recollections to fit their sermons;[2] and he does not say what reason there is to trust their memory, candour or intelligence. He also admits that the compilers may have modified and embellished the traditions they derived from the preachers. Indeed, his theory implies that this is what happened. He says that the early preachers had no occasion to refer to biographical detail. But if they alone supplied information to the compilers of the gospels, where did the latter find their additional facts? If there was no authentic oral tradition which reproduced Jesus' teaching, then the gospel sayings and stories about him originated in the later Church. Teeple goes so far as to accept this implication and to declare that 'the theory of an authentic oral tradition that moved from Jesus' teaching to the disciples to the churches and the NT is one of the most serious errors in biblical scholarship' (386, 58). Although few other theologians would endorse this, many would agree that each evangelist is more than a mere compiler, and that he supplemented the material he received and stamped it with a theology of his own. I shall later have occasion to illustrate this constructive editorial activity.

In spite of these weaknesses, form-criticism is today widely regarded as having definitively established that Jesus really existed, in that it has traced Mk. (supposedly written before AD 75) to preachers' formulae which were supposedly current as early as AD 50, this date being, it is argued, far too near Jesus' supposed actual lifetime for wholesale invention to have gone unchallenged. It would on the contrary be truer to say that what is valid in the form-critics' theory reveals that the very sections of the gospels which used to be regarded as most likely to be a true historical record can no longer be accepted as such.

This can be illustrated from the instructions to the twelve when they are sent out to 'heal the sick, raise the dead, cleanse lepers and cast out demons'. They are warned that they will be persecuted during their mission, and will 'not have gone through all the towns of Israel before the Son of man comes' (Mt. 10:8 and 23). The 'Son of man' is a redeemer who was to come down from the clouds at the end of time to judge mankind (Mk. 13:24–8). Early this century Albert Schweitzer pointed out that Jesus' prophecy was not fulfilled: the Son of man did not bring the world to an end while the disciples were on their way casting out demons. Nor were they persecuted, but returned to him unharmed (cf. Mk. 6:30). Schweitzer's point was that, since Matthew himself shows that these prophecies were erroneous, the whole speech in which they occur must have been actually delivered by Jesus; for no evangelist would invent a speech full of prophecies and then go on to provide the evidence that they were illusory.

Form-critics have replied that Mt. 10:5ff, so far from representing a real discourse, is – in the words of Harvey – 'an artificial composition by Matthew' (201, p 50), and includes logia which are set in quite different contexts by Mark and by Luke.[3] It is a compilation of rulings on matters of importance to Christian missionaries at the end of the first century. The instructions concern the founding of Christian communities (as is clear from Mt. 10:11ff) in missionary activity spread over a long period, and are not intelligible as directives given to disciples who soon return to the speaker (as the twelve are represented as doing). It is, for instance, stipulated that when they are persecuted the missionaries are not to court martyrdom, but to flee to another town and work there. The need for a ruling on such a practical problem naturally led to the conviction that the Lord had laid down what was to be done, and hence to the formulation of a Jesuine utterance. As for the coming of the Son of man, Matthew (writing at least fifty years after the supposed date of Jesus' speech) knew quite well that this had not yet occurred. It is not plausible to assume that an evangelist who manipulates his material freely would faithfully record doctrines he regarded as mistaken. Traditions which stamped Jesus as deluded would not have been uncritically preserved by evangelists who treat him with such deference that they do not allow even his enemies to reproach him directly. (His opponents criticize his disciples when speaking to him, and complain about him when speaking to his disciples or to each other, but they do not call him to account directly.)[4] It is, then, more reasonable to assume that Matthew understood Jesus' pronouncement concerning the Son of man not as a delusion, but as something acceptable. As Haenchen has noted (191, p 232) this will be the case if we assume that he meant the speech where he placed it to include instructions not only for the particular mission of the twelve which forms its context, but also for all future missions of the Church.

Another such composition, which gives rulings on matters of concern to the Christians of the evangelist's day, can be seen in Matthew's supplement (18:15–17) to a string of Jesuine instructions taken from Mk. 9:33–50. The supplement provides rules for dealing with dissensions within the Christian community or ecclesia (which did not even exist at the time when Jesus is supposed to have spoken!), and it is obvious that the evangelist is here writing in the belief that practices of the Christians of his own day were ordained by Jesus. The same, we saw (above, p, 28), is true of Mk. 10:12 where he rules that if a woman divorces her husband and marries another, she commits adultery. Some gospel sayings of Jesus can be traced to the liturgical needs of Christian communities. An obvious case is the Lord's Prayer – absent from Mk., given different settings in Mt. and Lk., and expanded by Matthew so as to make it appropriate for communal worship (121, p 5). In Mk. 7:1–23 Jesus bases an argument against the Pharisees on the Greek translation of the OT, where the Hebrew original says something different which would not have supported his case. That a Palestinian Jesus should floor orthodox Jews with an argument based on a mistranslation of their scriptures is very unlikely. The whole incident is, however, perfectly intelligible if we suppose that it was fabricated in Mark's gentile Christian community, which naturally read the OT in the Greek version, and ascribed to Jesus its own understanding of these scriptures. Bornkamm designates the process with the disarming phrase, 'the tendency of the word of Jesus to become contemporary' (55, p 18). This 'tendency' was at work even among the earliest Christians, whose 'prophets' claimed to be spokesmen of the risen Jesus, and represented him as giving through their mouths ordinances which later Christians transferred to the historical Jesus. The tendency to anchor later doctrines and customs to his supposed life-time played a considerable role in building up his biography.

Form-criticism, then, tends to sever the gospel material from the historical Jesus. One can understand Leaney's comment (119, p 252) that this result is 'less welcome' to conservative Christians than the discovery which of his recorded sayings are authentic – a result with which the form-critical method has commonly been credited.

(ii) Palestinian Elements
Professors Black (46) and Jeremias have defended the authenticity of

Jesus' sayings in the gospels by giving evidence that some of these Greek logia are discernibly based on an underlying Aramaic original. In such matters we are dependent on what has been called 'a small band of Aramaic experts' within the larger body of NT scholars, and, although the band consists of persons unlikely to propound theories disturbing to a settled orthodoxy, it is noticeable that they 'often disagree, largely from uncertainty concerning the Aramaic of the first century AD' (384, pp 55–6, 64–5). Furthermore, as many theologians have themselves observed, 'Aramaic' is not to be equated with 'authentically spoken by Jesus'. Against Jeremias it has been noted that an Aramaic-speaking community could as well invent 'words of the Lord' as a Greek-speaking one (400, p 66 and note); and that Aramaic terms and Semitisms do not even necessarily represent an early stage in the development of the tradition:

> 'Some Semitisms had entered the Hellenistic Greek language in general; early Christians adopted Semitisms from the Septuagint; many Christians in the first and second centuries knew Aramaic. Therefore these linguistic characteristics could appear in late Christian tradition and writing as easily as in primitive Christian tradition. In the same later period Jewish influence continued to be exerted on Christian tradition through the OT and through Christians familiar with Judaism.' (386, p 60)

Jeremias has also argued that some sayings of the gospel Jesus contain features which are not merely Aramaic, but also unique, in that they are unrepresented in the Jewish traditions of the period, and are therefore, he supposes, to be taken as proving that the sayings are genuine. For instance, Jesus in Gethsemane (Mk. 14:36) addresses God with the Aramaic word 'abba' (father). Mark supplies no witnesses who could have heard what was said, and also finds it necessary to put into Jesus' mouth the Greek translation of the word (making him say: 'Abba, Father, all things are possible to thee'). Nevertheless, Jeremias insists that the logion is genuine since in Jewish traditions God is never addressed simply as 'abba' without some additional qualifying phrase, such as is preserved in Matthew's 'our father who art in heaven' (225, p 89). To this the adequate reply has been made (191, p 493) that Paul's references to an early Christian practice of crying 'Abba, Father' (Rom. 8:15; Gal. 4:6) show that 'abba' followed by its Greek translation was a formula current in Hellenistic Christian circles, and that Mark has simply put it into Jesus' mouth. And a leading Jewish scholar (Vermes, 398, pp 210–11) has given evidence that 'abba' was used in the prayer language of the Judaism of the day in precisely the manner in which Jeremias and other Christian scholars have declared to be 'unthinkable'.

A second feature which Jeremias thinks authenticates some Jesuine sayings is the way they are prefaced with 'Amen, I say unto you' – for the word 'amen' is, in Judaism, never used to introduce sayings. Jeremias is himself aware that on two occasions this 'genuine' word has been added secondarily by Matthew to sayings in Mk. which are without it. He supposes that Matthew introduced the word because he recognized it as Jesus' way of speaking. But it is also the case — as Jeremias admits — that the whole formula has frequently been deleted in the reworking and editing of the earlier synoptic material. This must mean that the authors of the later layers of this material did not recognize the formula as genuinely Jesuine — unless we suppose that what they recognized as Jesuine was of no interest to them! Hence, as Hasler has observed, the reasons given by Jeremias for the later additions do not square with the 'tendency' to deletion that he correctly observes in the later layers. Some of the thirteen sayings introduced with the formula in Mk. are obviously suspect — e.g. 9:1 (on which see p 84 below); and 10:27, where the reference to sacrificing all for the sake of 'the gospel' suggests the standpoint of a persecuted Christian community, not the conditions in which Jesus is supposed to have lived. (Marxsen has shown (290, pp 77–83) that it is characteristic of Mark to impose the word 'gospel' onto the material he edits.) Hasler has made a good case for regarding the amen-formula as originally a form of words used by early Christian prophets in order to introduce sayings which, they supposed, had been communicated to them supernaturally by the risen Jesus (202, pp 181–3). Only at a later stage in the development of the tradition were, on this view, both formula and sayings ascribed to the earthly Jesus. Berger, writing independently of Hasler, shows that something very like the amen-formula was already available in the Septuagint and in Jewish apocalyptic literature, where it was used to introduce and to affirm the veracity of solemn statements. Like Hasler, he finds that the formula does not go back to a historical Jesus, but originated on the lips of prophets. But he prefers to regard the early Christian prophets not as spokesmen of the risen Jesus, but as making their forecasts about the end of the world on their own accounts, and for this very reason needing the formula to validate their utterances. In time, he argues, it was found that more effective validation was achieved by ascribing them to Jesus, just as many OT traditions came to be attached to Moses as a commanding figure of the past (38, 157–9).

(iii) Titles

The traditional view that the canonical gospels were written by eye-witnesses of the events recorded in them, or at least by men who had their information directly from such witnesses, is today almost universally abandoned. Haenchen notes that the Fathers of the Church could never have originated such a view if they had properly understood Lk. 1:1–4, which states that the 'eye-witnesses and ministers of the word delivered' their testimony orally, and that only then did 'many' (not alleged to have been eye-witnesses) 'draw up a narrative'. Luke 'thus knew nothing of gospels written by apostles. . . . The eye-witnesses . . . did not write but "only" preached'.[5] Today it is recognized (e.g. by Grant, 178, p 26) that the authors of the gospels are entirely unknown; that gospels, and other writings used for reading in church, at first existed without any titles, and were supplied with them only when Christian communities acquired more than one gospel and needed some means of distinguishing between them. The canon was unable to reduce the material to a single gospel for the reason that some influential communities had long used only one and some another.[6]

The ascription of titles, in so far as its basis can be inferred at all, seems to have been a haphazard business. Beare writes in this connection of 'second-century guesses' (32, p 13). Mk., for instance, acquired its title probably because 'my son Mark' is mentioned as a close associate of 'Peter the apostle' who poses as the author of 1 Peter (1:1 and 5:13). This epistle of the late first or early second century, influenced as it is by Pauline theology, introduces 'Mark' as a personage familiar from the Pauline letters (Coloss. 4:10) in order to create the authentic Pauline atmosphere. Nonetheless, it was probably this mention of Mark in a work ascribed to Peter that originated the tradition (preserved by Papias, AD 140) that Mk. was written by one Mark who took down the spoken recollections of Peter (191, p 8). This tradition was not finally discredited until the rise of form-criticism. At the beginning of this century orthodox commentators on Mk. still insisted that the gospel is a unitary composition, owing its unity to the author's dependence on the eye-witness Peter for all his information. The change in critical standpoint is at once obvious from comparison with Taylor's — also orthodox — commentary (first published in 1952), where stress is laid upon the great diversity of the traditions which Mark collected after they had already been used in the teaching and preaching of the Church.

Papias is also responsible for the ascription of the first gospel in the canon to 'Matthew', meaning presumably the Matthew named in all the synoptic lists of the twelve. But Mt.'s dependence on Mk., 'the Greek gospel of a nondisciple', is only one of the considerations which make this hypothesis 'completely impossible' (268, p 85). How fanciful the choice of title and author could be is equally well illustrated in the case of the third gospel. The second-century Church, aware that the author also wrote the book now known as the Acts of the Apostles, observed that some passages in Acts refer to Paul and his companions as 'we' and 'us', and on this basis selected Luke (mentioned in two epistles as a companion of Paul) as the author.[7] The fourth gospel is quite anonymous. The tradition that it was written by the apostle John, who was identical with the 'beloved disciple' mentioned in it, is unknown until the last quarter of the second century and, as Kümmel has shown (268, pp 166—7), the stages which led to this view can be reconstructed. The first twenty chapters include references to a 'beloved disciple', but do not name him nor represent him as the author. The final chapter 21, an appendix almost certainly by another hand, identifies this disciple as the author, but leaves him still anonymous. Later, Christians who knew all four gospels would readily suppose that 'the disciple whom Jesus loved' must be one of the three who, according to the synoptics, are most intimate with him, namely Peter and the two sons of Zebedee, James and John. (They alone witness the transfiguration, and go forward with him to Gethsemane: Mk. 9:2; 14: 33.) Since the fourth gospel names Peter in addition to the beloved disciple, and since James died early (Acts 12: 2), this leaves the authorship with John.

(iv) Sources and Dates

(a) Mark

Critical theologians are agreed that Mk. is the earliest extant gospel; that Matthew and Luke used it as one of their sources and are therefore of later date.[8] Mk. is clearly one of the earliest documents we have that sets Jesus' life in Pilate's Palestine, and its date is therefore of some importance.

External evidence of Mk. (i.e. mention of it by other authors) is not forthcoming until the middle of the second century. Neither Ignatius (AD 110) nor Polycarp (who perhaps wrote as early as AD 120, but more probably in AD 135) show any knowledge of it, although it must have existed when the latter wrote, for he used Mt., which presupposes it. Ignatius has much common ground with Mt., and many hold that he too used this gospel. If so, then Mk. (written before Mt.) existed by AD 110. Köster, however, thinks that Ignatius and Matthew were both drawing independently on traditions common to their backgrounds (cf. below, p 92).[9]

The long silence of external witnesses concerning Mk. is not surprising; for once Mt. had become available, it would naturally be preferred, since it includes nearly all Mk.'s material and very much more besides. Mk., then, must be dated before Polycarp's references to Mt. Let us see whether evidence internal to it permits a more precise dating.

Everyone must assume that the gospels are based either on the reports of eye-witnesses or on tradition. Even Mk. is today regarded as but a redaction of earlier traditions. The evangelist betrays in 7:31 an ignorance of Palestinian geography (see Harvey's admissions, 201, pp 146—7) hardly compatible with the assumption that he lived anywhere near the country. The Christian community for which he wrote is so remote from Jewish ideas that he has laboriously to explain Jewish practices, as when he states that 'the Pharisees and the Jews in general never eat without washing the hands . . . . And there are many other points on which they have a traditional rule to maintain' (7:3—4). Such passages also betray that, in Mark's day, the freedom of gentile Christian communities from the Jewish law was taken for granted, and that he therefore wrote considerably later than Paul, for whom this matter was still a burning issue.

The traditions which Mark redacted were not exclusively oral. Taylor's evidence for his use of earlier written sources includes the 'literary doublet' of two miraculous feedings, of the 5,000 and of the 4,000. The story of the 5,000 is clearly pre-Marcan, since it 'bears none of the signs of

Mark's literary activity within the body of the narrative' (1, p 279). That two separate incidents are involved is hard to believe, since in the second the disciples – who are represented as having recently witnessed the first – have so completely forgotten it that they think it impossible for food to be supplied to thousands in a desert place (8:4). The doublet is best explained by assuming that a tradition of one such feeding existed in two slightly different written forms, and that the evangelist incorporated both because he supposed them to refer to different incidents. Different written, and not merely different oral forms, underlie such doublets. Two oral traditions that are slightly discrepant can easily be combined into one story. But as soon as a tradition is fixed in writing, discrepancies between it and a kindred tradition can result in both these literary forms of the story being told. Another doublet is the dual reference to deceivers in a single Jesuine discourse (13:5–6 and 21–3), and 'the presumption is that Mark has taken them from two different sources' (384, p 515).

To allow time for the post-Pauline traditions (collected and arranged in a sequence by the evangelist) to have developed, a date of composition earlier than about AD 70 is unlikely, and is today seldom alleged. Some commentators think that Mk.12:9 (where Jesus predicts that God will 'destroy the tenants' of his vineyard because they have murdered his 'beloved son') presupposes knowledge of the destruction of Jerusalem in AD 70. Brandon has pressed for AD 71 as the date of Mk.'s composition, although all his evidence is consistent with a later date. He argues that Mk. was written at Rome – a view which is open to objection[10] – and he supposes (66, p 227) that Jewish payment of tribute to the Emperor (encouraged in Mk. 12:13–17) was of vital concern to Christians in Rome about AD 71. But in fact injunctions to Christians to submit to the authorities and pay taxes are not indicative of any particular place or date, and are found in Rom. 13:1–7 (which, if genuine and not interpolated,[11] is pre-Marcan), as well as in epistles of the late first and early second century (see above, p 46). The inconclusive nature of Brandon's evidence is clear also from his argument that Mark's unexplained reference (15:38) to the rending of the temple curtain presupposes that his readers knew what it was; and that he was therefore writing for citizens of Rome, who had seen it displayed (according to Josephus' account) in the triumphal procession through the city after the Roman victory in the Jewish War. It does not appear from what Brandon says that the curtain thus displayed was rent: and in any case the gospel reference to its rending would be universally understood as signifying a catastrophic end to the Jewish cult.

Ch. 13 has been made the basis of many attempts to date the gospel more precisely. It begins with Jesus predicting the destruction of the temple at Jerusalem:

'As he came out of the temple, one of his disciples said to him, "Look, Teacher, what wonderful stones and what wonderful buildings!" And Jesus said to him, "Do you see these great buildings? There will not be left here one stone upon another that will not be thrown down".'

Any observer of the strained relations between Jews and Romans might conceivably have guessed, almost at any time during the first century, that Jerusalem and its temple would be destroyed as a result of Roman action against an insurgent people. But it is nevertheless quite likely that the logion 'no stone will be left upon another' first arose in a Christian community which knew of the destruction of the temple (which occurred in AD 70) and wanted to believe that Jesus had predicted it. The narrative frame in which this saying is placed is patently artificial. Palestinian Jews, even those living in Galilee, would have been familiar with the temple since childhood, since it was the custom to go there for the greater festivals. It is therefore naive to make one of them speak as though he were seeing it for the first time. Here we can detect the hand of Mark, writing for gentile Christians who had never seen the temple.

The next verse changes the scene. Jesus is now sitting 'on the Mount of Olives opposite the temple', and is no longer accompanied by 'his disciples', but only by four intimates, who ask him: 'When will this be?'. Luke was obviously worried both by the implausibility of the Palestinian Jew marvelling at the temple, and by this discontinuity; for he eliminated both these features by combining the two episodes into one, and by making not disciples but unspecified 'people' admire the building (Lk. 21: 5—7). The two features eliminated by Luke do suggest that the saying 'not one stone will be left upon another' was a logion that existed as an independent unit before Mark. Thus Beare concedes that the two verses in which it occurs in Mk. are 'a self-contained narrative, centred in the prediction; the introduction is merely a frame for the saying' (32, p 215). This saying probably did not come into being until after the destruction of the temple, and Mark's assimilation of it, i.e. his composition of his gospel, must have occurred still later.

Nevertheless, most scholars insist that Mk. must have been written before AD 75[12] because 13:4 and 14 are held to imply that the end of the world is to follow shortly after the destruction of the temple. In verse 4 Jesus is asked (in response to his statement that 'no stone will be left upon another'): 'When will this be, and what will be the sign when these things are all to be accomplished?'. The 'accomplishment of all things' is a technical term in apocalyptic literature for the end of the world, and he does in fact answer the question by telling what signs will presage it. The apocalyptic discourse that follows is thus clumsily introduced by a question about 'all these things', when he has in fact spoken only of the temple. The wording of 13:4 betrays, then, that the evangelist links an event of AD 70 with the end of the world only because he decided to use the floating logion about the temple as an introduction to an apocalyptic discourse derived from another tradition which measures time on a different scale. Beare speaks of the 'glaring lack of concord' between the two (33, p 173).[13] The original connection between them was merely that both are concerned with some form of destruction. Such 'catchword connections', as they are called in critical theology, are often the only links between individual items in speeches by Jesus. We see now the importance of the form-critics' analysis of the gospels, which is admitted to have established that, before Mark, 'the traditions about Jesus were transmitted as brief self-contained anecdotes or sayings'; and that 'when they came into his hands, there was no sure indication of the order of events' (32, p 14). Mark's location of the apocalyptic discourse on the Mount of Olives suggests that he was following a *written* tradition which already specified this locality. Otherwise he could have recorded the discourse without changing the scene from that of the previous verses, where Jesus speaks of the end of the temple.

Jerusalem is not again mentioned explicitly in Mk. 13, but verse 14 is often understood as another reference to events in the city of about AD 70:

> 'When you see the desolating sacrilege set up where it ought not to be (let the reader understand), then let those who are in Judaea flee to the mountains.'

The corresponding passage in Mt. (24: 15) explains that 'the desolating sacrilege' was something mentioned in the book of Daniel, where the phrase is used (11: 31) to allude to the heathen altar which the Syrian Seleucid ruler Antiochus Epiphanes built in the temple over the altar of burnt offering in 168 BC. The writer was a contemporary of Antiochus, but pretends to have lived centuries earlier and to prophesy the events of his reign (see JEC, pp 79–81). He refers to them in such a veiled manner that the Christian evangelists supposed that they had not yet occurred, and that Daniel's 'prophecies' in fact referred to events which would come to pass in their own day and age – events which were to presage the end of the world: for according to Daniel, the sacrilege is to inaugurate a period of unprecedented distress, after which the end will come (12:1, 11–13). Mark, then, is telling his readers that' some event will shortly occur which will fulfil Daniel's prophecy, and that people in Judaea are then to 'flee to the mountains'. Why Mark, who was not writing for Jews, should wish to tell Judaeans what to do at a particular moment is not at all obvious. To explain this – and also the fact that the whole chapter (immediately before the passion narrative, but quite independent of it) is devoted to a discourse by Jesus, whereas the evangelist elsewhere makes very little attempt to record his teachings – it has often been assumed that he has here incorporated an earlier Jewish document (or Christian document addressed to Jews) which interpreted Daniel's prophecy as a reference either to the Emperor Caligula's threat in AD 40 to have a statue of himself placed in the temple, or to some desecration accompanying the destruction of the building in AD 70.[14] But whether Mark merely assimilated the passage or wrote it himself, he certainly goes on to say in verse 24, that the world will end 'in those days after that tribulation'. If, then, he expected the end soon after the distress caused by the sacrilege, and if this latter refers to an incident during the rebellion of AD 66 to 70, then he must have written his gospel within a few years of AD 70.

In JEC I did not dispute that Mark interpreted the sacrilege in this way although I was at a loss to see how his gospel could have existed at such an early date, as none of the Christian epistles (in or outside of the NT) which are dated within the first century shows any knowledge of it, or of its material. Furthermore, Mk. 13: 7—10 suggests that the writer is offering an explanation as to why the end of the world did *not* come during or soon after the Jewish rebellion. He here makes Jesus urge his audience not to be alarmed when they hear of wars and rumours of wars, for such things are but the birthpangs of the new age, and the end must be preceded by a long and painful period of missionary activity during which they will be indicted in courts, flogged in synagogues, and summoned to testify to their faith before governors and kings. It may be argued that the 'wars' of this passage are too vague to be construed as an allusion to the rebellion of AD 66 to 70. But the additional statement of verse 10 that before the end 'the gospel must first be preached to all nations' is directed against expectations of an immediate end, and is hardly consonant with expecting it to come soon after the destruction of the temple.

It is of course possible to suppose that Mark has simply strung together alien traditions without noticing or caring about their contradictions. The discourse certainly does include contradictions which are best explained by 'use of disparate tradition' (384, pp 498—9; 638). For instance, after having explained that the end of the world will be heralded by unmistakable signs, Jesus adds that it will take men by surprise (13; 7—31, 32—3). But it is surely uncharitable to suppose that Mark went about all his editorial work completely unintelligently. And as he himself couples his mention of the desolating sacrilege with an exhortation to the reader to 'understand', we must assume that he intended to convey some coherent and intelligible message. In fact the apparent contradiction between verses 10 and 14 disappears if the reference to the sacrilege can be understood as an allusion to an event later than the war of AD 66 to 70. And this, I think, is the case.

1 Maccabees, which gives a historical account of the reign of Antiochus Epiphanes (175—164 BC), tells (1: 54) that 'the desolating sacrilege was set up on the altar'; that pagan altars were built throughout the towns of Judaea, and that death was the penalty for refusal to comply with the king's decree to offer sacrifice at them. Evasion was possible only by 'fleeing to the mountains' (2: 28). Christians of the first century would not have suspected that the events openly reported here are the same as those prophesied in veiled manner in the book of Daniel. But Mark's reference to the sacrilege and to the necessity of 'fleeing to the mountains' when it arrives does suggest that he had the incidents of 1 Maccabees in mind. Haenchen has argued (191, p 447) that what Mark envisaged was a future attempt by a Roman Emperor to force pagan worship on Christians as Antiochus had done on his subjects. The book of Revelation (13:12)

reckons with such a possibility. The point is not baldly stated, as open criticism of the imperial power would have been dangerous not only for the author, but also for the community in which his book was used. (For this reason he sometimes (14:8) writes 'Babylon' when he means 'Rome'). Mark had to be equally discreet, and himself hints that he is giving his message in coded form by his words 'let the reader understand'. Haenchen decodes the message to read: as soon as preparations (e.g. the setting up of an image or altar) are seen being made for a compulsory sacrifice to a pagan god or to the Emperor himself; as soon, then, as the sacrilege is seen standing 'where it ought not to be', then 'those in Judaea', i.e. Christians, are to 'flee to the mountains'. Judaea is named because Mark is keeping within the framework supplied by Daniel; but in reality he had in mind the whole Roman Empire. And flight is necessary because, if Christians wait until they are brought before the heathen image or altar, they will be left with a choice only between compliance or death. If Haenchen is right, Mark is looking — not back to an event of AD 70, but forward to a danger that has not yet materialized. And so there is no conflict between his reference to the sacrilege and his insistence that before the end 'the gospel must first be preached to all nations'.[15]

Haenchen is anxious to interpret Mark as envisaging future, rather than present Roman persecution, since he agrees with the great majority of theologians who date the gospel at about AD 70, whereas persecution of Christians by the Roman state does not seem to have occurred at this time, but only later, in the reign of Trajan or, at the earliest, Domitian (cf. above, p 42). But in fact there is much in Mk. to suggest that persecution is already a reality. In 8:27–9:1 Jesus labours the need to stand firm under persecution, and 13:13 implies a situation in which the 'name' of Christian, i.e. merely professing to be a Christian, is a capital offence. Now we have seen that, although it is hazardous to try to link a Christian writer's references to persecution with any particular time or place, the situation implied by Mk. 13:13 is consistent with what could well have happened not infrequently from ca. AD 90. Winter (412) correlates this passage with Pliny's mention of the *nomen Christianum* when he asked Trajan in AD 112 whether the 'name' of Christian was sufficient evidence of the guilt of a defendant.

In Mk. 13:30 Jesus says that 'this generation' will live to see the end of the world. If he really said this, then he was deluded, and commentators who accept the logion as genuine try to avoid this implication by supposing him to be speaking not of the end of the world, but of the fall of Jerusalem; or by taking 'this generation' to mean the people of God, which will survive until the end of time.[16] More convincing is the argument that Jesus' assurance to 'this generation' was put into his mouth at a time when many Christians had begun to feel uneasy because the end of the world (represented as imminent in the earliest Christian writings) had failed to occur. This militates against the view that Mk. is earlier than AD 70, but does not exclude a date of composition twenty or thirty years later, when a few people who had been alive about AD 30 were still alive. In 9:1 Jesus says that only 'some' of his contemporaries will experience the end. This saying has only a 'catchword' connection with the preceding verses and none at all with those that follow, and has been regarded as originally a remark of an early Christian preacher which was later credited with the authority of Jesus (185, pp 89–90). Mark did not think in terms of historical precision, but regarded both this logion and the statements in ch. 13 (which he himself put together from various sources to form a continuous speech) as addressed to the Christians of his own day and age. Every reader would feel that he belonged to 'this generation' of 13:30 (cf. 191, p 451).

To sum up: Mk. must have been written between AD 70 and the date of composition of Mt., which used it as a source. Mt. was probably not known to Ignatius (AD 110), but was certainly known to Polycarp, who wrote not later than AD 135. Scholars who date Mk. in the earlier part of the period between AD 70 and 135 have, as internal evidence, only Mk. 13 (which I consider not to the point) as support; whereas there is cogent evidence (the ignorance of the substance of Mk. apparent in all the Christian epistles of the first century) in favour of a date in the middle of this period.

(b) Matthew and Luke

Both Mt. and Lk. were unknown to Clement of Rome (who wrote at the end of the first century, or a little later); Ignatius (ca. AD 110) certainly did not know Lk., and probably not Mt. either; but both gospels are quoted by Polycarp not later than AD 135. Luke may have written somewhat later than Matthew – not much later, because he knew nothing of Matthew's work.[17] McNeile dates Mt. after AD 80, and Kilpatrick and Grant favour a date after AD 90.[18]

Mt. and Lk. have a good deal of material in common (apart from what they took from Mk.). Most theologians agree that neither evangelist could have taken this material from the other, since they both wrote quite independently, and that their gospels overlap because they both used as sources not only Mk. but a second Greek document not now extant and usually called Q (Kümmel, 268, pp 50ff summarizes the evidence). Q consists mainly of sayings of Jesus, and it sets his life in first century Palestine by associating him with John the Baptist, but makes no mention of Pilate, nor of Jesus' passion and crucifixion. It may be earlier or later than Mk., of which it is independent; but it cannot be a very early document, for it presupposes material of different provenance which it has collected and arranged by means of 'catchword' connections. It has also abandoned the early Christian idea that Jesus' second coming is to occur in the immediate future (176, p 218; 283, p 85). Semitisms in the Greek logia of Q have been made the basis of arguments that it derives from an early record of authentic utterances of Jesus. But such 'Palestinian' Semitisms can be explained without this hypothesis.[19]

Q helps us to date Mt. and Lk. because each of these gospels have introduced minor variants of their own into the material taken from it, and these variants sometimes betray the standpoint or circumstances of the evangelist. For instance, in 22:7 Matthew introduces into a parable a statement of his own (absent from the Lucan parallel) that the king — the reference must be to the king of heaven — sent his troops and burned the city of those who had killed his servants. This is generally admitted to be an allusion to the destruction of Jerusalem in AD 70, an event which Matthew interprets as God's punishment to the Jews for slaying Jesus and his apostles.[20] Another indication that Matthew wrote after AD 70 is his report of Jesus' declaration to the scribes and Pharisees:

'Therefore I send you prophets and wise men and scribes, some of whom you will kill and crucify, and some you will scourge in your synagogues and persecute from town to town, that upon you may come all the righteous blood shed on earth, from the blood of the innocent Abel to the blood of Zechariah the son of Barachiah, whom you murdered between the sanctuary and the altar. Truly I say to you, all this will come upon this generation'. (23:34—6)

The prophet Zechariah, the son of Berechiah, cannot be meant, for he did not suffer martyrdom. Some commentators have supposed the reference to be to Zechariah the son of Jehoiada who was murdered in the court of the temple (2 Chronicles 24: 20—1); for, as 2 Chronicles is placed last in the canon of Hebrew scriptures, this Zechariah is the last of the OT martyrs and so — it is argued — is appropriately contrasted with Abel, the first. But it is senseless to suppose that Matthew intended to limit the guilt of the scribes and Pharisees to 'canonical' murders, the last of which occurred 800 years before Jesus, when the context makes it clear that some of the victims are to be Christian missionaries 'sent' by him. The reference is obviously to the Zacharias the son of Baruch who, as Josephus tells (232, 4:5, 4) was put to death by Jewish zealots 'in the middle of the temple' in AD 68. This man would, in Matthew's vision, appropriately be the last of the martyrs whose blood was to 'come upon' the Jews in 'this generation' when Jerusalem was destroyed two years later.

That Matthew looked back over some considerable interval to AD 70 is suggested by his evident concern to avoid any implication there may be in Mk. 13:1—4 that the destruction of the temple is connected with the end of the world. We recall that Jesus here speaks of the temple, is then asked when 'all these things' will be accomplished, and replies with a discourse about the end of the world. Matthew, however, is careful to make the disciples meet his words about the temple with two distinct questions — one about the temple and the other about 'the sign of your coming and of the close of the age' (24: 2—3). To make quite sure that any linkage with the temple is eliminated from the eschatological discourse thus introduced, these two questions are addressed to Jesus 'as he sat on the Mount of Olives' — not, as Mk. has it, 'as he sat on the Mount of Olives opposite the temple'. Similarly, the Marcan references (13:9) to persecution by Jewish authorities have been dropped in Matthew's account (24:9—14) of the events presaging the end. Matthew envisages persecution by Jews at an earlier stage (10:17; cf. below, p 109), whereas the end is to come after the annihilation of the Jewish state in AD 70, when only gentiles are left with the power to put Christians to death. This is clearly the situation of the evangelist's own time.[2][1] Indeed, that he restricts Jewish persecution to the period of Jesus' ministry and excludes it from the more distant future which he represents Jesus as foretelling, may well point to a date of writing later than AD 90; for it was about then that Christians were effectively excluded from synagogues — not by formal decree, but because a curse on heretics was at that time proposed as an insertion into synagogue worship (see below p 92) and in due course put into practice. Wherever it was implemented, Christians naturally found difficulty in continuing to attend the services (cf. Frend, 164, p 179; Hare, 198, pp 54—5). Thus the 'floggings in synagogues' of Mt. 10:17 are, for the Christians addressed by Matthew, a thing of the past (198, pp 105, 148). If they were outside the synagogue, they were no longer liable to its discipline.

At 23:13 Jesus' complaint against the Pharisees is not that they persecute, but that they prevent Jews from turning Christian. The situation here envisaged seems to be that of the evangelist's own times: 'Woe to you, scribes and Pharisees, hypocrites! Because you shut the kingdom of heaven against men; for you neither enter yourselves, nor allow those who would enter to go in'. That Matthew here designates as hypocrisy behaviour which sprang from religious conviction is typical of his lack of detachment throughout ch. 23, where the scribes and Pharisees are repeatedly reproached as hypocrites, whether or not the reproach in question can justly be made of both groups, and whether or not the behaviour criticized can justly be called hypocrisy (Haenchen, 191, p 424).

This ch. 23 begins, incongruously, with Jesus' endorsement of their teaching: 'The scribes and the Pharisees sit on Moses' seat; so practise and observe whatever they tell you, but not what they do; for they preach but do not practise' (verses 2—3). This logion was surely not invented by Matthew, but assimilated by him from a Jewish-Christian source. It nevertheless represents a degraded (and therefore late) tradition; for in Luke's version of the woes, the ordinary members of the Pharisaic party are carefully distinguished from their rabbinic leaders, whereas Matthew fuses the two groups throughout ch. 23, and makes 'the scribes and the Pharisees sit on Moses' seat' — as if the lay members of the Pharisaic party were all authoritative exegetes of the Torah (198, p 81)! Hare (p 125n) finds it incredible that Matthew should have left these opening verses standing if he had written much later than the effective application of the cursing of heretics proposed as an innovation in the synagogue liturgy ca. AD 90. But the verses are in flagrant contradiction with other material in ch. 23 (and elsewhere in the gospel). 16:5—12 expressly condemns 'the teaching of the Pharisees'. 12:33—5 tends in the same direction, and at 15:14 they are called 'blind guides'. If, then, the evangelist was content to allow internal contradictions to remain, we cannot suppose him to have been sensitive to rabbinic liturgical modifications. In ch. 23 itself the opening endorsement of the Pharisees' teaching is soon retracted; verse 4 designates this teaching as a 'heavy burden'. (A writer who really accepted it as god-given would not thus complain of its burdensomeness.) Matthew is clearly making logia which were originally independent of each other into a continuous speech. Verses 8—12 imply that Christians need no Rabbis, but have direct access to God. This too negates the doctrine of the opening verses and probably reached Matthew from sectarians who made Jesus speak on these lines because they believed that all Christians were directly inspired by the holy spirit and were therefore all 'brethren' who had no need of other 'teachers' or 'masters' (191, pp 422—3). Some commentators think that these verses 8—12, which stipulate that Christians have but one master, explain why Matthew allowed the contrary endorsement of Rabbinic teaching in verse 3 to stand; namely because verses 8—12 show that the material assimilated as verse 3 is no longer actual. Matthew, then, 'preserves a positive tradition which has been passed on to him, but at the same time he also intimates that in his community this tradition hardly functions any more' (Tilborg, 388, p 137; cf. Walker, 402, p 69n). Another example of this method — incorporating a tradition and then immediately denying its truth — is Jn. 4:1—2 (on which see p 202 below).

Mt. 23:38—9 (which is without Marcan parallel) clearly aims at interposing an interval between AD 70 and Jesus' second or final coming. Here, in Jerusalem just before his arrest, he cries: 'O Jerusalem, . . . Behold your house is forsaken and desolate. For I tell you, you will not see me again until you say, "Blessed be he who comes in the name of the Lord" '. On this, Montefiore makes the apposite comment:

'Probably the words are not authentic. Jerusalem had fallen: Jesus had not come. Therefore the men of a later generation felt that he must have predicted that an interval would lie between the fall of the city and his second coming, during which time it would remain in ruins. Hence the present verse.' (303, II, 307)

Luke also records this saying, but without the word 'desolate', which is also missing in some ancient mss of Mt. The logion was thus probably taken by both evangelists from Q, where it would not have included the words 'and desolate', but expressed the idea that Wisdom, who dwelt in the temple, had 'forsaken' it (see 381, p 69). Luke makes Jesus speak it before he has reached Jerusalem, and without the 'again' included in Mt.'s statement 'you will not see me again until you say, "Blessed be he" ', etc. Thus in Lk. Jesus' words could conceivably refer to his own triumphal entry into the city. Their position is a good example of how 'catchwords' guided the evangelist in his arrangement of his material: for Jesus has just said (Lk. 13:33) that a prophet can perish only in 'Jerusalem', and this word allows the logion about its temple to be appended.

Whether the reference is to Jesus' triumphant entry or to his final coming, other evidence shows unambiguously that Luke wrote considerably later than AD 70. In adapting Mk. 13, Luke writes not of the 'desolating sacrilege', but of 'the desolation of Jerusalem', effected by the armies encompassing it. And after describing the fall of the city as the result of a siege, he makes Jesus declare — not that the end of the world will follow immediately, but that the gentiles will trample down the city 'until their times are fulfilled' (21:24). Then will come a time of 'distress' — not, however, now for Israel but for the gentiles, and amidst convulsions of nature the Son of man will come.[22] Luke retains (21:32), as Matthew also does (24:34), the doctrine of Mk. 13:30 that 'this generation will not pass away before all these things take place'. Yet he shows signs of embarrassment in that he is nevertheless concerned to represent Jesus as declaring that the end will come later than Mark envisaged.

At the beginning of this century Schmiedel gave evidence (348c), which so eminent a scholar as Cadbury has described as 'very persuasive' (92, p 357), that Luke not only wrote later than the fall of Jerusalem, but also that he almost certainly utilized the *Antiquities* of Josephus — a work not available before AD 93. A recent commentator on Lk., Professor Ellis, is able to date the gospel earlier than AD 70 only by making light of this evidence and disregarding some of it.[23]

Lk. alone of the synoptics represents Jesus as applying to himself the words of Isaiah: 'He has anointed me to preach good news to the poor, . . . to proclaim release to the captives and recovering of sight to the blind, to set at liberty those who are oppressed, to proclaim the acceptable year of the Lord (4:18–19). Luke's purpose in including this emerges from comparison with 2 Cor. 6:2, where Paul quotes similar words from Isaiah about 'the acceptable time' and 'the day of salvation' and adds: 'Behold, now is the acceptable time; now the day of salvation'. Luke, however, in making Jesus, on a past occasion, identify the time of salvation with his own ministry, represents it as past. He was writing when the end of the world, regarded as imminent by Paul, had signally failed to occur; and so he had to make Jesus' earthly life not the final period of history, but an epoch of salvation which would be succeeded by the epoch of the Church (the evangelist's own times). The former epoch of course influences the latter. Jesus' activities on earth are the basis of the hopes of salvation entertained by the Church. But with Luke, Jesus' message is not the Marcan one (Mk. 1:15) that the kingdom is near, to come shortly, but that it 'is in the midst of you' (Lk. 17:21), that it has come in the person of Jesus, whose life is a guarantee of our future salvation.[24] This necessity (caused by the continuing absence of any indication that the world was reaching its end) to look back to Jesus' life, as much as forward to his second coming, in order to understand the nature of the kingdom and of salvation, was a very important motive for the creation of biographical details which supplemented the meagre Pauline account.

That the synoptics were written in the order: Mk., Mt., Lk. can also be illustrated by the statements which they represent Jesus as making at his Sanhedrin trial about the timing of the end of the world. There is no need to regard these statements as historical, as the motive for putting them into his mouth is perfectly clear. Christians of the late first century knew that the Jews refused to accept him as the Messiah; and this provided a basis for a narrative in which he tells the Jewish authorities that he is the Messiah, and has this claim rejected. Thus Mk. has it that he answers the high priest's question whether he is the Messiah with the words:

'I am; and *you will see* the Son of man seated at the right hand of Power, and coming with the clouds of heaven.' Then the high priest tore his garments and said . . . 'You have heard his blasphemy.' (14:62–4; Italics mine)

Commentators point out that Jesus' words were not blasphemous, and this again makes the narrative look like legend rather than history, particularly as there is an obvious reason for the formation of such a detail.[25] The suggestion that his interrogators would live to 'see' the Son of man come down from heaven to end the world embarrassed later evangelists. Matthew somewhat clumsily amended it to: 'Hereafter you will see the Son of man seated at the right hand of Power, and coming on the clouds of heaven' (26:64). Luke's emendation is more radical, and is meant to exclude the suggestion that the end would come soon enough for Jesus' contemporaries to witness it. He is made to say: 'From now on, the Son of man *shall be seated* at the right hand of the power of God' (22:69). The fourth gospel does not represent him as having been brought before the Sanhedrin for trial, and so there is no parallel passage in Jn.

Finally, I should mention the theory of 'Proto-Lk.'. We saw that the commonly accepted view is that both Matthew and Luke expanded Mk. by supplementing it with Q. Each includes, additionally, some material unrepresented in the other. Mt. thus consists of Marcan material, Q material (i.e. non-Marcan material shared with Lk.) and material unique to itself (and therefore called M). If Mt. thus consists of Mk. + Q + M, Lk. likewise consists of Mk. + Q + L (where L represents material unique to Lk.). Now although the dependence of Lk. on Mk., and hence its lateness, is hardly disputed any more, some have urged that the Marcan material was inserted into it only at a late stage. These critics, instead of regarding Lk. as an expansion of Mk., posit a 'Proto-Lk.' (not now extant) consisting of Q + L, and hold that, when Mk. became available, this Proto-Lk. was expanded into Lk. as we now know it by the insertion of blocks of Marcan material (and by the addition of the two new opening chapters – the present Lk. 1–2). The point of the theory is, of course, to authenticate some elements in the present gospel by making them pre-Marcan and therefore supposedly early enough in their origin to have been based on eye-witness reports. The theory has, however, not found much favour. Kümmel gives reasons (268, pp 92—5) for dismissing it as untenable. One of these is that Lk.'s passion narrative (which certainly could not have come from Q, in which all references to the passion are lacking) includes sections where Marcan phrases appear in the middle, although the sections in other respects differ considerably from Mk. Creed puts the matter as follows: 'These signs of Mk. are intelligible if the Lucan narrative is a recasting and expansion of the Marcan text. If, however, Luke had already written or found a full and independent non-Marcan narrative, it seems unlikely that afterwards he would have interpolated occasional sentences and verses from Mk.' (110, p lviii).

Although, then, Luke expanded Mk. and did not work Mk. into a document already independently completed, his copy of Mk. was incomplete and lacked Mk. 6:45—8:26, which has no equivalent in Lk. Immediately before this section comes the miraculous feeding of five thousand with five loaves and two small fishes — a story common to both gospels. Jesus then took leave of everyone and 'went into the hills to pray' (Mk. 6:46). In Luke's copy of Mk. these words seem to have been followed immediately by Mk. 8:27, where he 'questioned' his disciples in such a way as to elicit Peter's confession that he is the Christ; for Luke, after the story of the five thousand, passes straight to Peter's confession and introduces it with the verse: 'As Jesus was praying alone, the disciples were with him and he questioned them' (9:18). It is not said that they *came* to him, but that they *were* with him whilst he was alone! Haenchen calls this verse a 'desperate attempt' by Luke to run together Mk. 6:46 and 8:27 — an attempt which is intelligible only if the intervening Marcan material had been absent in Luke's copy of Mk. And he adds that recently discovered papyri show that it is not unusual for leaves to be missing in the middle of a codex (189, p 104; 191, pp 303—4).

(c) John

The fourth gospel is regarded as later than the other three. It was not known to a number of early Christian writers who knew and even quoted the others. However, this silence could be due not to ignorance, but to hostility towards a gospel which is so much at variance with the others; and even ignorance of a gospel might be due simply to its *local* circulation. More conclusive evidence of a later date is that John shows a tendency to enhance features which the synoptics adumbrate — for examples see JEC, pp 127—9 — and that his theology is more advanced. For instance, his elimination of the idea of a literal second coming from the clouds suggests a later stage than that represented in the synoptics. Mk. 9:1 makes Jesus say that 'there are some standing here who will not taste death before they see that the kingdom of God has come with power'. Mt. 16:28 and Lk. 9:27 give the saying with slight variations, but all three use the phrase 'will not taste death'. John does not record this saying, nor the context which the synoptics give it; but he does make Jesus affirm (8:52): 'If anyone keeps my word, he will never taste death'. The aim is clearly to break with the synoptic doctrine of a second coming, and to make eternal life dependent only on keeping Jesus' word. In the fourth gospel Christ's second coming no longer means his appearance in the sky as judge, but the coming of the holy spirit into the hearts of believers.[26]

Although Jn. is thus of later date than the synoptics, there is little in it to suggest that the author was acquainted with them, or even with the traditions on which they are based. His independence is particularly apparent in 'the peculiar character of the Jesuine discourses he puts together' (Käsemann, 238, p 193). This independence is understandable, for we cannot assume that, as soon as the synoptics were written, they were available in all major Christian communities. As we saw (p 77), it is quite likely that, in the first century, each community held by one gospel and did not have recourse to others. John's independence of the synoptics is not to be taken (as it is by Dodd) as implying that his gospel is based on traditions which are more ancient than those underlying the synoptics and therefore of great historical accuracy; for he seems to have drawn on what were more developed, more exaggerated and — in some cases — degraded forms of the traditions represented in them. Haenchen (190, p 110n) illustrates all three of these features by comparing with its synoptic parallels Jn.'s version of the story of the anointing of Jesus' feet. In Lk. 7:36–50 a harlot wets them with her tears, which she dries with her hair; then she anoints the feet with ointment. John does not leave her anonymous, but names her as Mary. This accords with his practice elsewhere. For instance, the synoptics report, without naming the participants, that the ear of the high priest's slave was cut off; but John states that the name of the slave was Malchus, and that the one who wielded the sword was Simon Peter. These are obviously details of growing legend. Exaggeration is apparent when Mary is made to pour a whole pound of ointment onto Jesus' feet. There is no mention of her tears, and it is the ointment that she wipes away with her hair (12:3–8). An equally senseless trait, betraying John's use of a degraded tradition, is Jesus' statement (after Judas has protested that she has wasted all the oil): 'Let her keep it for the day of my burial'. In Mk. the protest comes from some anonymous observers; Matthew ascribes it to 'the disciples', while John complicates matters by making it a hypocritical comment from Judas, who wanted the perfume sold, ostensibly for the benefit of the poor, but in fact (as treasurer of the group) in order to pocket the proceeds.

Jn. cannot be much later than the synoptics, for a papyrus fragment of it, found in Egypt, has been dated about AD 125 and constitutes the earliest preserved fragment of the NT (see 333). Like the synoptics it was written at a time of violent enmity between Jews and Christians — indeed the Johannine Jesus foretells that his followers will be excluded from the synagogues (16:2); and in one narrative the evangelist declares that 'the Jews had already agreed that if any one should confess him [Jesus] to be the Christ he was to be put out of the synagogue' (9:22). The reference is ostensibly to conditions obtaining in Jesus' lifetime, but it seems more likely that the evangelist wrote in knowledge of the synagogue's official cursing of heretical Jews by means of an insertion into its chief prayer authorized by Rabbi Gamaliel II ca. AD 90. This gave a formal basis to whatever earlier *ad hoc* decisions against Christians there may have been (cf. 310, pp 144—6). Throughout the fourth gospel Jesus speaks of the Jewish law as though he himself were not a Jew and had no connection with it (8:17; 15:25). For John he is no Jew, but a divine personage who existed before the Jewish nation came into being: 'Before Abraham was, I am' (8:58). Dodd, who believes that the 'basic tradition' from which John created his gospel was shaped before the Jewish War of AD 66, nevertheless affirms that it was written after the other three, and near the year 100 (133, pp 424—6). Grant argues for 'a date early in the second century', and notes that resistance to this view comes mainly from those who are 'reluctant to abandon the possibility that John the son of Zebedee was, if not the author of the gospel, at least in some sense responsible for it.' (178, p 175).

(d) Summary

The latest of the four gospels existed by AD 125 and the earliest of them was written between AD 70 and this date. Christian scholars have, for obvious reasons, been anxious to date Mk. at the very beginning of this period of fifty-five years; but the evidence allows that it was written about the middle of this period. Probably no great interval of time separates this, the earliest of the four, from Jn., the latest; for (i) John is ignorant of the other three, which therefore are unlikely to have had a wide and extended circulation when he wrote; (ii) Clement of Rome (ca. AD 96) fails to refer to any written gospel and regards as authoritative only the OT and 'what the Lord said'. The words of the Lord which he quotes are not taken from the synoptics and, according to Köster, represent an *earlier* layer of tradition — something analogous to Q (261, p 23). Furthermore (iii) Ignatius (ca. AD 110) did not know Lk., and although he has common ground with Mt. at many points, his dependence on Mt. is by no means proven. Mt. later became the most read gospel because it was most widely acceptable — and this because it included (more so than did other gospels) widely accepted traditions. It is with such traditions that Ignatius overlaps (*Ibid.*, p 61). Only with Polycarp (ca. AD 120—135) do we reach a writer who is really likely to have used both Mt. and Lk., which of course presuppose Mk. (For the relative positions of Clement, Ignatius and Polycarp in time, cf. the chart on p 47 above). The effect of this evidence is to narrow the time-gap between Mk. and Jn. considerably.

Notes to Chapter Three

1 Winter's study of the narratives of the arrest, trial and crucifixion led him to comment on the great 'variety of diverging and repeatedly conflicting accounts' of

these events (411, pp 5–6). And Harvey concedes that it is 'impossible' to fit the gospel resurrection accounts together into a single coherent scheme (201, p 297).

2 Such adaptation for preaching purposes is today admitted to underlie e.g. Mk.'s account (1:16–20) of the call of the first disciples. Jesus meets fishermen he has never before seen, and they 'immediately left their nets and followed him' after he had said: 'Follow me, and I will make you become fishers of men'. Keck concedes that this story 'does not report the actual process by which he acquired disciples', but was told by Christian preachers in order to inculcate in their audiences what the proper Christian response to the call of Jesus should be (245, p 24). The parallel passage in Lk. (5:1–11) tries to make the readiness of the men to drop everything and follow him more plausible by representing them as already having heard him preach, and as witnessing a miracle he works.

3 Any synopsis (such as the one by Sparks, 376) which prints corresponding gospel passages side by side, will show of Mt. 10 that verses 5–15 conflate Mk. 6:8–11 with other material, whereas Luke (9:1–6 and 10:1–6) has kept the two separate; that verses 17–22 have been taken from the apocalyptic discourse which Mark made Jesus deliver much later in his career; and that verses 24ff have material which occurs in various other contexts in Mk. and Lk.

4 See Mk. 2:16 and 24; Lk. 5:30. According to Bultmann (78, p 172) Jesus is made to face criticism of his disciples rather than of himself because an early Christian community was reproached over its attitude, e.g. to fasting and keeping the sabbath, and therefore needed traditions in which he defends the behaviour of his followers on these matters. But Christian communities were quite capable of representing him as having himself set an example, and the evangelists' failure to record direct criticism of his behaviour does seem due to their respect for him.

5 191, p 2. Luke himself is later in time than the 'many' who had already written gospels. He castigates the inadequacy of these earlier gospels when he says that he proposes to settle the truth (1:4). He does not suggest that he will do so by drawing on them; rather does he claim to institute an independent inquiry (verse 3). His prologue makes clear that, by the time he wrote, the relation of gospels to the events recorded in them had become a problem for the Christian community (see the searching discussion by Klein, 128, pp 206–7, 214).

6 There is, for instance, 'reason to believe that only Mt. was at all widely read in Palestine; that there were Churches in Asia Minor which only used Jn. from the very outset; that in Egypt only the [extracanonical] Gospel of the Egyptians was accepted as valid among the Gentile Christians' (115, pp 45–6), while the Jewish Christians of Alexandria used the Gospel of the Hebrews (28, pp 51–2).

7 See 92, p 261 and 188, pp 7–8. The discerning reader will find the facts admitted in Dodd's last book where he says that the author of Lk. 'has been identified, *from the time when the NT writings were first collected* [italics mine], as the Greek physician Luke who was for some years on the "staff" of the apostle Paul, and this may be right' (135, p 17).

8 Within the material that they have in common with Mk., Mt. and Lk. agree in the sequence of the events only in so far as they agree with Mk. Where they diverge from Mk., each goes his own way. From these facts Lachmann argued in 1835 that all three evangelists copied a lost original gospel which is best preserved by Mk. This argument from the order of events for the priority of Mk. still stands (*pace* Farmer, 152, p 66), even though the postulate of an original gospel underlying all three has today been replaced by the view that Mt. and Lk. used Mk.; since, in numerous instances, the divergence of Mt. and Lk. from Mk. in sequence can be made understandable, but not the divergence of Mk. from Mt. and Lk. (268, pp 46–8).

9 Ignatius does indeed say that Jesus was baptized by John 'that all righteousness might be fulfilled by him'. Somewhat similar words were added by Matthew to the Marcan account of Jesus' baptism, and Ignatius' phrase therefore suggests that he knew Mt. (cf. JEC, p 171). Köster, however, thinks that Ignatius did not take

the phrase directly from Mt. but from a confessional formula which was known both to him and to the evangelist (261, p 60).

10 Clement of Alexandria (d. ca. AD 251) is the first clearly to link Mk. with Rome. Eusebius declares that an earlier statement (not now extant) of Papias (ca. AD 140) confirms Clement. By about this time Peter had come to be regarded as having preached in Rome, and Mk. as we saw (above, p 77) was early associated with Peter. Again, the 'Mark' mentioned in 1 Peter 5:13 is said to be with Peter in Babylon − the code name used by early Christians for Rome (cf. above, p 83). Clement and Papias' view of the origin of Mk. was surely based on nothing more than inference from these tendentious traditions (as is betrayed by Eusebius' comments; see e.g. 149, Bk. 2, ch.15). If Mk. was in fact written in Rome, it must have originated after AD 96, for 1 Clement, written there at about that date, shows, as Evans notes, 'no sign of any knowledge of Mk.' (150, pp 6−7; cf. 261, p 23). Schulz thinks that the gospel may well have been written at Tyre, Sidon or in Transjordan (361, p 9), and Taylor finds that a case can be made for Antioch (384, pp 5, 32). In other words, all we can affirm with confidence is that it was written in an important and respected Christian community. This much seems to follow from the fact that, although Matthew and Luke smoothed what Trocmé has called the 'grande rusticité' (394, p 56) of Mark's style, they nevertheless respected the substance of his work sufficiently to make it the basis of their own accounts.

11 Rom. 13:1−7, which urges subservience to the authorities, and which even designates them loyal servants of God, has long been recognized as a self-contained unit independent of its context, indeed breaking the connection between the ethical admonitions which precede and follow it. Nevertheless, Kallas' reasons (244, pp 365−74) for setting it aside as a second-century interpolation are not fully convincing.

12 A notable exception is Farmer, who thinks Mk. may have been written as late as AD 100 or 125; but he also argues that it is later than and dependent on Mt. and Lk. (152, pp 200, 226). Trocmé proposes AD 85 as an upper limit for the final redaction of Mk., but he dates the first thirteen chapters as early as AD 50 (394, pp 193, 203).

13 Grässer (176, p 155n) and others have noted that it is possible to explain this lack of concord by supposing that Mark substituted the words 'all these things' for what was originally only a reference to the temple; and that he thus aimed to correct an earlier idea that the destruction of the temple would be followed directly by the end of the world, and to affirm that it was only one link in the chain of final events. If Mark was in fact correcting an earlier tradition in this way, it is probable that the need for such correction arose because the temple had already been destroyed (without bringing about the end of the world) and that Mark was therefore writing after AD 70.

14 Some commentators (see refs. in 231, p 215) interpret 'the desolating sacrilege set up where it ought not to be' as a reference to the coming of the Antichrist − a demonic figure expected before Jesus' second advent as the final persecutor of Christians, and sometimes identified with the 'son of perdition' of 2 Thess. 2:1−12, who takes his seat in the temple. The roots of this conception are probably to be found in the (originally Babylonian) legend of the battle of God with a dragon-like monster − a legend of which traces are to be found in various parts of the OT. One reason for linking the 'desolating sacrilege' with the Antichrist is that Mark qualifies this neuter phrase with a masculine participle − lit. 'set up where *he* ought not to be'. Equally allowable is the rendering of the RV: '*standing* where he ought not'; and Brandon thinks that this refers to an outsider who intruded into the temple. He takes it as an allusion to Titus' entry into the innermost sanctuary in AD 70, when the victorious Roman troops assembled in the temple court and sacrificed to their standards, which bore the

image of the Emperor. He regards this verse as the evangelist's own composition, and not as incorporated from an apocalypse of slightly earlier date (66, pp 232–3).

15 Branscomb (70, p 233) reaches this same conclusion from slightly different premises. He notes that the pre-Christian references to the 'desolating sacrilege' (in Daniel and Maccabees) link it with the temple; and he argues that Mark was editing an apocalypse which likewise mentioned the sacrilege in connection with the temple; and that, since the evangelist was writing after AD 70 (when the temple no longer existed), he deleted explicit mention of it and substituted the less definite statement that the sacrilege was 'set up where it ought not to be'.

16 The embarrassment of commentators on Mk. 13:30 and its synoptic parallels is illustrated by Dodd's argument that the passage is an example of 'shortening of historical perspective'. 'When the profound realities underlying a situation are depicted in the dramatic form of historical prediction, the certainty and inevitability of the spiritual processes involved are expressed in terms of the immediate imminence of the event' (132, p 55).

17 That Luke did not know Mt. is clear from his failure to include any of Matthew's additions to Mk. It is also unlikely that, if he had used Mt., he would have broken up Jesus' discourses as given there (particularly the Sermon on the Mount), omitted some of the fragments thus formed, and scattered others throughout his own gospel.

18 For evidence supporting the statements made in this paragraph see JEC, pp 165–74; 261, pp 23–4, 61, 122; 179, p 302; 249, pp 6–7, 127, 131; 292, p xxviii.

19 Even so mystical a logion from Q as Mt. 11:25–7 = Lk. 10:21–2 is claimed by Jeremias (228) as 'Palestinian', and is in fact paralleled in the Dead Sea Scrolls (see Davies, 122, pp 136ff). Most commentators agree that it is a piece of Church writing based on a number of OT quotations and put into Jesus' mouth. Here, says Vermes, 'contemporary exegetical scepticism joins forces for once with common sense' (398, p 201).

20 Rengstorf (145, pp 116, 125) has objected that the 'burning of the city' was a literary cliché common in parables concerning kings, and in historical narratives which relate the capture and destruction of a town in the briefest possible way; and also that it fails to bring out the salient events of AD 70. But if Matthew is in fact here using a cliché, this would explain why his allusion to these events is not more precise.

21 Cf. Walker, 402, pp 83–4, 115. On the other hand, Matthew's adaptation of Mark's statement about the 'desolating sacrilege' seems to work in precisely the opposite direction, and to link the events of AD 70 with the consummation. For he says not (as Mark does) that the sacrilege will be 'set up where it ought not to be', but that it will be seen 'standing in the holy place' (24:15). This certainly looks like a reference to the desecration of the temple at the end of the rebellion. The evangelist adds (verses 21 and 29) that 'then there will be great tribulation' and that 'immediately after the tribulation of those days' the end will come. Some commentators have, however, argued that 'the holy place' does not mean the temple at all. Bonnard notes that Matthew's retention of Mk.'s 'let the reader understand' hints that there is a hidden meaning in the prediction and indicates that Christians are to interpret 'the holy place' in a special way – as a veiled allusion to the Church. The 'desolating sacrilege' standing there would thus be a reference to idolatry, revolt or the coming of Antichrist in the Christian community (51, p 351); cf. Hill, 207, p 321 and Bacon's argument (11, pp 68–9) that Matthew 'makes no prediction that the Second Coming will follow "immediately" after the *fall of Jerusalem*. He predicts (what is much more to the purpose for his readers) that it will come immediately after the worst sufferings of *the Church*'.

22 The 'immediately' of Mt. 24:29 has no equivalent in Lk. 21:25. And Luke has also dropped the statement of Mk. 13:20 (preserved in Mt. 24:22) that the days preceding the end shall be shortened for the elect's sake.

23 He will not admit that Luke's version of Jesus' speech about the fall of Jerusalem is a 'prophecy after the event' (144, p 57). While *Biblica* (348, § 16) notes that Lk. 19:43 alludes to an actual incident in the destruction of Jerusalem, Ellis makes no comment on that verse, although the old commentary he is revising refers its readers to the incident as described by Josephus.

24 See Conzelmann, 105, pp 30–1; 106, pp 150–1. In JEC (p 87) I wrongly asserted that Lk. 12:54–6 makes Jesus take a different attitude, and encourages his audience to look forward to momentous signs which will announce the advent of the end of the world. More plausible is the argument of Klein that 'the present time' in verse 56 means the situation in the Church from the death of Jesus until the time of Luke – a period characterized by divisions (verse 52). The sense of the passage is that 'to judge the present time aright' one must take the Christian side (254, p 385). There is no reference to the end, although there was in the saying which Luke was reworking. (The Matthean form, 16:26f, is clearly more eschatological).

25 Jesus' true status was the principal point of dispute between Jewish and Christian communities late in the first century. The Christians regarded him not merely as supernatural, but even as divine, and such a claim was certainly, from the Jewish standpoint, blasphemous. (cf. Jn. 10:33 where the Jews try to stone him 'for blasphemy; because you, being a man, make yourself God'). Hence the origin of a Christian narrative in which Jews are represented as rejecting as blasphemous his affirmation of what, for Christians, constituted his true status. As Bousset observed (59, p 51), Mk. 14:64 derives from Christian dogma, not from Jewish legal ideas. Other features of the whole passage also show that it originated in a Christian community of sophisticated Christology, and that Jesus could not have said what Mark here ascribes to him (see below, p 114).

26 Jn. 14:16–18; 16:7 and 13. The way such crass contradictions are glossed over by apologists is well illustrated by Grant's statement that 'in regard to Christology and eschatology, the point of view of John is somewhat different from that of the synoptic evangelists' (182, p 154).

4 Christologies

(i) From Paul to Mark and Q

How did it come about that Paul's view of Jesus was succeeded by the very different one of Mark? I shall try to show that Mark's portrait combines what Paul believed with very different ideas put out by Christian teachers who had disputed his authority.

Paul believed in a supernatural Jesus who assumed human flesh and was crucified on earth at the instigation of evil supernatural powers. Paul was utterly unconcerned with when or where this happened – he does not give it a historical setting – because he was convinced that Jesus lived an obscure life on earth; so obscure that, until he manifested his true power at the resurrection, even the demons failed to recognize who he was: had they known the truth, 'they would not have crucified the Lord of glory' (1 Cor. 2:8). In coming to earth Christ 'emptied himself' of his divine form, and humbly assumed 'the form of a servant' (Phil. 2:7). His life culminated in a shameful and ignominious death on the cross in 'weakness' (2 Cor. 13:4). The weakness and obscurity of the earthly Jesus is surely also implied when Paul insists – in a context where he equates keeping the Jewish law with 'slavery' – that Jesus was 'born of woman, born under the law' (Gal. 4:4).[1] Paul does not know who Jesus' human enemies were and how they had him crucified. Even in the synoptics, only the later layers of the tradition (e.g. comments supplied by the evangelists, as editors, to link the pieces of tradition they took from their sources) identify Jesus' opponents as scribes, Pharisees, Sadducees, or Herodians. In the earlier layers the opponents figure merely as 'they' or as 'the Jews' (see Bultmann's evidence, 83, pp 54–6).

The obscurity of the Messiah is a doctrine which one would expect to find in earliest Christianity, if in fact this Messiah is a fiction. Christians believed (against the Jewish view) that he had already been on earth. But as it was obvious that practically no one had heard anything about him, he could not have come in triumph, but must have achieved his destiny unnoticed. His open triumphs would have to be reserved for a second coming.

This portrait of Jesus as obscure and rejected would accord well with the Jewish 'Wisdom' traditions, to which, we saw (above pp 38, 55), Paul is indebted. He had additional grounds of his own for preaching an inconspicuous Christ, namely to show how worthless are the things of which men are normally proud. In submitting to live in obscurity and die in shame, Christ 'made foolish the wisdom of the world' (1 Cor. 1:20). Paul deplores any attempt to 'boast' before God of human achievements (Rom. 3:27), and declares that for him the cross has put an end to such boasting (Gal. 6:14). Hence he calls Christians who had boasted of their spiritual experience and powers 'enemies of the cross of Christ'. He wishes to 'share Christ's sufferings, becoming like him in his death, that if possible I may attain the resurrection from the dead' (Phil. 3:10–11 and 18; cf. Rom. 8:17). Thus he acknowledged only shame, humiliation and pain as attributes of Jesus' earthly life, and thought that these qualities ought to be reflected in the lives of his advocates.

Christians scholars argue that a crucified Jesus was very inconvenient to the early Christians, and was accepted only because the brute fact of the historical crucifixion could not be denied. Paul of course realized that the crucifixion of the Messiah was unacceptable to orthodox Jews, but far from being embarrassed by it, he made it his whole basis for demonstrating the superiority of the new faith; for he complained that Jews 'boast' before God of their righteousness in keeping the complicated stipulations of the Jewish religious law; whereas he himself has 'no righteousness of my own based on law' (Phil. 3:9). And he goes on to link his own renunciation of these values with Christ's death, which has abrogated all worldly standards.

It is in such contexts that Paul states his conviction that believers are 'not in the flesh' (Rom. 8:9), meaning that they do not guide their conduct by standards which are valued highly in this world. Thus he writes disparagingly of — I give a literal translation — 'fleshly wisdom' (2 Cor. 1:12) and of people who are 'wise according to the flesh' (1 Cor. 1:26). He complains of opponents who judge a man by externals, such as his position, rather than by his inner worth. And he adds that he will in future regard no one — not even Christ — 'according to flesh'. English Bibles render this by such phrases as 'from a human point of view', or 'judged by worldly standards'. That this is the meaning is clear from the context:

'Christ died for all, that those who live might live no longer for themselves but for him who for their sake died and was raised. From now on, *therefore*, we regard no one from a human point of view; even though we once regarded Christ from a human point of view, we regard him thus no longer'. (2 Cor. 5:15–16)

The 'therefore' I have italicized suggests that all lives must be judged not by their outward success, but by the extent of their unselfish dedication. A life of obscure suffering is therefore not to be dismissed as worthless, even if — before his conversion — Paul himself thought nothing of Jesus' life on these grounds. 'From now on' refers back to Christ's death as the decisive event which enabled the believer to enter upon a new life. Paul says (verse 14): 'We are convinced that one has died for all; therefore all have died'. All, then, have died to the old values of 'flesh'. He is defending himself against opponents who appear to have complained that he lacks obvious powers and capacities to be expected of an apostle (cf. below, p 100). He replies that their criticism fails to take account of the fact that 'all died', that Christian existence is of a new kind which has abrogated human standards of judgement. It is therefore inappropriate 'to regard anyone according to flesh'. His opponents have judged him by standards which no longer hold.

It will now be obvious why many theologians (see the most recent discussion in Blank, 47, p 323) decline to interpret Paul's statement that he no longer knows Jesus 'according to flesh' as meaning that he once knew a flesh and blood Jesus, but is no longer interested in the Jesus of history. Paul is arguing, as Harvey has shown, that men's lives 'are, therefore, like Christ's life, not to be judged by worldly standards, such as power, eloquence and wisdom, but only by the extent to which they are dedicated and transparent, lived in the service of God and man' (201, p 585). There is, however, no doubt that the gospels represent Jesus' life as one of power, eloquence and wisdom, even though Paul is saying that it in fact displayed none of these qualities.

Paul's weak and obscure earthly Jesus is, then, incompatible with the gospel portrait of him as a worker of prodigious miracles. Indeed, as we saw above (p 19), Paul comes very near to expressly denying that he was the miraculously powered Messiah of Jewish expectation. Equally incompatible with the statement that the demons had him crucified because they failed to recognize him is the gospel allegation that it was precisely the demons who recognized his true dignity and status. For instance, the 'unclean spirit' he drives from a man says to him: 'I know who you are – the Holy One of God'. And when he 'cast out many demons' he would not let them speak, 'because they knew him' (Mk. 1:24 and 34). Paul knew of no traditions of this kind. He is not merely silent about them, but his express statements exclude them.

Where, then, do these very unpauline traditions, strongly represented in Mk., come from? Now it is obvious from what Paul says that other Christian teachers did not share his stress on humility. He wrote the first of his two letters to Corinth because he was faced with what Bornkamm describes as:

'the sudden appearance in the life of the Church of people filled with the spirit ("enthusiasts"). These fanatics boasted that they, and they alone, had already reached the state of "perfection" and were in possession of "spirit" and "knowledge" (2:6; 3:1ff; 8:1). The latter does not mean intellectual knowledge, but knowledge derived from revelation, which, as in mystery religions and gnosticism, allowed them already to share in the power of the divine world.' (56, p 71; cf. Schmithals, 352, p 173)

In his second letter to Corinth he joins issue with rivals of similar tendencies, although this time they were not local people but Christians of

Jewish origin (11:22) who had intruded into the Corinthian Church. They designated him as weak and themselves as men of power, able to perform miracles and receive visions. He replies that his own achievements include all this (2 Cor. 12:1–6 and 11–12), but that he would rather not boast about such matters, since in his view the Christian missionary authenticates himself not by visible demonstrations of power, but by undergoing the humiliation and persecution that characterized the life of Jesus (2 Cor. 4:9–11). Some of his rivals, however, preached what he calls 'another Jesus' (2 Cor. 11:4). The late Professor Brandon has based a great deal of his theory of early Christianity on the supposition that this 'other Jesus' was the historical Jesus of the Jerusalem Christians who – so he interprets 2 Cor. 5:13 – accused Paul of being 'beside himself'. Brandon supposes their argument to have been that, while they were sober followers of a historical preacher, Paul's religion was based on unreliable visions. But study of his epistle shows that his rivals were more given to ecstatic experience than he, and that the difference between him and them in this respect was that he regarded such experience as part of the private religious life, not (as they did) as the basis of public missionary work. Thus he writes to his flock that if he is 'beside himself', it is for God; while if he is in his 'right mind' it is for them. The doctrine implied here is the same as that stated openly in 1 Cor. 14:2 and 18–20, where he says that when a man is using the language of ecstasy, he is talking with God, not with men, for no man understands him, and that it is therefore preferable in the congregation to speak five intelligible words, for the benefit of others, than thousands of words in the language of ecstasy.

Paul does not even say that the rival teachers he is criticizing are the Jerusalem Christians, or in any way connected with them.[2] How are we to understand the 'other Jesus' of these rivals? As he complains of their self-confidence and their claims to miraculous powers, it is quite likely that they regarded Jesus as having led a life like their own – a life of power, eloquence and wisdom. They will have agreed with Paul that the pre-existent Christ did come to earth as the man Jesus, but not that he displayed his true strength by living in weakness and obscurity. If they asked themselves at all what sort of life he had lived, they would surely have assumed that he – from whom they derived their great powers – had worked miracles and had been as conspicuous as they themselves were. Traditions of this kind, on the part of such men, surely helped to originate the very unpauline tradition, strongly represented in the gospels, that Jesus was a man of signs and wonders.

The kind of teachers of whom Paul complains were familiar figures in the Hellenistic world. The pagan philosopher Celsus wrote about AD 178 of itinerant Jewish prophets known by the term 'divine man' who introduced their unintelligible utterances with such formulas as 'I am God' or 'a Son of God' or 'a divine spirit' (318, p 402). There is evidence that such men were active in the first century (374, p 180), that they were not repudiated in the Talmud, and were certainly acceptable to Hellenistic

Judaism (Vermes, 398, pp 69ff, and Hull, 213). Paul's Christian rivals were thus missionaries who had adopted the methods of Hellenized Jewish propaganda. When they arrived in a Christian community, they presented themselves, so Paul implies, with 'letters of recommendation' (2 Cor. 3:1), and these have been interpreted (e.g. by Köster, 264, p 234) as documents in which miracles they had worked were recorded and certified by the Churches they had visited. It would have been easy for traditions which stamped a historical Jesus as a 'divine man' to find acceptance in such communities.

Even Paul himself, for all his stress on humility, claims to have won gentiles to Christianity 'by the power of signs and wonders' (Rom. 15:19). He also includes the working of miracles among the 'gifts of the spirit' and adds that God has appointed 'miracle workers' within the community (1 Cor. 12:10 and 28). His suggestion, then, is that mighty works may be expected wherever the Christian mission goes: and so it was natural that a later generation would have little understanding for the idea of a weak Jesus who had lived incognito, and would find the Christology of Paul's rivals more to its taste.

If we turn to the NT epistles of the early second century, we do in fact find that the Christ hymns included in them differ from the Pauline ones precisely by representing Jesus' life on earth as a manifestation, and not a concealment, of the divine glory. 1 Peter 1:20 says that 'he was made manifest at the end of the times', and 1 Tim. 3:16 that 'he was manifested in the flesh, . . . [was] preached among nations and believed on in this world'. We saw that, while both these epistles differ from the Pauline ones by maintaining that Jesus lived in the recent past, 1 Peter knows nothing of the historical background to Jesus' life, whereas 1 Tim. quite explicitly associates him with Pilate. This latter kind of tradition, bringing him into conflict with a recent ruler of the country, would naturally follow quickly once Christians had come to believe that he had lived not only recently, but also in eminence instead of obscurity.

The most prominent characteristic of Mk. is that it is an attempt to combine these two incompatible traditions of an obscure and a prominent Jesus. The first half of the gospel presents him as *the* thaumaturge, whose appearance is *the* event wherever he goes. Mark and later evangelists give prominence to such miracles because Christian communities of the late first and early second centuries needed them as proof that he was genuinely 'sent by God' (cf. Jn. 3:2; Acts 2:22). To authenticate him they had to be even more impressive than those appealed to by rival sects, i.e. than those of the 'false prophets' who 'will show signs and wonders to lead astray . . . the elect' (Mk. 13:22). In Mk. 1:27 he is accepted because he has unique power, and the implication is that his power surpasses that of other miracle men.[3] It also shows the advent of the Messianic age, that 'the kingdom of God is at hand' (1:15); for the sickness he cures is the work of the evil supernatural powers which rule the world, and whose powerlessness to resist his healing activity presages their final dispossession.[4] Great emphasis is also laid upon his teaching – not because its content is of interest (it is seldom indicated at all) but because, like his miracles, it displays his power: 'He taught them as one who had authority' (1:22). In the final chapters, however, he works few miracles, addresses himself to disciples rather than to a crowd, and is finally deserted even by them. Here he is the lonely suffering figure of Pauline Christology, and the evangelist's message is the Pauline one that the Christian's lot is to share this suffering (8:35; 10:29; 13:11). At his death he is utterly alone, deserted even by God. To show both the magnitude of the burden he assumed and his strength in bearing it alone, the evangelist makes him speak from the cross the opening words of Psalm 22, 'My God, why hast thou forsaken me?' (Mk. 15:34; cf. 191, p 533). This Psalm supplied the early Christians with other details of their passion narrative; e.g. it is used, a few verses earlier (Mk. 15:29) to express the mockery of Jesus by passers-by. His cry of dereliction from the cross is often taken as expressive of complete despair (and as therefore unlikely to have been invented). But Mark surely did not intend to suggest that one who quoted a word of the Bible in prayer had lost faith in God! Luke's motive for deleting it may well have been that *he* found it despairing and therefore offensive; but this does not mean that it was so to Mark.

Mark tries to bring the two halves of his work, with their very different portraits of Jesus, into consistency by introducing what has become known as the 'Messianic secret'. It is not a very apt phrase, as the title of Messiah is only one of many used to indicate Jesus' true supernatural status. The point is that this status is not understood by the people who come into contact with him, not even by his closest disciples. Hence Dibelius has designated Mk. 'the gospel of secret epiphanies'. Although in the opening chapters Jesus works one miracle after another, only supernatural powers (e.g. the demons he casts out) recognize his divine status; and he repeatedly orders the people to keep silent about the miracles, and the demons not to betray that he is the Son of God (1:34; 3:11–12, etc.). On the two occasions when his disciples recognize that he is more than human (8:30 and 9:9), they too are told to keep silence – in the latter case 'until the Son of man should have risen from the dead'. This is in accordance with the Pauline view of a Jesus whose true strength was revealed only after his crucifixion – a view which is also emphasized by Mk.'s story of the centurion who, seeing the supernatural signs attending Jesus' death, cried: 'Truly, this man was a son of God' (15:39). There is wide agreement that Jesus' injunctions to keep silence about his miracles and his Messiahship – even in circumstances where the injunction could scarcely be obeyed because the miracle was so public[5] – is an artificial and doctrinal factor governing the whole gospel, and a feature which shows that the work is not an uncomplicated and straightforward record of events which can be taken at its face value as history. It is a device which enabled the evangelist to synthesize the incompatible Christologies of earlier Christianity. Its artificiality is clear from an incident such as the cure of the demoniac in the Capernaum synagogue in ch. 1, where the people are represented as, for some reason, taking no notice of the demon's disclosure of Jesus' supernatural status, and as wondering only at the cure.

The contradictory nature of the traditions which Mark brings together is well illustrated by the incidents where Jesus, contrary to his normal practice, orders a man he has cured to promulgate the fact (5:19), and where he flatly refuses to give the Pharisees 'a sign from heaven', saying that 'no sign shall be given to this generation' (8:12), whereas in other episodes he works wonders under their very eyes. Again, the evangelist wishes to attribute Jesus' death to Jewish malice, and so, as we shall see, he has sometimes (against his more general doctrine of the Messianic secret) to allow Jesus' real nature to be manifest to the Jews, who could otherwise be excused on the ground that they perpetrated their crime in ignorance.

The demons' acknowledgement that Jesus was divine – one of the unpauline features of Mk. – arises naturally when Jesus is put into a historical context. The Pauline Jesus is first and foremost a supernatural being, and the demons failed to recognize him during his sojourn on earth (the time and place of which is not specified) because he had assumed a temporary disguise. But the Marcan Jesus lives the life of a man in a specific historical situation, and the evangelist had to safeguard against any suggestion that he might be just a man, and not supernatural at all. The problem was particularly acute because the Messianic secret compelled Mark to represent human beings as blind to his true status. And this left only supernatural beings – the demons, and the voice from heaven at his baptism and transfiguration – to authenticate him.

Jesus is not actually said in Mk. already to have existed as a supernatural personage before he came to earth; but such a pre-existence does seem to be implied. He is introduced as 'Lord' (1:3), is attested as 'son' by a voice from heaven (1:11 and 9:7) and is ministered to by heavenly beings (1:13). Some have held that the divine voice at his baptism *adopts* him as son on that occasion, prior to which he was a mere man. But it is surely more likely that the intention of the passage is to illustrate the fact that he proceeded from God and came to earth from the heavenly world. Furthermore, as Boobyer has observed (53, p 53), why does Mark in 2:10 call attention to the fact that the Son of man had power *on the earth* to forgive sins if he was not thinking of his heavenly pre-existence? The expression 'son' of God – used at Jesus' baptism and transfiguration – recurs in the parable where the owner of a vineyard lets it out to tenants and sends his 'beloved son' to them; but instead of giving him the owner's share of the fruit, they kill him (12:1–9). Here, Jesus the beloved son figures as a pre-existent being, 'sent' to mankind, as the redeemer of Paul, of Jn. and of gnostic myth is sent for our redemption (cf. Schreiber, 359, p 167). Thus, as Käsemann admits, the earliest of our gospels 'makes the life-history of Jesus almost the subject of a mystery drama' (238, p 193). Instructive in this connection is Mark's version of the temptation. 'Immediately' after his baptism 'the spirit drove him out into the wilderness. And he was in the wilderness forty days, tempted by Satan; and he was with the wild beasts: and the angels ministered to him' (1:12—13). There is no reference to fasting or hunger (which are specified in the later accounts of Matthew and Luke). On the contrary, the 'ministry' of the angels (which the tense of the Greek verb shows to have been continuous) could only have consisted in supplying food (as angels fed Elijah (1 Kings 19) when he was in the wilderness for forty days). Nor does Mark (again unlike Matthew and Luke) state wherein the temptation consisted. But the wilderness is the traditional haunt of evil spirits (319, p 455), and the background to Mark's story is clearly 'the current belief that the Messiah was the divine agent for the overthrow of Satan and all his powers, and that therefore a tremendous battle, or trial of strength, between him and Satan would form an integral element in the last days' (314, p 63). This idea that evil spirits constitute a realm whose destruction Jesus is about to accomplish is, we saw, stressed in Paul's letters (see above, p 20) and appears also in the incident (Mk. 1:24) where a demon asks Jesus: 'Have you come to destroy us?'. The Jesus of Mark's temptation story is still relatively close to the Jesus of Paul, in that his contest with evil lacks the concrete and quasi-historical details supplied by such younger traditions as the parallel accounts in Mt. and Lk. When Mark wrote, says Schweizer, 'Jesus was a mere name', and the message of salvation might as well have been connected 'with Hermes or Attis or any other saviour' (365, p 421). The gnostics, he adds, 'were about to draw this consequence'. And he clearly implies that Mark wrote in order to prevent them from doing so. If we turn from Mk. to 2 Peter — the latest document in the NT canon — we see evidence that the struggle against heresy has even led Christians to express positive uneasiness about the Pauline Christology; for the writer of this second-century epistle complains that Paul's letters contain 'some things hard to understand, which the ignorant and unstable [i.e. heretics] twist to their own destruction' (3:16).

For all their differences, Paul and Mark agree in ascribing supreme importance to Jesus' passion and crucifixion. But we saw (above, p 39) that this is not true of some of the pre-Pauline material in the epistles. A non-passion Christology is also represented in Q (the hypothetical document which is independent of Mk. and which, in addition to Mk., underlies Mt. and Lk.; cf. above p 84). Q sets Jesus' life in first century Palestine by associating him with John the Baptist, but it makes no mention of Pilate, and gives not the slightest hint of the passion and crucifixion. Nor, on the other hand, does it represent Jesus as a great miracle worker, but rather as an obscure and rejected preacher. Only two miracle stories are included and the principal of these emphasizes the faith of the person who requests the cure rather than the healing itself (Mt. 8:5—13 = Lk. 7:1—10). The earthly Jesus of Q suffers in so far as he is rejected by men, but his suffering has no atoning power. The suffering stressed in Q is the tribulation which is to befall men in the last days, and has no redemptory effect. Q consists mainly of sayings in which Jesus predicts the coming of the kingdom and insists that only those who accept him and do what he says will be saved when the 'Son of man' comes to inaugurate it. He also provides a moral code ('love your enemies', 'judge not') by which men are to live in preparation for the coming judgement. There is evidence that some of these sayings in which he performs the two functions of warning and moral guidance were originally utterances of Christian prophets who believed that he was speaking through them.[6] Convinced as they were that the end was nigh, they 'heard the voice of the resurrected Lord pronouncing already proleptically the decision of the future day of judgement upon specific situations of the present' (339, p 86).

Many elements in Q's portrait of Jesus can be explained as motivated by the 'Wisdom' traditions, which we have already seen to have had an important influence on the pre-Pauline hymns and on Paul's own thinking. Proverbs 1:20–30 presents Wisdom as a street preacher, who comes to man in order to warn him of an impending catastrophe. But man rejects her, and she will in turn reject his pleas for aid after the catastrophe has begun. A reader with thoughts of the end of the world on his mind, like an early Christian, would naturally suppose that due warning of this end had been given. Q seems to have been compiled for a Christian community which believed that Jesus was a supernatural personage sent to earth to provide such a warning, in words of wisdom, and who had returned, rejected, to heaven. The author presumably knew from Wisdom of Solomon 7:27 that Wisdom had become incarnate in a series of men. And since he knew of and respected John the Baptist, he represented him as also a preacher of imminent doom and judgement. (Q in fact stresses this preaching when writing of the Baptist, almost to the exclusion of his baptising activity; cf. below, pp 154f). In Q both men are designated children of wisdom (Lk. 7:33–5), but Jesus' superiority is asserted by making him the later of the two, the *final* envoy of Wisdom who announces that 'this generation' will be required to answer for the rejection of previous envoys (Lk. 11:49–51). It may, then, be the Jewish Wisdom literature that gave the author of Q, who knew independently of John, the idea that Jesus must have lived later than John.

Q, then, and some pre-Pauline Christians, envisaged Jesus as rejected on earth, but not as an atoning sacrifice. Paul's Christian rivals probably thought of him as a triumphant miracle worker. Paul himself had yet other ideas. Small wonder that an eminent theologian has designated early Christological thinking as 'fluid' (339, p 86). The only factor which these Christologies have in common is that they all regard Jesus as a supernatural personage.

(ii) Evangelists Later than Mark

In Mt. the supernatural status of the earthly Jesus is less emphasized, and he appears as the Messianic king of Israel, the descendant of David predicted by scripture. Matthew also differs from Mark by repeatedly introducing quotations from the OT, for the purpose of representing Jesus as the culmination of revelation. And he adapts Mark's account of arguments with orthodox Jews in such a way as to bring Jesus' standpoint closer to what is acceptable to them.[7] All this has often been understood to imply that Matthew wished to inculcate in his readers (of the late first or early second century) the belief that Jesus was still to be accepted by them as the Messiah of Israel, and that salvation is only for Jews and for those who keep the Jewish law, every fraction of which is expressly endorsed (5:17). The ruling of 18:17 — that erring brethren who refuse to obey 'the church' are to be ostracized like 'a gentile and a tax collector' — supports such a conclusion, as does Jesus' statement (10:23) that his second coming will have occurred before the disciples have missionized all the cities of Israel. This verse is an isolated saying (only loosely connected with its context) which must have arisen as a promise and consolation to Christians attempting to convert Jewish communities — assuring the missionaries that they would not have to endure Jewish persecution for long (see Tödt, 389, p 61). That Matthew assimilated the saying suggests that he envisaged Christianity as appealing to Jews rather than to gentiles. He also (unlike Mark) mentions Jewish customs without elucidating them, and this has been taken to indicate that he was writing for a Christian community which itself practised them, or which was at any rate well acquainted with them.

In Mk. 13:18 Jesus tells the disciples to pray that, in the tribulation of the last days, their flight 'may not happen in winter'. To this Matthew (24:20) adds 'or on a sabbath', and this is usually taken to mean that he is sufficiently Jewish to represent Jesus as endorsing the keeping of the sabbath. Haenchen, however, has argued that the very opposite may well be implied; that Matthew means to say that those who flee on a sabbath betray by this action that they are not Jews but Christians, and are thus revealed as such to the Roman authorities from whom they are fleeing (191, p 454; cf. above, p 83).[8] More obvious evidence of an *anti*-Jewish attitude in Mt. is Jesus' statement (to a Jewish audience) that 'the kingdom of God will be taken away from you and given to a nation producing the fruits of it' (21:43; cf.8:11). No one particular nation is meant, for 'this gospel of the kingdom will be preached throughout the whole world, as a testimony to all nations' (24:14; cf. 28:19). Furthermore, immediately after endorsing every jot and tittle of the Jewish law, Jesus introduces amendments to it! His amended version is mainly concerned to supplement its requirements with more stringent ones (and thus to stipulate (5:20) a 'righteousness exceeding that of the scribes and Pharisees'), but it also excludes such specifically Jewish features as ritual cleanliness (cf. 15:17—18) and 'an eye for an eye', and makes no mention of circumcision or sabbath (cf. Walker, 402, pp 135—6).

Mt. is also characterized by fierce hostility towards all Jewish authorities. The scribes and Pharisees are called hypocrites and 'serpents' (23:29 and 33). The 'Pharisees and Sadducees' are repeatedly introduced as if they were a uniform group (whereas Mk. and Lk. mention the Sadducees on but one occasion) and abused together. In a typical passage Matthew represents them as seeking baptism from John, who, however, turns them away, calling them a 'brood of vipers' (3:7). Hill concedes (207, p 92) that 'the likelihood of members of the two parties being associated in a common desire for John's baptism is small: the combination is a literary device to denote representatives of Israel' — of an Israel which, in this gospel, appears as uniformly hostile to Jesus from beginning to end. The news of his birth, welcomed by 'wise men from the east', throws not only Israel's king, but 'all Jerusalem with him' (2:3) into consternation. The scribe of Mk. 12:28—34, whom Jesus declares to be 'not far from the Kingdom of God', is made by Matthew into an enemy out to ensnare Jesus with a question (Mt. 22:35). Matthew evidently could not believe a scribe capable of approaching the Lord in good faith, nor that Jesus could praise such a person. In the temple Jesus is arraigned by 'the chief priests and the elders of the people' (Mt. 21:23; the evangelist has added 'of the people' to Mk. 11:27). All the people (27:22) demand his crucifixion — the 'all' is a significant addition to Mk. 15:13 — and in a verse without synoptic parallel 'all the people' answer Pilate's plea for clemency with: 'His blood be on us and on our children' (27:25). This text has been made the basis of ferocious Christian persecution of Jews, to which the Second Vatican Council has belatedly put an end by ruling that no Jews alive today are to be understood by Matthew's phrase 'our children'. What the evangelist had in mind was surely simply that the generation of Jews represented by the 'children' of the speakers in 27:25 bore the horrors of the Jewish War, AD 66—70, and in this way paid for their fathers' murder of the Messiah. Again, the story of Judas' suicide (absent from the other gospels) is adapted by Matthew so as to magnify the guilt of 'the chief priests and the elders'. Judas is at least penitent, and confesses to them that he has 'betrayed innocent blood'; to which they callously reply: 'What is that to us?' (27:4). And finally, only in Mt. does the Jews' rejection of Jesus extend beyond his lifetime and include an attempt to discredit his resurrection (28:12—15).

How can we explain this mixture of pro- and anti-Jewish material — the contradiction, for instance, between the idea that the Christian mission must be confined to Israel (10:23) and the universal mission advocated elsewhere in the gospel? Carlston supposes that Matthew was writing from a gentile standpoint, but was drawing on material of a strongly Jewish-Christian flavour which he occasionally failed to tone down or modify to serve his own ecclesiastical interests.[9] This hypothesis entirely fails to account for the way in which Matthew adapts Mk.'s version of Jesus' arguments with Jewish authorities so as to bring him closer to an orthodox Jewish standpoint. Hummel finds the key to the problem to lie in Jesus' statement that he has come 'not to abolish the law and the prophets, but to fulfill them' (5:17). This means that, in Matthew's view, what is to be accepted is not the law, but the law as interpreted by Jesus. Matthew, who repeatedly quotes Hosea's dictum that God desires 'mercy, not sacrifice', seems to regard the Levitical command to love one's neighbour as the most imperative stipulation (5:43—8) in the light of which others must be interpreted; it restricts the validity of the law about the sabbath (12:1—14) and implies the complete abolition of the law of talion (5:38—9). The evangelist is here following the method of orthodox Jews, who disguised the fact that their new interpretations of the law often contradicted it by alleging that they went back to the 'real' sense of the scripture. Matthew's attitude to Jesus' teaching is revealed by the way he manipulates Mk. 1:21—8. He turns verse 22 ('they were astonished at his teaching, for he taught them as one who had authority and not as the scribes') into a comment (Mt. 8:29) on the Sermon on the Mount (which is not in Mk. at all). He does not, however, describe this 'teaching' which caused astonishment as 'new', but carefully deletes the following verses in Mk. in which it is designated 'a new teaching' (Mk. 1:27). This, says Davies, is significant evidence that the teaching of Jesus for Matthew was not radically new (121, p 100).

It is in particular against the Pharisees' interpretation of the law that Matthew protests. His version of the arguments with them shows that he was nearer to the Jewish standpoint than was Mark, and yet that his conflict with those who held this standpoint was far more acrimonious. He does not so much argue with them as abuse them. The implication is that he is not appealing to them in the hope of converting them, but asserting his own independent position in the face of Pharisaic criticism. After AD 70 the Pharisees emerged as the leading force in Judaism and, at Jamnia, led initially by Rabbi Johannan ben Zakkai, they systematized their beliefs. Davies regards Matthew's Sermon on the Mount as 'the Christian answer to Jamnia', as the outcome of 'the desire and necessity to present a formulation of the way of the New Israel at a time when the rabbis were engaged in a parallel task for the Old Israel' (121, p 315).

In accepting the law (suitably interpreted) Matthew naturally opposes those who reject it altogether. (The Greek word for 'lawlessness' occurs in the gospels only in Mt. — e.g. at 24:12 — and is unequivocally repudiated.) This does not mean that he was attacking the gentile Churches in general, and we have seen that he in fact accepts Christianity's gentile mission. His remarks may well have been directed against a particular group of antinomians in his immediate environment (Hummel, 214, p 65).

Walker has plausibly argued (402) that it is in order to show the heinousness of the Jews' behaviour to Jesus that Matthew represents him — with greater emphasis than any other evangelist — as the Messianic king of Israel, the son of David who takes special pains to bring his message of salvation to Jews, even — in the first instance — to the exclusion of gentiles; for he dispatches the twelve with instructions (in a passage unique to Mt.) not to go to gentile lands, nor to any Samaritan town, but 'rather to the lost sheep of the house of Israel' (10:6; cf. 15:24). No account is given of what they did on the mission, which is never again mentioned. The evangelist does not expressly record their return from it, but re-introduces them (12:1) without explanation. This makes it clear that he is not interested in it as an event which occurred during the Galilean ministry, but in Jesus' instruction that the proclamation of the gospel is to be restricted to Israel. As this restriction is not included in the parallel passages in other gospels, it is often assumed to represent the attitude of the Church for which Matthew wrote. Harvey makes this suggestion in a discreet way, saying: 'Perhaps the Church he knew was one engaged in a difficult mission to the Jewish people, tempted to abandon the task, but needing to be recalled to its first duty' (201, p 49). But the instruction can be equally well understood as evidence of the Jews' special guilt in rejecting the salvation offered in the first instance specifically to them; for Jesus adds that they will be as 'wolves' to Christian missionaries, and will flog them in 'their synagogues'. His references to 'their synagogues' or 'their scribes' (substituted in 7:29 for Mark's 'the scribes') when addressing disciples, and to 'your synagogues' when addressing Jews, shows how deep was the rift between synagogue and Church. The result of the Jews' rejection of Jesus is that his period as Israel's king is at an end. The 'children of Jerusalem' will not see him again until they say: 'Blessed be he who comes in the name of the Lord' (23:39), i.e. until he returns to earth as their judge. This may imply that they can still be saved if only they accept him. In sum, Matthew's Christology — in so far as it concerns the earthly Jesus — differs from that of the other evangelists by being consistently Messianic: Jesus is the Messianic king of Israel. Matthew's purpose is, however, to show that Israel, by rejecting him, has brought about its own annihilation and inaugurated the mission to gentiles, so that the Church now consists of Jews and gentiles. What we see in Mt. is thus a Jewish Christianity universally orientated and permeated with Hellenistic ideas, which does not regard a mission to Jews or gentiles as irreconcilable alternatives, and which has overcome this rigid position by accepting the Torah, interpreted not Pharisaically, but as implying the supremacy of the command of love of neighbour in a way acceptable to all except the antinomians among the gentiles (cf. Hummel, 214, p 166).

Matthew's suggestion that the gentile mission is a consequence of the Jews' rejection of Jesus is a natural development of the early tradition represented in the epistle to the Romans. Paul, who regarded the earthly Jesus as a Jew (cf. above, p 18), naturally spoke of him as 'a servant to the circumcized' (Rom. 15:8). He knew that the Jews refused to accept him as the saviour, and so said that 'through their trespass salvation has come to the gentiles' (11:11). Matthew has transformed these ideas into a definite historical sequence.

Luke's Christology is far removed from Paul's in that the evangelist distinguishes sharply between God and Jesus, and 'never employs such concepts as pre-existence, creation or rulership over the universe' (42, p 126). Jesus was born a man, and only after his resurrection did God make him 'both Lord and Christ' (Acts 2:36). At Lk. 1:32–3 the angel tells Mary that 'the Lord God will give to him the throne of his father David, and he will reign over the house of Jacob for ever'. In Acts (2:33) it is made quite clear that this enthronement did not occur during his lifetime, but only at his ascension, when he was 'exalted at the right hand of God'. The earthly Jesus of Lk. can therefore be called king – as he is at his entry into Jerusalem (Lk. 19:38) – 'only proleptically' (Burger, 85, p 139). What characterizes his life on earth is his miraculous power. In Lk.-Acts the 'miracle man' Christology is stressed almost to exclusion of the Pauline tradition. Not only does Jesus perform mighty works, but also, in Acts, the leading Christians of the early Church perform works of the same calibre. Stephen legitimates himself as a missionary by miracles (6:8); Philip wins a convert by the same method and impresses even a rival by his 'signs and great miracles' (8:6 and 13). Even Paul – the same Paul who wrote his second letter to Corinth *against* such an understanding of the apostolic ministry – has now become a primary example of the missionary who is a miracle man. 'The elements which are constitutive for the image of the missionary in ... Acts correspond exactly to those found among Paul's opponents in 2 Cor. – powerful preaching, spiritual exegesis of Scripture, performance of miracles, visionary experiences' (Köster, 264, p 235).

Correlative to this stress on powerful works, Luke lacks all passion-mysticism and regards Jesus' suffering and death as necessary incidents in God's plan for man's salvation but not as effecting forgiveness of sins. Luke carefully deletes the statement of Mk. 10:45 that 'the Son of man also came not to be served but to serve, and to give his life as a ransom for many'. Luke replaces these words with: 'For which is the greater, one who sits at table, or one who serves? Is it not the one who sits at table? But I am among you as one who serves' (22:27). In not associating any redemptive significance with Jesus' death, Luke is following a tradition we have seen represented in Q.

The Christology of the fourth gospel agrees with that of the Pauline letters in representing Jesus as a pre-existent redeemer who came to earth, died and rose again; but John varies the older pattern by interpreting the second of these three phases as a period of power and triumph. Whereas for Paul Jesus' life on earth was emptied of deity (Phil. 2:6–11), for John the pre-existent Logos brought his divine glory into the world and sought to reveal it there. That he is the Messiah is (in contrast to what we are told in Mk.) no secret: for when a Samaritan woman speaks to him of Christ who 'when he comes will show us all things', Jesus replies: 'I who speak to you am he' (Jn. 4:25–6). John's Christology makes his passion story very different from Mark's which, as we saw, presents a suffering and humiliated figure akin to the Jesus of Paul. John replaces the cry of dereliction from the cross with sayings of a very different kind because he

110

is so concerned to represent the crucifixion as a triumph (e.g. Jn. 16:31–3) that he gives hardly any indication of the suffering involved.

(iii) The Messiah and the Son of Man

The Hebrew word for 'Messiah' means 'anointed', and was originally used to designate kings and high priests, who were always anointed with oil. The term did not, at this stage, signify a future redeemer, but denoted the reigning king, and is used frequently in the OT to designate Saul and David. Later, the inadequacies of their kings caused the Jews to look forward to a future which would bring them more worthy monarchs, and David, as the most successful king of the past, naturally became the prototype of what was expected. Hence the hope, expressed by the prophets, that a 'son of David' would govern them. When the nation lost its independence, the historical kingship ceased to exist; and Jews reading the Psalms, where the phrase 'the anointed' is often used to denote the Davidic king as such (without reference to a particular person) would then suppose that, since there were no more kings in the old sense, the Psalmist's reference must be to another king or Messiah, perhaps in heaven. In sum, the term 'Messiah' originally meant any anointed person, but came in time to mean a particular individual who was expected, either as a human being who would restore the old kingship, or as a supernatural personage who would descend from heaven.

The latter kind of redeemer is not often called 'the Messiah' but has come to be known by other titles, of which in Christian literature 'the Son of man' is the best known. By the end of the first century AD this phrase had come into use in Jewish apocalyptic writings (revelatory writings which disclose the secrets of what is to happen in the 'last days'), probably as a result of a misunderstanding of the phrase in Daniel 7:13 about 'one like a son of man coming with the clouds of heaven' (cf. JEC, pp 82–3). In ch. 13 of the Ezra apocalypse (ca. AD 96) the seer has a vision of 'the form of a man flying with the clouds of heaven' who annihilates a hostile army with his breath of fire and then establishes for the Jews a kingdom of power and glory. 'Son of man' is not here used as a title, but the man in this passage is, as Vermes agrees, 'the preserved, hidden, heavenly Messiah'. Vermes also notes that in the second century Rabbi Aqiba identified Daniel's 'one like a son of man' with the Christ (398, pp 171–2); and in the section of the book of Enoch known as the 'Parables' or 'Similitudes' of Enoch, probably written some time between 63 BC and AD 70,[10] there is mention of 'the Son of a man' – a supernatural being in heaven who has existed there with God from the beginning ('before the creation of the world'). The title 'anointed' or 'Messiah' is occasionally used in contexts which suggest that it refers to him, and he is certainly represented as one who will perform Messianic functions: he will terminate the gentile rule over the earth, introduce a new age or new kingdom, be king over all nations and a light to the gentiles.[11] Vermes disputes that 'Son of man' is used as a title even in Enoch. He points out that obvious titles like 'the anointed' or 'the Lord of the Spirits' are used in the work without explanation, whereas 'Son of man' is always explained, e.g. by an added phrase such as 'born unto righteousness'. But the step from such usage (where the term is still relatively unfamiliar and requires a gloss) to titular use is small, and is intelligible as a result of its increasing popularity.

The Son of man is thus a heavenly, supernatural Messiah in contrast with the human Messiahs of earlier Jewish lore. This development of the idea of the redeemer resulted not only from the abolition of the historical kingship, but also from the changed international political situation. When the OT prophets wrote, the world they knew consisted of God's people, a number of small nations (Edom, Moab, Syria), and the two large powers of Egypt and Assyria at opposite ends of the geographical horizon. The Jews could measure their strength with the small kingdoms, and even the two large ones were so countered by one another that Israel could always turn to the one for protection against the other. In these political conditions, the redeemer could be regarded as no more than a man, as a powerful king who would lead the country to independence. But with the rise of Alexander the Great's Empire, which extended from Greece to Persia, and later with the even more extensive Roman dominion, the Jews found themselves facing a situation where political independence was out of the question. The old hope of national prosperity under the Messianic king had to fade, and it was not surprising that they began to think that only a cosmic act of God would have the power to break the vast empires oppressing them. The result was that the prophetic literature, which was concerned with the nation's political freedom under a Davidic king, was succeeded by apocalypses, which foretell a deliverance accompanied by the stars falling from heaven, and the whole natural order passing away. Even in the literature which still regarded the Messiah as human he is described in such exaggerated terms that a later generation could easily think that the person possessing such powers must be supernatural. For instance, numbers 17 and 18 of the Psalms of Solomon (from the first century BC), borrowing words and ideas from Isaiah 11, speak of the coming son of David as one who will 'destroy the godless nations with the word of his mouth'. For all these reasons the redeemer began to be regarded as a supernatural figure who would descend from heaven in the last days in order to annihilate the gentiles. He was also expected (cf. above, p 20) to dispossess and destroy the evil angelic governors of the world, who would naturally not relinquish all that they held in bondage without furious resistance. This again would encourage the view that Messianic times would be a period of unprecedented woe and of cosmic catastrophe.

Of course, older ideas concerning the Messiah survived alongside these newer ones, and this lack of uniformity constituted an important characteristic of Messianic thinking at the beginning of our era. As G.F. Moore long ago said (in words which have repeatedly been endorsed), 'there was no generally accepted opinion, no organized and consistent teaching, above all no orderly Messianic doctrine possessing the faintest show of authority. The thing itself was of faith, all the rest was free field for the imagination' (in Jackson, 218, p 356; cf. O'Neil, 317, p 156). The apocalypse of Ezra (7:29) shows how the old national Messianic hope could actually be combined with apocalyptic ideas. The Messiah, we are there told, will reign 400 years on earth – this resembles the old idea of a vindication of Israel with a millennium of peace – and will then die, and all other men with him. After seven days of silence God will awaken all for the final judgement. Here, then, the *reign of the Messiah* has been linked with the newer idea of *God's Last Judgement* of all nations according to their righteousness. Resurrection properly pertains only to the latter idea, yet here an attempt is made to introduce it into the former. In Christianity this linkage between Messiah and resurrection becomes much more pronounced; for Paul, the resurrection of the Messiah presages and guarantees the general resurrection of mankind. Rev. 20:4–6 offers a further variant: the millennial reign of the Messiah is to be a post-resurrectional kingdom. Those who were martyred for Christ are to be raised and given the special privilege of reigning with him for a thousand years, after which will follow the final defeat of Satan and the resurrection of the rest of mankind.

Many scholars have insisted that the Christian idea of the Messiah as a supernatural personage is totally unjewish and could not have been derived from the Jewish environment. What they have in mind is that, up to AD 70, the Phasisaic-rabbinical literature avoids apocalyptic ideas and uses the word 'Messiah' – if at all – in the old sense of a human king who is to come and rule. The Pharisees, as realists who accepted the Roman rule, were sceptical of Messianic, let alone apocalyptic expectations, while, correlatively, the apocalyptic sects characteristically used terms other than 'Messiah' to designate their supernatural redeemer. However, the different words all denoted redeemers of some kind, and it is only to be expected that the newer, apocalyptic ideas would retain some of the ideas associated with the old Messiah,[12] and sometimes even use the old *term* in the new sense. The book of Enoch supplies evidence that this in fact happened. Early Christianity was clearly an apocalyptic sect, and would therefore also incline to give the old term a new meaning. Christian scholars have often supposed that it was Jesus who equated such terms as Messiah and Son of man. But if Jesus could do this, so could Christian writers of the first century, and then put appropriate words into his mouth.

In Christian literature earlier than the gospels, the term 'Son of man' is almost unknown. Paul never uses it, and unlike other titles (such as son of David, Messiah and Son of God) it does not occur in any Christian formula summarizing the faith. In the gospels (except in Jn. 12:34) the term occurs only in sayings of Jesus. Whether Jesus existed or not, these gospel Son of man sayings cannot be authentic; for, as Teeple notes, in early Christian literature (prior to the middle of the second century when the gospels were employed as sources) they 'are not quoted or even alluded to outside the gospels, even when the writers are dealing with Church problems — such as Jesus' death, the parousia, apostasy — which are dealt with in the Son of man logia. Since these problems were very often discussed by the Christian writers, it would be very strange that they did not know and employ these sayings if the latter were authentic words of Jesus'. Particularly significant is the failure of early Christian writers to allude to the Son of man sayings about Jesus' parousia or second coming, which are very prominent in the synoptics. The problem of the time and manner of the parousia is a frequent theme in early Christian literature other than the gospels; and if a historical Jesus 'had actually discussed the coming of the Son of man, surely Christian writers other than the evangelists would have referred to it when they discussed the problem of Jesus' return' (386, pp 226, 237). And the relevant synoptic sayings can sometimes be seen to be clearly of literary origin. For instance, the high priest asks: 'Are you the Christ, the son of the Blessed?' Jesus replies: 'I am: and you will see the Son of man sitting at the right hand of Power, and coming with the clouds of heaven' (Mk. 14:61—2). The explicit identification of the three titles — Messiah (or Christ), son of the Blessed, and Son of man — and the obvious use of Daniel 7:13 and of Psalm 110:1, betray what Vielhauer calls 'an advanced stage of Christological reflection' (400, p 172; cf. above, p 96).

The gospel sayings in which Jesus speaks of the Son of man fall into three classes:

1. Statements that the Son of man will come at the end of time as judge, e.g. Mk. 14:61—2 (which I have just quoted); Mt. 24:44 'You also must be ready, for the Son of man is coming at an hour you do not expect'; Mk. 8:38 'Whoever is ashamed of me and my words in this adulterous and sinful generation, of him will the Son of man also be ashamed when he comes in the glory of his Father with the holy angels'. Statements of this kind have been explained by supposing that the spiritual messages received by Christian prophets from the risen Jesus were viewed as words of the heavenly Son of man of Jewish apocalyptic thought; and that these messages were in due course ascribed to the teaching of the Messiah Jesus prior to his crucifixion. The last of the logia just quoted probably originated at a time when Christians were required to stand before courts and there to confess or deny Jesus (400, p 79); Q as well as Mk. contains a saying of this kind (Mt. 10:32 = Lk. 12:8) and makes the mode of origin even clearer by stating that those who 'deny Jesus before men' (and not simply those who 'are ashamed' of him) will be punished at the final judgement. Those who deny him have presumably been asked whether they are Christians, and have returned a negative answer in order to escape persecution. The word rendered as 'before' is the standard expression for standing before a judge in a court. If we regard such a logion as genuinely from Jesus, we have to assume that he was able to foresee a situation

which arose only about sixty years after his death, namely that a profession of allegiance to his person would be regarded by human courts as decisive evidence for securing the conviction of the accused.

Having foretold the coming of the Son of man 'in the glory of his Father with the holy angels', Jesus goes on to promise that the 'kingdom of God' will soon come 'with power' (Mk. 9:1). Matthew changes this into a promise that the 'Son of man' will soon be seen 'coming in *his* kingdom' (Mt. 16:28). Here, then, the Son of man has taken over what was, in the earlier document, a function of God. Such a detail illustrates the developing Christology of NT times. The Pauline view that Jesus will finally 'deliver the kingdom to God the Father' (1 Cor. 15:24) was in time replaced by a Christology which regarded Jesus not merely as supernatural but as the equal of God.

In these gospel sayings about the coming of the Son of man as judge, the speaker (the earthly Jesus) is not expressly identified with the Son of man who is to come. From the point of view of the evangelists, the two were only potentially identical – the former was not yet the Son of man, but would soon be returning to earth in this capacity. For this reason, then, Jesus is made to speak of the Son of man in the third person, as if the reference were to someone other than himself.

2. Statements in which Jesus speaks of the suffering, death and resurrection of the Son of man. This group of sayings is also not authentic, for in them Jesus predicts his passion and resurrection in a way that displays such detailed knowledge of what is to happen that the sayings simply must have originated as *vaticinia ex eventu*, as 'prophecies' after the events had occurred or were believed to have occurred. Thus he tells (Mk. 10:33–4) that the Son of man is to be handed over to the chief priests and scribes at Jerusalem, who will condemn him to death, pass him on to heathens, who will mock, scourge, spit upon him, and kill him, three days after which he will rise again. All this can be accepted as what a real person actually said only by those prepared to credit him with divine foresight. And even then, if he had actually said these things to his disciples – repeatedly according to Mark, who puts similar predictions into Jesus' mouth on two other occasions – the complete confusion of these same disciples after his death would be incomprehensible.

This group of sayings is quite separate from the first group – those which predict his parousia (his final coming in glory, with his angels, from the clouds). Thus Mk. 8:31, 9:31 and 10:33f specify his suffering, death and resurrection (with no mention of his parousia), while the reverse is true of Mk. 8:38, 13:26ff and 14:62. These latter logia about his parousia in no way suggest that he is already on earth, and must first die, be resurrected and elevated to heaven before he can come down from heaven to bring the world to an end. The reasonable inference is that Jesus' resurrection and his parousia were originally quite independent traditions; that logia (familiar in Jewish apocalyptic thinking) about the final coming of the Son of man have been put into the mouth of a personage who was believed to have died and have risen again. The identification of such a personage with the coming Son of man is not surprising. If he had risen from the grave and had joined God, then he could readily be equated with the Son of man who was to come down from heaven.

3. Jesus' statements that the Son of man is already active on earth: e.g. 'The Son of man has nowhere to lay his head' (Mt. 8:20 = Lk. 9:58). This group of sayings (represented in both Mk. and Q) seems to embody a later stratum of tradition, when the term Son of man had come to be regarded as a solemn manner in which the earthly Jesus referred to himself. In the saying quoted, the Son of man appears as humiliated and rejected on earth, not as a powerful and glorious being who is to come. This is not what one would expect from Jewish apocalyptic literature. Admittedly, some Christian scholars (e.g. 282, pp 87–8) have urged that, from Daniel onwards, humiliation and suffering as well as glory are involved in the Son of man's struggle against the forces opposing him. But Vermes denies that this is true either of the Daniel passage or of Jewish exegesis of it. He regards this third class of gospel 'Son of man' sayings as authentic on the ground that in Galilean Aramaic 'Son of man' occurs, from the second century AD, as a circumlocutional reference to self in contexts implying awe, reserve, or humility. Nothing, he adds, suggests that this idiom was a second century innovation, and was not in use earlier. He rejects as inauthentic only the other two classes of gospel 'Son of man' sayings, which he regards as 'eschatolizations' of this neutral speech-form, effected by 'the apocalyptically-minded Galilean disciples of Jesus by means of a midrash based on Daniel 7:13' (398, pp 168–86). From this we see that evidence which would establish that Jesus was in fact active in Galilee (which will be discussed below) is of some importance to the question of his historicity. Vermes has shown that, if Jesus was in Galilee, he could have used a speech-form which was both genuinely Aramaic and restricted to Galilee. On the other hand it would have been equally possible for Aramaic speakers who had never known him to have put this speech-form into his mouth. Furthermore, the Wisdom traditions, which represent Wisdom as humiliated and rejected, may also have been of influence on this third class of gospel 'Son of man' sayings. It is true that Wisdom was not, in pre-Christian literature, identified with the Son of man; but the Son of man was the possessor of divine wisdom in the highest degree, and was *the* wise man (193, p 28; 306, p 208). And as he who was to appear at the end of the ages to introduce the new aeon, the Son of man could readily be identified with him who was considered to be the *final* envoy of Wisdom (cf. above, p 105). The book of Enoch itself provides a precedent for identifying a human being (namely the Patriarch Enoch) with the apocalyptic Son of man; for on his arrival in heaven Enoch is greeted as 'the Son of man' (71:14).

(iv) Son of Man and Son of David

Paul, we saw, never uses the term 'Son of man'. He designates the earthly Jesus as son of David, but (unlike the OT prophets) he regards this personage as a pre-existent supernatural being. It is therefore not surprising that later Christian writers (e.g. the evangelists) saw fit to apply to him the title 'Son of man', which was in use in the Jewish background to designate the supernatural redeemer. Indeed, since 'son of David' could still be understood in its old, exclusively human sense, the two titles were to some extent in conflict. The fourth evangelist seems to have regarded them as incompatible, for he represents Jesus as the pre-existent Son of man and Logos, and suggests that he is not of Davidic lineage; at any rate, he does not attempt to refute the Jewish charge he records against Jesus, namely that he cannot be the Messiah because he comes from Galilee, and not from David's 'village' of Bethlehem (Jn. 7:41–2). In his gospel he consistently represents Jesus as from Galilee, and makes no mention of any connection with Bethlehem.

Mark also records an incident where Jesus is rejected as a nonentity because his family connections are known to be perfectly ordinary (Mk. 6:1–3; cf. below, p 150). The tradition, then, that Jesus had Davidic connections, although early, was in competition with traditions incompatible with it. Mark, however, unlike John, is anxious to represent Jesus as son of David, although very little of the material at his disposal could be made to serve this end. Mark does not introduce the term 'son of David' until the incident where the blind beggar Bartimaeus is made to address Jesus with the title in 10:46–52, and to add the request: 'have mercy upon me!' This is unlikely to be historical; nowhere else in the Bible is this latter phrase used to address a human being, although it is frequently employed in the Psalms by suppliants addressing God. For Mark it would therefore constitute an appropriate way of speaking to Jesus, and the evangelist presumably added both this phrase and the appellation 'son of David' to material concerning the miraculous cure of the blind beggar which reached him from tradition. His purpose seems to have been to show by these additions that Jesus was recognized as son of David immediately before his entry into Jerusalem (recorded in the next chapter), and thus to prepare the way for the words of acclamation with which he is greeted as he rides into the city:

'Hosanna!
Blessed is he who comes in the name of the Lord!
Blessed is the kingdom of our Father David that is coming!
Hosanna in the highest.' (11:9–10)

This again is a literary construction of the evangelist; for 'hosanna' is another cry of supplication, deriving from the Psalter. Mark seems to have been unaware of what it meant, and to have taken it for a cry of joyous exaltation which he could appropriately put into the mouth of the crowd (see Burger, 85, pp 47–50). The next sentence is a verse from Psalm 118 which was understood by the Jews of the time as a blessing upon pilgrims coming up to Jerusalem. The sentence that follows it in Mk. is designed as a comment on it and closely parallels it. (In literal translation from the Greek, 'blessed is the coming one', from the Psalm, is echoed by 'blessed is the coming kingdom'.) The wording of this comment is Christian rather than Jewish; for Jewish tradition speaks of the 'restoration', not of the 'coming' of the Davidic kingdom. From these facts Burger infers that a Christian narrator has made a traditional cry of welcome to Jewish pilgrims into a Messianic acclamation by adding a reference to David's kingdom which in fact ill accords with Jewish ideas (p 52).

Dependence on the OT is conspicuous in other details of Mark's story of Jesus' entry into Jerusalem. For his ride into the city he miraculously selects 'a colt on which no one has ever sat' (11:2). This makes no sense (even apart from the miracle) as a factual report – he would hardly have chosen an unbroken mount – but is quite intelligible as an echo of the Septuagint of Zechariah 9:9: 'Behold the king is coming ... riding on an ass and a young [lit. new] foal'. This OT passage specifies not only the animal and the entry but also the acclamation of the crowd: 'Rejoice ... daughter of Jerusalem'. Mark's narrative is thus 'not an eye-witness report of Jesus' entry into Jerusalem, but a story told by the later Christian community which allowed the OT to provide the material' (191, p 378). Dibelius regards the whole incident as a 'cult-legend', prompted by the 'holy words of the OT', read liturgically in the cult (125, p 119). There is certainly evidence that it was the duty of Christian ministers to read the OT in public worship (see Hanson's comment, 196, p 54 on 1 Tim. 4:13). Those who accept the triumphal entry as historical have to explain why both Jewish and Roman authorities failed to intervene.

Inside Jerusalem, Jesus is himself made to use the phrase 'son of David' in a discussion of Psalm 110:1 and its implications concerning 'the Christ'. He does not suggest that he himself is the Christ, but asks his audience:

'How can the scribes say that the Christ is the son of David? David himself, inspired by the Holy Spirit, declared, "The Lord said to my Lord, Sit at my right hand, till I put thy enemies under thy feet". David himself calls him Lord; so how is he his son?' (Mk. 12:35–7)

This looks like a flat denial of the Messiah's Davidic descent, and probably reached Mark as a tradition circulating in a Christian community which did deny Jesus' descent from David. That such communities existed is indicated not only by the fourth gospel but also by the non-canonical epistle of Barnabas, which was written after AD 70 – its ch.16 presupposes the destruction of the temple – but is not dependent on any of the canonical gospels (see JEC, pp 74–7). This eminently anti-Jewish work alleges that David was inspired to speak the words of Psalm 110 in order to provide means to refute those who 'in after times will assert that Christ is a son of David' (ch.12). This evidence shows that Christian use of the Psalm apropos of the descent of the Messiah did not derive from anything said by Jesus – the epistle does not allege that Jesus used the Psalm in this or any other connection – but from the doctrinal needs of a Christian community. Mark, however, has not only put the doctrine into Jesus' mouth, but in placing it after the Bartimaeus episode and the triumphal entry, he can hardly have meant it to be understood in its original sense as a denial of Jesus' Davidic descent. Mark's intention seems rather to indicate that 'son of David' is not a sufficiently exalted title for the Messiah, who is a supernatural being in heaven, sitting at God's right hand. (The same words from Psalm 110 are quoted in Hebrews 1:13 and Acts 2:34—5 in order to emphasize this.) He is therefore far superior to David, who himself acknowledges this by calling him Lord, and so cannot be subordinate to David (as his son). If, then, he is given the title 'son of David', he must nevertheless be regarded not as a mere earthly prince, but as transcendental Lord. Mark's criticism of the Davidic title may well be informed by the apocalyptic 'Son of man' idea. It is indeed noticeable that in Mk. 14:62 use is again made of Psalm 110:1, and this time in association with a specifically Son of man Christology.

In sum, then, by means of the incident with Bartimaeus and the triumphal entry, Mark represents Jesus as Son of David, and yet shows from Jesus' own words in Jerusalem that this title does not do full justice to him. In this connection Burger reminds us of the pre-Pauline formula 'son of David according to the flesh', but 'son of God in power according to the Spirit of holiness by his resurrection from the dead' (Rom. 1:3—4). Mark, says Burger, seems to have some such distinction in mind when he lifts the 'Messianic secret' to the extent of allowing Jesus' 'fleshly' status as son of David to become public at the time of his arrival in Jerusalem, while reserving the disclosure of his full dignity for the time when 'the Son of man should have risen from the dead' (Mk. 9:9). The evangelist's motive for this partial disclosure may have been to give the Jewish authorities some inkling of Jesus' importance, and hence some basis for their determination to kill him.

Matthew and Luke supplement the Marcan material with genealogies, which represent Jesus as of Davidic descent, and with stories of his birth in Bethlehem. The two accounts are mutually exclusive, and apart from these questionable introductions the two evangelists were entirely dependent on Mk. for what they say concerning Jesus as son of David. In Mt., for instance, Jesus is frequently addressed by this title, but the address has simply been introduced into passages taken from Mk. The sole exception is Mt. 9:27 where two blind men cry 'Have mercy on us, Son of David'. This incident is indeed peculiar to Mt., but is clearly a mere duplicate of Mark's story of Bartimaeus, which Matthew has also included in its proper place later (20:29—34). He needed to duplicate it here at 9:27 in order to justify Jesus' statement at 11:5 that, as a result of his activities, 'the blind receive their sight'.

We are now in a position to see how baseless is the argument (above, p 18) that Jesus' Davidic descent must be historical fact because it is recorded as early as the Pauline letters. Mark, we saw, at two points imposed the idea onto his material, and at a third adapted to his own purposes a tradition which expressly denied it. The rest of his gospel does nothing to link Jesus with David, and even includes material which militates against any such link. Matthew and Luke knew of no additional relevant traditions except their obviously legendary genealogies and birth stories. And John seems not to accept Jesus' Davidic origin at all. As for Paul, his statement on the matter is not put out as historical information, but is quoted from a confessional formula (Burger, 85, p 31).

(v) Summary

The Christology of the NT is far from homogeneous. The presentation of Jesus as a pre-existent redeemer and also as a miracle worker can be understood as an attempt to synthesize the views of Paul and of his Christian rivals. The pre-Pauline hymns and Q have a non-passion Christology, while the Christology of the Son of man who is to come in the future can be traced to Jewish ideas of the time. The existence of strongly divergent Christologies in early Christian times is a strong argument against Jesus' historicity. If he had really lived, early Christian literature would not 'show nearly everywhere churchly and theological conflicts and fierce quarrels between opponents' (Käsemann, 241, p 238) nor disagree so radically as to what kind of person he was.

Notes to Chapter Four

1 Paul's immediate concern here is admittedly not with Jesus' obscurity, but (as the context shows) to stress that in submitting to the law, he placed himself in the power of the evil angelic rulers of this world (cf. JEC, pp 299–300), before (at his resurrection) openly challenging and defeating them. Nevertheless, the earthly Jesus could have avoided any confrontation with the law and the angelic governors only by living inconspicuously.

2 He does indeed call his rivals 'superlative apostles' (2 Cor. 11:5), but this seems to be sarcasm, not deference towards those in Jerusalem who were apostles before his own conversion. He goes on to call them 'false apostles', and would hardly have referred to Cephas, James and John in this way. Commentators who refer the phrase 'superlative apostles' to them have to argue that the 'false apostles' mentioned a few verses later are a different group. Käsemann thinks (237, p 49) that they were not themselves the Jerusalem apostles, but depended for their authority on these 'original apostles' of Jerusalem. But Paul's complaint against them is that they 'measure themselves by one another', i.e. that they are boundless in their self-reliance and self-confidence, whereas he does not attempt to boast beyond his proper sphere (10:12–13).

3 Two cures recorded by Mark (7:33 and 8:22–6) involve the use of touch and spittle in a way well known from the behaviour of Greek and Jewish miracle-healers. (Taylor gives relevant pagan parallels, 384, p 354). This was too much for Matthew, who broke up these stories, dispersed and edited them so as to make them acceptable (see Hull's searching account, 213, p 138).

4 In Mk. 3:23–7 Jesus implies that he is the 'strong man' who has power to 'bind' Satan. Kallas notes that the 'kingdom of God' implies 'the cleansing of the contaminated world where Satan ruled by means of demons, suffering, sickness,

leprosy, blindness, famines, storms, etc. Why else would Mark concentrate, page after page, on these events if they were peripheral and not vital illustrations of the central message of the kingdom?' This comment is directed against attempts to make the miracles of healing and exorcism acceptable to the sophisticated reader of today by representing them as 'enacted parables illustrating a spiritual truth' (243, p 83).

5 Thus he enjoins silence (1:44; 7:36), but the people are unable to contain themselves. Again, having raised Jairus' daughter from the dead he 'strictly charged them that no one should know this' (5:43) — even though her death has already become public (verses 35 and 39).

6 There are, for instance, numerous examples of prophetic speech forms and phrases within Q. One of the latter is the Q equivalent to the OT 'thus says Yahweh', namely: 'Truly, I say unto you'. This formula 'functions as the mode of authentication for those who speak within the community not on their own initiative, but as spokesmen for the risen Lord' (142, p 255).

7 Hummel gives the following examples: (i) In Mk. 2:15–17 Jesus justifies his infringement of a Pharisaic practice with an appeal to his own authority. Mt. 9: 9–13 makes him preface this appeal with a quotation from Hosea. The effect is to show that his behaviour (his mission to sinners) reflects God's will as stated in scripture; and so the opposition between his standpoint and that of the Jews has been toned down: (ii) In Mk. 2: 23–8 Pharisees accuse the disciples of 'doing what is not lawful on the sabbath'. Matthew again quotes Hosea in order to show that they are 'guiltless' (12:7), i.e. their behaviour is within the (properly interpreted) Jewish law: (iii) Mt. 15: 17–20 is indeed not compatible with the law; but the evangelist is careful not to state the incompatibility as bluntly as Mark had done.

8 Matthew's omission of Mk. 2:27 ('the sabbath was made for man, not man for the sabbath') is not significant, since Luke (whom no one suspects of partiality to Jewish ideas) also omits it.

9 Carlston instances the impossibility of harmonizing 23:3 ('The scribes and the Pharisees sit on Moses' seat; so practise and observe whatever they tell you') with the rejection of handwashing in 15: 1–2 and 20 as 'only a special instance of what the author must have faced again and again in coming to terms with materials more rigidly Jewish-Christian than he was himself' (95, p 91).

10 140, pp 299–300; 373, p 38. From the fact that the Similitudes have not been found at Qumran (although every other part of the book of Enoch has), Leivestad infers (274, p 246) that they are of later date. But the Essenes of Qumran held by a Davidic Messiah, and may for this reason have ignored or rejected writings which proclaimed a Son of man Messiah. Dr Hooker rightly repudiates as 'without foundation' the suggestion that the Similitudes are Christian. And even if the work is later than the Ezra apocalypse, the beliefs it embodies about the Son of man may well have been current before (206, pp 15, 99; 210, p 48).

11 See Enoch 48:4–10; 52:4; 62:13–16; 63:6–10.

12 Scholem has recently reminded us (357, p 8) that 'Jewish Messianism is in its origins and by its nature . . . a theory of catastrophe' which 'stresses the revolutionary, cataclysmic element in the transition from every historical present to the Messianic future' (e.g. Isaiah 2 and 4). Hence the apocalypses represent a 'genuine continuance of Messianism'. He adds that this continuance was denied by the great Jewish scholars of the nineteenth and early twentieth centuries because they pleaded for a purified and rational Judaism to which apocalypticism was distasteful. Christian scholars concurred because anxious to claim all combinations of Messianism and apocalypticism as Christian (pp 9, 19).

5 The Twelve

(i) The Twelve as Companions of Jesus

The twelve disciples are often regarded as guarantors of Jesus' historicity, although we are told nothing of most of them except their names, on which the documents do not even agree completely. In Mk. and Mt. the list of names is also very clumsily worked into the text.[1] All this makes it obvious that the *number* is an older tradition than the *persons*; that the idea of the twelve derives not from twelve actual disciples, but from some other source – quite possibly from the expectation that Jesus, as Messiah, would command twelve men as leaders and judges of the new Israel. Thus the epistle of Barnabas (written some time between AD 70 and 145) says (ch. 8) that 'those whom Jesus empowered to preach the gospel were twelve in number, to represent the tribes of Israel, which were twelve'. The fourth gospel (unlike the synoptics) does not even list the names. From 6:60 we learn that the disciples are 'many', and a few verses later Jesus is suddenly made to address 'the twelve'. There has been no previous hint of choosing the number. Clearly, then, John knew of a tradition that there had been twelve disciples, but was unable or unwilling to elucidate it and is therefore not a valuable witness to its historical accuracy. In the synoptics, Peter, James and John are Jesus' most intimate disciples, but in the fourth gospel Peter plays but a minor role, and James and John are not mentioned at all. (Jn. 21 – generally admitted to be an appendix added to the solemn conclusion of the gospel recorded at the end of ch. 20 – does indeed mention 'the sons of Zebedee', but even here they are not named as James and John.) On the other hand, the fourth gospel makes disciples of personages who are not mentioned in the synoptics (Nathanael, Nicodemus). All this is clear evidence that the traditions on which the fourth evangelist drew were aside from the synoptic stream.

Mk. refers much more often to Jesus' 'disciples' – the whole body of his followers – than to the closer group called the twelve. The term 'disciples' is first introduced in 2:15, where he is at table 'with his disciples', who are included among the 'many who followed him'. In 3:7 this is increased to a 'great multitude', and in verses 32–4 his true family is said to be with the 'crowd' sitting round him. It is these same people who, with the twelve, question him about the parables (4:10), and to whom he explains the parable of the sower. And so 'when it is said (4:34–5) that he never spoke to them apart from parables and that he interpreted in private to his own disciples, any distinction between an inner group, a larger entourage, and the multitude, has become blurred' (Evans, 150, p 57). Evans adds that this picture of Jesus permanently accompanied by a vast train of personal adherents is not historically plausible; and that he has clearly been made into 'a paradigm of the Lord and his Church in Mark's own day'.

Nearly all Mk.'s references to 'the twelve' occur in passages which Taylor designates as 'Marcan constructions' (384, p 620). A typical example is 4:10: 'When he was alone, those who were about him with the twelve asked him concerning the parables'. It seems odd that the evangelist finds it necessary to say that those 'who were about him' included his twelve close companions, and this clumsiness is explained if the original reading was simply 'those who were about him', and if a reference to the twelve was added later, when the idea arose that he was always accompanied by them. Again, Mk. 11:11 ('as it was already late, he went out to Bethany with the twelve') was written by Mark himself to serve as a link between two independent episodes which he took from his sources, namely the triumphal entry into Jerusalem (verses 1—10) and the cursing of the fig tree (verses 12—14). Neither episode mentions 'the twelve', but only 'the disciples'. The absence of any reference to the twelve in the second episode (after the linking verse which does mention them) is very instructive. 'They' are said (verse 12) to return from Bethany the following morning and to hear him cursing the tree; but in verse 14 'they' are identified not as 'the twelve' but as 'his disciples'. Evidence of this kind has suggested to theologians that 'the twelve did not originally belong in the Jesus traditions' and that Mark tried hard to introduce them into material which resisted this constructive editorial activity (352, p 69; 400, p 69).

The conventional view that after the resurrection the twelve exercised a decisive influence is not borne out even by the Church's own account of its early history in Acts, where they rapidly disappear from the narrative. The author ascribes the greatest importance to them; yet he mentions them as a group only in the opening chapters, and ch. 9 is the last occasion where they appear as the sole leaders of the Jerusalem community. The whole book gives information about only one of their number, namely Peter. Clearly, he was the only one about whom stories were circulating in the Christian communities – stories on which the author could draw.[2] They are no more than half a dozen in number, and are yarns of miraculous cures and of a raising from the dead rather than historical reminiscences. Even Peter does not appear after ch. 15, by which time the twelve share the leadership of the Church with 'elders' and with one James whose identity is not explained.[3] After 16:4 we hear no more of the twelve, and from then on James and the elders are the sole leaders in Jerusalem (as is clear from 21:18).

These facts suggest that the author of Acts stresses the importance of the twelve not because they were prominent in any historical records he was utilizing, but because such stress suited his theological purpose, which was (as we shall see) to silence heretics by representing the true Christian proclamation as the prerogative of men who had been life companions of Jesus on earth, or at least the immediate pupils and subordinates of such men.

Now that we have seen that neither gospels nor Acts give convincing evidence that Jesus was accompanied by twelve disciples, we may turn to Paul's much earlier statement that Jesus, after his resurrection, appeared to Cephas and afterwards 'to the twelve' (1 Cor. 15:5). If these words were really written by Paul, then it looks as though he was aware that Jesus chose twelve disciples; and if Paul in this respect corroborates what the gospels say, then it would be reasonable to infer that he also knows the principal facts of Jesus' life, as detailed there, in spite of his silence about them. In JEC I gave reasons for setting aside this, Paul's only reference to the twelve, as interpolated into his epistle by someone acquainted with the tradition that Jesus had twelve disciples. But the evidence for interpolation is far from decisive, and the unpauline features of the context are generally attributed to the fact that he is here quoting an already existing Christian creed (cf. above, p 37). As he mentions the twelve nowhere else, he obviously did not know them: for him, they could only have been personages named in this creed – deriving from a primitive Christian community – which specified witnesses of the resurrection. The community which formulated this pre-Pauline creed would have known them not as companions of a historical Jesus, but as a group of enthusiasts who, having heard of the appearance of the risen Jesus to Cephas, thought that it presaged a general resurrection of the dead (cf. above, p 34). In the exalted state of mind which went with such expectation, the group would have become convinced that Jesus had appeared also to them, but have fallen apart when the hope that had led to its inception was not fulfilled (352, pp 70, 82). If it had persisted as an important group, Paul would surely have mentioned it again, and not merely have named it once in a passage which was, for him, a quotation. That Paul's mention of the group he calls 'the twelve' is not dependent on knowledge of the traditions which were later recorded in the gospels is also apparent from the fact that, according to the evangelists, the risen Jesus did *not* appear to his twelve disciples, but to eleven of them (Judas having defected). Mt. 28:16 and Mk. 16:14 are quite specific on the matter, and record appearances not to 'the disciples' but to 'the eleven'.

Paul does mention Cephas in other contexts, and it is quite clear from these references that he knew Cephas as a Christian teacher and rival at Jerusalem. It is significant that he knows nothing of 'twelve' as leaders of Jerusalem Christians, but names these leaders as Cephas, James and John. Cephas may have been the same person as the 'Peter' mentioned in a single Pauline passage (Gal. 2:7–9, although Paul does not equate them); for 'Cephas' is not a proper name but an Aramaic word meaning 'rock', while 'Peter' is a translation of this word into Greek. In the synoptics there is no mention of Cephas, but the most prominent disciple is called Simon, and – in different circumstances in each gospel – Jesus gives him the title 'Peter'. There is nothing in Paul's writings to support the view that the Cephas he mentions had the career and connection with Jesus alleged of Peter in the gospels. Paul has occasion to resist the pretensions of Cephas, and calls him a dissembler (Gal. 2:13); yet he makes no use of information to Peter's discredit recorded in the gospels – the designation of him as Satan (Mk. 8:33), his sleeping in Gethsemane and his denial of his Lord with curses. This latter story is of the most damning kind, yet Paul, anxious to establish his authority against that of Cephas, makes no mention of it. This suggests that, if the gospel Peter is the same person as the Cephas of Paul's epistles, the details of his career (particularly his association with a historical Jesus) were invented only after Paul's time. The sequence could well have been that an early Christian leader acquired the title of 'rock' of the Church because his vision of the risen Jesus antedated all others, and that, at a later stage in the development of Christianity, it was felt necessary to retroject his pre-eminence into Jesus' lifetime (see Dinkler, 127, p 199). In this way, 'the authority of Peter as the first Easter witness in the most primitive Christian community became institutionalized as the authority of the first of the twelve' (Klein, 256, p 315). It is primarily Acts which links Peter with both the earthly and the risen Jesus, and Peter there describes himself as one of the men who had kept Jesus' company from his baptism to his ascension. But those who accept such Petrine speeches as an accurate historical record have yet to explain why in them Peter appeals to the Jews of Jerusalem with proofs from scripture which presuppose the Greek translation of the OT and are not available in the Hebrew original (188, p 148). Klein has noted that, from this alone, it is clear that what Peter says in Acts cannot be taken as a true reflection of the ideas of the Jerusalem Christians he is supposed to have led, but could only have been drawn up in a Hellenistic community.[4]

It is in Mt. that Jesus addresses Peter as the 'rock' on which he will build his Church, and promises him 'the keys of the kingdom of heaven: and whatever you bind on earth shall be bound in heaven, and whatever you loose on earth shall be loosed in heaven' (Mt. 16:18–19). Mt. is the only canonical gospel which records a specific teaching about the Church, and which makes Jesus use the word. The further mention of the Church and of the powers of binding and loosing in 18:15--18 (where they are accorded to 'the disciples' as a whole) shows that what is meant is the power of excluding persons from the Christian community, and the power to remove such a ban. And as the evangelist links the 'Church' on earth with the 'kingdom' in heaven, the implication is that only members of the Christian community can enter the kingdom. Bornkamm thinks that Matthew's purpose here is to set up an authority to determine what is acceptable Christian doctrine, 'in conscious criticism of all free pneumatical behaviour' which was without respect for law and order (128, p 184) – the kind of charismatic behaviour which had unsettled the communities to which Paul wrote. And Matthew's method of achieving his aim was to make Peter (who is given more prominence than in Mk.) the guarantor of Jesus' instructions. On this view, then, Matthew was writing for a community which believed: Peter has commanded us to do certain things, and his orders are valid because he heard Jesus give them (see also Hummel, 214, p 60).

Conservative theologians of course continue to affirm that — in the words of Dr Meye, their most recent spokesman — 'the NT picture of the twelve as the company of Jesus is not at all open to doubt', and that the reliability of the earliest of the gospels in this particular gives 'momentous support' to its whole witness (300, p 209).

(ii) Disciples and Apostles

Most people take for granted that Jesus had twelve close disciples, and that it is appropriate to call them 'the twelve apostles'. But theologians — whether or not they accept the historicity of the twelve — have recently shown that they were not apostles in the sense in which the term was used in the early Church, and that Luke is the first Christian writer who consistently refers to them as 'apostles'.

Paul's reference to the twelve (which I have quoted in its context, above, p 30) distinguishes them from apostles. He is giving a list of those to whom the risen Jesus has appeared, and he mentions 'the twelve' as witnesses of the second appearance, and 'all the apostles' as witnesses of the fifth. From his use of the term, it is clear that for him an 'apostle' is someone who has had a supernatural experience of the risen Jesus and has been called to his service by such a vision. Thus he defends his own claim to be an apostle by asking: 'Have I not seen Jesus our Lord?' (1 Cor. 9:1). And he also describes himself as 'called to be an apostle' (Rom. 1:1). It is agreed that these references are not to meetings which he had with Jesus before the crucifixion, but to the visions of the risen Jesus which converted him to Christianity. In 2 Cor. he controverts Christian preachers who claimed that they, and not he, were apostles because only they could produce heavenly revelations, miracles and convincing manifestations of the spirit (cf. above, p 100). He calls them false apostles, and discusses how the true ones are to be distinguished from them. Such discussions would have been unnecessary if it had been generally acknowledged that the only true apostles were twelve men who had kept Jesus' company on earth. There is thus no connection between the historical Jesus and the apostolate. Paul and his Christian opponents concur in the view that an apostle is a missionary called to office by the risen Jesus.[5]

Even Mk. and Mt. do not normally call Jesus' followers 'apostles', nor do they suggest that 'apostle' designates a particular office — although Lk.–Acts certainly does.[6] The way Luke imposes the word 'apostles' on his material is well illustrated by his reference (11:49) to 'prophets and apostles', where the corresponding passage in Mt. has 'prophets, wise men and scribes'. Lk. contains a mere half dozen mentions of 'apostles', for the author was restricted by sources which did not call the disciples by this term. But in Acts he was under no restriction, and there he repeatedly uses the term in a technical sense as a title for the twelve. A clue as to Luke's motive is provided in the farewell speech which Paul is made to deliver in Acts to the 'elders' of the Church of Ephesus, where he disclaims all responsibility for future divisions, which, he foretells, will rend the Church, and declares that he has preached the true doctrine, 'the whole counsel of God' (20:27). Haenchen, whose commentary on Acts is one of the outstanding achievements of post-war NT scholarship, is surely right to say (188, pp 528–9) that such a warning is not intelligible as a genuine Pauline utterance of about AD 60. The very fact that it is addressed to 'elders', a governing body within the Church, presupposes a more sophisticated Church organization than is indicated in Paul's own epistles — one which is more akin to that advocated in the Pastoral epistles of the early second century. Luke, then, writing late in the first or early in the second century, puts the warning against heretics into Paul's mouth because by then they had begun to rend the Church. Klein thinks that they had even begun to claim Paul as their own (as Marcion was to do a little later when he appealed to Pauline doctrines in order to justify his total rejection of the OT). According to Klein, Luke wishes to retain Paul for orthodoxy and at the same time to make him quite useless as an authority to whom heretics can appeal. Paul is therefore represented as subordinate to twelve apostles who enjoyed the advantage of being instructed by Jesus in his life-time. Such subordination is very different from the manner in which Paul himself, in his own writings, represents his position, and comparison of these with Lk.–Acts betrays the tendencies of the latter.

Paul represents himself as having been far above average in his zeal for his native Jewish faith (Gal. 1:14), and as having persecuted Christians for this reason. His purpose is (as the sequel in Galatians shows) to convince his readers that it required more than human means to convert him to Christianity. If he was a particularly zealous Pharisee, and a persecutor of Christians, then only a supernatural revelation (and not mere human instruction from the Jerusalem Christians) could have sufficed, so he insists, to win him for the true faith. In Acts, however, Luke represents him as a quite average Jew, who, before his conversion was not more 'zealous for God' than were others (22:3; 26:4ff), but who as a persecutor of Christians was positively ferocious: who beat, fettered and delivered to prison both men and women, breathed fire and slaughter, and consented to murder (8:1 and 3; 9:1–2; 22:4 and 19). This is hardly historical portraiture, for the Roman authorities would not have permitted such Gestapo activities.[7] Luke, then, lowers Paul's stature by representing him as having been but moderately devout as a Jew, but almost maniacal as a persecutor. The same tendency to depress Paul's standing is visible in Luke's account of his conversion. Paul himself, in his own letters,

127

attributes this to a supernatural vision, and not to any human agency. But Acts (9:3ff and 22:6ff) represents the risen Jesus merely as telling him to go to Damascus where 'you will be told what you are to do', and where he is duly told by 'a disciple ... named Ananias', who fills him with the Holy Spirit. Thus whereas Paul's own account says nothing of Ananias, Luke subordinates Paul to a representative of the existing Church. In one of the speeches he is made to deliver in Acts, he does not even allege that the risen Jesus had appeared to him at all, and says only that after the resurrection 'for many days he appeared to those who came up with him from Galilee to Jerusalem' (i.e. to the disciples who were with him when he was crucified), and that *they* 'are now his witnesses to the people' (13:31–2). Furthermore, Acts has it that, soon after his Damascus experience, Paul went to Jerusalem, where Barnabas introduced him to the apostles (9:27); and it is in the temple at Jerusalem, by means of a second vision of Jesus, that according to Acts 22:17–21 he is given his vocation to preach to the gentiles. One point of these narratives is to subordinate him to Jerusalem and to its Christian authorities. His own story, in Gal. 1:15–17, is that he had nothing to do with Jerusalem and its apostles for years after his conversion.

Lk.–Acts is the earliest extant document which both stresses the idea of the 'twelve apostles' and also depresses the stature of Paul. Klein argues that the coincidence of these two factors betrays the origin of the former; that Luke's purpose was to show that the only true apostles are those who were companions of Jesus throughout his whole ministry. This purpose is betrayed in the incident in Acts where a new twelfth 'apostle' is chosen to replace the traitor Judas. Peter on this occasion declares (1:21–2) that Judas' place must be taken by 'one of the men who have accompanied us during all the time that the Lord Jesus went in and out among us, beginning from the baptism of John until the day when he was taken up from us [i.e. the day of the ascension] – one of these men must become with us a witness to his resurrection'. We saw that originally an apostle was someone who had 'witnessed the resurrection' as Paul had done, by a vision of the risen Jesus. To this original condition of apostleship Luke adds a second which has the function of guaranteeing continuity between the risen and the historical Jesus; and he has no compunction in making this second condition stringent enough to contradict the older tradition of Mk. 1:14ff, according to which the disciples began to keep Jesus' company not from the day John baptized Jesus, but only after John's imprisonment.[8] The whole speech of Peter in Acts in which the two conditions of apostleship are enunciated is obviously unhistorical, for it represents him (1:19–20) as explaining in Greek, for the benefit of the Aramaic-speaking Jews of Jerusalem, the meaning of one of the words of their language, and as presenting them with a proof by prophecy which depends on the Septuagint and which the Hebrew OT text does not permit.

Luke, then, to make Paul inaccessible to heretics, made the twelve disciples into 'apostles' and subordinated him to them. No aversion to Paul is implied, who in Acts is allowed to perform miracles as spectacular as Peter's. Indeed, Luke needed such traditions for his account of the spread of the Church; for he knew of no missions by Peter, or any of the twelve, outside Palestine. It is only Paul who fulfils the command of the risen Lord to bear witness 'to the end of the earth' (Acts 1:8). But his missionary activity was acceptable to Luke only if he worked in conjunction with the Jerusalem community, and accordingly some of its prominent members (Silas, and Barnabas: 4:36) are represented as accompanying him.

Finally, the NT Apocalypse or book of Revelation, which consists of a redaction of early and late material,[9] contains a reference to the 'twelve apostles of the lamb', whose names are on the twelve basement courses of the New Jerusalem (21:14). In the vision of the writer, the New Jerusalem represents the perfected religious community, and he makes the city a square of side 12,000 stadia, having a wall 144 cubits high, with twelve gates, twelve angels at them, and the names of the twelve tribes inscribed on them. His prime concern is clearly to show the importance of the number twelve in the perfect community; and it may be that he postulates twelve apostles not because he knows of twelve original apostles, but because, when writing of the relation between the twelve tribes and the apostolic faith, he envisages twelve apostles as appropriate for his ideal community — however many there may have been in the empirical Christian community known to him. If, however, we take the view that he could only have regarded the twelve names as inscribed on the foundations of the new world because he and his readers knew of a tradition that the apostles on earth were twelve, then we can (with Haenchen, 188, p 677) understand this tradition as a development of the logion of Q (Mt. 19:28 = Lk. 22:30), where Jesus promises his 'disciples' (Mt.) — Luke has changed this to 'apostles' — that 'in the new world . . . you who have followed me will . . . sit on twelve thrones, judging the twelve tribes of Israel'.

(iii) The Twelve and the Seven: Jesus and the Jewish Law

Even the tendentious Acts, anxious to establish that 'the company of those who believed were of one heart and soul' (4:32), nevertheless betrays that the early Jerusalem Church did not consist of an undivided community under the direction of 'twelve apostles'. A disagreement is mentioned (6:1) between the 'Hellenists' of Jerusalem, i.e. those Jewish Christians who spoke Greek, and the 'Hebraists'. The former complained that no provision had been made to feed their widows. That the charitable organization overlooked only Hellenists suggests that these formed in some sense a separate group, as is understandable. Apart from the language difference, the Hellenists (deriving as they did from the Greek cities of the Diaspora) were used to practising a certain accommodation to pagan ideas and customs, and this could easily lead to friction between them and the Hebraist Christians of Jerusalem. The author is doubtless glossing over these differences when he restricts them to the question of feeding the poor. He goes on to relate that the dispute was resolved by choosing seven men to feed all the poor (not only those of the Hellenist group), thus leaving 'the twelve' free to devote themselves exclusively to prayer and preaching. In the sequel, however, Stephen and Philip (both members of the seven) proceed to make public appearances as preachers; Philip becomes so prominent a missionary that he is even designated 'the evangelist' (21:8). It is clear from this that the seven are not in fact officers exercising a subordinate function within a single community ruled by the twelve, but a group with the same functions as Peter and the rest of the twelve. Furthermore, all the seven have Greek names, and are therefore likely to have been the leaders of the Hellenists.

In ch. 7 Stephen incenses the orthodox Jews, who put him to death and then persecute the whole Christian community of the city, with the result that all the Christians 'were scattered, except the apostles'. Strange indeed that the rank and file should be persecuted, but the leaders left unmolested. But Luke would have spoiled the continuity of the Church if he had said that the apostles left Jerusalem. Furthermore, the sequel does not bear out the allegation that, apart from them, the whole Christian community suffered persecution. For in 9:31 we read that the persecution was over: 'the church throughout all Judaea and Galilee and Samaria had peace', yet 'those who were scattered' (alluded to again in 8:14) are in 11:19 still on the move, and begin a mission to gentiles in Antioch. They are said to include 'men of Cyprus and Cyrene'. It really looks, then, as if it was only the Hellenists, indeed only the leaders of the Hellenists, who had been driven from Jerusalem. The 'apostles', i.e. the twelve, are expressly exempted, and the narrative (we saw) goes on to show the Church in Judaea at peace, while Hellenists are scattered abroad. But if the orthodox Jews of Jerusalem persecuted only the Hellenist Christians, these, under the seven, must have preached doctrines which gave offence in a way in which the Hebraists, under the twelve, did not. What the Jews found offensive in the Hellenists is obvious from their indictment against Stephen (a prominent member of the seven), namely that he abused the temple and the law. So the Jerusalem Christians consisted of Hellenists who disrespected the Jewish law, and Hebraists who kept it. There was thus, side by side with those led by the twelve, a primitive group led by seven men which had other doctrines. Could the Christian community have been thus divided into two factions if the twelve had really been what Luke represents them as being – chosen for their office by Jesus at the beginning of his ministry, witnesses of his resurrection, who will one day sit upon twelve thrones judging the twelve tribes? Luke's position seems to have been that he could not in Acts afford to tell the whole truth about the twelve and the seven. If he had admitted that the seven were leaders as much as the twelve, he could not also have maintained that the twelve were uniquely qualified to be leaders. But on the other hand he did not wish to ignore the tradition of the martyrdom of the Hellenist Stephen;

and so he made him a member of a group of seven which he represented as mere deacons, feeding the poor, within the community ruled by the twelve.

These are agreed to be the facts of the case by such eminent theologians as Haenchen and Conzelmann. Both these scholars of course believe that the early Christians based their views on the precepts of a historical Jesus. It is however of interest that Haenchen admits (188, p 221, and more emphatically in the first edition of his commentary, 187, p 226) that it is not possible to say whether Jesus took the stringent attitude to the law of the Hebraist Christians, or whether he was more permissive, since the gospels represent him as contradicting himself hopelessly on this matter — saying now that every jot and tittle of the Jewish law is permanent, now that whole aspects of it are obsolete.[10] He obviously could not in fact have adopted both attitudes. I know that preachers contradict themselves, but hardly to this extent. We should not readily believe that Bertrand Russell publicly proclaimed, in one season's addresses, that Britain ought to atom-bomb every city in Russia and also unilaterally renounce nuclear weapons. It is generally supposed that there was a historical Jesus who took either a stringent or a permissive view of the law, and that the opposite to what he said was also put into his mouth in the course of the composition of the documents. But if he had committed himself on the law, one way or the other, then surely the issue could not have divided the early Church into two opposing factions. Carlston summarizes the evidence as showing that (i) 'the "historical Jesus" in the strict sense was at a very early stage in primitive Christianity simply unrecoverable'; (ii) 'for many communities' (not including the Pauline Churches, which did not base their doctrines on the teachings of a historical Jesus) 'he was also in some sense unavoidable. In other words, side by side with an inability to repeat Jesus' teaching was an insistence that Christianity was inseparably tied to that teaching' (95, p 95). Each faction was, then, impelled to invent 'words of the Lord' which committed him to its party standpoint. The facility with which this occurred suggests that the historical Jesus 'very early became unrecoverable' because there was nothing to recover. The early Christians who respected the law would have felt convinced that Jesus had done so too, and so they assumed that he had endorsed it in his speeches. The faction which did not wish to preserve the law would, arguing from opposite premises, reach the reverse conclusion; and in this way sets of mutually contradictory statements could come to be ascribed to him and eventually be brought together in one gospel, written by a redactor of available traditions.

If this is how his statements on the law are to be explained, it is understandable why some of the texts represent him as abrogating it, yet not attempting to justify the changes he demands. If, on the other hand, such rulings were made by a historical Jesus who was a real man, and not an incarnation of God, then they are merely presumptuous. In Mt. 5:21—44, for instance, they are introduced with the phrase, 'I say to

131

you'. Schweizer regards these sayings as 'among those that are most likely to be genuine', and he does not dispute that here 'the "I" of Jesus speaks in the place of God' (367, p 14). It is open to any man to criticize the prevailing standards and customs, but he should give reasons for his views, and not merely — as Jesus does — demand changes on his own authority. Commentators who accept his rulings as genuine have to excuse his dogmatic attitude by positing a 'unique consciousness of authority as a trait of his character' (so Trilling, 393, pp 46, 94). Trilling cannot of course defend all his incompatible pronouncements on the law as valid, and finds that 'it is in the last analysis a matter of prior faith and of judgement which of the texts one regards as weightier and which of less validity' (p 87).

(iv) Judas and His Place in the Passion Narrative

Standard Christian works of reference today admit that what Judas betrayed and why he betrayed it are insoluble problems.[11] Most people nevertheless believe that the story is too unedifying to be a Christian invention. In fact, however, Cheyne long ago showed that this is not so. He wrote in the *Encyclopaedia Biblica*:

> 'Supposing that the original tradition left the ease with which the capture of Jesus was effected unaccounted for, Christian ingenuity would exert itself to find an explanation. Passages in the Psalms (41:9 and 55:12–14) which spoke of the Righteous Man as treated with brutal insolence by his own familiar friend would suggest the originator of the outrage; the betrayer of Jesus must have been a faithless friend.'

Paul knew only that Jesus had been 'delivered up'. That much had been extracted from Isaiah (see above, p 25). Christians were convinced that the OT was a revelation of God's plan for the world's salvation, and so they naturally sought in it further indications of the details of Jesus' fate. The evangelists all use the Pauline verb 'deliver up' (paradidomi) in connection with the activities of Judas, and not the usual Greek verb for 'betray', which would be 'prodidomi'. (English translations misleadingly represent Judas as 'betraying' Jesus. In fact, only at Lk. 6:16 is Judas called a 'traitor' (prodotes) in the Greek.) This shows that the evangelists were reworking an older tradition derived, via Paul, from the OT. Mark, then (or his source), is clearly interpreting a tradition which had not specified when, by whom or to whom Jesus was delivered up, so as to make it mean Judas' handing over of Jesus to the Jewish authorities on the night of the passover. And not only the Psalms to which Cheyne referred, but also other OT passages guided the process of reinterpretation. Enslin has said that 'the conspiracy of David's son, and the plan urged by David's former confidant Ahithophel of how they might lay hold of David, would seem to be the background for the story of the treacherous act of Jesus' disciple' (148, p 141). A number of traits in the Judas tradition are paralleled in rabbinic sayings about Ahithophel, and these similarities show that

Christian thinking about Judas 'fits well into the "betrayer categories" which the Jews took from the OT Scriptures' (168, p 39). Even the name Judas, and his position as one of the twelve, selling his master for money, is 'scarcely accidental, but would seem a clear reflection of the act of the earlier Judah (Greek 'Ioudas'), one of the twelve brothers, urging the selling of Joseph to the Ishmaelites for twenty pieces of silver' (148, p 141). 'Iscariot' could have any of half a dozen meanings, and one suggestion is that it represents the Aramaic word for 'deceit', 'falsehood': in which case Judas would be named 'the false one'.

Those who assert that no Christian would have invented a traitorous disciple need to be reminded of the statement in the epistle of Barnabas that Jesus 'chose his own apostles from the worst type of sinners, since it was not his mission to call saints but sinners'. I showed in JEC (pp 175–6) that the author took this not from the gospels but from a tradition only partly parallel with them. No one today believes that what he says is true, that Jesus' closest followers consisted exclusively of 'the worst type of sinners'. Here, then, we have a Christian invention of precisely the kind which is today confidently asserted to be an impossibility. The intellectual environment in which this invention arose would naturally favour, as a further development, specific charges of evil-doing against named intimates. And what could better suit the anti-Jewish attitude of many early Christians (including the evangelists) than the betrayal of their Lord by one Jew and his denial by another?[1][2]

In the gospels the betrayal story occurs in the wider context of the passion narrative of the closing chapters, the only long and continuous narrative found anywhere in these works. Time and place, treated so cavalierly elsewhere in the synoptics, are indicated with great detail here. If we follow Mark's account from the beginning of his ch. 14, we shall see that the narrative nevertheless comprises a number of units of tradition which were obviously independent of each other before he welded them into a whole.

1. 'Two days before the Passover and the feast of Unleavened Bread' the chief priests and scribes conspire to take and kill Jesus. This is 'the first precise date in the gospel' (Dodd, 133, p 22), although not as precise as Mark thought, since the passover begins on 14th Nisan and the feast of unleavened bread only on 15th; and so no given day can be 'two days before' both. The priests decide not to proceed 'during the feast, lest there be a tumult of the people'. But the sequel represents them as in fact acting against Jesus during the festival, and no indication is given that would explain a change of mind. Some commentators have therefore suspected that Mark has combined together independent units of tradition which did not agree as to chronology. Luke obviously perceived the inconsistency between the narrative that follows and Mk.'s statement that Jesus was not to be seized 'during the feast'; for he deleted these words, saying merely that the priests 'were seeking how to put him to death; for they feared a tumult of the people' (Lk. 22:2).

2. Jesus is anointed at Bethany in the house of Simon the leper. This is a unit of tradition independent of the passion narrative, and containing in itself no indication of when during Jesus' life the event occurred. Mark has inserted it here — breaking the natural connection between 1. and 3. — but Luke and John have given it different contexts. Mark represents a woman as pouring costly ointment over Jesus' head, whereupon some witnesses ask indignantly why it was 'thus wasted' and not 'sold for more than three hundred denarii and given to the poor'. Jesus defends her, saying: 'Wherever the gospel is preached in the whole world, what she has done will be told in memory of her'. Commentators concede that this perspective of world-wide evangelism hardly goes back to Jesus himself, and that the very phrase 'preach the gospel' belongs to the missionary vocabulary of the later gentile Church (314, p 372; cf. p 76 above). The words may have been put into Jesus' mouth in order to settle a controversy between Christians who considered the relief of the poor and Christians who considered worship the most important concern of the Church. Mark assimilated the story in order to show — in his usual way — that Jesus' Messianic dignity (as the true anointed one) remained unperceived by the majority. The woman's act is perceptive, but 'in the eyes of those who do not know the mystery it is only extravagance. Thus, as in the story of the triumphal entry, the secret of the Messiahship is apparently straining after a mode of open expression which, however, it cannot yet receive save in the form of a symbolic action' (87, pp 253, 255–6).

3. Judas, 'one of the twelve', offers to 'deliver up' Jesus to the priests, who promise him money. In Mt. this is further interpreted, on the basis of 'prophecy' in Zechariah 11:12, as a specific sum (thirty pieces of silver). Mark does not say that Judas' motive was financial, but that he went to the priests 'in order to deliver him up' and that they thereupon offered him cash. Matthew, in an attempt to make his behaviour more intelligible, attributes it to desire for money, and makes the traitor ask the priests: 'What will you give me if I deliver him to you?'[1][3]

4. The next incident takes place 'on the first day of Unleavened Bread, when they sacrificed the passover lamb'. In fact the Jewish practice was to sacrifice the paschal lamb on the day preceding the first day of the unleavened bread feast. (Matthew, better informed concerning Jewish customs, has deleted Mark's phrase 'when they sacrificed the passover lamb'). The incident consists in Jesus' dispatch of two disciples into the city to prepare the passover meal for himself and his disciples in an upper room. The word 'disciples' — rare in Mark's passion narrative, which refers instead repeatedly to 'the twelve' — occurs four times in this short passage, and this in itself suggests that we have here an independent unit which Mark has inserted. Jesus tells the two that they will find persons in the city who will enable them to make the necessary preparations, and his supernatural foresight 'has numerous parallels in legends and fairy tales' and also 'unquestionable affinity' with the 'difficult passage' 11:1–6,

where he sent two disciples to obtain a colt for his triumphal entry into Jerusalem (Nineham, 314, p 376). The present passage thus seems to be a tradition modelled on 11:1–6, and which the evangelist has likewise utilized as an introduction to an important incident (in this case, the Last Supper). A very important feature of the present passage is that it is the only indication that the evangelist wishes the Last Supper which follows (as 6. below) to be understood as a passover meal, although in fact it is by no means identical with a normal Jewish passover meal. The presumption is that the Christians for whom Mark wrote did not keep the passover as the Jews did, but celebrated a eucharist which they regarded as the true passover meal, and represented it as instituted by Jesus (cf. below, p 188).

5. 'And when it was evening he came with the twelve'. In view of the previous incident, one would have expected him to have come to the upper room with only ten (two having preceded him there). This suggests that the present incident was a tradition originally independent of the previous one. 'As they were at table eating' Jesus predicts that 'one of the twelve', 'one who is eating with me, will deliver me up'. Commentators concede that Jesus would hardly have said 'one of the twelve' (but rather 'one of you'), and that the whole wording shows the evangelist to have had Psalm 41:9 in mind: 'Even my bosom friend in whom I trusted, who ate of my bread, hath lifted his heel against me'. (In the fourth gospel this passage is actually quoted in this connection). In other words, it had been inferred from the OT that Jesus would be betrayed by someone who shared table-fellowship with him, and on this basis a scene was constructed where he sits at table with his closest associates and prophesies the treachery. Mark introduces not only this incident, but also the next one he records, with the words 'as they were eating'. The repetition would be unnecessary in a single composition and betrays that he is combining two separate units. Judas is not here mentioned – the culprit is merely said to be 'one of the twelve'. We may infer, then, that scrutiny of the OT had, before Mark, given rise to a tradition that Jesus would be delivered up by an intimate, and to a further tradition that Judas was this intimate. Mark has assimilated both, and by placing the latter earlier in his narrative (as 3. above), he invites the reader to identify the culprit, unnamed in this present pericope, with Judas. (Matthew expands Mark's narrative so as to make Jesus identify the traitor as Judas, and thus show his omniscience. But it then becomes unintelligible that the eleven do nothing to restrain the person identified in their presence as the future betrayer.)

6. The Lord's Supper is instituted 'as they were eating'. This is an independent unit of tradition which Mark has inserted here (see above p 27 and below, p 188).

7. The party goes to the Mount of Olives, where Jesus predicts the defection of the disciples (and says it is in accordance with prophecy) and his own resurrection appearance in Galilee. The latter prediction is obviously independent of the other material here and was inserted as an alien body into this context by Mark; for Peter, replying to Jesus, ignores

it, and only remonstrates against the prediction that they will 'all fall away'. This latter can be understood as a product of the persecuted Church of Mark's own day. Peter's experience, says Beare, 'was a continual reminder to the Church in the days of the persecutions to resist both undue self-confidence and undue pessimism over the lapsed. If the Prince of the Apostles could deny his Lord, every man must fear his own ability to stand fast; and if one who had denied his Lord could yet become the Prince of the Apostles, there was no need to despair of the restoration of any who renounced their faith under trial, and no justification for unforgiving severity towards the lapsed' (32, p 229).

8. 'They went to a place which is called Gethsemane'. Nothing is known of such a place. Mark presumably took this story from a tradition in which Gethsemane was already named, and, by including it here, he invites the inference (from 7. above) that Gethsemane is in the vicinity of the Mount of Olives. 'And he said to his disciples, "Sit here, while I pray".' But instead of doing so, he takes Peter, James and John with him further, and then tells them to wait behind and watch while he goes, alone, even further forward. Only then does he begin to pray. It seems, then, that Mark is combining a tradition which made him pray in the vicinity of disciples (not specified as the twelve in this incident) with a tradition which made him do so in the vicinity of three. The audience, according to Mk., is not only at a distance, but has fallen asleep. But, though there was no one to overhear Jesus' prayer, Mark knows and quotes its substance; and Luke, who has simplified the narrative by deleting all reference to these three companions, is able to record that an angel appeared to Jesus as he prayed. It is likely that Mark derived this prayer from a development of the tradition, recorded in Hebrews 5:7, that 'in the days of his flesh, Jesus offered up prayers and supplications, with loud cries and tears to him who was able to save him from death'. Such a tradition originated probably as an attempt to make clear, by drawing on material in the Psalms, the magnitude of the burden which Jesus took upon himself for our sakes. Mark, we saw (above p 102), insists that Jesus assumed this burden alone and deserted. This is one reason why the evangelist represents the disciples as asleep at Gethsemane. Luke stresses the weight of the burden even more than does Mark, for the angel who in Lk. appears to the praying Jesus has come to 'strengthen' him as his sweat 'became like great drops of blood falling down upon the ground' (Lk. 22:43–4). The fourth evangelist, on the other hand, evidently thought that a plea from Jesus to be spared death would depress his dignity; and so in Jn. there is no Gethsemane scene, and hesitation on Jesus' part to face death is reduced to a rhetorical question when he says (immediately after his triumphal entry into Jerusalem): 'Now is my soul troubled. And what shall I say, "Father, save me from this hour"? No, for this purpose I have come to this hour' (Jn. 12:27).

In Mk. Jesus returns at intervals to the sleeping disciples to admonish them, on one occasion with the words: 'watch and pray that you may not enter into temptation; the spirit is indeed willing but the flesh is weak'. This reads like an edifying construction of the Christian community. Schille, for instance, thinks that the injunction to 'watch', although ostensibly addressed to the disciples, really reckons with an audience of Christian worshippers (to whom the whole passage was ritually read) who are thereby urged not to be caught off their guard at the Lord's return. And Nineham quotes Rawlinson to the effect that 'for the martyr Church of Mark's day, the example of Jesus in the Garden, as contrasted with the behaviour of the three disciples, must have had special value as setting forth the spirit in which the vocation to martyrdom should be approached' (314, p 390).

9. 'Judas came, one of the twelve, and with him a crowd with swords and clubs'. Judas has already been introduced as 'one of the twelve' (see 3. above), and the repetition of the phrase here suggests that this story of Jesus' arrest was another originally independent pericope which Mark has woven into his whole. This impression is confirmed when we find that no hint has been given that Judas left the party during or after the Last Supper. (Only the fourth gospel motivates his appearance now at the head of an armed party by saying that he 'went out' after Jesus had earlier identified him as the one who will 'deliver' him.) The mob led by Judas has come from 'the chief priests and the scribes and the elders'. In the next chapter it is 'the chief priests, with the elders and scribes and whole council' who deliberate about Jesus. These all-inclusive lists are anti-Semitic rather than historical. They 'surely reflect the early Christian desire to emphasize the wide and general Jewish responsibility for Jesus' death' (Nineham, 314, p 411). Judas had told the mob that 'the one I shall kiss is the man'. But the narrative itself goes on to represent Jesus and his movements as well-known, and therefore Judas' role in helping the authorities to find and identify him as superfluous. For Jesus addresses his captors with the words: 'Have you come out against a robber with swords and clubs to capture me? Day after day I was with you in the temple teaching, and you did not seize me'. Of these two sentences, the first purports to make clear that he is not an insurgent; the second is inappropriate as an address to the mob, and the evangelist probably had the Jewish authorities in mind. (Lk. 22:52 alters Mk. so as to make Jesus direct his reproach at them.) Jesus adds: 'But let the scriptures be fulfilled'; and the incident is then terminated with the words: 'And they all forsook him and fled'. That he faced death completely alone and deserted is a feature which Mark reiterates and which guides his presentation of the passion material. This whole account of the arrest may well be but an imaginative expansion of the one idea that 'they all forsook him'.

In Mk. this is the last we hear of Judas. Matthew gives a supplementary legend about his death and Luke (in Acts) yet another legend about it. Mark concludes his ch. 14 with Peter's denial and Jesus' trial and condemnation by the Sanhedrin, and I will not repeat the account I gave of these incidents in JEC. From the beginning of Mark's ch. 15, the time is carefully marked off in three hour intervals. We learn, first, that the Sanhedrin 'held a consultation' and 'delivered' Jesus to Pilate. No indication is given here that this body has (according to the previous chapter) just completed a detailed 'consultation' concerning Jesus, and has condemned him as deserving death, so that any further consultation is unnecessary. Thus ch. 15, with its time-markers, is independent of what has preceded, and is complete in itself. (Bultmann regards the detailed Sanhedrin trial and condemnation of ch. 14 as a later, imaginative expansion of the bald tradition, preserved in 15:1, that the Sanhedrin 'held a consultation'. Mark, who knew both traditions, included both because he wrongly supposed them to refer to different incidents.) The sequence in ch. 15 is as follows:

1. The Sanhedrin 'delivered' Jesus to Pilate 'as soon as it was morning'.
2. He is crucified at 'the third hour' (i.e. 9 a.m.).
3. Darkness covers the whole land from the sixth to the ninth hour (noon to 3 p.m.).
4. At the ninth hour Jesus utters his last cry and dies.
5. 'When evening had come' (6 p.m. in Jewish reckoning) Joseph of Arimathea asks permission to take down the body from the cross.

These precise indications of time have often been explained by supposing that early Christian preachers had to be more definite about Jesus' passion than about his ministry in order to explain away his shameful death (cf. above, p 71). But Schille justly says that such apologetic teaching would not need to specify time (nor place) so closely, and that these specifications are better understood from the assumption that they were intended to give the gospel passion narrative a dramatic character. Earlier this century J. M. Robertson explained the undoubted dramatic features in the narrative by arguing that it is a transcript of what was originally enacted as a play (see JEC, pp 240–1). Schille offers the not entirely dissimilar explanation that the narrative was composed in order to be read to the community at the cultic celebration of the Lord's death. It would, he says, be made more dramatic by its precise references to time and place, and, in particular, the time of incidents specified in it as having occurred on the day of Jesus' death (hearing before Pilate, crucifixion, supernatural darkness, death and burial) would reflect phases of the community's annual protracted 'Good Friday' memorial service. And he stresses that, apart from the fact that the passion story does not in itself reflect historical interest in Jesus' biography, we are not entitled to presuppose such interest (conspicuously lacking in the first century epistles) as a basis for the cultic celebrations. On the contrary, the awakening of interest in the history at a certain stage of the development of the cult is one of the things to be explained (347, pp 170–98).

Both Robertson and Schille are able to offer impressive but not decisive evidence in support of their hypotheses; and in any case, as Burkill has rightly noted against Schille, Mark's passion narrative 'has a comprehensiveness which resists explanation in terms of a single type of motivation', and certainly includes elements devoid of liturgical import (89, p 246). Here, as elsewhere in the NT, the narrative as it at present stands is the outcome of a long process of redaction, which was inspired by mixed and even conflicting motives.

But I must return to Judas. I have tried to show that what was available to Mark was a number of traditions about the circumstances in which Jesus was 'delivered up', and that he has fitted these -- without, however, making clear what Judas betrayed, nor why – into a passion narrative which was moulded by complex factors (cultic interests, desire to encourage a persecuted Christian community, etc.). The isolated and even conflicting nature of the units of tradition, and the evangelist's failure to make Judas' behaviour plausible, are to be expected if the betrayal story is a legend. Earlier this century it was widely so regarded, and today Professor Enslin sets aside both Judas' betrayal and Peter's denial of Jesus as 'details added by Mark to make even more vivid the picture of the dreadful aloneness of Jesus, abandoned by all, even by his closest band, and of the bleak and unbroken despair, which the act of Easter was so tremendously to reverse' (148, p 139).[14] It seems to be quite generally the case that, if a hero is superlatively great, then his supporters invent a false friend who betrays him. So it is with King Arthur, with Roland, Siegfried, and many others. Mark's technique, then, so far from certificating his narrative as true, is almost universal as an effective device to heighten the tragic injustice of the hero's death.

Because the Judas incidents in Mk.'s passion narrative have only a loose connection with the whole, they have sometimes been set aside as interpolations. But they could not have been added to Mk. long after its completion, for they were obviously present in the Mk. on which Matthew and Luke drew, and which these two later evangelists adapted. And form-criticism has shown that loose connections are to be expected between gospel pericopes. Another argument that has been advanced in support of interpolation is that three Christian apologists of about the mid-second century write in such a way as to exclude the betrayal story from Jesus' biography. Aristides (who was familiar with a written gospel which included the virgin birth story) wrote ca. AD 140 that Jesus had twelve disciples, and that after the resurrection 'these twelve' went forth to preach the gospel. Justin Martyr (d. ca. AD 165) failed to mention Judas, even though he wrote in detail of the Last Supper and of Jesus' arrest. And in the extant fragment of the apocryphal Gospel of Peter, which gives a full account of the crucifixion and resurrection, the narrator tells how, after Jesus' death, 'we, the twelve disciples of the Lord, were weeping and were in sorrow' – no hint being given of defection by a member of this group. On the other hand, Papias mentioned Judas ca. AD 140.[15] It seems, then, more likely that the Judas story was distasteful rather than unknown to those writers who excluded it, who were certainly capable of adapting their facts to their apologetic needs.

Aristides, for instance, addressing his Apology for Christianity to the Emperor, says that Jesus was 'pierced by the Jews'. He may well have deemed it discreet to make no mention of Roman involvement. All these writers, including Papias, do not rely exclusively on the now canonical gospels for their information about Jesus. At that time, then, it was possible both to look beyond these four gospels, and to be selective in accepting their stories. That a gospel was not immediately regarded as definitive is obvious from the ways in which Matthew and Luke edit Mark's version of Jesus' life. And we shall have occasion to note further instances where later writers found an incident distasteful, even though it had been earlier acceptable.

Finally, modern critical discussion of Judas serves to illustrate how, in perfect good faith, purely imaginary biographies of Jesus can be constructed and offered as fact. Glover, for instance (in a book that has gone through many editions) is sure that Judas turned against Jesus the moment the latter admitted to his disciples that, although he was the Messiah, he would be rejected and put to death (Mk. 8:27–32). There is, in this gospel passage, no mention of Judas. But Glover writes:

> 'From that moment we may date the falling away of Judas, and what this man's constant presence must have meant to Jesus, ordinary experience may suggest. Shrewd, clever and disappointed, he must have been a chill upon his Master at all hours. His influence upon the rest of the group must have been consciously and increasingly antipathetic. Night by night Jesus could read in the faces which of them had been with Judas during the day. . . . And night by night he had to undo Judas' work. . . . The daily suffering involved in trying to recapture the man, in going to seek the lost sheep in the wilderness of bitterness, may be imagined.' (174, pp 128–9).

It can scarcely be other than 'imagined' in view of the total silence of the evangelists. (The synoptics pick up Judas – apart from including him in their lists of the twelve – only at their passion narratives.) If incidents in Jesus' life can be thus constructed, by extrapolation from 'ordinary experience', by scholars of the twentieth century, we can readily understand how much invention will have occurred, unchallenged, in less disciplined minds at the beginning of our era.

Notes to Chapter Five

1 Matthew's names (10:2–4) have often been set aside as an interpolation; for in verse 5 the evangelist has to work back to the topic of verse 1 by repeating instructions about healing and casting out spirits already specified there. Mark's list is likewise only tenuously connected with its context. The statement 'he appointed twelve to be with him' (3:14) is senselessly repeated (with an added definite article) in verse 16: 'And he appointed the twelve' (omitted in the RSV). The continuation, where he gives Simon his new name, does not lead naturally into the list which then follows (I give a literal translation): 'He gave a name Peter

to Simon, and James the son of Zebedee and John the brother of James . . .'. If this material was interpolated, Mark himself was the interpolator, for it was present in the Mk. known to Matthew and Luke, who straightened out what Kirsopp Lake calls the 'remarkably clumsy' Marcan text (269, p 95).

2 Of nine of the twelve, Acts reports nothing but the names. We learn (12:2) that Herod Agrippa beheaded James the son of Zebedee, and there is no further mention of his brother John. The few incidents which include John bring him in as an extra, accompanying Peter. Thus 3:4, reporting the cure of the cripple, tells that 'Peter looked on the lame man, with John'. Published English translations smooth this into something like: 'Peter fixed his eyes on him, as John did also' (NEB). But even this hardly disguises the fact that John's name was added as an afterthought, and that, in the tradition which reached the author of Acts, it was Peter who performed the cure.

3 He is not the son of Zebedee whose execution has been reported in ch. 12. The James who leads the Jerusalem community in Acts may reasonably be identified with the Jerusalem personage Paul calls 'James the Lord's brother' (Gal. 1:19); but I have disputed (see above, p 21) the usual assumption that this means the brother of Jesus.

4 253, p 364. In Acts 15:13ff James likewise appeals to the Christian Jews of Jerusalem by quoting a passage from the Septuagint which distorts the Hebrew original (see Harvey's admission, 201, p 456). And his purpose is, by such means, and in front of such an audience, to justify the mission to the gentiles!

5 Paul does indeed mention two 'apostles of churches' (RSV 'messengers of churches'); and he calls the Philippians' messenger to him their 'apostle' (RSV 'messenger'). These men are (as the Greek allows) apostles only in the sense of 'envoys' – persons sent on specific missions to carry out specific duties. But when he applies the term to himself, or writes of an 'apostle of Jesus Christ', he is using it in a technical sense to mean someone called to Christ's service by a supernatural revelation (24, p 45; 255, p 55; 352, pp 60–1).

6 There is a single occurrence of 'apostle' in Mk. and another in Mt. (I do not include Mk. 3:14, 'he appointed twelve, whom also he named apostles', as the subordinate clause is missing from most manuscripts and, as Taylor says (384, p 230), 'is probably an assimilation to Lk.'. It is given only in the margin of the RV and RSV and is omitted altogether by the NEB.) Mk. 6:30 records the return of the disciples with the words: 'the apostles returned to Jesus'. In Greek, 'apostle' means literally 'person sent out'; and the corresponding verb is used in verse 7 where Jesus sends the disciples out. Mark, then, is simply saying that those who had been sent out returned. Barrett (24, p 29) and Schmithals agree that there is here no implication that the disciples were 'apostles' in the sense that they held a particular office, and that it is our familiarity with Lk. that inclines us to read such a meaning into Mk.

Matthew's single use of the term occurs when he introduces his list of the twelve with the words: 'these are the names of the twelve apostles'. An important ancient manuscript (the Sinai-Syriac) has Mt.'s usual term 'disciples' here, and so some scholars hold this reading to be the original one (352, p 72). Even if 'apostles' is the correct reading, it occurs here in a passage which must be ascribed to Matthew's own editorial hand. (The list of names may be regarded as traditional material, which he assimilated, but the introductory words, 'these are the names of the twelve apostles', constitute his own editorial setting and so reflect ideas of his own day.) This would imply that, when Matthew wrote, the twelve had only just come to be known as apostles. If so, Luke, in insisting that they were apostles, was not introducing a totally new idea, but developing and exploiting a tradition which had originated very shortly before him.

7 Hare notes (198, pp 35–6) that Paul's own writings never suggest that he had been responsible for the death of any Christian, and that neither he nor other orthodox Jews would readily defend Torah by committing so great an offence

against Torah as murder. Bornkamm agrees that Paul the Pharisee could not have exceeded the penal power granted to synagogues, which allowed only scourging, ban and excommunication (56, pp 15—16). Later Paul the Christian was himself scourged by the synagogue (2 Cor. 11:24).

8 Mk. 3:13 further represents Jesus as choosing the twelve from a crowd, and this permits the inference that some of them could have been strangers to him up to that moment. Lk. 6:13 significantly excludes this possibility by making him choose them from men who were already his disciples.

9 Rev. in its present, final form is widely supposed today to have been written at the close of Domitian's reign, about AD 95. This tradition goes back to Irenaeus, who was guided in his choice of date by the references in the work to persecution, and by his belief that Domitian persecuted Christians (on which see above, pp 41f).

10 In a later work (191, p 266) Haenchen takes the view that Jesus abrogated the law. But he has to admit that 'Paul does not seem to have known of this and took the same decisive step on his own initiative' (cf. above, p 19).

11 Well-known is Schweitzer's theory that Judas betrayed to the priests not Jesus' identity (which they knew already) but the secret (known only to the twelve) that he claimed to be the Messiah; whereupon the priests were easily able to persuade the mob to regard him as a blasphemer and demand his execution. If Schweitzer were right, it would not in fact have been necessary for Judas to accompany anyone into the presence of Jesus, nor to kiss him. This confrontation implies identification of Jesus, not the passing on of some secret information about him. In any case, the 'Messianic secret' is, we saw (above, p 102), not part of the biography of a real Jesus, but an artificial element introduced by Mark. And Schweitzer is also wrong to suppose that one who claimed to be the Messiah would necessarily be denounced as a blasphemer. Bar Cochba, who made the claim, had it accepted by Rabbi Aqiba, the greatest of the Pharisaic leaders of the time. Robertson has noted, against Schweitzer: 'To assert that the Jewish people had long collectively expected a Messiah, and that at the same time they held it blasphemy for *any one* to claim to be He, is to put a flat counter-sense' (334, p 48).

12 Some have argued that it is no accident that 'Judas' is so nearly 'Judaeus', that he is in fact a mythical figure which represents the Jewish people. Gärtner (168, p 23) has noted that, even if one does not accept this theory, it is undeniable that the evangelists (particularly John) contrive 'a certain parallelism between Judas and the Jews' by stressing that the latter refused to accept Jesus and instead handed him over to Pilate (e.g. Jn. 18:35).

13 The price specified by Matthew is 'ridiculously low' (168, p 16) and the only other text which represents Judas as greedy is Jn. 12:4—6 (on which see p 91 above). Having thus excluded financial inducement as unhistorical, Gärtner concedes that 'the texts tell us nothing about Judas's own motives'.

14 Enslin sees that the silence of Paul, anxious to establish his authority against Peter, has very great force in showing that the story of Peter's denial cannot be historical (cf. above, p 125).

15 For the relevant information concerning Aristides, Justin, etc., see JEC pp 130, 179—83. In JEC I myself inclined to the view that this evidence stamps the Judas story as a late addition to the gospels.

6 Galilee and John the Baptist

(i) Nazareth and Jesus' Family

It is often asked why, if Jesus never existed, he was linked with so unlikely a place as Nazareth in Galilee. There was a strong Jewish tradition that the Messiah would be born as a descendant of David, and David is said (1 Samuel 16) to have hailed from Bethlehem in Judaea. Mt. and Lk. — the two gospels with birth stories — locate Jesus' birth there, even though the two narratives are in almost all other respects mutually exclusive.[1] The objection I have to answer is: while an association with Bethlehem can be explained as an inference from the OT, an association with Nazareth seems to be a brute historical fact which the evangelists did not find particularly edifying, but which was too well attested to be denied.

Now it is quite wrong to suppose — as many do — that there was any uniform view of the Messiah among Jews of the first century AD, and that traditions which did not give him one particular set of qualifications would be universally rejected (cf. above, pp 112f). We saw evidence (p 118) that it was not even agreed that he was to be of Davidic descent. Nor did the advocates of a Davidic Messiah all believe that he would come from Bethlehem. For Matthew, as for Jewish tradition up to his time, Jerusalem, not Bethlehem, was 'the city of David'. According to the OT, David spent his youth in Bethlehem, but there is no suggestion that he was there as king. Matthew, who lays great stress on Jesus' descent from David, does not say that Bethlehem was the home of David, nor does he mention the place at all in his account of Jesus' ancestry and birth in ch. 1 of his gospel. He introduces Bethlehem and names it as the place where Jesus was born only in ch. 2, in connection with the story of the magi, their visit to Herod and his slaughter of the innocents. When the evangelist explains that the birth took place there in fulfilment of prophecy, he quotes Micah 5:1ff which states (without mentioning David) that a ruler of Israel shall come forth from Bethlehem. Burger infers from all this (85, p 105) that Matthew took the name Bethlehem from traditions about Herod's dealings with wise men from the east and about his ferocious behaviour towards royal pretenders. Christians who knew such legends would also know Micah's promise of a ruler from Bethlehem, and the statement of 1 Samuel that Bethlehem was David's home. This would enable them to link the material concerning Herod with stories about Jesus' birth as a descendant of David. Matthew effected such a linkage, but the suture lines between the originally independent material of his chs. 1 and 2 are still visible.

Mark never mentions Bethlehem, locates Jesus' ministry not in Judaea but in Galilee and its environs alone, and makes him go to Jerusalem (seventy miles to the south) only once, at the end of his life. Later evangelists change this. Luke makes him equally active in Galilee and Judaea,[2] and John has it that he worked predominantly in Jerusalem, and made only occasional visits to Galilee.

Again, Mark (and Matthew who follows him) site the resurrection appearances exclusively in Galilee, while Luke confines them to Jerusalem. We had a striking instance (above p 71) where Mark imposes a reference to Galilee onto his material, and many agree that 'all the Galilee passages in Mk. are editorial' (361, p 28), that the editor's knowledge of Palestinian geography was imprecise and sometimes led him to posit itineraries (e.g. 7:24ff and 10:1) which 'baffle the commentators' (150, p 24). It is also widely accepted that Mark's purpose in stressing the importance of Galilee was to controvert Christian communities orientated towards Jerusalem. Galilee was an unsophisticated area, regarded with disfavour by strict Jewish piety because of gentile elements in its population and the consequent infiltration of Greek ideas and ways of life. Jerusalem, on the other hand, was the home of the Pharisees and the priestly orthodoxy. Galilee is thus appropriately made the source of a divine revelation whose ultimate destination is the gentiles – Mark was certainly writing for them – while Jerusalem is the location of its opponents. The theological representatives of Judaism, the scribes, are twice pointedly said (when they argue matters of doctrine with Jesus) to 'come down from Jerusalem' (3:22; 7:1). Lohmeyer has said that, for Mark, Galilee is 'the holy land of the gospel', as against Jerusalem, 'the city of deadly enmity to Jesus, of sin and death' (279, pp 29, 34). Some have found this formulation exaggerated, as he is well received when he enters Jerusalem, and is not unopposed in Galilee. But Mark does seem to associate Jerusalem with hostility in so far as he thinks of it as the seat of the religious authorities. The geography of the story is adapted to the theological need of underlining Christianity's break with Judaism, and of showing that the message of salvation is for lowly ones, in the despised Galilee of the gentiles.

Mark, then, was written at a time when Christian tradition had developed sufficiently to bring Jesus into conflict both with the Roman and with the Jewish authorities in Jerusalem. These facts alone would make it intelligible that the evangelist could think of him as a Galilean; for throughout the first century Galilee was notorious for its opposition to the authorities, while correlatively any person with a popular following in Galilee was, for them, suspect. Vermes, reviewing the evidence for unrest in the area, concludes that 'the conflict between Jesus and the religious and secular authority outside Galilee was at least in part due to the fact that he was, and was known to have been, a Galilean' (398, pp 43—4). It is equally possible to argue that, if this conflict is a legend, a Christian who accepted it as a datum could explain it to himself by *supposing* that Jesus had been a Galilean. That association with Galilee may thus be merely a stage in the developing tradition is suggested by Vermes's own observation of the 'remarkable' failure of the synoptics to mention any of the larger Galilean towns (Sephoris, Gabara, Tarichaeae, Tiberias). The link with Galilee, because it is invention, remained thin; just as the conflict with the Jerusalem authorities remains implausible since – again on Vermes's own showing (pp 36–7) – the synoptics represent the Sanhedrin as 'breaking every rule in the book' at their trial of Jesus, which in turn is poorly linked with his trial before Pilate; for the chief priests do not ask Pilate to confirm their own findings, but hand him over to the governor with a fresh charge.

Mark's Galilean orientation meant that he would not be interested in traditions about the birth of the Messiah in Bethlehem of Judaea, even had they been available at the time when he wrote. He seems to be following another and very different Messianic tradition – and I have stressed how varied these were – according to which the Messiah was to appear from some unknown place of concealment. This idea is voiced by the Jews who in Jn. 7:27 reject Jesus on the ground that 'we know where this man comes from', but 'when the Christ appears no one will know where he comes from'. In the apocalypse of Ezra of slightly earlier date the Messiah is symbolized by the figure of a man arising out of the sea, and the Most High explains the analogy by saying that, just as 'it is beyond the power of any man to explore out the deep sea . . ., in the same way no one on earth can see my Son . . . until the appointed day' (13:52). Again, the identity of the Messiah of the Similitudes of Enoch has been kept secret, but has been revealed by God to the righteous (62:7). These two apocalypses are particularly relevant as they embody a 'Son of man' Messiah which Mark favoured against the older view of a Davidic Messiah (cf. above, p 119). He would also have viewed traditions about a Messiah of obscure provenance more favourably than the well-known expectations concerning Bethlehem, for he is anxious to show that Jesus was not recognized as Messiah during his lifetime (cf. above, p 102). All these considerations would naturally lead the evangelist to make Jesus come from an obscure locality in Galilee.

It will perhaps surprise my readers that Nazareth (which is not named in any document earlier than Mk.) is mentioned only once in this, the earliest of the gospels. After the section on John the Baptist, we read that 'in those days Jesus came from Nazareth of Galilee and was baptized by John in the Jordan' (1:9). In four later passages (1:24; 10:47; 14:67; 16:6) he is given the title 'Nazarene', and this is almost invariably rendered in English Bibles as 'of Nazareth'. The English reader will thus, wrongly, suppose that Nazareth is repeatedly mentioned by Mark. The translators have obviously assumed that 'Nazarene' must necessarily mean 'the man from Nazareth'. But the assumption is arbitrary, as theologians are well aware. Bauer's standard dictionary states (27) that it is difficult to 'bridge the gap' linguistically between Nazarene and Nazareth, and that it is not unlikely that 'Nazarene' meant something else before it was interpreted as meaning 'of Nazareth'.

'Nazarene' is used in some extant documents as the title of a sect, not as a name having geographical associations. 'Jesus the Nazarene' is thus equivalent to, say, 'Henry the Quaker' or 'George the Methodist' (248, p 132). In Acts 24:5 the hostile Jews describe Paul as a 'ringleader of the sect of the Nazarenes'[3] – which does not here mean 'people from Nazareth' but 'Christians'. In the Talmud too the term is used as a Jewish term of abuse for Christians. It is an intelligible word-formation – *Nazoraios*, formed like *Pharisaios*, both denoting a sect. Some commentators hold that 'Nazarene' derives from a root NSR of a Hebrew word for 'observe', and means 'observant', 'devotee' – a term which could have been applied to any strict Jewish sect. And Epiphanius (d. AD 403) mentions pre-Christian Jewish sectarians called Nazarenes. They seem to have been ascetics, and Black thinks they may have been a sectarian survival of the old Nazirite. This word is derived from another Hebrew root, NZR, and means 'separated', 'consecrated'. It was used in ancient Israel to designate those who, like Samson, had devoted themselves to Yahweh by vowing certain abstinences. In Judges 13:7 an angel tells the mother of the yet unborn Samson that he will be 'holy to God from the womb'; and in verse 5 this is equated with 'a Nazirite to God' from the womb. This suggests that 'Nazirite' and 'Holy One of God' are synonymous. Now in Mk. 1:24 a demon calls Jesus both 'Nazarene' (not, admittedly, Nazirite), and 'Holy One of God'. This latter phrase is not known as a Jewish Messianic title, and is also rare in early Christian literature. The obvious parallel is with the phrase 'holy to God' in the book of Judges. And so some have inferred that the title 'the Nazarene, the Holy One of God', had originally nothing to do with Nazareth, but arose from regarding Jesus after the model of OT Nazirites like Samson (see 145, pp 90–3). Black has argued that the earliest Christians included groups which had taken Nazirite vows (44, pp 69, 74), and Lohmeyer points to accounts which represent not only John the Baptist but also James the brother of the Lord as Nazirites. It is thus possible to hold that the adjective 'Nazarene' originally designated a strict pre-Christian sect out of which Jesus and the Church emerged.

Theologians have shown (as we shall see) that the followers of John the Baptist constituted a sect which rivalled early Christianity. And his followers seem to have been Nazirites. This is reflected even in the NT, where John's birth is miraculously announced (in Lk.) in the same terms used by the angel who had foretold Samson's birth, and where his disciples are said to practise fasting. We shall see that there are episodes in the gospels which are today understood as Christian polemic against this rival baptist sect. And interpreting the term 'Nazarene' as meaning 'pertaining to Nazareth' is perhaps a case in point. In sum: Jesus is said, at the beginning of Mk., to come to John 'from Nazareth of Galilee'. Later he is four times referred to as 'Jesus the Nazarene'. It looks, then, as though Mark wishes us to understand 'Nazarene' to mean 'from Nazareth'. Kennard suggests that he has deliberately introduced this as a new interpretation of the term – an interpretation more acceptable to him than its older meaning, which was 'man belonging to some kind of ascetic sect', in particular to the sect which venerated John the Baptist. In order to give Jesus an importance of his own, and to raise him above such Nazarene movements, Mark has made him a Nazarene in a new and geographical sense (248, p 135). And the reason why the evangelist retained the old word (and did not simply change 'Nazarene' to 'of Nazareth') is, according to Kennard, that the word was important in exorcistic formulas. A survival of such a formula may be seen in Peter's ability to perform a cure 'in the name of Jesus Christ the Nazarene' (RSV 'of Nazareth', Acts 3:6).

I do not wish to be dogmatic, and freely admit that we do not know for certain what 'Nazarene' meant. But Mk.'s one mention of 'Nazareth of Galilee' does occur in a gospel which utilizes Galilee for theological purposes. And my point is that the case for linking Jesus with Nazareth is really no stronger than that in favour of the Bethlehem traditions; for both alike can be explained as inspired by theology. It is unjustified to contrast the two, as is usually done, by supposing that theological motive is obvious in the one case, but out of the question in the other.

When we pass from Mk. to later gospels, we find Jesus more firmly linked with Nazareth. In Luke's birth story, Jesus' mother lives there, and the evangelist has to introduce the myth of the census (on which see JEC, pp 25–8) to engineer his birth in Bethlehem. And we shall see (below, p 151) that in Lk. Nazareth is the point of departure for his whole ministry. His rejection there by his neighbours sends him out on his mission. In Mt., however, his family comes from Bethlehem, and settles at Nazareth unexpectedly, and only after his birth, whereby 'might be fulfilled what was spoken by the prophets', namely that 'he shall be called a Nazarene' (Mt. 2:23). There is no such prophecy in the OT, and so this verse is something of a puzzle. Black thinks that it is 'an intentional allusion to the manner of birth of Samson as analagous to that of Christ; and more particularly to Samson's vocation as a Nazir prefiguring that of Christ' (44, p 83). However we interpret Matthew's statement, it is clear that he has advanced from Mark's position by quite explicitly linking Nazareth with Nazarene. And this is not a surprising advance. Matthew's problem was to conclude the birth and infancy narrative (which he added to Mk.) in such a way as to ease the transition to the next chapter, which gives the material contained in Mk.'s opening chapter about Jesus' first public appearance, when he came to John for baptism 'from Nazareth of Galilee' (Mk. 1:9). Thus, after the birth in Bethlehem in fulfilment of scripture, a connection with Nazareth must be established, and this could be effected by representing residence in Nazareth as also a fulfilment of scripture, and by using the title 'Nazarene' (recorded in Mk. but not expressly in connection with Nazareth) for this purpose.

Jesus' association with Nazareth is not the only gospel detail that has been regarded as too unedifying to have been invented. At the beginning of this century Schweitzer (cf. above, p 73) and Schmiedel (348b, § 139) specified others which, they thought, would not have been recorded but for the fact that they were supported by a strong and ancient tradition. Schmiedel's examples of such 'pillar passages' from Mk. include Jesus' refusal to be called 'good', and his professed ignorance concerning the day when the world will end (13:32). In fact, these details are not as unedifying as Schmiedel supposed. In not allowing himself to be called good, Jesus is not ranking himself with mere sinners. Such an interpretation is 'not only unnecessary in itself, but is at variance with the entire synoptic portraiture' of him (Taylor, 384, p 426; cf. above, pp 73f). Jesus' point is that 'no one is good but God alone' (Mk. 10:18). Haenchen (191, p 356) instances three passages in Job where even heavenly beings are said to be imperfect compared with God. The fact that Matthew was disturbed by the Marcan passage and accordingly 'altered the sense of Jesus' remark' (Harvey, 201, p 164) does not mean that Mark intended anything derogatory. And, as Grant points out, Jesus' profession of ignorance as to when the world would end may have been concocted 'by the Church in order to counteract enthusiasm for eschatological timetables'.[4]

Another passage regarded as so unedifying that it must be true is the statement in Mk. 3:21 that 'the ones from beside' Jesus 'went out to seize him, for they said, "He is beside himself" '. Many English Bibles translate the phrase 'the ones from beside him' as 'his friends', but the meaning in this context is 'his family', for when they reach him in verse 31 they are identified as his mother and brothers. Matthew and Luke edit Mk. so as to suppress this hostility altogether,[5] but the Marcan tradition reappears in Jn. 7:5 as 'even his brothers did not believe in him'. Mark was obviously not its originator, for he tries to obscure the facts by an insertion between verse 21 and the natural continuation (verse 31), which furthermore reports the arrival of the mother and brothers in such a way as to suggest that the occasion is a mere family visit: they are said to be 'outside asking for him', with no suggestion that their purpose is to take him into custody. Even in verse 21, the evangelist, as we saw, avoids saying plainly who 'the ones from beside him' are. Mark, then, has toned down what was obviously an earlier tradition, and the question is, how could it have arisen if it was not true? Some commentators interpret 'being beside himself' to mean not madness but the kind of mystical exaltation which Paul contrasts (using the same verb) with being in one's 'right mind' (2 Cor. 5:13). But Mark may well have understood the comment to be really derogatory, and have included the incident because of his conviction that the Messiah would necessarily be 'despised and rejected by men' (Isaiah 53:3). He expressly makes Jesus remind his audience, in another context, that the scriptures say of the Son of man 'that he should suffer many things and be treated with contempt' (9:12). The narrative about the hostility of Jesus' family could thus be an example of the familiar tendency of early Christian writers to — in Grant's phrase — state the facts of Jesus' life 'as they could be inferred from the OT'.[6] Even if it is not, its origin is not hard to explain. It has been observed that early Christian prophets (on whom see above, p 28), or a community which held them in high regard, would have excellent motives to invent a scene in which Jesus is so preoccupied that he does not eat (Mk. 3:20), and whose friends consider him deranged and come to seize him; for these prophets were surely themselves subjected to just such a response. 'They too became over-wrought and would neglect to eat; their erstwhile companions would wonder about their sanity, and they would hear the derogatory charge' of being 'beside themselves' (54, p 510). Finally, we know that the earliest (the Pauline) references to Jesus' life on earth represent it as lived in obscurity, suffering and humiliation: and from such a premiss a tradition could easily arise that he had been rejected even by his own family.

The same can be said to account for the origin of another incident commonly adduced as inconvenient or distasteful to the evangelist — the story of Jesus' rejection (Mk. 6:1–6) in his 'own country' (RSV) or 'home town' (NEB) — Nazareth is not expressly mentioned. There is mention of 'the wisdom given him' (6:2). Jewish Wisdom literature tells (cf. above, p 105) of a series of agents of God's saving purpose who came to earth and were rejected by man. Hamerton Kelly discreetly suggests that 'the myth of Wisdom's messengers exercised some influence on Mark's Christology here' (193, p 50). Dodd points out that the divine men of Greek lore were commonly represented as rejected by their homeland. He quotes from a letter ascribed to Apollonius of Tyana: 'What wonder is it if, while other men consider me equal to God, and some even consider me a god, my native place, so far, ignores me?' (134, p 325).

Some of the details in this incident of Jesus' rejection were obviously added by Mark as embroidery to a more primitive tradition. Grässer has pointed to certain artificialities which betray the evangelist's editorial hand. Jesus is represented as (1) arriving at the scene of the action with his disciples; (2) teaching there in the synagogue on the sabbath, and (3) (initially) astounding the people by his teaching, the content of which is not indicated. This sequence seems to be a stereotyped schema which Mark has invented, for he has already used it on an earlier occasion, when narrating Jesus' activity in Capernaum (1:21–8). Equally stereotyped is the expression of the audience's astonishment. In both the Capernaum pericope and the one about his rejection in his own country, this astonishment is first stated in general terms, and is then said to have been occasioned by Jesus' teaching and by his miracles. Thus the people in the Capernaum synagogue say: 'What is this? A new teaching! With what authority he commands even the unclean spirits!' (1:27). This sequence — general surprise, reference to teaching and then to miracles — is appropriate at Capernaum, where he has both taught and cured. It is, however, inappropriate in the other pericope, where he teaches but is not alleged to work miracles. His audience is nevertheless represented as responding with the same sequence of three comments: 'Where did this man get all this? What is the wisdom given to him? What mighty works are wrought by his hands!' (6:2).

This astonishment then turns to hostility. How, they ask, can this person, known to be quite ordinary, have such powers? ' "Is not this the carpenter, the son of Mary and brother of James and Joses and Judas and Simon and are not his sisters here with us?" And they took offence at him'. He reacts by saying: 'a prophet is not without honour, except in his own country, and among his own kin, and in his own house'. A similar proverb is recorded as a saying of his in the Oxyrhynchus papyri and also in the Gospel of Thomas (cf. above, p 71), and Bultmann regards Mark's narrative as an ideal scene constructed from the proverb (83, p 30), but only very imperfectly adapted to fit it; for the incident does not take place in Jesus' 'house', nor are his 'kin' included among those who take offence at him here. ('His sisters' are said to be present, but are distinguished from those who reject him).

After Jesus has spoken the proverb, we are told that 'he could do no mighty work there, except that he laid his hands upon a few sick people and healed them. And he marveled because of their unbelief'. This again does not fit the proverb. If he thinks it normal for a prophet to be rejected at home, it is not consistent of him to be surprised at it. But this final sentence, which links his failure to perform miracles with the unbelief of the people, shows that one purpose of the whole story is to inculcate in the reader the importance of true faith. The evangelists repeatedly argue for the necessity of faith in him, both by making him himself declare it essential, and also by representing him as able or willing to help only those who believe in him.

It seems, then, that a tradition to the effect that Jesus preached without success in his own country was all that was available to Mark, and that the concrete details of the rejection there are the evangelist's own construction. It may well have been the missionary experience of the Christian communities of his own day that led him to assimilate and embroider such a tradition. They had come to regard Jesus as the first and as the ideal missionary, and naturally believed that he had experienced the disappointments and frustrations which they themselves knew went with missionary work. It is surely significant that, immediately after Jesus' rejection, the evangelist makes him dispatch the twelve on missionary work with the instruction: 'If any place will not receive you and they refuse to hear you, when you leave, shake off the dust that is on your feet for a testimony against them' (6:11).

The way in which Matthew and Luke adapt Mark's narrative shows how freely they manipulate their source for theological ends. Mark, we saw, has it that Jesus *could* do few miracles there, and that he 'marveled because of their unbelief'. Matthew (13:58) alters this in such a way as to stress more clearly the importance of faith in him: 'And he *did* not do many mighty works there, because of their unbelief'. Luke's adaptation of the story is highly instructive. First, he specifies the locality as Nazareth and transposes the incident to the very beginning of Jesus' ministry (4:16–30. Mark had placed it late in Jesus' activity in Galilee, perhaps because this rejection in his 'own country' helps to motivate his withdrawal to his own circle of disciples). In consequence Luke cannot (as Mark does) represent the disciples as witnesses, for they have not yet been called to Jesus' service: so in Luke's version he has to come to Nazareth alone and there is no mention of either disciples or family. Furthermore, Mark, who seldom gives any indication of the content of Jesus' preaching, had made a typically cryptic reference to his 'teaching in the synagogue' (6:2), without saying what he taught. Luke expands this by making him read the lesson at the sabbath service; but the passage allegedly read from the OT turns out to be a mixture of material from two different chapters of Isaiah, beginning with the words 'the spirit of the Lord is upon me because he has anointed me'. Jesus interprets this (4:21) as applying to himself, and Luke's motive in placing this incident so soon after his reception of the 'Holy Spirit' at his baptism (3:22) may have been to stress the importance of the spirit in his mission – as is reiterated in Acts 10:38: 'God anointed Jesus of Nazareth with the Holy Spirit and with power'.

Luke's account of the rejection discusses not only the prophet's relation to his home town, but also to Israel as a whole. Jesus gives two instances in which OT prophets were sent by God to help non-Israelites instead of their own people. The implication is that his work will save gentiles rather than Jews: and it is only at this point that the crowd, which has hitherto 'wondered at his gracious words' (4:22) becomes angry with him. Their anger is thus attributed to a cause of which there is no trace in Mk. In Lk. 'it is not so much that Jesus goes elsewhere because he is rejected, as that he is rejected because he announces that it is God's will and his mission to go elsewhere'. Luke has clearly 'reinterpreted the grounds for the rejection in the light of his own theological views' (Tannehill, 146, p 62).

(ii) John the Baptist

That the narratives of Jesus' birth and infancy (given only in Mt. and Lk.) were composed as prefaces to supplement Mark's account of Jesus' public career is obvious enough: for Matthew can report nothing of his life between his infancy and his baptism, and Luke knows of only one incident with which to fill this gap (the story of the twelve-year-old Jesus in the temple). Such prefaces were urgently needed to deal with heretics. Mark's silence concerning Jesus' life prior to his baptism as a full-grown adult enabled some of them to suppose that he had come straight from heaven, in human form but without a normal human body.[7] The two birth narratives also pursue the very different aim of showing that Jesus is the Son of God, and this is why they represent him as without a human father. As a divine personage he must needs have a divine father, even though his human mother is designed for the purpose of showing that he has a normal body.

Theologians who concede all this hold that, with Jesus' public ministry, we are on more solid biographical ground. Let us therefore investigate the incidents with John the Baptist, with which in the gospels this ministry begins.

The historical Baptist was a preacher with a following of his own which persisted in some areas into the second century, as is evidenced by Christian polemics against it (368, pp 201–2). He is unmentioned in the Talmud, probably because, like the Essenes (also not mentioned there), he was on the very fringe of orthodox Judaism. However, the Jewish historian Josephus mentions him as a 'good man' who exhorted the Jews to 'join in baptism' and was put to death by the tetrarch who feared the seditious effect of his preaching. The passage is almost certainly genuine. It is true that the text of Josephus was retouched by Christian scribes in other passages; but if this one had been interpolated by a scribe familiar with the gospels – the only other early source of information about the Baptist – then its account of the motives for his imprisonment and execution would not (as they in fact are) be entirely different from those specified in the gospel version of these events (cf. 360, p 346).[8]

That Jesus is associated in the gospels with this person whose historicity is attested by Josephus does suggest – so it is usual to argue – that Jesus too is historical. Against this, it is important to note that Josephus (whether his two references to Jesus are genuine or not) does not, in his single mention of the Baptist (in quite another passage), associate the two men; and that they are certainly not linked in the first century Christian epistles. Paul, who makes it clear that early Christianity was a baptist sect, never mentions John. In fact in none of the NT epistles, which refer so often to Jesus' suffering and death, is there so much as passing reference either to the mission of John or to Jesus' Galilean ministry. The gospels, which do link the two men, do so for theological reasons. Let us study the evidence.

The evangelists make the Baptist a prophet, since the revival of capacity to prophesy was expected in Messianic times. He speaks (Mk. 1:7) of a 'mightier one' who is to 'come after' him. 'He that cometh' is, in Christian usage, a Messianic title, probably derived from such passages as Psalm 118:26: 'Blessed is he that cometh in the name of the Lord' – words which were originally addressed to pilgrims coming up to the temple, but which Christians interpreted as referring to the Messiah. To prove that John is a prophet Mark introduces him with a quotation from the Septuagint of Isaiah 40:3 about 'the voice of one crying in the wilderness'. (The passage is available in the form required by Mark only in the Septuagint, and not in the Hebrew original). The 'wilderness' is where some of the Jews of this time expected the Messiah to appear. The idea was that the eschatological age of salvation would correspond to the early history of Israel, and a number of Messianic fanatics felt that they were called as the second Moses or Joshua to bring things to a head in the wilderness. Josephus tells (cf. above, p 69) of men who conducted multitudes there, and the association of wilderness and Messiah is alluded to when Jesus warns against 'false Christs' and against their supporters who say: 'Lo, here is the Christ! . . . Lo, he is in the wilderness' (Mt. 24:23–6). The Baptist, then, is located there because his activities denote the imminence of the end of time.

Mark and Matthew show how soon they expect the world to end by representing the Baptist as Elijah returned to earth (in accordance with the prophecy of Malachi concerning the last days).[9] Luke, however, writing when this expectation had faded, omits the passages in Mk. which hint that the Baptist is to be equated with Elijah,[10] and puts the Baptist to quite different use by making him the son of a priest and also of the priestly tribe through his mother, who is 'of the daughters of Aaron'. The Dead Sea Scrolls have revealed that a priestly Messiah of Aaron's line was among the manifold expectations of that time (see 229, pp 120–31), and Luke's purpose is – in the discreet words of a recent commentator (144, pp 69–70) – to 'clarify' these expectations by explaining that 'there is no Messiah of Aaron, but that in the Baptist the priestly tribe does contribute to the Messianic hope'.

For Mark, the Baptist as a new Elijah is forerunner of Jesus. Wink has shown that Mark designates John the *beginning* (1:1) of the gospel of Jesus because Elijah must come *first* (9:11) to restore all things; and that in Judaism this 'restoration' had come to be conceived as a mass repentance on the part of Israel. Hence Mark's allegation (1:5) that 'all the country of Judaea and all the people of Jerusalem went out' to John who was preaching repentance. This is agreed to be not history but eschatology: it emphasizes what was expected to happen at the appearance of the herald of the end of the world, and also shows this herald as Elijah. If 'all' have repented at his word, then he is clearly Elijah who is to come. Mark is so concerned to make John Jesus' forerunner that he insists that John was removed from the scene by imprisonment before Jesus began to preach: 'After John was arrested, Jesus came into Galilee, preaching the gospel of God' (1:14). This reference to John's arrest is not appropriate here – his fate subsequent to arrest is narrated only much later (6:14ff) – except as a device to separate his activities from those of Jesus. The same end is served by the statement of 6:14–16 that Herod, on hearing of Jesus' miracles, regarded him not, as some did, as Elijah, but as John the Baptist returned to life. In 8:28 Jesus is again taken for the resuscitated John. As Wink observes, 'those who expressed this opinion could not have seen the two of them working together or known of Jesus' baptism by John' (410, p 9). In fact the opinion could have been rationally held only by those who believed that Jesus had been born after John's death.

Whatever the origin of this tradition, it enabled Mark to introduce his story of John's death. As it is not easy to discern what motives underlie this story, commentators have vigorously defended its historicity. An exception is Haenchen, who, after noting the discrepancies between the accounts of Mark and Josephus, points to obvious legendary elements in the former. Herodias' daughter dances before Herod and his 'chiliarchs', and so pleases him that he offers to give her whatever she asks, 'even half of my kingdom'. Herod was in fact not a king, but a tetrarch. He had no kingdom to give away, and could do nothing without the consent of Rome. The mention of 'his chiliarchs' (commanders of 1,000 men) gives another legendary embellishment of his real power. Mark may have been glad to include the story in order to fill the gap between Jesus' dispatch of the twelve on their mission of preaching repentance, and their return to him. Without this story of the Baptist's death, the 'going out' of the twelve recorded in 6:12 would be followed directly by their return in 6:30 (191, pp 239–42). Furthermore, one motive from which Mk. was written was to encourage Christians to remain steadfast under persecution (cf. above, pp 62, 83). From this premiss it is understandable that John should be portrayed as 'Elijah incognito whose sufferings prepare the way of the Lord and serve as an example to the persecuted Christians' (Wink, 410, pp 13, 110). John is said in the Greek to have been 'handed over' (1:14) – a catchword which is used apropos of Jesus' passion (cf. above, p 25); and the story that Pharisees *and Herodians* combined against Jesus (3:6 and 12:13) is likewise inspired by a contrived parallelism between him and John: his typical opponents join with the people of the man who had the Baptist executed in order to plot his death (cf. 257).

Mark's narrative (1:2–8) about John's public preaching makes no mention of Jesus and forms a unit complete in itself, in a gospel which is agreed to consist largely of short and originally independent stories. Some Christian scholars hold that this particular unit is pre-Christian, and belonged originally to a document of the sect which venerated the Baptist. For although Mark naturally means us to understand Jesus as the 'mightier one' who is to follow John, the original reference may have been to a purely supernatural figure, or even to God himself; for 'might' is a common predicate of the divinity (e.g. Rev. 5:12 and 7:12). In Mk. 1:4 John's baptism figures as a sacrament effecting forgiveness of sins – no mean function, as we see when Jesus' claim to perform it is designated 'blasphemy' by the scribes, on the ground that God alone can forgive sins (Mk. 2:7). There is thus no room for a human Messianic figure to follow the Baptist; the judge of the world will shortly appear to ratify the classification of men effected by his baptism.

This impression is confirmed by the way Matthew and Luke supplement Mk. 1:7, drawing on ancient material from the common source Q they used in addition. This part of Q could well have been originally a Baptist document: it tells that the coming mightier one 'will baptize with fire', i.e. will destroy in a terrible judgement, very shortly to occur, all who do not repent and submit to John's baptism. The coming one is here said to have 'his winnowing fork in his hand, and he will clear his threshing floor and gather his wheat into his granary, but the chaff he will burn with unquenchable fire' (Mt. 3:11-12; Lk. 3:16—17). Jesus is introduced immediately after these accounts of John's preaching, and by this juxtaposition the evangelists contrive to give the impression that he is the coming mightier one. But they may have simply combined traditions about the Baptist with Jesus-traditions with which they had no original connection.

Another tradition absent from Mk. but present in both Mt. and Lk. is the Baptist's inquiry from prison whether Jesus is 'he who is to come, or shall we look for another?' (Mt. 11:2—6). This tradition has also been regarded as reflecting not the historical situation of the Baptist and Jesus, as the evangelists allege, but rather that of their followers of a later generation who were in competition. Jesus replies to the Baptist's query by alluding to his own miraculous powers, and then declares that John (presumably because he is Jesus' predecessor) is greater than any ordinary mortal, yet inferior to 'the least in the kingdom of heaven' (Mt. 11:11). Those in the kingdom are surely, for Matthew, the members of the Christian community, and the view here ascribed to Jesus is intelligible as a Christian attempt to discredit a man venerated by a rival group. A narrative in Acts betrays the same tendency very clearly. It tells of a convert to Christianity in Ephesus who 'knew only the baptism of John' (18:26) and had in consequence never heard of the Holy Spirit. Paul then explains to the Ephesians generally that John had taught belief in 'the one who was to come after him'; and they thereupon allowed themselves to be 'baptized in the name of the Lord Jesus; and ... the Holy Spirit came upon them' (19:4—6). The point of the story is to make clear to Christians the value of true Christian baptism and so render them immune to the propaganda of the Baptist sect.

The most elaborate attempt in the synoptics to link John and Jesus is the account of the birth and infancy of the two in Lk. 1—2. (This has no parallel in the other gospels, and is placed before the details of John's public ministry in ch. 3 which Lk. has in common with Mk. and Mt.) Luke begins (1:1—4) with a prologue in 'elegantly worded Greek, on the model of the prefaces to ancient histories such as those of Herodotus, Thucydides and Polybius'. But the rest of ch. 1 and the whole of ch. 2 (comprising the two birth and infancy narratives) are written in a clumsy style; 'the grammar, vocabulary and thought forms are unmistakably Semitic' and include 'phrases which no Greek author in his senses could have written' (368, pp 49—50). The opening of the third chapter reads like the beginning of a new book: 'In the fifteenth year of the reign of Tiberius Caesar, Pontius Pilate being governor of Judaea, and Herod being tetrarch of Galilee and his brother Philip tetrarch of . . .' etc. It thus seems highly probable that the infancy stories existed separately before they were assimilated by Luke into his gospel. Furthermore, the story of Jesus' supernatural conception given in ch. 1 seems to have been originally quite independent of the narrative of his birth and infancy in ch. 2;[11] and there is wide agreement that not all of the material relating to the Baptist in ch. 1 was originally Christian. In particular, 1:5–25 (the angel's announcement of the Baptist's birth to his father, the priest Zechariah) lacks anything specifically Christian, and exalts the Baptist to the point of designating him the forerunner not of the Messiah, nor of 'the Lord' (as in 1:76, where the word can be taken to mean Jesus) but of God himself: John will 'go before him [God] in the spirit and power of Elijah' (1:17).[12] Such a statement would seem to represent non-Christian material which Luke has assimilated.

The fourth gospel brings Jesus and the Baptist into close contact, making their ministries overlap. In the synoptics they meet only at Jesus' baptism, after which John is removed from the scene by imprisonment before Jesus begins preaching. But the fourth gospel insists that, at the beginning of Jesus' ministry, John was still free and still baptizing (Jn. 3:22–4). By making the two simultaneously active, the fourth gospel is able to stress that Jesus had a much greater effect than the Baptist (4:1) and also that the latter ungrudgingly acknowledged Jesus' superiority by encouraging his own disciples to transfer their allegiance to him (1:35–7). Why the Baptist nevertheless went on baptizing in independence of Jesus (as 4:1 alleges) is not made intelligible. That the first disciples whom Jesus called were formerly disciples of the Baptist is alleged only in the fourth gospel. It may well be historical that some early Christians had formerly belonged to the sect which venerated him. This would form an intelligible basis for a later Christian narrative which made him himself refer his followers to the historical Jesus.

In the fourth gospel there can be no question of any inquiry from the Baptist (of the kind recorded in Mt. and Lk) to ascertain which of the two men is the greater. His inferiority is emphasized even in the prologue, where he is said to be 'not the light'; he merely 'came to bear witness to the light' (1:8). He is then made to hail Jesus with a series of Messianic and divine titles, and to argue for Jesus' priority by positing his pre-existence: 'After me comes a man who ranks before me, for he was before me' (1:30). It is widely agreed that such evidence establishes that the evangelist is concerned to refute the claims of the sect which took the name of John the Baptist, and which seems to have been a dangerous rival of the early Church in some areas.

Jesus' baptism by John is often included (e.g. by my critic the Rev. Dr D. P. Davies) among the gospel details which – it is alleged – so far from betraying why they were invented, seem inconvenient to the evangelists. Jesus' submission to baptism is said to constitute an admission of John's superiority which runs counter to the evangelists' theological expectations. Thus Mark, having said that John proclaimed 'baptism of repentance for the forgiveness of sins' (1:4), goes on to introduce Jesus and to represent him as simply submitting to it. If these two traditions could be proved to have been originally connected, the argument would have more force. But I have given evidence that the phrase characterizing John's baptism occurs in a tradition about the Baptist that was possibly independent of all traditions concerning Jesus. Mark is able to link it without embarrassment to his account of Jesus' baptism, probably because he was aware of the Jewish belief that the Messiah would be unknown as such to himself and others until anointed by his forerunner (see JEC, p 319); and also because his attention is centred on the supernatural phenomena accompanying the incident, which enable him at the very beginning of his gospel to make clear Jesus' divine status (1:10–11).[13] I am surprised that Dr Davies, who is among those of my critics who accused me of not being up to date in my reading, should rely on an argument which goes back to Schmiedel's 'pillar passages' (discussed above, p 148), when eminent theologians today concede that the story of the baptism may well have 'been formed in the tradition of the Church, as a result of later reflection upon the person and work of Jesus as a whole' (Evans, 150, p 12). Haenchen regards the story as a legend inspired by the baptismal practices of Christian communities. They believed that baptism imparted the spirit, and so they naturally assumed that Jesus himself had received it at baptism. Mark's account is thus based 'not on an old historical tradition, but on the projection of early Christian experience onto the life of Jesus' (191, p 62). As Burkill discreetly puts it: in Mk. 1:10, where he at baptism receives the spirit, we have 'the prototype of Christian baptism' (86, p 14).

(iii) Conclusion: the Evangelists as Editors

Paul, who was converted to Christianity about AD 35 and wrote his extant epistles before AD 70, knows nothing of Jesus' association with John the Baptist, nor with Nazareth, and never calls him a Nazarene or a Nazirite. Other epistle writers of the first century are equally silent. Mark, whose gospel is conventionally dated at about AD 70, but who may well have written much nearer the end of the century, wrote very differently of Jesus. When one considers the immense changes in the life of the Church which occurred between Paul and Mark – changes in its constituent elements, its geographical extension, and in its religious outlook – we cannot be surprised to find that Mark alleges things which were unknown to earlier writers. We should be ill-advised to accept them as authentic.

That evangelists had no hesitation in making Jesus say and do what is in fact representative of their own theology is apparent from comparison of their gospels. What we are to understand him to have said at the Last Supper, on the cross, and by way of instruction to the eleven after his resurrection, depends entirely on which gospel we consult. One of the most instructive examples is Matthew's report of the Last Supper, and to appreciate it we must go back to the narratives of Jesus' baptism. Mk. 1:4 has it that John preached 'a baptism of repentance for the forgiveness of sins' – even though, in the view of the Jewish lawyers who speak in 2:7,

157

God alone can forgive them. Matthew was obviously not prepared to credit the Baptist with such powers, and assigned to Jesus the function of 'saving his people from their sins' (1:21) by the sacrificial shedding of his blood in death. Matthew seems to have subscribed to the standpoint of Hebrews 9:22: 'Without the shedding of blood there is no forgiveness of sins' – a proposition which may represent Christian polemic against a baptist sect. And so he studiously deleted the phrase 'for forgiveness of sins' in his adaptation of the Marcan account of the Baptist's activities – he mentions (3:6 and 11) the 'repentance' specified by Mark, but not the forgiveness – and inserted it into the report of Jesus' words at the Last Supper. In Mk. 14:24 this reads: 'This is my blood of the covenant, which is poured out for many'. To this Mt. 26:28 adds 'for the forgiveness of sins'. This is conscious literary adaptation of an existing text, not historical reporting.

Such details show how unwise we should be to place reliance even on the earliest extant gospel. If later evangelists were prepared to adapt the written Marcan account with considerable freedom, we must allow that Mark may have treated his sources (which have not come down to us) with the same lack of respect. Indeed, we were able to discern some features in his account (the Messianic secret, the contrast he points between Galilee and Jerusalem) which are artificial and which would not be present if his aim had been simple and straightforward reporting. Furthermore, we must allow for much greater freedom on the part of innumerable teachers and preachers before Mark, who transmitted the tradition as they remembered it, as they had heard it from another, not as it lay fixed in written form.

I am not imputing fraud to these early Christians. Neither preachers nor evangelists were detached historians, and their criterion of the truth of what they related was not the correspondence of their reports with what actually happened, but rather the faithfulness of these reports to the Christian community's picture of Jesus, which itself was determined by the manifold forces reviewed in this book. These writers were convinced that they had a higher basis for their understanding of Jesus than that of mere historical fact. It was not dishonest of Luke to change the sequence of events posited by his source material so as to make Jesus deliver an inaugural sermon in Nazareth (see above, p 151). If an event had to occur at a particular moment in order to have the theological importance that he attributed to it, then the evangelist will have felt confident that it did occur at that moment, even if this meant a critical approach to his sources. Such adaptation of the Marcan narrative is no more dishonest than the practice of Christians of today who reject or interpret symbolically those gospel traditions which they find unpalatable. According to the late Professor Dodd, for instance, the modern Christian knows 'instinctively' that Jesus could not have cursed the fig tree (130, p 213) although two gospels represent him as doing so. Such 'instinctive' insight was surely as strong in the formative years of Christianity as today.

1 That the birth and infancy narratives of Mt. and Lk. 'contradict each other in essential features' (Kümmel, 268, p 38) is no longer seriously disputed. Stendahl concedes that their differences are 'more drastic' than any other in the canonical gospels, even than the discrepancies between the synoptics and Jn. (145, p 96). I discussed this whole matter at length in JEC.

2 For instance, the statement of Mk. 1:39 that Jesus preached in the synagogues of 'all Galilee' is corrected to 'the synagogues of Judaea' in many ancient manuscripts of Lk.

3 While Mark uses the form 'Nazarene', Mt. has 'Nazorean', and Lk.-Acts uses both. They are regarded as not significantly different, and the Marcan one as an example of the 'Latinisms' which characterize his work, and which were not uncommon in the Greek of the Roman Empire (see Bacon, 11, p 164) as a result of continual contact with military, fiscal and civil authorities.

4 182, p 286. Cadbury includes Mk. 10:18 and 13:32 among logia inspired by the idea of 'Not I, but God', reflecting 'a feeling for the humility and human kinship of the Son of man' (93, pp 120–1). He implies that gospel readers of today are apt to assume that the opposite standpoint (that Jesus is to be linked as closely as possible with God) must necessarily dominate the synoptic tradition. But he rightly insists that in fact 'mixed motives' are discernible in it, and that none of them can be singled out as embodying traditions which are necessarily primitive, let alone historical.

5 Matthew and Luke did not incorporate Mk. 3:20–1 into their gospels, and they deleted the words 'among his own kin' in their adaptation of Mk. 6:4. Acts 1:14 designates Jesus' mother and his brothers as zealous believers.

6 178, p 35. It is true that Mk. 9:12, which echoes Isaiah, does not seem to fit its context and is often set aside as an interpolation. Bultmann thinks it was inserted by someone familiar with the parallel passage in Mt. 17:12 (82, p 31; cf. Nineham, 314, p 240). And Hooker has recently shown that there is little in Mk. (or even Mt. – in contrast to Lk.-Acts) that links Jesus with the suffering servant of Yahweh in Isaiah. Alfaric (3, p 95) traces Mark's account of Jesus' rejection to Psalm 69:8: 'I have become a stranger to my brethren, an alien to my mother's sons'.

7 Cf. above, p 48. That Luke's birth story was written to refute 'Docetist' heresy of this kind is suggested by the fact that, soon after, Marcion rejected Luke's first two chapters because he held that Jesus descended to earth in adult form at the date assigned by Lk. 3:1 to the beginning of his public ministry. To establish the reality of Jesus' body, Luke goes so far as to make him parade his 'flesh and bones' even after the resurrection (24:39).

8 233, Bk. 18:5, 2. Scobie (368, pp 21–2) has given a good summary of the reasons for not accepting as genuine the passages about Jesus and the Baptist in the version of *The Jewish War* (Josephus' other major work) written in a dialect of Old Russian, and extant in manuscripts of the fifteenth and sixteenth century which were discovered in 1866.

9 The identification of the Baptist with Elijah is explicit in Mt., but only hinted at in Mk. According to Malachi 4:5 and Ecclesiasticus 48:1ff Elijah is to prepare the way for God himself in the last days. According to some rabbinical traditions, however, he is to prepare the people for the Messiah. Here, as in other respects, Jewish thinking about the end of the world is far from uniform.

10 Mk. 9:9–11 and Mt. 11:14 have no equivalent in Lk., nor has Mk. 15:35, where the dying Jesus is interpreted as calling on Elijah. Mk. 1:6, where John's dress is described in a way that is meant to be reminiscent of Elijah's, is also cut by Luke, who will allow only that John was a prophet *comparable* with Elijah, possessing the latter's 'spirit and power' (1:17).

11 The annunciation story of Lk. 1:26–38 represents Mary as the virgin who knows

no man, and who is totally at a loss to understand how she is to bear a child. In 2:7 and 48, however, Jesus is said to be the first born son of Joseph and Mary. Luke tries to harmonize the two narratives by introducing Joseph as Mary's fiancé in 1:27, but this makes nonsense of her statement to the angel in verse 34 that she has no acquaintance with a man which could lead in due course to her bearing a child (cf. JEC, p 14). Thus, 1:26–38 and ch. 2 were originally independent of each other. (2:21 was added by Luke to provide a link with the material of the first chapter.) Ch. 2 itself consists of three originally independent stories: the homage of the shepherds at Jesus' birth; Simeon's recognition of him as the saviour when he was presented in the temple; and the astonishing teaching of the twelve-year-old boy in the temple. Each of the stories aimed to show exactly when it was that his true significance was recognized, and Luke has simply combined them into a sequence (see 128, pp 217–18).

12 Thyen takes the description of the Baptist in Lk. 1:78 as 'light from on high' as also of Baptist (not Christian) origin, and argues that it means 'the redeemer come from heaven'. He points to parallels in the way the priestly Messiah is described in the Qumran literature and the Testaments of the Twelve Patriarchs. His conclusion is that 'this late Jewish literature is the reservoir from which devotees of the Baptist drew the material to make a Messiah of their master' (128, pp 116–17, 123; cf. Vielhauer, 400, pp 37–40).

13 Matthew does show signs of embarrassment, for he omits Mark's phrase about remission of sins, and represents the Baptist as hesitating to baptize Jesus; while the Lucan wording deliberately disguises the fact that it was John who performed the baptism (Lk. 3:21–2). The fourth gospel retains only the descent of the Holy Spirit (1:32) and omits the baptism altogether, together with other synoptic episodes which might be understood as depressing Jesus' dignity. However, we have already had examples to show that what was embarrassing to later evangelists need not have appeared so to Mark.

7 Was Jesus a Political Rebel?

(i) Introduction

A number of recent scholars have argued that Jesus was executed as a rebel against Roman authority; that the evangelists, in order not to offend the Romans, tried to suppress all mention of his political activity and pretended that he was condemned by Jews for heresy — not by Romans for sedition; and that evidence of his revolutionary behaviour and connections nevertheless shows through the gospels, even though they have been most carefully edited to erase it.

When Christians began to believe that Jesus had suffered under Pilate, it is intelligible enough that some of them should also have supposed that Pilate had executed him as a political rebel (cf. above, pp 59ff). There is thus no difficulty in accounting for the origin of such traditions, and even for their partial survival in the gospels (although, as we shall see, the evidence adduced to show that certain gospel incidents are to be interpreted as such survivals is often far from convincing). There are, however, three obvious difficulties against the supposition that a historical Jesus was actually executed as a rebel:

(i) All Christian documents earlier than the gospels portray him in a way hardly compatible with the view that he was a political agitator (see chapter 2 above).

(ii) If his activities had been primarily political, and the evangelists were not interested in — or deemed it inexpedient to mention — his politics, then what was the motive for their strong interest in him? How did they come to suppose that a rebel, whose revolutionary views they tried to suppress in their gospels, was the universal saviour?

(iii) If such an episode as the cleansing of the temple was not a religious act (as the gospels allege) but an armed attempt to capture the building and to precipitate a general insurrection, then why does Josephus say nothing of it? As Trocmé has observed (395, p 16), a military attack on the temple would not have been ignored by this writer who was so concerned to show the dangers of revolt and violence. Josephus' silence is corroborated by the positive affirmation of Tacitus that there was no disturbance in Palestine under Tiberius (AD 14–37), whereas the preceding and following reigns were characterized by rebellion and unrest there (*Historiae* 5:9).

The advocates of a politically orientated Jesus fail to give an adequate solution of these three obvious difficulties of their case. Mr Maccoby, the

161

most recent writer to make Jesus into a freedom fighter, supposes – in answer to the first difficulty – that early Christian documents give gentile distortions of Jesus' life, and were written by 'death-worshipping mystagogues' who 'exalted the Roman cross into a religious symbol' and saw 'more meaning in Jesus' death than in his life' (285, p 136). He names Paul as the chief culprit in this connection. But if the earliest literature is the least reliable, how are we to learn the true facts? Mr Maccoby thinks that 'the only NT document which appears to have survived . . . with only slight Paulinist revisions is the Epistle of James, which is the work of . . . Jesus' own brother' (p 236). I should like to know what evidence supports the view – rejected by many Christian commentators – that it was written before the very end of the first century, let alone by Jesus' brother. The author of this epistle, which exhibits what Beare has called 'the finest Greek in the whole NT' (34, p 59), does not even himself claim to be Jesus' brother (see above, p 40). He has nothing at all to say of the man Jesus (see JEC, pp 151–3), and so Maccoby has to reconstruct the 'facts' by divesting the canonical gospels of what he takes to be their Pauline veneer. He is confident that he can distinguish 'the facts of Jesus' life and death' from 'the interpretations . . . added by the gospels' (p 124), which he approaches with the conviction that 'there must be some kernel of truth' (p 22). He even knows of anti-Roman elements which Jesus' preaching 'must have contained' even though 'omitted from the gospels' (p 130). This does not prevent him from censuring other scholars when he finds them propounding 'a highly imaginative theory based on nothing whatever in the text' (p 298).

The second difficulty I have specified – why Christians should wish to turn a political rebel into what Maccoby calls 'an ineffectual angel and eventually an object of worship' (p 209) – he answers as follows. Jesus' immediate supporters at Jerusalem refused to believe he was dead, and thought that he 'had been brought back to life like Elijah, and would soon return to lead a new attack on the Romans which this time would be successful'. This resurrection would not make him divine, for 'the same belief had been held about previous figures in Jewish history without involving any belief in their divinity' (p 219). But when his story fell into gentile hands, the idea of his resurrection enabled it to be assimilated to pagan mystery cults and their divine dying and rising saviours. It is clear that this solution to the difficulty involves Maccoby in assumptions about post-crucifixion Jerusalem Christianity which, we saw in chapter 2 above, are not substantiated by what documentary evidence is available. The third difficulty – Josephus' silence – he meets by supposing that Jesus' rebellion was too insignificant to be noted (p 199), and was based more on apocalyptic expectations than on military preparedness. For instance, he issued 'only two swords' to his disciples to defend him from arrest because he was expecting God to intervene on his side – for such a miracle he prayed in Gethsemane (p 194). The incident of the two swords is given only in Lk., and we shall see below whether Maccoby is justified in his confident affirmation that 'Luke could have had no possible motive in inventing it' (p 188). Here I am concerned with the silence of Josephus, and Maccoby admits (p 93) that this historian does note the activities of other relatively insignificant rebels whose activities were tempered by apocalyptic ideas. Furthermore, the more insignificant Jesus is made, the harder it is to understand why Paul and others should so rapidly have come to regard him as a supernatural being. (If, on the other hand, he was from the first so regarded, and in fact never lived on earth, then his earthly insignificance – on which Paul insists – is a natural corollary: cf. above, p 97).

Mr Maccoby is avowedly attempting no more than 'to make available to the reader a good deal of recent scholarly work on the *political* significance of the events described in the gospels' (p 9). So I may appropriately turn from him to the principal scholar on whom he relies, namely the late Professor Brandon.

(ii) The Temple Cleansing and the Barabbas Incident

Brandon holds that the temple 'cleansing' was a revolutionary act, and the direct cause of Jesus' arrest (66, pp 331 ff). Mk.'s version of the incident runs (11:15–18):

> 'And they came to Jerusalem. And he entered the temple and began to drive out those who sold and those who bought in the temple, and he overturned the tables of the money-changers and the seats of those who sold pigeons; and he would not allow any one to carry anything through the temple. And he taught, and said to them, "Is it not written, 'My house shall be called a house of prayer for all the nations?' But you have made it a den of robbers". And the chief priests and the scribes heard it and sought a way to destroy him; for they feared him, because all the multitude was astonished at his teaching.'

The temple sacrifices were of sheep or (in the case of poorer Jews) pigeons. Pilgrims purchased them in the temple forecourt instead of bringing them to Jerusalem, for if the animals were injured in transit the priests would reject them as unfit for sacrifice. Hence the presence of 'those who sold and those who bought in the temple'. Money changers had also to be there, since it was not permitted to pay the temple tax in pagan coins: these had to be exchanged for coins minted in Tyre (regarded as the nearest approximation to Jewish currency in a Judaea which, under Roman rule, was not allowed its own mint). Commentators agree that the sale of animals and the exchange of money were 'unobjectionable institutions' (Harvey, 201, p 173), and that is extraordinary that Jesus should condemn them as 'robbery'. Furthermore, the OT quotations on which this condemnation is based do not, in their original sense, support it. Jesus quotes Isaiah 56:7 as if it meant that the temple should properly be a place of prayer, not of sacrifice; and that the concomitants of sacrifice (sale of animals and exchange of money) have made it a den of robbers. But what Isaiah is in fact saying is that foreigners who have adopted the Jewish faith may, with Jews, offer sacrifice in the temple to Yahweh, who here declares: 'Their offerings shall be acceptable on my altar'. It is in the light of these words that the following ones (which Jesus quotes) must be understood: 'For my house shall be called a house of prayer for all the nations'. Just as little to the point is Jesus' reference to Jeremiah 7:11. What is there said is that Jews who commit robbery and other crimes must not think that they will be safe from Yahweh's wrath merely because they come and stand before him in his temple: if they do, they are making the temple a den of robbers. Mark, then, is using OT passages in a sense they will not bear. Either the episode is historical — i.e. Jesus distorted scripture in the interests of his own polemic — or a Christian community, accepting a tradition that he had proceeded in some way against the temple, tried to find scriptural justification for his behaviour and, in the usual manner, paid but scant attention to the real meaning of the biblical passages resorted to.

A legendary tradition that Jesus cleansed the temple is perfectly intelligible. Jeremias has shown (224, pp 35ff) that Jesus thinking linked the renewal of the temple with the enthronement of the Messiah; and the sense of Mark's story would thus simply be that 'the kingdom of God is at hand' (Grässer, 176, p 28). As history, however, the story is 'not without its difficulties' (Nineham, 314, p 301). For instance, how could Jesus — single-handed according to Mk. — have driven out both buyers and sellers and have controlled the whole floor space ('He would not allow any one to carry anything through the temple')? Nineham notes that 'St. Mark probably thought of Jesus as exercising the supernatural power which would naturally belong to "the Lord" when "he suddenly comes to his temple" '. Quite so. The difficulty of understanding how Jesus, unaided, could have done what Mark reports, did not exist for an evangelist who saw his behaviour as 'fulfilment' of Malachi 3:1, Zechariah 14:21 or Hosea 9:15. Nineham summarizes: 'The story corresponds very closely to OT prophecies, and some critics have traced its whole origin to them'. Commentators who try to discern some historical incident underlying it have to suppose that Jesus did not act alone, but was aided by a crowd of supporters. But this supposition raises its own difficulties. Why did the temple police not intervene? (Brandon answers: they probably did, but the record has been 'carefully edited' so as to suppress the fact.) Why was there no reaction from the Roman garrison occupying quarters overlooking the temple, and strengthened at the time of passover to deal with rioting? (Brandon calls this Roman inaction 'curious'.) Why was the whole matter not mentioned at Jesus' trial? To this Brandon supplies a complicated and ingenious answer, based on Mk.'s statement that 'false witnesses' accused Jesus, at his trial, of having threatened to destroy the temple:

'And some stood up and bore false witness against him, saying, "We heard him say 'I will destroy this temple that is made with hands, and in three days I will build another, not made with hands' " ' (14:57—8).

This passage is an incident in the wider context (14:55—65) of Jesus' unanimous condemnation by the Sanhedrin for blasphemy. Some theologians regard this nocturnal Sanhedrin trial (absent from Lk. and Jn.) as 'a report inserted by the evangelist himself, without recourse to any received tradition' (88, p 334 and refs. cf. above, p 138). Whether this is so or not, Jesus' reference to 'three days' does not inspire confidence in the historicity of the logion, and suggests that it was concocted by someone familiar with the tradition of the resurrection. It is a floating logion (set in other contexts by other evangelists), and is clearly Messianic; the renewal of the Jerusalem temple is the sign of the Messianic age (Ezekiel 40—48). Mark has adapted this idea to Christian use by making the renewed temple signify the resurrected Jesus. At the same time he cannot represent the words as genuinely spoken by Jesus, but only as a Jewish calumny; for if Jesus had really threatened to destroy the temple, the Jews' condemnation of him would not have been the monstrous crime which Mark represents it to be. Brandon's interpretation of the narrative is that Mark took it from a document composed by the original Jerusalem Christians who were anxious to persuade the Jews that Jesus had never threatened the temple, and who to this end put out a version of his trial in which the accusation that he had made such a threat was clearly repudiated as 'false witness'. Brandon further infers that, if the early Jerusalem Christians had to rebut such a charge, the historical Jesus must have said or done something which occasioned it; and that this something was in fact his 'revolutionary act' in attacking the temple trading system — an attack which 'was achieved by the aid of an excited crowd of his supporters and was attended by violence and pillage', and which led to his arrest (66, pp 332—5). Brandon thus posits (i) a revolutionary Jesus and (ii) Jerusalem Christians who gloried in his nationalist behaviour, but were embarrassed by his attack on the temple, and who therefore set about to convince Jews, some of whom must have witnessed or heard of his revolutionary act, that he had never committed it. On this view the truth must be reached by correcting not only Mk. but also Mk.'s hypothetical Jerusalem source.

Even if Mark wrote as early as AD 70 about a Jesus who had in fact been crucified about AD 30, his gospel represents a redaction of oral and written tradition which had accumulated during a period of forty years. As Bearman has pertinently asked (36, p 276), what kind of accuracy can be expected of such a document or of such underlying material? According to Mark himself, Jesus' disciples forsook him and fled at his arrest, and so Christian knowledge of his trial could be nothing but hearsay. Can we really presume to correct not merely Mk. but the scraps of material on which he drew?

Brandon's use of Mk. 15:6—7 and 15 illustrates how he seizes on any scrap which seems to betray that Jesus existed, although not as the person the evangelist alleges him to be:

> 'Now at the Feast he [Pilate] used to release for them any one prisoner whom they asked. And among [Greek 'meta', i.e. 'with'] the rebels in prison, who had committed murder in the insurrection, there was a man called Barabbas. . . . . And Pilate, wishing to satisfy the crowd, released for them Barabbas, and delivered Jesus . . . to be crucified.'

Mark does not explain what 'insurrection' he has in mind. Brandon takes the passage as evidence that, at the time when Jesus led an attack on the temple, a zealot insurrection occurred; that both attacks failed, so that Jesus was crucified by the Romans for sedition with two zealot conspirators at his side. Now Mark's account does not stand much scrutiny. Pilate leaves the Jews free to choose between Jesus and Barabbas, even though the high priests have brought a heavy charge against Jesus, who himself has not denied Pilate's imputation that he is 'king of the Jews'. Furthermore, as Brandon is of course well aware, there are reasons for supposing that 'Barabbas' originally figured in the gospels under the name of 'Jesus Barabbas' (the reading of Mt. 27:16 given in the NEB; cf. JEC, pp 245–6). Maccoby has plausibly argued (285, pp 214–15) that Mark introduced this person into his narrative in order to discredit an earlier tradition which had made a multitude of Jewish supporters of Jesus Christ unsuccessfully demand that Pilate release him. According to this earlier tradition, then, Pilate was guilty and the Jews innocent of Jesus' murder. (Maccoby takes this earlier tradition to be historical fact, but I see no reason to follow him here.) Mark's answer to this earlier tradition is that the person whose release the Jews had demanded was another Jesus, Jesus Barabbas. This name, which means 'Jesus son of the father', seems ideally adapted to Mark's purpose and allows him to concede that the Jews did indeed press for the release of a man whose name bore some resemblance to that of Jesus Christ, but that they were nonetheless hostile towards the latter. Mark may well have utilized a tradition about a zealot named Barabbas who had been involved in an uprising and pardoned, and this tradition may even have been true. But Mark's use of it — his linking it with Jesus Christ — is visibly guided by the desire to burden the Jews (particularly the high priests) with responsibility for Jesus' death. To that end they are represented as urging Pilate to set a murderer free and to have the true saviour executed. In sum, there is no need to take the reference to insurrection and murder as Mark's unwitting betrayal of a tense political atmosphere. The story can be understood as deliberately introduced by him for the purpose of establishing a theological tenet.

(iii) Luke's Adaptations

A serious weakness, then, in Brandon's exegesis is that it treats evangelists as mere collectors of traditions, and supposes not only that they assembled their gospels from shreds and patches (which, as form-criticism has established, they certainly did), but also that they put the shreds together carelessly, without much editorial attempt to make a coherent story. Critical theologians, particularly in Germany, today rightly insist that, when an evangelist combined diverse traditions into a narrative, he intended the whole to present an intelligible message to his readers.

Study of the way later evangelists assimilated and supplemented the Marcan material has revealed how carefully it is adapted to serve particular theological purposes of overriding importance. Let us consider some examples.

In Mk. 12:14—17 certain of 'the Pharisees and of the Herodians' ask Jesus: 'Is it lawful to pay taxes to Caesar or not? Should we pay them, or should we not?' He replies: 'Render to Caesar the things that are Caesar's, and to God the things that are God's'. There is no need to suppose that a historical Jesus made such an utterance. Mk. was written late in the first century for a Christian community which believed in a historical Jesus, and which needed a clear ruling on what attitude to take to the Roman rulers. Under these conditions it was natural for a dictum to be invented which decreed that Christians were to pay taxes, but not to join in any act of worship of the Emperor. Jesus' words constitute a clear rejection of the zealot nationalist position which regarded payment of Roman taxes as a crime.

In Lk. he is asked the same question by 'the chief priests and scribes' and returns the same answer. But in Luke's version of Jesus' trial, these same 'chief priests and scribes' accuse him before Pilate of 'forbidding us to give tribute to Caesar' (23:2). This passage has been added by Luke to the material he took from Mk., and those who believe that Jesus was a political rebel think that Luke is here less 'circumspect' than Mark, and has let the cat out of the bag, betraying the real reason for Jesus' condemnation. Against this, Conzelmann has shown that Luke is concerned not only (as Mark had been) to put the blame for Jesus' execution onto the Jews, but also to stamp the Jewish leaders as the real rebels against Rome, in contrast to Jesus, whom he represents as politically innocuous. The passages already studied exemplify the first of these two tendencies. Luke changes Mark's account not only by adding a Jewish indictment that Jesus was a rebel, but also by ensuring that the Jews who make this indictment are *the same persons* as had been informed by Jesus that he was not a rebel. We saw that, while in Mk. it is certain of the 'Pharisees and Herodians' who ask him about tribute to Caesar, in Lk. the question is asked by 'the chief priests and scribes'; and it is they who later (in the passage without Marcan parallel) indict him to Pilate as a rebel. Luke's purpose is clearly to stamp this indictment as a deliberate Jewish calumny. It is quite unnecessary to assume, as does Brandon (66, p 348) that Luke has committed an indiscretion, and has inadvertently assimilated material which betrays what 'really' happened.

The second of the two tendencies which Luke follows in his adaptation of Mk. is evidenced in the Barabbas narratives. We recall that in Mk. the multitude demanded the execution of Jesus and the release of Barabbas, who was in prison 'with the rebels' (15:7). The Greek does not explicitly say that he was a rebel – only that he was in jail with rebels. Luke, however, expressly says (23:19) that he 'had been thrown into prison for an insurrection started in the city'. Scholars looking for political dynamite in the gospels have supposed that Mark suppressed proper mention of Barabbas' political misdeeds, and that Luke has betrayed more of the true atmosphere of political foment which formed the background of Jesus' arrest. But again closer scrutiny shows that Luke is here writing purposefully. He deliberately represents Barabbas as a rebel in order to show that the Jewish leaders who demand his release are, like him, rebels against Rome; that they, and not Jesus whom they lyingly accuse, are the true rebels. The care Luke takes to make his point is shown by his laboured repetition. Having said (verse 19) that Barabbas was in prison because he had committed murder in an insurrection, the evangelist adds that Pilate, pressed by the Jewish leaders, 'released the man who had been thrown into prison for insurrection and murder, whom they asked for' (verse 25). This, then, we are to understand, is the type of person they sympathize with!

Luke not only edits Mk. so as to paint the Jewish leaders as unfaithful to Rome; he also, and correlatively, deletes from Mk. any suggestion of such infidelity on the part of Jesus. Mk.'s account of the triumphant entry into Jerusalem represents Jesus as greeted by the crowd as the Messianic king, with OT quotations and shouts of 'Blessed be the kingdom of our father David that is coming!' (11:10). Theologians recognize serious difficulties in the narrative, particularly apropos of its use of the OT (cf. above, p 118). The OT 'prophecies' which the Christians of the late first century understood as referring to Jesus, were regarded as of absolute reliability – of far greater value than eye-witness reports about him, even if these had been available at the time. Mark clearly intends the episode as a Messianic demonstration; but we saw that he was not recording an actual event, but rather partially lifting the veil he had hitherto thrown over Jesus' exalted status, with the result that he was recognized as son of David (although not as son of God) at the time when he entered the city, and the Jewish authorities were thus provided with some basis for their hostility to him (see above, p 119). Now Luke had his own specific understanding of the OT prophecies concerning a Davidic Messiah. We saw (above, p 110) that in his view they refer not to the earthly activities of Jesus, but to his enthronement after his resurrection. It is for this reason that Luke carefully deletes any political undertones there may be in the Marcan story of the entry into Jerusalem. In Luke's version of the incident there is no mention of David, and so there can be no suspicion that Jesus is acting rebelliously towards Rome. The same purpose is served by Luke's studied failure to ascribe to Pilate any act of condemnation of Jesus. In Mk. 15:15 'Pilate delivered him to be crucified' and Roman soldiers proceed to carry out the sentence. But in Lk. Pilate merely delivers him up to the will of the Jews (23:25) and 'they' led him away to execution. 'They' are not expressly said to be Roman soldiers, as is the case in Mk.

Another Lucan passage well illustrates how interpreters have seized on details which allegedly betray truths unpalatable to the evangelist, without pausing to ask whether he was trying to say something intelligible and coherent to his readers by including these very details. Just before his arrest, Jesus says to the twelve:

' "When I sent you out with no purse or bag or sandals, did you lack anything?" They said, "Nothing". He said to them, "But now, let him who has a purse take it, and likewise a bag. And let him who has no sword sell his mantle and buy one. For I tell you that this scripture must be fulfilled in me, 'And he was reckoned with transgressors'; for what is written about me has its fulfilment". And they said, "Look, Lord, here are two swords". And he said to them, "It is enough" ' (22:35–8). (22:35–8).

This passage occurs in no other gospel. Rylands, who believed (as indeed I do) that Jesus never existed, argued that 'sword' here 'properly signifies a long knife, . . . such as would be used for a sacrifice'; and that the injunction to 'procure knives' is immediately followed by the words 'this scripture must be fulfilled in me', pointing directly to the sacrifice. Rylands concludes: 'Possibly we have here a reminiscence of an ancient ritual' (342, p 48). The advocates of a political Jesus, on the other hand, take the injunction to buy a sword as a tell-tale incident which betrays the important fact that, at the time of his arrest, 'Jesus made sure his disciples were armed' (66, p 340). But before we thus accuse Luke of random assimilation of traditions concerning ancient ritual practices, or of indiscreet betrayal of inconvenient political facts, we will do well to look at the context in which he sets Jesus' injunction. Conzelmann rightly emphasizes that the evangelist's purpose here is to make a distinction between the time of Jesus' public ministry (represented as an idyllic period, free from persecution and even from want), and the time of the nascent Church. The latter is the evangelist's own time (which is probably as late as the early second century), and he represents it as a period of hardship and of persecution which was inaugurated by Jesus' own arrest and execution. In all three synoptic gospels Jesus sends out the disciples as preachers early in his public ministry, and tells them to take nothing for their journey – no bread, money nor extra clothing (Mk. 6:8 and parallels). Whatever Mark and Matthew may have understood by these instructions, Luke takes them to designate the care-free existence that Christian missionaries were then able to lead, eating and drinking whatever is given them (Lk. 10:7) – conditions which, as Jesus points out just before his arrest, are about to be succeeded by sinister times. It is here that he refers to the necessity of obtaining swords, and the context shows that he must be understood metaphorically. As Taylor says: 'Jesus is thinking of the position in which the disciples will find themselves after his death' (383, p 192). The disciples, it is true, take his words literally; but Luke's implication is that they have misunderstood him – as they have repeatedly done when, as here, he had tried to explain to them that it was necessary for the Messiah to suffer and die (Lk. 9:44–5; 18:32–4).

The term 'zealots', which I have used above without explanation, requires some comment. Josephus calls a group of militants, active from ca. AD 66, by this name (see Hengel's account, 203, pp 64ff), and Hengel and others trace their attitude of revolt to Judas of Galilee, who (again according to Josephus) taught in AD 6 that Caesar must be actively resisted; and also to the numerous 'sicarioi' (dagger-men) and 'lestai' (bandits) whom the same historian mentions as active from this time. (Resistance to the Romans was, until the outbreak of the war in AD 66, guerilla action, and would naturally be designated banditry by the disapproving Josephus.) Now Mark and Matthew's lists of the twelve disciples include one 'Simon the Cananaean'. In Lk. (6:15) the term is translated correctly into its Greek equivalent (zelotes) as 'Simon called the zealot' (to distinguish him from Simon called Peter). He is never mentioned again, and there is no suggestion that he acted as a zealot (in a political sense) after joining Jesus. Brandon and others have, however, insisted that, if one of the twelve was a zealot, Jesus himself could not have been without zealot sympathies. More orthodox Christian scholars have retorted that it is fantastic to make a disciple 'of whom no deed or word has been recorded' the basis of such an inference (Richardson, 330, p 43). Furthermore, another of the twelve is said to have been a tax-collector (Mt. 10:3), 'many' of whom were included in Jesus' following (Mk. 2:15; Mt. 9:10). Greater enemies than zealots and tax-collectors cannot be imagined, and the idea may have been to suggest that Jesus stood above such divisions, not that he sympathized with any one of them.

(iv) Recent Popularizations

Arbitrary interpretation of isolated passages is an obvious weakness of Carmichael's well-known popularization of Jesus' story in terms of political revolt. Let me give some examples. Lk. tells how various people, including tax-collectors and soldiers, came to John the Baptist for advice, and were told not to rob anyone, and to be content with their wages. For Carmichael, the fact that the word rendered as 'soldiers' can also mean 'combatants' implies that the Baptist 'was actually giving specific instructions for the conduct of a guerilla campaign' against the Romans (96, p 168). Jesus, after initially submitting to John's baptism – which of course constituted initiation into a para-military movement (p 174) – broke with him and led an independent rebellion. The two men thus became rivals, and when we read in the fourth gospel that the Baptist ungrudgingly acknowledged Jesus' superiority, saying of him 'He must increase, but I must decrease' (Jn. 3:30) – a statement quite in accordance with the evangelist's theology (cf. above, p 156) – we must realize, insists Carmichael, that what the infuriated and jealous Baptist really said, after Jesus had abandoned him, was exactly the opposite. Pacifist statements recorded of Jesus in the gospels may represent his opinions after his break with John, when he was 'still gathering support for his new enterprise' (p 179).

The nature of this enterprise is revealed when he asks his captors in Gethsemane why they arrest him, since 'day after day I was with you in the temple teaching and you did not seize me' (Mk. 14:49). Carmichael takes (p 40) 'day after day' to imply that he had an armed force powerful enough not only to seize the temple, but also to hold it for some time. In Lk. 13:1–5 (without synoptic parallel), Jesus, on being told (well before he reaches Jerusalem) of Galileans 'whose blood Pilate had mingled with their sacrifices', comments that their fate does not prove them to have been more sinful than Galileans who did not so perish, any more than the eighteen inhabitants of Jerusalem killed by the fall of the tower of Siloam (on the city wall) are to be supposed particularly wicked citizens. For Carmichael, the fall of the tower – which Jesus mentions as a thing of the past before he ever sets foot in Jerusalem – 'may be an echo of the siege operation that must have been executed by the Romans in order to recover control of the Temple Hill after it had been taken by Jesus and his insurgents'. The Galileans executed by Pilate – also, according to Lk., before Jesus' arrival in the city – 'may well have been the group who took and held the Temple'. The two men crucified with him were perhaps the insurgents in command at the tower of Siloam and the temple respectively. Barabbas was a member of the temple hierarchy, arrested in error with Jesus and his insurgents – hence Pilate's offer to set this innocent man free (pp145–6). Why did Jesus have disciples at all? Obviously, they were his lieutenants, in a military sense. What Judas betrayed was the hiding place to which he had withdrawn after his defeat by the Roman cohort (p 150). That he was arrested by a cohort, commanded by a tribune, is a detail peculiar to the fourth gospel – a detail which, Carmichael insists, 'could never have been invented after the event', since 'the whole early Christian tradition tended to take the blame away from the Romans' and ascribe it to the Jews (p 22). But it has long been clear to theologians that the fourth evangelist introduces all manner of details for the purpose of stressing Jesus' divine powers, and his story of the Roman arrest gives him the splendid opportunity to allege that a whole cohort of armed soldiers fell to the ground at the majesty of the appearance of the unarmed Jesus (Jn. 18:6. Carmichael purports to deal with the objection that the evangelist introduced the cohort for dramatic effect. He supposes that what effect there is must be due to the use of the words chiliarchos (tribune) and speira (cohort), and is therefore negligible, since these words contribute 'nothing to the exaltation of Jesus'!).

After all this Carmichael blandly tells us (p 163) that he has 'resisted the temptation of "filling in" this shadowy picture with persuasive, imaginatively elaborated details', and that those who reject the historicity of Jesus' occupation of the temple — an event which the evangelists have 'softened' and 'spiritualised out of all reality' — offer only 'naive' reasons for their view (pp 138–9). These reasons are not stated by Carmichael, who suggests that such scholars simply infer deductively that, since the occupation must have been a major enterprise, requiring force, it never took place. Carmichael, for his part, is not naive; he knows that 'the relationship of Jesus to the Temple is so central a theme in the Gospel story, it is so obviously the springboard for his arrest and trial [sic], that its historicity must be taken for granted'. Non-Christian evidence is adduced in support. Tacitus 'simply takes it for granted that from the point of view of Rome Jesus was an enemy' (as though that enhanced the value of his testimony!); Sossianus Hierocles, the prefect of Egypt who persecuted Christians under Diocletian and was 'so in a way a successor of Pontius Pilate', said that Jesus 'was the leader of a band of highway robbers numbering more than 900 men' (250 years lie between Pilate and Hierocles; could the latter have derived his view from independent inquiry, or did he gladly allege it to justify his own activities as persecutor?); 'a mediaeval copy of a lost version of a work of Josephus also reports that Jesus had more than 2,000 armed followers with him on the Mount of Olives' (p 141). In fact, this statement occurs in the mediaeval Jewish *Toldoth Jeshu,* a violently anti-Christian work. I was at a loss to know what Carmichael had in mind until I discovered that Eisler (one of the nine authors listed in his bibliography) alleged that the statement in the *Toldoth* represents 'a lost passage in *Josippon*' — a fifth century Hebrew paraphrase of Josephus — some manuscripts of which still include other anti-Christian passages which Eisler regarded not as inventions of Jewish malice, but as derived from copies of Josephus (no longer extant) which had escaped Christian censorship (143, pp 100, 107, 370n). Carmichael's link between the Galileans killed by Pilate, the tower of Siloam and the two men crucified with Jesus, is also taken from Eisler, and, as a recent critic has observed, one may admire the skill and imagination with which Eisler fuses such isolated gospel details into a unified dramatic story, while one must recognize that such reconstruction has nothing to do with sober historical scholarship (48, p 41).

Carmichael's whole reconstruction of Jesus' biography is based on the premiss that the earliest traditions about him must have consisted in recollections of his ordinary human existence, and that these were gradually overlain by later ideas which represented him as divine. From these presuppositions he infers that 'any fragment we can manage to isolate' in the gospels which runs counter to their prevailing tendency of exalting Jesus, anything which suggests that he was merely a rather unoriginal Jew, is likely to be authentic. Carmichael asks (p 14) why all four gospels — he later (p 26) notes that Lk. has in fact to be excepted — in spite of their obvious desire to inculpate the Jews, nevertheless report that it was the Romans who in fact sentenced Jesus to crucifixion and

172

carried out the sentence themselves. He obviously thinks the only rational answer is that Roman involvement was too well attested to be denied; whereas my case is that it was simply an earlier stage of tradition which had been itself preceded by yet other traditions which did not link Jesus with Pilate's Palestine. He is, of course, aware that the Pauline letters (with their portrait of a supernatural Jesus of whose human career next to nothing is known) were written much earlier than the gospels. Yet, in the interests of his theory, he has to maintain that they represent later ideas than those informing the synoptic tradition (pp 47, 61, 221); and he does not discuss at all the epistles which are intermediate in date between Paul and the gospels. Paul, he supposes, gives us Jesus' story 'transposed to a hellenistic terrain' (p 191), and therefore sullied by pagan thinking, whereas the synoptics are based on 'Palestinian tradition' (p 64) and even Jn. on an Aramaic original (p 186). Lk. and Acts — whose Christology (on which see pp 109f above) suits Carmichael's thesis better than that of Mk. and Mt. — 'were written in fairly close connection with the events of Jesus' career'. The prevalence of such uncritical statements on such a crucial matter justifies my devoting some space in this present work to an inquiry into the dates of the various NT books.

I will conclude with a brief account of two further attempts to portray Jesus as a rebel — those of Levin and Cohn. Dr Levin was kind enough to send me a copy of his book, published in 1969. Its principal theses are (1) that the fourth gospel, generally considered the latest, was in fact written first; (2) that miracles, ethical teachings and warnings that the world will shortly come to a catastrophic end are wrongly ascribed to Jesus in the gospels, and in fact represent actions and sayings of John the Baptist. On the first of these two points the evidence offered by Levin is quite inconclusive. He supposes that the denigration of John the Baptist in the fourth gospel would have been pointless 'after the year 70 when the Qumran baptists were no more' (275, pp 22–3). But he himself later (p 97) refers to Christian polemics against second-century disciples of the Baptist who regarded him as the Christ. The anti-Baptist attitude of Jn. does not, therefore, establish that it was written before AD 70. And although its portrait of Jesus is, for Dr Levin, more reliable than that of the other gospels, he has to admit that its author was 'more interested in mysticism and metaphysics than in history' (pp 22–3), and so the actual life of Jesus has — after all — to be reconstructed principally from the synoptic gospels.

This reconstruction is effected by very free interpretation. When Mark records (11:11) that Jesus, on entering Jerusalem, went into the temple and 'looked round about upon all things' (RV), Dr Levin takes this to mean: Jesus 'proceeded to survey the defences of the temple area' (p 51). The cleansing of the temple on the next day is interpreted as an armed attempt to capture the building and to precipitate a general insurrection; for, Levin says, no Roman governor would have permitted the breach of the civil peace that Mark represents the cleansing to be. Levin nevertheless asks us to assume that Jesus' preceding triumphal entry into the city, which he interprets as a political demonstration, was permitted by the Romans, who further allowed him to survey the temple's fortifications before attacking it in force the following day!

If Jesus was a rebel, then any of his recorded actions or doctrines which are politically indifferent, or which counsel political quietism, cannot have stemmed from him. It is on this basis that Levin argues that it was not Jesus but John the Baptist who worked miracles and delivered the Sermon on the Mount and the 'eschatological' discourses which promise this world a speedy and catastrophic end. The process of amalgamating the two men into a single figure began, he says, during Jesus' lifetime (p 84) — it is hard to see why, when the thesis is that their respective doctrines were wholly incompatible. Here we see why Levin has been at pains to establish the reliability of the fourth gospel, for, to explain the fusion of the two men, he says that they 'must have been very close, must have collaborated often, met often, exchanged followers, perhaps even resembled each other (physically)' (pp 83, 85). It is, we saw (above, p 156), only the fourth gospel which knows of a period of contact between Jesus and the Baptist and tells that some of the Baptist's disciples transferred their allegiance to Jesus. Levin regards this as historical fact — not as part of the evangelist's 'anti-Baptist polemic' — and infers that, after Jesus' death, his followers, *while still respecting him,* returned to their first allegiance', i.e. to the Baptist (p 89). The phrase I have italicized is an attempt to explain why they did not just drop Jesus but amalgamated his ideas with those of his forerunner. The result was a post-crucifixion Jerusalem Church which believed a mixture of activism and quietism. 'The change to passivity was by no means complete', and that Peter did not altogether abandon his former sabre-rattling is evidenced by his rough handling of Ananias and Sapphira (pp 45, 90)!

Cohn, like other writers on Jesus' trial and death, has no difficulty in showing that the gospel standpoint that the Jews were responsible for Jesus' death is tendentious fiction; that the Jews are not guilty of deicide, and that the centuries of Christian persecution of them on this ground is sheer prejudice. However, his concern to vindicate the Jews leads him to argue that what really happened was that they tried to save Jesus' life. Let us recall what the gospels say. Matthew and Mark allege that Jesus was both tried and sentenced by the Sanhedrin; Luke that he was tried but not sentenced by that body; John that he did not appear before it at all. Cohn agrees with the many scholars who reject the historicity of the Sanhedrin trial, but he does not accept John's version that the court did not meet at all. He posits a meeting — not because there is any real evidence for it, but because it constitutes a concession to the view which makes the Jews responsible for Jesus' death. He is thus 'assuming the burden of an "admission against interest" '; the meeting 'is an assumption against us' (102, pp 95–6). Having certificated the meeting as historical on the ground that it is not in his 'interest' that it should be historical, he proceeds to argue that it could have had only one purpose, namely 'to prevent the crucifixion of a Jew by the Romans, . . . of a Jew who was loved as a worker of miracles, healer of the sick, consoler and redeemer of the poor and persecuted, castigator of corruption, and . . . sworn enemy of the rich' (p 76). To believe this is to take for granted the truth of a very great deal of the gospel accounts which Cohn elsewhere finds so unreliable.

What the Sanhedrin attempted was, in Cohn's view, to persuade Jesus not to plead guilty when brought before Pilate. But when he insisted that he was the Christ, it was obvious that the Romans were bound to condemn him for setting himself up as a king; whereupon the high priest rent his clothes – in grief at the failure of his rescue bid, according to Cohn, even though Mark and Matthew (the only gospels which record the incident at all) attribute the rending to indignation at the blasphemy of Jesus' claim. Cohn shows that, from the Jewish standpoint, the claim was not blasphemous at all, and that 'the easiest way to unravel the riddle, as with most problems arising out of the gospel reports, is to dismiss the whole incident of the rending of the High Priest's garments as unhistorical' (p 133). But this he declines to do, and throughout he implies that to deny the basic historicity of the gospel story is too cheap a method, is a mere 'simple expedient' which betrays 'reluctance to grapple with the diffi-culties presented by the gospel inconsistencies' (pp 21–2). Here again is evidence of an attitude that is scarcely scientific. The scientist holds that the true explanation is the simplest one which will account for all the relevant facts. Whether in any instance it will turn out to be simple or complicated depends on the instance under investigation, and one cannot, in advance of inquiry, prescribe a certain level of complexity. Further-more, although it is a simple matter to say that the gospels are all untrue, it is in fact far from simple to explain how, in that case, they came to be composed. Theorists who explain Christianity without positing a historical Jesus are normally accused of introducing unnecessary complexities, not of over-simplification. Equally unscientific is Cohn's argument that if all four evangelists agree on a particular matter, 'one might presume that they had a satisfactory and conclusive source' (p xix). In truth, the fact that in many points they agree loses its value as corroborative evidence when it is recognized that parallel passages in the first three gospels are often verbally identical, and must therefore have been copied either from one another or from a common source. Again, Cohn says: 'A tradition reported in an earlier Gospel which the later evangelists, or any of them, saw fit to dismiss by contradiction or exclusion as untrue or unreliable may well be viewed with suspicion'. Theologians and rationalists alike have often worked on the very opposite principle – that an unedifying statement in an early gospel which a later evangelist has tried to tone down or suppress, has a strong claim to authenticity. Not that this principle is any more acceptable than Cohn's (cf. above, p 148).

Another example of interpretation based on passages taken arbitrarily from their context is Schonfield's *The Passover Plot*. I discussed it in JEC (pp 325–8) and will not repeat myself. A generation or more ago there was some excuse for this kind of exegesis, namely the form-critics' demonstration that evangelists assembled their gospels from disparate traditions. But today it has been established that they were meticulous editors. What Conzelmann has shown in the case of Lk. has been shown to be true of Mt., and even of Mk., where the evidence is far less clear, as none of Mk.'s sources is extant on which to base a comparison. In each case there is an overriding theological purpose (not, of course, identical in all three evangelists) which guides the assimilation of earlier material.

(v) Conclusion

It is customary now to dismiss with contempt many nineteenth-century lives of Jesus on the ground that their authors simply found in him all the qualities which they themselves considered estimable. But the wide circulation today of books which portray him as a rebel seems yet another illustration of the same phenomenon. Brandon himself noted that 'owing to the temper of our times', many people have welcomed his arguments that 'Jesus did really involve himself in politics' (69, pp 13–14). So instead of the Pauline co-agent of all creation, or the liberal who 'went about doing good', we now have the radical patriot who staged his 'demo.'.

8 The Pagan and Jewish Background

(i) Religious Development

The difficulty most people find in even contemplating the possibility that Christianity arose without a historical Jesus is that they cannot on this basis conceive how the gospel narratives could have arisen. Many are willing to believe that these contain some unhistorical elements, but it is generally assumed that, while inaccuracies of detail are comprehensible, it is necessary to believe in a nucleus of fact upon which the unauthentic elements were grafted; for elaborate stories sincerely related which yet have no basis whatever seem unaccountable.

Yet no one doubts that – whether the gospels are a case in point or not – stories with no factual basis have found widespread and lasting acceptance. Some Roman historians regarded Hercules as a historical figure who went about doing good. Herodotus reports (Bk. 1, § 34–5) that Attis was the son of a king of Lydia, and was killed on a hunting party; and also (Bk. 2, § 144) that the god Horus (son of Isis and Osiris) was once the ruler of Egypt. Even the early Christians did not deny the historicity of these pagan saviour gods: in the second century Clement of Alexandria called them 'mere men' and in the fourth Firmicus Maternus declared that Osiris and Typhon were 'without doubt' kings of Egypt (see Simon, 64, p 146). William Tell was accepted as historical for centuries, and even today many are unaware that historians are well-nigh unanimous that he did not in fact exist. So we are faced here with a problem which is much more general than that of Christian origins; namely how do men come by such entirely erroneous beliefs?

In explaining myths we are mainly concerned with the way in which man constructs his view of past or remote events. The lore of savages concerning the origin of the world, of man and of various human institutions, struck the nineteenth-century anthropologists as so ridiculous that they found it necessary to assume that the minds of savages work quite differently from ours. It was overlooked that they had made many practical and useful inventions (e.g. fire, pottery, weaving and agriculture) and showed no tendency at all to romance when the problem was to build a canoe or design weapons for hunting. It was also overlooked that many beliefs prevalent today are just as absurd as those which astonish the anthropologist, but as they are familiar and often shared by him, they do not strike him. The truth seems to be that man, whether civilized or not, has those of his beliefs which concern practical affairs continually corrected by his experience; but where the belief concerns a remote past or a future life after death, experience cannot so readily correct it, and in some cases cannot do so at all. A fireman who acts on the belief that ether is a good extinguisher will have a rude shock, and if he survives it, the belief will not survive with him. But he can readily retain for the whole of his life all manner of fantasies concerning conditions remote from him. Thus we have *practical* beliefs, which are subject to experimental control and which are accordingly modified and corrected until they are found to be adequate; and another kind of beliefs which are not controlled in this way, and which may be such as to flatter or comfort, or, in general, to satisfy some emotional requirement, to resolve some state of tension. This kind of belief plays a large part in religion.

The belief – common in the Middle East in the first centuries of our era – that at some unspecified time in the past a saviour God (Osiris, Tammuz, or whatever his local name) had been on earth to suffer, die and rise again, is obviously an erroneous inference that once made would not be corrected by everyday experience. The problem, then, is to understand how it was made in the first place. My answer is, briefly: religious symbols and rites handed down through many generations are no longer understood in terms of the conditions which gave rise to them. Hooke writes of a process of 'degradation', as when 'a symbol or fragment of ritual persists after its original meaning has been lost' (208, pp 6–7). Such elements receive new interpretations in terms of contemporary ideas, and the fantastic results of such interpretations fail to be corrected because they refer to past events which no experience can directly reproduce.

Frazer and his contemporaries summarized these developments as a series of clearly distinct phases. Today it is conceded that the actual evidence for some of the phases in this sequence is – in the words of Brandon – 'curiously vague and unsatisfactory' (63, p 269). But the whole sequence is still widely accepted (e.g. by James, 221, pp 291–2) as providing an intelligible origin of religious ideas which are otherwise hard to explain. It is as follows: first there was an elaborate magic ceremonial devised according to the lights of the wiser or more influential members of the tribe over a long series of generations; e.g. human sacrifice as a magical means of bringing about the rebirth of animal and vegetable life at springtime. The winter was regarded as an enfeeblement of the god or spirit of vegetation, and it was believed that it could be renewed by killing a human being representing it, and transferring it from him to a younger and more vigorous individual.[1] Such ritual killing was a method which uncivilized man employed in order to renew vegetation, i.e. to get good crops in the coming year. At no stage, probably, was the whole ceremony intelligible to those who conducted it, for there was a large element of tradition which had to be accepted. We may, however, say that each element had a rational origin, i.e. it was first introduced because it seemed calculated to produce some desired effect. But none of these elements could be tested for their efficacy, and this constitutes a great distinction

178

between *ritual* and *practical* activities such as fishing, hunting or building. In these latter cases, the relation between purpose and means employed is understood and clearly seen, and so the benefit or otherwise of a change of method can also be seen and judged. But changes and irregularities and innovations in a ritual believed to be efficacious in encouraging the growth of crops have no immediately visible effect, and there is no practical test of efficacy. Since on the whole the traditional practice seems to ensure a fair crop, it is better to keep to it as accurately as possible. This is the psychological basis of the special sanctity of the archaic in religious practices.

Sooner or later some elements in a ritual, or even the whole of it, will have to be reinterpreted, for the reason that, over the generations, their original purpose has been lost from sight. The new explanations of traditional rites may assume various forms, but commonly myths are invented to make the rites intelligible. Typically, such myths would allege that the practice was established by so-and-so on such and such occasion, and that it has ever after been done in commemoration of that person or that event. Returning to my example: the annual killing of the vegetation god aimed originally at stimulating the growth of crops. When the purpose of the ritual ceased to be understood, it was reinterpreted as a memorial ritual to commemorate his death, which had occurred on one particular occasion in the past, and in the manner (beheading, hanging, crucifixion) portrayed in the ritual. It is in fact one of the fundamental principles of modern anthropology that ritual explains the myth, not vice versa; i.e. ritual tends to persist long after its original purpose and significance have been lost from sight, and among the worshippers myths then arise to explain it, although in fact it explains them. Thus, in the case of the ritual killing of the god, all the attributes of a vegetation god who died annually came eventually to be ascribed to an individual, who was held to have died only once and whose death the ritual commemorated.

A further stage, which may precede, accompany or follow the reinterpreting of the ritual, consists in modification of the original rite, which has become repugnant or difficult to perform. Human sacrifice (as a magical means of bringing about the rebirth of animal and vegetable life in the spring) may in time be modified, either because of the difficulty of procuring victims or because of increasing repugnance on the part of the participating people. The modification may substitute an animal or an image for a human victim. Alternatively, a real execution of a man may be replaced by a mock-killing, and this would involve an elaborate dramatic performance in which the man impersonating the god dies and then comes to life again in a more vigorous form. If at a later stage the purpose of the ceremony (to revive vegetation) ceases to be understood, then it will be reinterpreted as a memorial enactment of the death and resurrection of the deity on a particular historical occasion in the past.

Insofar as the sacrifice was originally accompanied by cannibalism, that is to say eating the sacrificed victim in order to acquire his special fertilizing virtue, the modified form of the rite will use some edible figure as the substitute, for example a cake fashioned in the required form (see Jensen, 223, p 187). The persistence of such a symbolic sacrifice and of such ceremonial eating in more civilized times will require a special explanation, for even if the true origin is clearly indicated by the survival in neighbouring countries of the original rite, the celebrant of the modified rite will be reluctant to admit any connection between them. At this point myth intervenes to give a more acceptable explanation of the altered ceremonial. The ritual of eating the cake will be said to have been instituted by the command of the deity, who will be represented as saying: 'Do this in remembrance of me'.

It is a fundamental assumption of this account of the development of religious rites that their original purpose should at some stage be lost from sight. I might be content to leave this assumption unsupported, since nothing is more common than to find even today details of religious ceremonies carried out by people who have no idea what purpose they serve. How many church-goers could say what point there is in turning east at various moments in the liturgy, or in the use of incense? But I can in fact support my assumption by showing that a drastic change in social conditions occurred which made it very understandable that the rationale of old rituals should cease to be understood — namely urbanization. The change from village life in contact with the seasonal changes of nature, when the dependence of man on the ripening of the crops is manifest to all, to city life where these matters were more remote and the problems of life had another aspect, was a vital factor in the development of the great pagan religions of salvation. The new urban conditions gave the old rites a new meaning. The concrete concern with agricultural actualities was replaced by psychological problems of a different order. In the small village communities the condition of different individuals may not differ very greatly. But the growth and differentiation of society, the emergence of large classes of thwarted and depressed persons whose normal instincts could not, in the existing social conditions, find proper satisfaction, meant that religious rites, instead of being the accepted method of ensuring certain material requirements (e.g. crops), became a means of replacing them. They became a substitute. In the mystical interpretation of old rites, depressed and impoverished persons were able to find an 'ideal' satisfaction. This might partly consist merely in the belief in a future life of retribution and recompense, to be ensured by participation in the magic ceremonial and by observance of certain norms of behaviour. To return to my example of the dramatic portrayal of the death and resurrection of the god, we may say that the town-dweller, who had come to hope for his own resurrection in a future, happier existence, would regard his participation in the ritual as a means of ensuring his own desired immortality. The connection was obvious. Just as the ritual portrayed the god's death, and his triumph over death, so the participant, who had faith in the god, could hope that the ritual would magically ensure his own eternal life.[2] In this way, rites which in the original agricultural conditions aimed at making the crops grow, could in conditions of urbanized poverty be resorted to in order to ensure a blessed immortality (see Frankfort, 162, pp 18–19). Brandon indicates the evolution when he says that Osiris, 'the vegetation god *par excellence* of Egypt', became 'the Saviour to whom men and women turned for the assurance of immortality' (63, p 275).

The idea of personal immortality, which is foreign to early Jewish and early Greek ideas, was greatly encouraged by the absorption of formerly independent communities into large empires (first the Greek and then the Roman). In the older days religion could still be a national, not an individual matter. The tribe or the city-state could expect its deity to succour it in affairs which concerned the well-being of all, such as the growth of its fortunes in war. But when such a community ceased to exist as an independent unit, its deity could no longer be a tribal appurtenance, and, as the God and ruler of *all* men, he would be regarded as favouring not a particular tribe, but rather particular individuals. Bell has said (37, p 65) that, in the first centuries of our era, this increased emphasis on personal religion, as against the communal ideas of the older cults, was a prominent trend in the Graeco-Roman world generally. And it produced similar effects in Hellenistic, Jewish and Christian religious thinking. For instance, in some Christian epistles written late in the first century or early in the second, baptism is designated 'regeneration' – the baptized person has acquired new life. Knox notes that the same idea can be found in the pagan mystery cults of the period; and he infers that the concern of both the Christian and the pagan cults with personal religion was leading, in the theology which explained them, to the independent development of such metaphors (259, p 94).

A significant feature of the religious life of the first century was the multiplication of private brotherhoods, cult associations (sodalitates, thiasoi) devoted to the worship of a certain god.[3] Statements by Epictetus, Celsus and Josephus suggest that a certain standard of behaviour was required in these brotherhoods.[4] Poverty and humility are likely to have been stressed, for it seems reasonable to expect that the least fortunate in this life will reap the highest rewards in the other – a widespread idea which underlies all kinds of asceticism and mortification. But there is also a principle of reciprocity which life in a community teaches. 'Do unto others as you would they should do unto you' is a precept which must naturally suggest itself to all social animals. An injury provokes retaliation, while a friendly gesture will often be returned. This applies in particular to the weaker individuals, to whom other methods of ensuring due consideration are not available. Meekness, courtesy, affability are attitudes naturally assumed by the weak in the presence of the strong because it is felt that they are more likely to elicit sympathetic and friendly treatment than arrogance and rudeness. The same motives do not apply in the case of the powerful in the presence of the weak. Thus it is that humility, kindness, generosity are virtues especially developed among the poor and depressed classes and it was to these classes in the Roman Empire that Christianity especially appealed. In the first three centuries of its existence it 'made little impression on the aristocracy' and in its early days 'most of its adherents were persons of low degree and little or no education' (302, pp 20, 37). Non-resistance to evil, inculcated by Jesus, represents the extreme of meekness and humility. I am not, of course, suggesting that such preaching was delivered by a historical Jesus. If there had been such a person, why is he also represented as indulging in continuous vilification of the Pharisees?

I have tried, then, to account for belief in the historicity of saviour gods in terms of erroneous inferences – religious rites and symbols, being no longer understood, were given new interpretations. Another kind of erroneous inference which has been important in religious evolution is that written descriptions of some event (historical or imaginary) may be read by persons who know nothing of the real subject represented, and who freshly interpret the document in accordance with their own knowledge. In this way they may take the writing to refer to people entirely unknown to the actual writers. In the Psalms, for instance, the term 'the anointed' or 'the Messiah' is used to designate the reigning king. Later generations, reading the Psalms when the historical kingship had ceased to exist, nevertheless assumed that the meaning of the Psalmist had some relevance to present times; and that since there were no more kings in the old sense, his reference must be to another king or Messiah, perhaps in heaven (cf. above, p 111). An example important for Christian origins of this kind of reinterpretation of old documents is the way Paul and other early Christian writers interpret OT passages as references to Jesus. It has long been appreciated that a great deal of Jesus' biography was constructed from OT models. Later, Paul's writings were in turn interpreted by Christians who were too remote from the earliest Christian times to properly understand them. He had written of the practice of speaking in 'tongues' of ecstasy (1 Cor. 14:5). The author of Acts took this to mean the speaking of foreign languages, and explained the apostles' ability to speak them by his story of the miracle of Pentecost (2:1–13). Such misinterpretations and misunderstandings meant that the original traditions were completely remoulded in perfectly good faith – deliberate falsification or fraud was not involved. What is essential to my thesis (that there was no historical Jesus) is that such misinterpretations should fail to be corrected. And the reason for this is that they refer to past events which no experience can directly reproduce.

(ii) The Pagan Resurrected Saviour God: Baptism and Eucharist

Some scholars have recently urged that the main efflorescence of pagan cults worshipping saviour gods came only in the second and third centuries AD – 'much too late to have provided Christianity with its fundamental doctrines' (180, pp 77–8). Fuller, however, concedes that this 'attractive' suggestion 'does not quite fit the facts', since mystery cults were active in the very areas missionized by first century Christians: 'Antioch was in close contiguity with the Adonis cult, Ephesus with the Cybele and Attis cult, Corinth with the Eleusinian mysteries' (166, pp 91–2). It is, however, true that, although the cults of Attis and Adonis can be proved to have included from immemorial times ritual lamentation of the god's death, celebration of his resurrection is not unambiguously attested in literature until the second century (that of Attis by Plutarch, and that of Adonis by Lucian). The cult of Attis was encouraged at Rome by Claudius (d. AD 54), and included the ritual mourning of a felled pine tree, symbolizing the vegetation god. But the festival may not originally have also included a later day of rejoicing (Hilaria) celebrating his resurrection, for Hilaria is not attested until about AD 200, and there is even some dispute as to whether it celebrated the god's resurrection, although this is indicated by its date (25 March) — the first day of the year when the day is longer than the night. Archaeological evidence, however, suggests that the legends of Attis (which represent him as dying and remaining dead) were supplemented by the idea of his resurrection before Christian times.[5] Tammuz was also originally worshipped only as a dying god, and whether the idea of his resurrection was added to his cult before our era is still disputed. He was, in any case, not at any early date believed to confer immortality, since the idea of human immortality was foreign to the Babylonians (cf. below, p 202).

That gods in whom natural forces are personified should suffer and even die is quite intelligible. Nature seems benumbed in winter, so gods who personify it were believed to suffer imprisonment or injury. In hot climates the summer sun also has deathly power, and the generative force of nature is thought to reside not in the sun but in the earth and in its water. In the mythologies of the ancient Near East a god such as Adonis 'represents the brief spring, a sudden blooming of indescribable loveliness which withers in a few weeks' in the summer heat. And the earth figures as a goddess – the mother, sister or wife of the suffering and dying god whom she mourns. As she personifies nature's prolific fertility, she recovers from the annual injury which the loss of the god-child symbolizes; but her recovery does not necessarily entail the resurrection of the god, although in some myths he is represented as returning to earth to restore her fecundity. [6] In yet others the recovery of nature was attributed directly to the resurrection of the god, and the goddess relegated to a less important role. Thus the resurrection of Osiris 'personified the resurgence of vitality which becomes manifest in the growing corn, the waxing flood, the increasing moon' (161, p 197).

Wagner holds that in the second and third centuries AD the cults of Attis, Adonis and Tammuz were assimilated to the Osiris cult and to the Eleusinian mysteries in the general syncretism of Imperial times. This theorem leaves the Osirian and Eleusinian rituals unimpugned as early rites, based on belief in a resurrected god, which mediated a blessed immortality (cf. below, p 202), and which in time came to have great

183

influence on other cults. Lambrechts, who also denies that Attis and Adonis were originally regarded as resurrected, agrees that Osirian influence was important, and that in early Egyptian rites the festivals of mourning were always followed immediately by jubilation at the discovery of the fragments of the god's mutilated body, and at its reconstitution (270, p 238). The resurrected Osiris did not, of course, return to earth (any more than the resurrected Jesus resumed his earthly life); both, after an unjust death, rose to rule over the kingdom of the dead as saviour and judge.

Brandon has studied the rituals used from the third millennium BC to confer immortality on dead Pharaohs (68, p 45). The desired result was thought to be achieved by 'assimilating' the deceased to Osiris, i.e. by performing on the corpse acts which, it was believed, had caused Osiris to rise from the dead. Thus the mouth was opened, and the whole body bathed in water (a life-giving substance in the view of primitive peoples, and also the substance which daily rejuvenated the setting sun). The deceased was also directly identified with Osiris, being addressed by this name and told to 'wake up'. This mortuary ritual was in time extended from kings to lesser folk, and 'continued to be practised until the forcible suppression of paganism in favour of Christianity in the fourth century AD'. This process of making a dead person one with the god by means of ritual acts was 'so natural and therefore so necessary that it recurs in the practice of other later religions' (64, pp 25—9). Brandon instances Christianity as a case in point. Paul supposed that Jesus' crucifixion, accomplished in ignorance of his true character by demons (see above, pp 19f) had potentially broken their hold over mankind. But he naturally asked himself how the triumph won over them by Christ could be made available to those who accepted him as saviour. His answer was: by means of baptism. He thus interpreted the ritual lustration already known in Palestine (see Thomas, 387) as 'a ritual of mystic assimilation whereby the neophyte was to be united to Christ both in his death and resurrection' (64, p 31). There are three actions in a baptism of total immersion, and Paul regarded them all as symbolic. Entering the water signified death, immersion beneath it meant burial, and emergence from it resurrection (Rom. 6:1—8). This ritual of death and resurrection was carefully provided for in the baptismal rites of the early Church. Candidates undressed, descended into the water, and emerged to be reclothed in white robes, given a new name and receive mystic food of milk and honey (68, p 41). This view of baptism, deriving from Paul, invokes that same 'principle of ritual assimilation that had for so many centuries operated in the Osirian mortuary cult'. In sum:

'The Osirian ritual was designed to secure post-mortem salvation for the dead: the Christian baptismal ritual was performed to place the living in a state of salvation. But each was concerned with a common task, namely of mediating new life that had been won by a divine saviour (Rom. 6:8—11; Coloss. 2:20; 3:2—4). To accomplish that task each ritual was significantly based upon the principle of mystical (or magical) association' (64, p 33).

Paul, then, knew baptism as an existing Jewish rite to which he gave his own Christological interpretation. Later it was natural to explain the origin of the Christian rite by representing it as instituted by Jesus or at least as modelled on his own practice. The former course is taken by Mt. 28:19, which makes the risen Jesus enjoin baptism in a trinitarian formula which shows that this verse embodies a late idea. The latter course is taken by Jn. 3:22 and 4:2 which (in contrast to the synoptics) make both Jesus and his disciples baptize.[7] Jesus' own baptism by John the Baptist, narrated (with significant variations) in all three synoptics, can also be viewed as a legend inspired by the baptismal practices of the early Christians (cf. above, p 157).

Not only baptism but the eucharist existed as pre-Christian rite. Metzger, who urges 'caution' in linking Christianity with paganism, concedes that Mithraism 'appears to have had something which looked like the Christian eucharist. Before the initiate there were set a piece of bread and a cup of water, over which the priest muttered a ritual formula' (298, pp 12, 14–15). Mithra came to earth to labour for man, and then reascended. He is thus a suffering and rising, though not a dying, god, for there is no evidence that his ascension was preceded by death. According to Plutarch, the Romans first encountered him in Pompey's campaign against the Cilician pirates in 67 BC. The evidence for his cult (summarized by Vermaseren, 391, pp 253–4) is mainly archaeological, and the following incidents in his life can be inferred from monuments. He is born from a rock as a sun god. (Light is shown streaming from the celestial vault in representation of his birth.) He delivers mankind from drought, and catches and kills the bull whose blood fertilizes the earth. (The animal's fertilizing power is shown by representations of his tail ending in ears of corn). He and his followers drink the bull's blood and eat its flesh; and finally he ascends and returns to the realm of light.

While the material result of killing the bull is 'the burgeoning of new vegetative life', the spiritual result is the obtainment of after-life. This is apparent from some recently discovered vases in a Mithraeum which are dated AD 202 and on which is written 'you saved us by having shed the eternal blood'. This same literary evidence also establishes that – at any rate at this late date – bread and wine had replaced the meat and blood of the sacred meal. Water sometimes replaced the wine. There is nothing to suggest that Mithra was identified with the bull, or in other words that in killing the bull he sacrificed himself for mankind. It is, however, certain that the Mithraists believed that the practice of eating the meat or bread and drinking the blood or wine was favoured by the god, and ensured them a happy after-life. 'In this way bull-slaying and the sacred meal influence each other. From the outset the purpose of Mithra's birth and deeds was to save mankind from the realm of darkness and confusion' (391, p 254).

Baptism and eucharist, then, existed as pre-Christian rites, and the earliest Christian documents show them already established as Christian ones. The early Christian eucharist was a full meal and included a rite of breaking and eating a loaf consecrated by prayer. The purpose was to bring believers into true fellowship and give them the assurance that they would participate in the banquet which the Messiah was to give the elect at his final coming. Theologians have shown (see JEC, pp 263–9) that the Pauline view – that the meal necessarily included wine as well as bread, and brought about communion with the dying and resurrected Christ (the bread symbolizing his body and the wine his blood) – was not part of the earliest tradition. Paul, however, in stressing the wine as a symbol of Jesus' blood, naturally emphasizes the link between the meal and his death (the occasion on which he provided his blood). Hence, having quoted words of Jesus (given above, p 26) which instituted the meal, Paul adds: 'For as often as you eat this bread and drink the cup, you proclaim the Lord's death until he comes' (1 Cor. 11:26). This occurs in a context where Paul is criticizing the eucharist of the Corinthian Christians; and it seems reasonable to infer that their eucharist did not imply reflection on Jesus' suffering and death, but was a bread eucharist which celebrated his power and glory – his resurrection (concerning which Paul is very noticeably silent in his account of what the eucharist should be like) and his future coming. Achtemeier has recently observed that Christian communities which regarded the historical Jesus as a powerful miracle-worker, a man of signs and wonders – as we saw (above p 101) the Corinthian Christian leaders may well have regarded him – can be expected to have had just such a eucharist. It would have celebrated not the death but the presence of the Lord in all his power. Whether or not they regarded the historical Jesus as a man of signs and wonders, they certainly believed themselves to be, by means of their ecstatic experience, in direct communion with the supernatural world (see above, p 100). They could well have understood the eucharist as providing the power to transcend the conditions of everyday life and attain the supernatural knowledge they valued (cf. 107, pp 58, 87).

Achtemeier also interprets the two miraculous feedings of the 4,000 and 5,000 in Mk. as evidence that a eucharist of a non-Pauline kind was not confined to Corinth. These two stories are not inventions of Mark, but traditions assimilated by him which therefore existed before he wrote (cf. above, pp 78f); both include four key words and actions which Mark also ascribes to Jesus at the Last Supper, namely taking bread, blessing, breaking and giving it. Nevertheless, the agreement between the eucharistic details in the two feeding stories and Mark's narrative of the Last Supper is far from exact and therefore pre-Marcan. Had the evangelist introduced these details deliberately in order to harmonize the feeding stories with his story of the Last Supper, he would have made them correspond more closely (Schweizer, 366, p 77). The feeding miracles are epiphanic – they show Jesus to be divine. In Achtemeier's view, the accounts of these miracles formed part of a liturgy recited at a eucharist which likewise stressed Jesus' strength and power: 'As he was revealed in his mighty acts as a *deus praesens,* so he is revealed in the meal as among his participants. This would have the further implication that, for the participants, the eschatological age has already begun, that the Christ whose reality was seen in the miracles was now at hand in the celebration of the eucharist' (1, p 208).

Communities, then, which saw power and glory in the earthly career of Jesus, could 'celebrate his glorious presence at their communal meals without the need to interpose an account of the inauguration of those meals specifically anchored in Jesus' death and subsequent glorification' (1, p 212). Paul's contrary view of the eucharist was, however, the one that prevailed and which found its way into the Marcan passion narrative; for Mark, we saw, accepted the Pauline view of an earthly Jesus who was distinguished principally by a shameful and lonely death. The evangelist subordinated contrary traditions to this view by the device of the Messianic secret (see above, p 102). In fact, the Pauline view of both baptism and eucharist could have provided the basis from which passion narratives, which form a substantial fraction of the gospels (particularly of Mk.) were in time developed. These narratives were certainly not written from biographical interest, which would have been better satisfied by an account of Jesus' earthly life (which is treated but sketchily in the gospels), than by a detailed description of the circumstances of his death. Rather do they reflect the special significance which the Church ascribed to his death. Baptism would, we saw, enable Christians to think of Jesus' passion, death and resurrection; and Schille has pointed out that there are a number of early Christ hymns (e.g. Phil. 2:6—11) which mention his passion (without dwelling on it) as part of such a sequence. The Pauline eucharist, however, would occasion reflections as to how much he had suffered in order to provide his redeeming blood; and Schille thinks that interest of this kind furnished the basis for a narrative about the details of his passion (347, pp 170–98).

Schille divides the Marcan passion narrative into two principal sections: the story of the final day of Jesus' life (Mk. 15), and the preceding account (14:17–72) of his last night alive, from the beginning of his last meal with his disciples until cock-crow the following morning. (The unity of this second section is broken by Jesus' eucharistic words 'this is my body', etc.) These two principal sections are strikingly independent, in that 14:17–72 contains repeated references to the 'night' on which the events there described occurred, but none at all to the events of the following day (the subject of Mk. 15). And the whole of the former section — from Jesus' prophecy at table that he will be betrayed, to Peter's weeping at cock-crow — seems to be an elaboration of what, according to Paul (1 Cor. 11:23ff), Christians should have in mind about the night when Jesus was 'handed over' (cf. above, p 25) when they are celebrating the eucharist. Schille thinks that the two sections of Mk. were written in order to be used at two cultic festivals of early Christian communities: the narrative of the last day of Jesus' life was composed, he thinks, to be read to the community each Good Friday (see above, p 138): and the preceding narrative of the night before his execution was written as a text to a eucharist celebrated on the previous night. Schille does not assert that these narratives, because composed for ritual purposes, reflect nothing at all that is historical about Jesus. He leaves the amount of historical fact in them an open question (p 200).

According to Schille, then, the gospel passion narratives drew out the implications of a particular kind of eucharist. This theory would certainly account for the fact that the eucharistic texts ('this is my body', etc.) are an independent unit within the narrative of Christ's suffering, death and resurrection. But Feneberg has objected that the theory fails to account for the further facts that the eucharistic texts have themselves been placed within the passion narrative; and that Mark, when detailing the preparations which Jesus orders to be made for the Last Supper, clearly represents it as a passover meal (see above, p 135), whereas the meal itself as reported later in the same chapter (with the eucharistic words) is by no means identical with a Jewish passover meal. Feneberg's theory (154, pp 113–38) is that the whole passion and resurrection narrative, including the eucharistic words, must be understood as derivative from the festival of Easter, the celebration of man's redemption through Christ's death and resurrection. Easter itself clearly derives from the Jewish passover festival, as is obvious from the coincidence of names and dates. The Greek word 'pascha' (from Hebrew 'pesach') means both passover and Easter. The early Christian 'Quartodecimans' actually celebrated Easter on the day of the passover (14 Nisan, on whatever day of the week that fell), and other early Christian communities on the Sunday immediately following; only later was a date calculated independent of Jewish reckoning. Easter, then, is the Christian way of celebrating the passover. The early Christians were Jews who did not drop the passover (any more than they did the OT), but understood it in their own way and in time (as they moved further away from Jewish ideas) refashioned it.

The passover had undergone many changes in the course of Jewish history, and by NT times had come to be understood as a commemoration of the Exodus from Egypt. The feast included a narrative – an interpretation of the various elements of the passover meal: the unleavened bread symbolized past misery, the bitter herbs slavery, and the lamb was a reminder of God's 'passing over' Egypt, and so on. The story of Yahweh's deliverance of his people from Egyptian captivity was not recited as historical reminiscence, but understood as a pointer to the final deliverance which was to come with the advent of the Messiah. Now the early Christians could not understand this coming redemption entirely in the manner of Jewish messianism or apocalyptic. For them, the final deliverance had already been made manifest in Christ's death and resurrection, and they eagerly awaited his return, his second coming. They would therefore make changes in the narrative part of the passover celebration. At the point where mention was made of Yahweh's deed of salvation towards his people, they would specify not only the deliverance from Egypt, but also that effected by the resurrection of Jesus. (And in time they would drop the Exodus narrative altogether.) Having taken this step, they would naturally proceed to modify the second part of the passover ceremony, the meal. They would consider it unnecessary to eat a lamb, as Christ had already shed his blood as a paschal sacrifice. (This idea occurs as early as 1 Cor. 5:7: 'Christ, our paschal lamb, has been sacrificed'.) The lamb would accordingly be replaced by a meal which had obvious symbolic reference to Christ's blood. The unleavened bread, which in the Jewish passover meal stood for the 'bread of affliction' eaten at the Exodus, could be retained; but it was reinterpreted and understood as symbolizing not the misery of the Exodus, but the body of Jesus which he had given to suffering and death. It is obvious that, on this view, the first Christians did not eat (symbolically) the flesh or drink the blood of Jesus at the rite, but remembered his sacrificial act. The idea of feeding on his flesh and blood was a later development.

Feneberg's theory is that the gospel passion stories 'historicize', in terms of a biography of Jesus, this Easter festival, with its two constituent parts of narrative and meal. The story of his suffering, death and resurrection is intelligible as an expansion of the narrative part of the festival. And the eucharistic words ('this is my body', etc.) represent the meal as instituted by the historical Jesus, so that they have to be placed in the gospels *before* his suffering and death, even though, in the festival, the meal *followed* the narrative. The process of 'historicizing' has taken different forms in the synoptic gospels and in Jn. The synoptics have linked Jesus' last meal with the passover (by representing it as a passover meal). The fourth gospel has linked his death with the passover, by making his last meal take place earlier and his death coincide with the slaughter of paschal lambs in the temple. Additional details of the gospel passion narratives, such as the stories of Judas' betrayal and Peter's denial of Jesus, can be understood as inspired by the experience of persecution and apostasy which Christian communities were then experiencing (cf. above, p 136).

(iii) Deified Men and Gnosticism
Individuals are necessarily always involved in the inauguration of a new religion, but the important personages in the world's great cults — Buddha, Paul, Mohammed, Fox, Wesley, Joseph Smith — are not regarded as gods but as prophets or inspired teachers. Greek lore includes 'heroes' (Hercules, Asklepios) who may have been originally conceived as mortal men and later deified, or who were originally regarded as divine and later provided with human biographies. In either case the period in which they

were extensively worshipped is much later than their supposed lifetime. Asklepios, for instance, figures in Homer as a skilful physician whose sons were doctors in the Greek camp at Troy. Only centuries later was he widely worshipped as a saviour god.

Some few men whose existence is better attested have also been deified long after their death, e.g. Imhotep 2,500 years after.[8] Others have demanded or received divine honours in or near their lifetime. The best known of these were men of considerable political or military influence, e.g. the Pharaohs, Lysander, Alexander the Great and his successors (see 43 and 327), and often their cults did not long survive their own political power. Gibbon notes (173, I, 69–70) that the same is true of the deified Caesars. Emperor worship had an obvious social function in the Roman Empire as the link which held its diverse parts together; and it was sincere to a point, for 'there were doubtless many who felt a genuine enthusiasm for the ruler whose power was their guarantee against external attack and internal anarchy' (37, pp 57–8).

Another group of men who sometimes claimed divine status were the itinerant prophets, preachers and miracle workers of the Hellenistic world. We saw (above, p 100) that the prevalence of such men created the intellectual climate in which Jesus could readily come to be regarded as a miracle-worker. Celsus gives a specimen of their teaching, as current in his own day in the region 'about Phoenicia and Palestine'. He tells that they posed as divine personages who 'would return with heavenly power' and 'save' those who accepted their doctrines from the general destruction which would be the lot of an iniquitous world (318, 7:8–9). We know little about such divine men, partly because their influence was ephemeral and their appeal to simple people, not to the educated class which wrote the extant literature; and partly because, if they did succeed in founding a viable sect, its records were later destroyed by rivals. The Simon Magus of Acts 8:6–24, and Apollonius of Tyana, if they existed at all, were men of this type and active in the first century AD.[9] Among men who 'said that they were gods', Justin (ca. AD 150) includes a certain Simon, active in Rome at the time of Claudius (AD 41–54) – he may or may not be the Simon Magus of Acts (the identification is made only by later Christian writers) – his alleged disciple Menander, and the undoubtedly historical Marcion, who died ca. AD 160 (235, 1:26; cf. Wetter, 407, for details).

Such men often were (or came to be regarded as) exponents of some form of gnosticism. The hypothesis that gnosticism existed before Christianity and influenced it has naturally been resisted, and many Christian scholars prefer to accept the patristic view that all gnosticism is a heretical deviation from true Christianity. But views alluded to by Paul suggest standpoints in some respects like those known from the gnosticism of later centuries. Yamauchi concludes his highly sceptical survey of the evidence by accepting 'the presence of an incipient gnosticism slightly later than the genesis of Christianity'. By this he seems to allow that 'Paul and John interacted with and combated a rudimentary form of gnosticism'

(417, p 185). It is therefore plain that some form of gnosticism existed as an influential factor in the environment when Christianity originated.

A detailed picture of the nature of gnosticism can be constructed only from later evidence; it may, of course, have been different in the first century. In Persia there still exist people who call themselves Mandaeans ('gnostics'), whose religious texts were already ancient at the time of the Moslem conquest (137, p 9). There is wide agreement that the roots of this religion 'belong to the chronological and spatial proximity of primitive Christianity, and either originated directly from a Gnosticized Judaism, or at least appeared very early in a polemical exchange with syncretistic Judaism'. Mandaean influence on the fourth gospel has been particularly stressed. The available Mandaean texts are regarded as 'late and deformed witnesses for a Jewish gnosticism which took form on the edge of Judaism, and which is to be accepted as the spiritual background of Jn.' (268, pp 158–9).

It is a fundamental gnostic idea that individual human selves are fragments of one single heavenly being which was overpowered by evil forces, dismembered, and, after being robbed of all memory of heavenly origin, forced into individual material bodies (353, p 28). This heavenly being was often regarded not as the highest God, but as himself created by the supreme entity in the form of Archetypal Man – a spiritual, 'mystic' or 'secret' Adam in whose image the human Adam (physical man) was in turn made.[10] From these premises, man's task is to recognize that his true self, his soul, has this heavenly origin; and according to early gnostic thought, this is something that can be achieved by the individual without instruction from a redeemer figure who comes down from heaven. Later, however, the idea that the divine substance is present in all men was replaced by the view that it exists only in a few distinguished individuals, and these were then regarded as redeemers of the rest of mankind.

A transition between these two standpoints seems to have been represented by (or ascribed to) Simon Magus, who is alleged to have taught in the first half of the first century that angels had created the world and had imprisoned the divine substance in human beings. Acts (the oldest account of Simon) represents him as someone who, 'for a long time' before he heard anything of Christianity, had amazed the Samaritans with his magic. He declared he 'was somebody great', and the people heeded him, saying: 'This man is that power of God which is called Great' (8:9–11). All later traditions concerning Simon likewise record his claim to be 'the great power', a gnostic technical term for God. (Haenchen thinks that the author of Acts is interpreting the term when he writes of 'the power *of God* called great'.)[11] According to these later traditions, Simon taught that in him the 'great power' had come down to earth to reveal to men that their souls are also part of the 'great power'. His own claim to divinity thus did not exclude the divinity of other men. But in teaching, as he did, that salvation was to be attained merely by accepting his preaching, he made it possible for his followers to regard him as a divine saviour, as a redeemer who possessed divinity in a way that other men did not.

It is clear that all current predicates of divine or semi-divine beings could be ascribed to such a person, and Schmithals has shown, from the – admittedly late – evidence of Hippolytus (d. AD 235), that one of Simon's titles – whether he used it himself, or whether it was only later applied to him – was the Jewish religious term 'Christ' (i.e. Messiah). It was only the term that was borrowed, not the Jewish Messianic ideas associated with it. On this view, 'Christ' was used by pre-Christian gnostics as synonymous with the 'great power', and meant not a Davidic king nor a messenger from heaven (such as the Son of man Messiah of Jewish apocalyptic), but the Archetypal Man or Spiritual Adam present in all men. Schmithals argues that this transfer of the Jewish Messianic title 'Christ' to Archetypal Man (the principal figure of gnosticism) could have occurred only where gnosticism was trying to establish itself in an area dominated by Jewish ideas; and that the Jews of that area would not have objected to the equation Messiah = Archetypal man, since the old idea of a human Messiah (a Davidic king) was falling more and more into discredit at the time in question, and acceptance of the supernatural Son of man Messiah was accompanied by a general openness to gnostic ideas (353, pp 40–55; 69).

Schmithals has tried to reconstruct the ideas of gnostics of the first century AD from Christian attacks on rivals (352, p 115 and n). He finds that they believed in a redeemer who would come down from heaven. He did not usually figure as a man with human flesh, for gnostics regarded flesh as essentially evil. Often he barely comes into the world, but merely sounds a 'call' from outside it, or comes as 'word' from the beyond. Sanders has stressed the influence of such gnostic ideas, which he regards as pre-Christian, on a number of Pauline passages, e.g. Coloss. 1:15–20 and Phil. 2:6–11, where Jesus is depicted as a heavenly being who came to redeem us by his voluntary death, and was then exalted and enthroned, and the cosmic powers subjected to him (344, pp 24, 39, 96). In the Mandaean literature the redeeming revelation is brought by an anonymous messenger, whose appearance is vaguely assigned to primeval times. It is not uncommon for later gnostic traditions to place what was originally an anonymous word of redemption in the mouth of a redeemer regarded as a historical personage (352, p 126). In this connection, Schmithals and Bultmann have argued that the metaphysical discourses of the fourth gospel – long recognized as incompatible with Jesus' speeches as recorded in the synoptics – were taken by John from a literary source in which the speaker was an anonymous figure concerning whom one may not inquire as to the time and place of his appearing. All the names which this redeemer bears (light, soul, vine, life, way, good shepherd, etc.) are pictorial ones which portray his significance. The Revealer is in truth the Gnosis itself, not a historical figure. John has combated the gnosticism of his source-document by representing these speeches as the statements of a historical personage of flesh and blood. Kümmel agrees that John is appropriating to Jesus salvation-predicates (such as vine, shepherd, the envoy) which were ascribed to gnostic figures of relevation, and that the evangelist 'is considerably indebted for his conceptual world, especially as it appears in the Johannine Jesus discourses, to a heterodox Jewish-Gnostic milieu, which must be supposed on the edge of a Palestinian Judaism, and which was strongly influenced by a Syrian mythological Gnosticism' (268, pp 161–2).

(iv) Syncretism

The pagan mystery religions of the Roman Empire were not entirely new revelations, but adaptations of cults which reach back into prehistory. The worship of Jesus, however, is not documented before the first century AD, and appears as the cult of a new divinity. Why did it arise? I think the answer lies in the environment. Where men of different traditions, outlook and creeds are brought together in peaceful intercourse, existing religious beliefs begin to be eroded and replaced by others. All animals tend to be conservative in a constant environment, and new forms of behaviour arise only when conditions change. Man lives in a social environment, and his ideas are chiefly determined by those which prevail among his fellows. In an isolated society there may be almost complete uniformity in all ideas that are unaffected by personal daily experience, and it will be almost impossible for an individual to break away from the traditional beliefs. He necessarily believes what everyone else seems to believe, particularly in matters where experiment and personal investigation is difficult or impossible. But in the eastern provinces of the Roman Empire there was, when Christianity arose, no single established set of beliefs or practices but a chaos of both, made up of elements from Egypt, Assyria, Persia, Greece and other sources. Furthermore, the growth of this large empire, which had destroyed so many smaller communities, meant that groups and clubs of a non-political kind grew up, where the individual might find comfort or instruction or at least companionship. The religious brotherhoods which proliferated at the beginning of our era claimed to provide wisdom (sophia) and knowledge (gnosis). Not vulgar knowledge of everyday tangible things, but mystical truths. The epistle of James makes it clear (1:5–7) that, for such seekers after esoteric wisdom, doubt was a vice. Gnosis is the attempt to attain knowledge of God, of his nature, and of the nature and meaning of the universe. This very vague and intangible knowledge, when communicated to new recruits, would in all likelihood become even more muddled than it originally was. And this kind of distortion would occur readily because intercourse prevailed between persons of different mental capacity and cultural background, brought together by the mixture of peoples and cultures in the Roman Empire. Once again I must stress the distinction (cf. above, p 178) between practical and theoretical or religious beliefs. Where practical invention was concerned, skill was maintained by the discipline of practical results. In the case of theoretical beliefs there was no such preserving discipline, and the result was muddle and confusion. It is well illustrated in the works of Philo of Alexandria, and also in such works as the book of the Secrets of Enoch, written about AD 50 by an orthodox Hellenistic Jew who borrows from every quarter and incorporates Platonic, Egyptian and Zend elements into his system. Jews in Asia Minor fused the worship of Yahweh with that of Sabazius (the Phrygian Jupiter or Dionysus). Again, the Odes of Solomon (mystical hymns by an unknown second century author) give evidence of what Sanders calls 'a thoroughgoing eclecticism in their religious ideas', which he traces to an earlier Jewish sect, influenced, he argues, by the Adonis cult. These Odes, he says, seem to attest that, under such outside influence, Judaism could give birth to a myth of redemption similar to that enunciated in the pre-Pauline Christological hymns of the NT (344, pp 101–13). Such syncretism was not restricted to the Diaspora. Recent archaeological discoveries of synagogues and tombs from the second and later centuries have disposed of the rabbinical dogma that Palestine was an anti-Hellenistic oasis; they show that, even there, Jews used pictures and symbols from pagan sources and thus shared in oriental and Graeco-Roman culture (230, p 81; 316, pp 122–3). Lohse notes (281, p 89) that the Jews ascribed to pagan authors various doctrines they had themselves composed, and added Jewish sayings to the Sibylline oracles. In both cases the motive was to show the accordance of Jewish with pagan thought. And Qumran discoveries have shown that Pharisaic orthodoxy existed side by side with quite different forms of Jewish thought and life. Jewish gnostics had many ideas in common with the pagan mysteries. It is true that, while the gnostics regarded man's soul as essentially divine, and therefore called upon him to save himself by achieving true self-knowledge, the mystae *acquired* something of the divinity's nature as a result of a cultic act of mystic communion. In both cases, however, the result was to confer an assurance of immortality, and this was the point of contact which facilitated linkage and confusion between the two sets of ideas.

The early Christians were as much exposed to the influence of Jewish and pagan sects as these were to each other. The NT epistle of Jude does not hesitate to quote the Jewish book of Enoch as of equal prophetic value with words of Christian apostles (verses 14, 17). Bauer has given detailed evidence that, in a number of early Christian centres, the new religion rested on 'syncretistic-gnostic foundations'. That certain early Christian ideas and practices were closely related to pagan ones is clear from Paul's complaint (1 Cor. 10:21) that members of his flock were wont to attend both Christian and pagan rites, and therefore presumably found them not so very different. It is usual to discount pagan influence by supposing that early Christians would necessarily have despised anything that smacked of polytheism. Reviewers of JEC have asked incredulously how (if there had been no historical Jesus) a monotheistic Jew such as Paul could come to believe in a divine being called Jesus. But the Jewish thought of the period was not uniformly monotheistic, and Paul revised current beliefs about a 'pleroma' of supernatural beings so as to make of them an acceptable quasi-monotheism involving both God and Jesus (see JEC, p 290). The monotheism of much of the Jewish Wisdom literature is also questionable.[12] I would claim that, in this present book, I am able to show, more clearly than I did in JEC, how much there was in the Jewish (as against the pagan) background that makes the rise of Christianity intelligible without a historical Jesus. But in any case, even if pagan religious thinking had been as different from Judaism as my reviewers supposed, it would not follow that Paul would have been repelled by a Christianity which shared certain features with paganism; for when he became a Christian, his ideas underwent a change, presumably from orthodox Pharisaism to something very different. What this something was, and what connection it had with current Jewish and pagan ideas, is something to be investigated, not determined *a priori*.

Concerning the monotheism of early Christianity, it may be said that, while Paul was cautious enough to avoid actually calling Jesus God, some later NT writers spoke of 'our great God and Saviour Jesus Christ' (Titus 2:13; cf. 2 Peter 1:1). Furthermore, Paul characteristically says 'God raised' Jesus from the dead (Rom. 10:9 etc.; 1 Thess. 4:14 should also be thus interpreted, see Evans, 151, p 21). But many second-century Christians insisted that Jesus rose by means of his own power. Teeple notes that 'the primitive Christian view was consistent with the monotheism of Judaism, whereas the later interpretation was suggested by the triumph over death by pagan deities' (10, p 114).

What my reader will naturally ask is, how the Christian idea of a supernatural personage who has come to earth to suffer and die by crucifixion, and who will come again as judge in the future, can be understood as an amalgamation of elements in the intellectual environment. The first Christians were Jews, sharing the ideas and practices of orthodox Jews. Naturally, within this framework, they had ideas of their own, as did other Jewish groups such as Pharisees, Sadducees and Essenes. In time, Christian ideas became so markedly different from those of orthodox Jews that the Christians formed a separate body. What we have to try to understand is, what ideas, within the range of those acceptable to orthodox Jews, formed the starting point of this process.

Now the Jewish idea of the Messiah was the source for the view that the redeemer would come in the future. According to the Jewish apocalypse of Ezra, the Messiah will die after a reign of four hundred years, and all mankind with him; all will be resurrected a week later for God's final judgement. These are unchristian ideas, and the passage expressing them is unlikely to be a Christian interpolation. They also stimulated some Jewish protest, for the passage is omitted by the Arabic and Armenian versions, and in one of the Latin manuscripts 'adsumetur' has been substituted for 'morietur', thus bringing the passage into accord with the doctrine of the 'Syriac' apocalypse of Baruch, contemporary with it, where the Messiah is to return to heaven without tasting death, and then 'all who have fallen asleep in hope of him shall rise again' (2 Baruch 30:1–2; cf. Box, 61, p 117). What these passages show is a linkage, within Judaism, of the idea of the reign of the Messiah and the idea of resurrection. We saw (above, p 113) that this linkage is understandable as a synthesis of early and late Jewish thought about the end-time. In the Ezra passage the linkage has gone so far that death and resurrection are predicated of the Messiah himself. But his coming is still located in the future. Whence, then, the specifically Christian view that he had already lived and died? Obviously important in this connection were the pagan ideas of a god who had suffered and died on earth in the remote past. We saw that Paul's evaluation of the death of Jesus is 'based on concepts which were alien to the Jewish religion and akin to that of Osiris' (Brandon, 64, p 30; cf. above, p 184). And Rom. 6:2ff shows him interpreting the death and resurrection in terms of pagan mysteries and their sacramentalism.[13] Pagan ideas about a past redeemer could amalgamate readily with ideas embodied in Jewish Wisdom literature, where Wisdom figures as a pre-existent entity who had come to earth to warn and instruct man, and who is said to have been 'established in Zion' (Sirach 24:10) and to have died a 'shameful death' (cf. above, p 39). Such statements may have been originally mere metaphor, but the reader of the first century AD had lost all historical and critical understanding of this sacred literature, and had come to regard it as God's revelation to him and his age. The relevance of the Wisdom literature is obvious from Paul's allusions to the mysterious divine wisdom, which the angelic governors of the world did not recognize; for had they done so, they would not have crucified the Lord of glory (cf. above, pp 19f). The possible influence of Jewish gnostic ideas on early Christian thought may also have caused the redeemer to be regarded as a figure of the past; for gnostics assigned his journey to earth to primeval times (see above, p 192). Schmithals points in this connection to chapters 70 and 71 of the book of Enoch, where, he says, the Patriarch Enoch himself appears as the incarnation of the Son of man Messiah, who had therefore been on earth in the remote past. Placing the redeemer in the relatively recent past could have been suggested to early Christians by contact with the Essenes. The Dead Sea Scrolls show that the Essenes of the first century AD kept alive the memory of the sect's leader, who had been tortured and killed by the official priesthood of Jerusalem some time before 63 BC. Christianity thus originated in a Jewish environment which revered a past leader of Messianic proportions.

Jewish ideas about the Messiah may also have inspired the Christian view that the redeemer would suffer. The apocalypses of the first centuries BC and AD refer repeatedly to the 'birth pangs of the Messiah' or 'the Messianic travail', meaning the woes that will precede his coming. Klausner has observed (252, p 440) that 'by understanding the Hebrew expression too literally', it is possible to take it to mean 'sufferings endured by the Messiah'. It was a familiar thought that, when suffering was greatest, the Messiah would be nearest. It was no great step to suppose that he would himself experience some of the suffering. Again, Zechariah 12:10 mentions lamentations over a martyr 'whom they have pierced' after all heathendom gathered at Jerusalem and perished there. The Talmud interpreted the passage as a reference to the Messiah ben Joseph, who – certainly in post-Christian Jewish thought and possibly earlier – is placed alongside the Messiah ben David as a war leader, but as one who is to be slain in battle (and who thus suffers, but not by way of atonement). Furthermore, in the apocalypse of Ezra the Messiah is to die. It is true that his death is not attributed to disease, maltreatment, nor to any kind of suffering, but in the muddle and distortion to be expected in the religious thinking of the times, the idea of his death could be linked with the suffering and death of religious personages mentioned in the literature of the times.

Christ's suffering, although integral to all extant Christian literature, may well have become the established view only after a doctrinal struggle. We saw (above, p 100) that Paul controverted Christians who proclaimed 'another Jesus', possibly a Jesus of power and glory. We may infer that Christ's suffering was queried at an early date from Paul's invective against Christian worship of angelic powers who supplemented Christ's work and made redemption complete – a view Christians implied when Paul tells (Coloss. 2:7–10) not to pay attention to these powers, and when he insists that it is in Christ that Christians are brought to completion. The superiority of the angels presumably lay, for these opponents of Paul, in their immunity to human weakness and suffering. Against this view, Paul 'was concerned to demonstrate (2:13–15) that the passion of Christ was not tragedy and defeat, but the very event of triumph over every contrary force' (Craddock, 109, pp 95–6). That the suffering of Christ continued to be a theological problem after Paul is suggested by the polemic of the author of Hebrews against angel-worship (cf. above, p 52).

Whence, we may ask next, the Christian stress not only on the redeemer's suffering, but also on its redemptory effects? The Wisdom traditions do not suggest that the suffering of Wisdom's envoys had atoning effect. Death as an atoning sacrifice was, however, an idea well established in the Jewish cultus, and Paul's statement that God 'put forward Christ Jesus as an expiation by his blood' (Rom. 3:25) is quite in accord with Jewish religious thinking. Furthermore, the idea of vicarious suffering was not unfamiliar to pre-Christian Judaism. Flusser has pointed to 2 Maccabees 7:18 and 38 as examples;[14] and the Pharisaic Testament of Benjamin includes the 'prophecy of heaven' (which the author regarded as fulfilled by the Patriarch Joseph) that 'a blameless one shall be delivered up for lawless men, and a sinless one shall die for ungodly men' (3:8). This passage is so close to Christian ideas that a Christian interpolator easily adapted it by adding, after 'prophecy of heaven', the words 'concerning the lamb of God and saviour of the world' and, after 'ungodly men', the words 'in the blood of the covenant for the salvation of the gentiles and of Israel'. (The words are obviously Christian in nature, and are furthermore absent from the Armenian version of the text, which presumably escaped interpolation.) The Assumption of Moses, an apocalypse written shortly after the death of Herod, tells (9:1—7) how, after a period of godlessness and persecution, a man of the tribe of Levi named Taxo will, with his seven sons, surrender willingly to death in fidelity to the law, whereupon the time of salvation will appear. The idea is that his special fidelity has achieved so much atonement that this time could be delayed no longer. Such a passage could give rise to a belief that a great turning-point would come in a time of dire distress as a result of a voluntary death.

It was, then, a current thought among the Jews of the first century AD that the perfectly righteous man not only fulfils all the commandments but also atones, by suffering, for the sins of others, and that excess suffering is thus of service to others. All that was needed was that this idea should be applied to the Messiah. This application was natural enough, since the Messiah was believed to be a powerful and virtuous being, and the idea that suffering gives power and is associated with virtue is almost universal. The Indian Brahmins, for instance, practised self-inflicted suffering in the hope of attaining supernatural power, and many virtuous men or saints are reported to have endured great suffering. The idea may have arisen from the supposed connection between sin and punishment. Suffering is held to atone for wickedness, and suffering to excess is therefore like the opening of a credit account.

None of the factors I have so far specified helps to explain the origin of the idea that the redeemer died by crucifixion. There is evidence (see above, p 39) that this was not among the very earliest Christian traditions. It was, however, firmly established as early as Paul (possibly by him). How could it have originated?

It is commonly supposed that crucifixion was unknown in Palestine before the direct Roman rule which began in AD 6, and that Paul's reference to a crucified person must therefore point to someone executed after this date. In fact, however, as Stauffer and Bammel have made clear, 'the originally non-Jewish punishment of crucifixion had been used in Palestine since the second century BC — even by Jewish courts' (14, p 164; 377, pp 123—7). Josephus reports that both Antiochus Epiphanes (175—164 BC) and Alexander Jannaeus (103—76 BC) had crucified Jews in Jerusalem 'while they were still alive and breathing' (233, 12:5, 4 and 13:14, 2). Both periods of persecution are referred to in other Jewish literature (e.g. the Assumption of Moses, the Dead Sea Scrolls and the Similitudes of Enoch) and Jannaeus' crucifixion of eight hundred Pharisees left a particularly strong impression on the Jewish world. Thus Paul's environment obviously included traditions of the crucifixion of holy men one and two centuries earlier. If he had reason to believe that Jesus the descendant of David had already been on earth, he could well have thought of him as one of these victims. In this connection it is of interest that the dating of Jesus as a heretic who was put to death for misleading the people about 100 BC, under Jannaeus, is 'one of the most persistent elements of Jewish tradition concerning Jesus' and 'goes back to the floating mass of tradition' from which the Talmud drew (Mead, 293, pp 414—15: cf. Bammel, 13, p 321). Mead allows that this dating may have originated as a result of controversy between orthodox Jews and Christians of Pauline type, whose Christianity comprised 'a minimum of history and a maximum of opposition to Jewish legalism' (pp 419—20). In other words, if Pauline Christians thought of the earthly Jesus as a holy martyr of 100 BC, the Jews would have replied that he was a heretic of that time.

At a certain stage of such a debate between Christians and Jews, both sides may well have agreed that he perished by order of the Jewish authorities. Mk. 8:31 seems to represent a survival in the NT of such a stage of thinking. Jesus here foretells that 'the Son of man must suffer many things and be rejected by the elders and the chief priests and the scribes, and be killed, and after three days rise again.' It is generally agreed (see Strecker, 380, p 26) that the statement about his 'rejection' was inspired by the Septuagint of Psalm 117:22. And the whole verse in Mk. represents a tradition which existed before the evangelist wrote. That it is pre-Marcan is clear from the fact that the evangelist has but clumsily worked it into the gospel context, for (in the next verse) Peter 'rebukes' Jesus – as if he were protesting against the resurrection, and not merely against Jesus' forthcoming suffering and death (191, pp 295—6. Luke's adaptation of this passage (9:22—3) carefully omits Peter's rebuke). What is so striking about the saying of Jesus which Mark has assimilated here at 8:31 is that it attributes his death only to 'the elders, the chief priests and the scribes', i.e. the Sanhedrin, with no mention of Romans; whereas in 9:31 and 10:33—4, where the evangelist has repeated this saying, he has reworded it so as to bring it into better harmony with his own passion narrative. (In 10:34 there is a clear allusion to the part played by Romans in the condemnation of Jesus.) Mk. 8:31 represents a *post-Pauline* tradition (for it uses the title 'Son of man'), but nevertheless a stage of Christian thinking prior to traditions which link Jesus' death with Pilate. In this respect, the verse is comparable to 1 Thess. 2:14—15, where 'the Jews' are said to have killed Jesus. The verb used here for 'kill' is the same word as in Mk. 8:31, whereas, when Mark is writing on his own account, he prefers to say that Jesus was 'crucified' rather than 'killed'. I argued above (p 22) that this verse in 1 Thess. is a post-AD 70 interpolation into Paul's letter; but it nevertheless seems to represent an earlier layer of tradition than those involving Pilate. Mark, we saw above, drew *principally* on traditions blaming Pilate and rewrote them so as largely to absolve Pilate from guilt (see above, pp 63f). But at 8:31 he has assimilated a more ancient tradition (that only Jews were to blame), and the Jews in question were not necessarily (in the thinking which originally informed this tradition) those of the first century AD! The relevance of all this is that traditions about the circumstances of Jesus' death do vary substantially, and that this is just what one would expect if in fact he never existed.

I have already mentioned some of the factors which may well have led

Christians to think that the redeemer would not only — as was the case with the Jewish Messiah — come to earth in the future, but had already lived on it. An additional factor, probably of some importance, is that some of the crucifixions and atoning deaths mentioned in the apocalypses were future from the standpoint of the alleged writer of the work, but were meant to be interpreted by readers as past events. The Assumption of Moses, for instance, purports to be Moses' prophetic vision of the history of the Jews until the last days, i.e. the lifetime of the real author, and consists of an enumeration (in slightly veiled form) of striking historical events followed by the only truly prophetic part of the book — the account of the end of the world. The point of the preceding summary of the nation's history is that readers are to be so impressed by Moses' insight that they will be willing to accept his account of the real future. And this means that they must recognize his predictions as having been fulfilled in the nation's past. Thus the references in the work to a 'visitation' that is to befall Israel (involving the crucifixion of religious men) and to Taxo are both, according to Charles, clear allusions to events in the reign of Antiochus Epiphanes.[15] Now when the Jews saw that statements about the future really referred to the past, they might generalize this experience, and apply the principle even to those statements in the apocalyptic literature which the author genuinely wished to be understood with reference to the future. This could result in converting a future into a past Messiah.

This whole question of whether the tense of a verb — be it future or a past — is really to be understood literally, is of especial relevance to the so-called four servant songs in the second part of Isaiah which depict the exaltation, suffering and death of 'the servant of Yahweh'. Commentators are divided as to whether the servant is an individual person or a group. But whatever the writer's intention, his reference to the servant as 'a man of sorrows' who 'hath borne our griefs ... and was wounded for our transgressions' (Isaiah, 53:4—5) could easily have been understood as referring to an individual. Rowley argues that the suffering and death of the servant are to come in the future, even though the past tense is used — quite unambiguously in the Septuagint, as in the English version I have quoted.[16] Readers could therefore readily suppose the reference to be to suffering, death — and even resurrection — which had occurred in the past.[17] If they equated the servant with the Messiah, they would thus believe that he who was yet to come in triumph had come in the past to suffer and die. And some scholars have argued that the suffering servant and the Davidic Messiah were in fact fused into one conception in pre-Christian times.[18] Of this there is no proof, but it is undeniable that they lent themselves readily to fusion: for 'some of the predicates of the Davidic Messiah and of the suffering servant are common to both figures', which are thus 'related conceptions' with 'many points of connection' (Rowley, 341, pp 90—2).

Apart from the servant passages, there are many OT texts in the past tense which were, or may have been, interpreted Messianically. Alfaric instances 'Thou art my son; this day I have begotten thee' (Psalm 2:7). This was originally addressed to an actual king of Israel, but is understood by the writer of the epistle to the Hebrews as having found fulfilment in Jesus. The sufferer who speaks in Psalm 22 (which underlies some of the incidents in the gospel passion narratives) speaks in the past when he cries: 'My God, why hast thou forsaken me?'

It will perhaps be objected that, although the ingredients of early Christianity can be discerned in the religious environment, to suppose that all these disparate traditions were jumbled together is to ascribe to early Christians a state of delirium. The objection can be met by showing that the Christian evidence itself shows how the new faith arose as a result of emotional needs, mystical beliefs and contagious delusions, and how it was moulded in the meetings of the congregations under the influence of preachings, prophesyings and speaking with tongues. Paul tells that at Christian meetings anyone could stand up and promulgate a 'revelation' he had received; that some made ecstatic utterances, not understanding what they were saying, while others supplied an interpretation (1 Cor. 14:26–32). The interpretation of unintelligible utterances would easily lead to the establishment of all manner of doctrines among the members of a group. That the early Christians formed groups each of which had radically different ideas, and which were bitterly hostile to each other, is obvious from the NT, and intelligible on the same basis. Paul repeatedly controverts Christians of different persuasions and later epistle writers fulminate against false teachers. Non-canonical writers such as Clement of Rome and Ignatius were likewise surrounded by faction.

It is remarkable that scholars still insist that Christianity is so different from other religions, although they are often able to see not only that it encompassed these many factions with often contradictory doctrines, but also that its main ideas are traceable to the pagan and Jewish environment. This fact is even today sometimes attributed to what Brandon calls 'divine predestination' rather than to the influence of multifarious traditions (63, p 280). Of course, the parallels between Christian and earlier ideas are not exact, and there is no reason why they should be. In its particular combination of tenets drawn from various sources, early Christianity was unique, as is the combination of ideas which constitutes any creed. But this uniqueness is often taken to mean that it possessed elements which ensured its victory over its rivals. In truth, however, its triumph was largely due to political conditions in the fourth century. Until then it remained a minority sect; but the conversion of Constantine enabled the recently persecuted Church, supported by the newly Christianized government, to shift from defence to attack with a speed which has repeatedly called forth comment (see e.g. Bloch, 302, p 193). By forcibly suppressing pagan cults, and also by accommodating itself to pagan ideas and practices (for examples see Bury, 90, pp 366–73), it then rapidly became the dominant religion of the Empire, but failed to spread effectively to countries outside Roman influence.

1 Many scholars have held that, in the ancient Near East, the practice was widespread of killing the chief of a tribe when his virility (on which the fertility of the crops was thought to depend) showed signs of failing (see James, and Margaret Murray, 322, pp 63–4, 595–7; Engnell, 147, pp 25–35).

2 This reasoning was, of course, only possible to those who had already formed the idea of human immortality. The idea was foreign to the Babylonians, and so the salvation attained in the Tammuz rituals was from sickness in this life, not eternal well-being after death. However, the Osirian and Eleusinian rituals were early believed to mediate a blessed immortality (see Wagner's admissions, 401, pp 95, 121, and Brandon, 64). According to Apuleius' account (8, 11:6) the rites of Isis assured the mystae that they would see and venerate Isis in their after-lives. Wagner's allegation that this constitutes less than immortality is hard to understand (except as Christian bias), and there is an obvious parallel with the Christian's expectation that he will 'see God' (cf. Mt. 5:8) in the next world. Mylonas' recent critical account of the very popular Eleusinian mysteries accepts that they included 'a passion play' and 'gave the initiate confidence to face death, and a promise of bliss in the dark domain of Hades, whose rulers became his protectors and friends through initiation' (307, pp 263 f, 282).

3 Beare notes (30, p 9) that at, for instance, Philippi, 'we hear of an association of worshippers (cultores) of Silvanus, another dedicated to the worship of Cybele and to the imperial cult at the same time. There are *mystai* of Dionysus, *thiasi* (the Greek term Latinized) of Father Liber and *posiastae* of a Thracian god who ... receives the epithets of ... "He who saves" and "He who answers prayer" '.

4 Epictetus, *Discourses*, 3:21, 15 (written AD 90). Cumont (118, p 241) quotes Celsus' words (318, 3:59) as evidence of 'l'exigence d'une pureté à la fois rituelle et spirituelle'. And Josephus declares that Jews obey the law for their whole lives, whereas 'foreigners' are 'not able to observe such things for a few days' time, and call them "mysterious" and "sacred ceremonies" ' (234, Bk. 2:188–9).

5 Attis died emasculating himself under a tree; but ancient art includes 'scenes of the emasculated Attis dancing', indicating his resurrection (391, p 256). The oldest evidence is a Hellenistic Greek vase depicting 'the dancing Attis *hilaris* ... from the fourth century BC' (397, p 47). Vermaseren also instances two later statues from Ostia which point to the god's periodic resurrection. One (from Roman Imperial times) shows 'another young Attis standing ready to replace the dying one'. The other statue (dedicated in the second century AD) depicts the 'lying and triumphant Attis, his entire figure indicating the resurrection which is also shown by the decoration of various kinds of flowers and plants' (397, pp 35–6, 40).

6 See Frankfort, 161, pp 282–5. Lambrechts shows that the only joyful element in the early festivals of Attis concerned his brief return to earth – for a few days every year – when he consummated his marriage with the goddess, 'grande personification de la Terre nourricière qui a besoin de la semence mâle pour accomplir son destinée séculaire': i.e. the god 'redonne, par son union annuellement répétée avec la déesse, force et vigueur à la nature' (270, p 217).

7 These verses from Jn. are admitted to be 'difficult historically' because of their discrepancy with the synoptics (163, p 189). In Jn. 4:2 the statement that Jesus baptized is immediately denied in a parenthesis which 'ruins the sentence, and perhaps has a better claim to be regarded as an "editorial note" by a "redactor" than anything else in the gospel' (Dodd, 134, p 311n).

8 Imhotep lived about 2900 BC and was 'not ranked among the full gods of Egypt until the Persian period, dating from 525 BC', although during part of this long interval he was 'regarded as a sort of hero or demigod and received a semi-divine worship' (216, pp 29, 43). A similar process of gradual elevation occurred in the case of Amenophis the son of Hapu (124, p 130).

9   Leisegang has noted that the reports of Simon Magus' activities and doctrines are often contradictory and of doubtful reliability; that they do not make him an individual person, active at a particular time and place, but rather a type – the typical gnostic prophet and sect founder, seen through enemy eyes (273, p 83). Concerning Apollonius of Tyana, Lucian (about the middle of the second century) called him an imposter, and Apuleius (a little later) may have included his name in a list of magicians, although the relevant manuscripts do not agree, and the name written by Apuleius may not have been Apollonius at all (see 323, pp 19–20). The only full account of him is that by Philostratus, written about 150 years after his supposed existence, and today universally agreed to be highly untrustworthy. However, there is no reason why earlier writers should have taken much notice of Apollonius, and the paucity of second-century references does not prove that he is a fiction. On the other hand, there is no justification for *a priori* assertions, typified in the statement of Dr Witt, that 'Philostratus' *Life*, however lavishly embroidered, must have had some real facts behind it to lend it probability' (414). The purpose of Witt's argument is to establish that the gospels likewise 'must' portray a historical Jesus, however lavishly they embroider his career.

10 The myth of Archetypal Man can be read in *Poimandres*, the first treatise in the corpus of Hermetic writings which is dated by some scholars in the first century AD (417, p 71).

11 190, p 294. Haenchen thus holds that, although Acts portrays Simon as a magician rather than as a gnostic, this only means that the NT tradition has degraded him from a divine redeemer into a mere sorcerer. Yamauchi has objected that this involves 'assumptions' regarding the reliability of Acts which not every scholar would be prepared to entertain (417, p 61). But to suggest that Haenchen 'assumes' the unreliability of Acts is little short of grotesque. He has done more than any other commentator to demonstrate its unreliability. In another book (416) Yamauchi argues for the reliability of Acts on the basis of Ramsay's work (on which see JEC, pp 36, 161) and does not so much as mention Haenchen. Yamauchi's own standpoint appears from his uncritical use of Mt.'s story of the magi in ascertaining the date of Jesus' birth (see above, p 7).

12 That Jewish thought of the first century BC was not all strictly monotheistic is well illustrated by the pseudo-Solomonic Wisdom of Solomon, where Wisdom figures not merely as a personification of God's mind or will or as a principle pervading the universe, but sometimes as a hypostasis – separate from God and yet of the same substance, rather like the second person of the Christian Trinity. The writer of course 'never quite crosses the line into dualism by postulating a second Eternal' (109, p 35).

13 Wagner's denial (401) that the mystery religions are relevant to an understanding of Rom. 6 has been adequately met by Brandon's discussion of the Osirian ritual to which the one specified by Paul is so remarkably similar (see above, p 184). Kümmel finds Wagner's 'denial of all mystery-religion influence on Paul's baptismal doctrine as unconvincing as the denial of all gnostic influence on his conception of the Church' (267, p 174n).

14 391, p 233. Charles (98, p 202) refers additionally to 4 Maccabees 6:28–9, which 'belongs indeed to the first century AD, but expresses genuine Jewish thought on this question'. See also Lohse, 280, pp 66ff.

15 It is perhaps of interest that, in the extant manuscripts, these references are placed, as a result of a dislocation of the chapters, *after* the period of Herod (see Charles, 99, vol. 2, p 420). If this dislocation had already been effected in manuscripts which were being read late in the first century AD, then readers would obtain the impression that devout Jews had been crucified by the Romans shortly after Herod's time.

16 341, pp 10, 55. Klausner (252, p 165) explains the past tense used by supposing

the prophet to record what the persecutors of the servant will say when, in the end of days, they acknowledge their error.

17 The fourth song seems to imply the servant's resurrection by representing him as active after his death (Rowley, 341, pp 26, 36).

18 For details see Rowley, 341, pp 67, 70, 77, and Morgenstern, 304, pp 68–9.

Conclusion

If Jesus really lived on earth, he could have made little impact on his contemporaries, as no personal traits of his life and character found expression in the early literature about him. The first century literature which mentions him at all (i.e. the extant Christian literature earlier than the gospels) presents him as a supernatural personage who attracted attention not by his life on earth in human form, but by the appearances he made after his death. There is nothing in this pre-gospel literature which would establish (or even make probable) that those who experienced these appearances had known him alive. I have given evidence that even the earliest of the gospels may have been written only very late in the first century. If so, Jesus is not linked with a recognizable historical situation in any document (Christian, Jewish or pagan) that can be proved to have originated before about AD 100. Those who try to account for Christian origins without a historical Jesus are often accused of positing a complicated and involved series of processes in order to explain what can be much more simply explained by assuming the existence of a preacher who was crucified under Pilate. However, the correct explanation is not necessarily the simplest hypothesis that comes to mind, but the simplest one that can account for *all* the relevant facts. The facts represented by the literature of the first century are very hard to explain on the assumption that Jesus was active in Palestine at that time.

One of the principal reasons why the historical existence of Jesus is still accepted today is that he is assigned by the gospels to a definite historical situation, whereas this is not true of the pagan saviour gods who died and rose to redeem us. But this difference between paganism and Christianity is perfectly intelligible, even if Jesus is no more historical than Osiris. According to Budge, Osiris was the god of the resurrection in the earliest dynastic times (about 3,000 BC), and so his worshippers in the first century AD could not think of his death and resurrection as a recent event. None of the pagan mystery religions of the Roman Empire began as new revelations, but were adaptations of very ancient cults. If a god is worshipped by a primitive society before it acquires written records, there is no historical framework into which to fit him. The worship of Jesus, however, is not documented before the first century AD, and appears as the cult of a new divinity; and so the possibility of assigning his resurrection to a known historical situation was at least given. Indeed, it was really demanded. A god who was from the first regarded as the

Messiah descended from David had to fit somewhere into a known chronology, and sooner or later, in order to answer critical questions, his worshippers would have to be explicit about the where and when.

Many think that a theory of Christian origins without a historical Jesus is absurd because it necessarily implies that erroneous beliefs became widespread under conditions which ought quickly to have discredited them; that the elaborate gospel stories about Jesus and Pilate would at once have been seen to be false if Jesus had never existed. The answer to this objection again lies in the dates of the documents. Jesus was not linked with Pilate by writers contemporary with Pilate, but only by those of about seventy years later, when few who had lived through his administration were still alive to come forward and contradict them.

My critics will no doubt continue to deny that anything can be inferred from silence. But such denial is absurd. Supposing all documents (Marxist and non-Marxist) earlier than 1960 and relating to twentieth-century Russia, made no reference at all to Lenin's actions and to the specific situations in which they were performed; supposing also that every writer after 1960 assumed that he had organized the October Revolution of 1917. Then we should have strong evidence, from silence, that Lenin was a myth, for the silence would otherwise be inexplicable. In fact Lenin did live, and so many of the earlier documents do refer to his life, and one cannot point to a date, at a distance from his lifetime, when such references begin. Thus it must always be of important figures who really did exist.

People who are no more Christians than I am myself have told me that whether Jesus existed is a trivial matter, not worth writing a book about. To their minds, either there was a Jesus of whom we now know next to nothing, or there was nobody at all, and there is little to choose between the alternatives, neither of which has any more bearing on modern affairs than the fate of the little princes in the Tower. But I am not concerned to encourage my readers to choose between two 'irrelevant' alternatives. My point is that, if we wish to understand how Christianity began – and the manner of origin of one of the world's major religions is surely no triviality – then neither of these alternatives is helpful. Christianity is not explained by attributing it to an unknown founder, any more than to a non-existent one. If it were true (as most orthodox Christians believe) that we have a great deal of reliable information about Jesus, then it would make sense to say that he was responsible for Christianity, in the same way as Mohammed was responsible for Islam. But if Jesus (unlike Mohammed) is a mere cipher, then he explains nothing (cf. above, p 2). I have tried to make clear that the rise of Christianity must be understood in other terms, and to indicate what these are.

Finally, will the thesis that Jesus did not exist – if it comes to be accepted – have much effect on Christianity? I think not, if theologians play their hand carefully. 'I believe in God the Father Almighty' has already been revised by John Robinson to something like 'I believe in Ultimate Reality'. To reinterpret the further phrase 'and in Jesus Christ his only Son, our Lord' should not present insuperable difficulty. We shall, perhaps, be told that belief in Jesus is not at all the same thing as believing that he lived 1,950 years ago. Theologians have indicated that they are ready to apply their ingenuity to the problem, should the need arise. Zahrnt, for instance, has declared that, even if historical study managed to prove that Jesus had never lived, 'even then we theologians would succeed in finding a way out – when have we not succeeded in the past?' (419, pp 102–3). In this context, 'a way out' means a form of words. To prevent people from seeing the sunlight, one can place them in a dungeon. When this becomes impracticable, the same result can be achieved by creating a universal fog. Exponents of the 'new hermeneutic' have shown that they are ready to fulfil this function in the face of any problem.

Numbered List of References

A work listed here is referred to in this book by its number in the list.

Abbreviations (see also pp ix–xi above)
BJRL   Bulletin of the John Rylands Library
HTR   Harvard Theological Review
Int   Interpretation
JBL   Journal of Biblical Literature
JEC   No. 405 in the list below
NCB   New Century Bible
Nov Test   Novum Testamentum
NTS   New Testament Studies
RGG   No. 169 in the list below
ZNW   Zeitschrift für neutestamentliche Wissenschaft
Z ThK   Zeitschrift für Theologie und Kirche

1 Achtemeier, P. T. (Prof. of NT, Lancaster, USA), articles on 'Pre-Markan Miracle Catenae', *JBL*, 89 (1970), 265–91 and 91 (1972), 198–221.
2 Id., 'Gospel Miracle Tradition and the Divine Man', *Int*, 26 (1972), 174–97.
3 Alfaric, P. (ordained 1899, left the Church 1910, Prof. in Strassburg from 1919, d. 1955), *Origines Sociales du Christianisme*, Paris, 1959 (denies historicity of Jesus and explains the rise of Christianity largely in terms of class conflict: hence, no doubt, the East German translation, Berlin, 1963).
4 Allegro, J., *The Sacred Mushroom and the Cross*, London, 1970.
5 Allen, E. L., 'The Lost Kerygma', *NTS*, 3 (1956–7), 349–53.
6 Anderson, H. (Prof. of Biblical Criticism, Durham, USA), 'The Easter Witness of the Evangelists', in *The NT in Historical and Contemporary Perspective*, ed. H. Anderson and R. Barclay, Oxford, 1965, 33–55.
7 Anonymous, review of JEC in *The Times Literary Supplement*, 12 March, 1971.
8 Apuleius (born ca. AD 123), *Metamorphoses* (better known as *The Golden Ass)*, Loeb Classical Library, 1935.
9 Arvedson, T., *Das Mysterium Christi. Eine Studie zu Mt. 11:25–30*, Uppsala, 1937.
10 Aune, D. E. (ed.), *Studies in NT and Early Christian Literature*, Essays in Honour of A. P. Wikgren, Leiden, 1972; includes H. R. Moehring on 'The Census in Luke' (144–60); M. Rist on 'Pseudepigraphy and the Early Christians' (75–91); and H. Teeple on 'The Historical Beginnings of the Resurrection Faith' (107–20).
11 Bacon, B. W. (Prof. of NT, Yale, d. 1932), *Studies in Mt.*, London, 1930.
12 Baird, W. (teacher at Lexington Theological Seminary, USA), 'What is the Kerygma?' *JBL*, 76 (1957), 181–91.

13 Bammel, E. (Prof. of NT, Erlangen), 'Christian Origins in Jewish Tradition', *NTS*, 13 (1967), 317–35.
14 Id., (ed.), *The Trial of Jesus*, London, 1970; includes articles by R. Morgan (135–46) and E. Bammel (162–5).
15 Id., review of no. 324 below in *The Expository Times*, 85 (1974), 145–7.
16 Barclay, W. (Prof. of Divinity, Glasgow), *The Mind of St. Paul*, Fontana, 1965.
17 Id., broadcast criticism of JEC, 3 March, 1971.
18 Barnard, Rev L. W., *Studies in the Apostolic Fathers*, Oxford, 1966.
19 Barrett, C. K. (Prof. of Divinity, Durham), *The NT Background. Selected Documents*, London, 1956.
20 Id., 'Christianity in Corinth', *BJRL*, 46 (1964), 268–97.
21 Id., *Jesus and the Gospel Tradition*, London, 1967.
22 Id., 'Paul and the "Pillar" Apostles', in *Studia Paulina*, ed. Sevenster and van Unnik, Harlem, 1953, 1–19.
23 Id., *The Holy Spirit and the Gospel Tradition*, London, 1970.
24 Id., *The Signs of an Apostle*, London, 1970.
25 Id., *NT Essays*, London, 1972.
26 Bartsch, H. W. (Prof. of Theology, Frankfurt), article on 1 Cor. 15:3–11, in *ZNW*, 55 (1964), 261–74.
27 Bauer, W. (Prof. of NT, Göttingen, d. 1960), *Griechisch-Deutsches Wörterbuch zum NT*, 4th edn., Berlin, 1952; trans. by W. F. Arndt and F. W. Gingrich as *Greek-English Lexicon of the NT*, Chicago, 1957.
28 Id., *Orthodoxy and Heresy in Earliest Christianity*, trans. G. Strecker (et al.), Philadelphia, 1971.
29 Beach, C., *The Gospel of Mark*, NY, 1959.
30 Beare, F. W. (Prof. of NT, Toronto), *A Commentary on Phil.* (Black's NT Commentaries), London, 1959.
31 Id., *1 Peter*, Oxford, 1947.
32 Id., *The Earliest Records of Jesus*, Oxford, 1962.
33 Id., 'Sayings of the Risen Jesus in the Synoptic Tradition', in *Christian History and Interpretation*, Studies Presented to John Knox, ed. W. R. Farmer (et al.), CUP, 1967, 161–81.
34 Id., 'NT Christianity in the Hellenistic World', in *The Communication of the Gospel in NT Times*, London, 1961.
35 Id., articles on 'Jesus of Nazareth' and on 'The Mission to the Disciples', *JBL*, 87 (1968), 125–35; 89 (1970), 1–13.
36 Bearman, H. V., 'Scholarly Myopia', *The Modern Churchman*, 14 (1971), 273–80.
37 Bell, Sir H. Idris (Reader in Papyrology, Oxford, d. 1967), *Cults and Creeds in Graeco-Roman Egypt*, Liverpool, 1953.
38 Berger, K., *Die Amen-Worte Jesu*, Berlin, 1970.
39 Best, E. (Lecturer in Theology, St. Andrews), *1 Peter* (NCB), London, 1971.
40 Betz, H. D. (Prof. of NT, Claremont), 'Lukian von Samosata und das Christentum', *Nov Test*, 3 (1959), 226–37.
41 Id., *Lukian von Samosata und das NT*, Berlin, 1961.
42 Id., 'Jesus as Divine Man', in *Jesus and the Historian*, Essays in Honour of E. C. Colwell, ed. F. W. Trotter, Philadelphia, 1968, 114–33.
43 Bevan, E. R. (Lecturer in Hellenistic History, London, d. 1943), art, 'Deification' in *Encyclopaedia of Religion and Ethics*, ed. J. Hastings, 13 vols., Edinburgh, 1908–26.
44 Black, M. (Prof. of Biblical Criticism, St. Andrews), *The Scrolls and Christian Origins*, London, 1961.
45 Id., 'The Son of Man Problem', *BJRL*, 45 (1962–3), 305–18.
46 Id., *An Aramaic Approach to the Gospels and Acts*, 3rd edn., Oxford, 1967.
47 Blank, J. (Prof. of NT, Saarbrücken), *Paulus und Jesus*, Munich, 1968.
48 Blinzler, J., article on Lk. 13:1–5 in *Nov Test*, 2 (1958), 24–49.

49 Id., *Der Prozess Jesu*, 4th revised edn., Regensburg, 1969.
50 Boers, H. (Assoc. Prof. of NT, Emory Univ.), 'NT Christology since Bousset', *JBL*, 89 (1970), 450–6.
51 Bonnard, P. (Prof. of Theology, Lausanne), *L'Évangile selon Saint Matthieu*, Neuchatel (Switzerland) and Paris, 1963.
52 Boobyer, G. H., 'The Pre-Existence of Jesus in Mk.', *Expository Times*, 51 (1940), 393–4.
53 Id., *St. Mark and the Transfiguration Story*, Edinburgh, 1942.
54 Boring, M. E. (Phillips Univ., Enid, Oklahoma), 'Oracles of Christian Prophets', *JBL*, 91 (1972), 501–21.
55 Bornkamm, G. (Prof. of NT, Heidelberg), *Jesus*, trans. I. Frazer (et al.), London, 1960.
56 Id., *Paul*, trans. D. Stalker, London, 1971.
57 Borsch, F. H. (Prof. of NT, Evanston, USA), *The Son of Man in Myth and History*, London, 1967.
58 Bouquet, Rev Dr A. C., 'Freedom and Responsibility in Christian Commitment', *The Modern Churchman*, 15 (1971).
59 Bousset, W. (Prof. of NT, Göttingen, d. 1920), *Kurios Christos*, Göttingen, 1913.
60 Bowden, J., review of JEC in *Church Times*, 12 February, 1971.
61 Box, Rev G.H. (d. 1933), *The Ezra Apocalypse*, London, 1912.
62 Brandon, S. G. F. (Prof. of Comparative Religion, Manchester, d. 1971), *Time and Mankind*, London, 1951.
63 Id., 'The Myth and Ritual Position', in *Myth, Ritual and Kingship*, ed. S. H. Hooke, Oxford, 1958, 261–91.
64 Id., (ed.), *The Saviour God*, Comparative Studies Presented to E. O. James, Manchester, 1963, includes articles by Brandon (17–33) and by M. Simon (Prof. of History of Religions, Strassburg) (144–59).
65 Id., *History, Time and Deity*, Manchester, 1965.
66 Id., *Jesus and the Zealots*, Manchester, 1967.
67 Id., (ed.), *Dictionary of Comparative Religion*, London, 1970.
68 Id., 'Redemption in Ancient Egypt and Early Christianity', in *Types of Redemption*, ed. Zwi Werblowsky and Bleeker, Leiden, 1970, 36–45.
69 Id., *The Trial of Jesus*, London, 1971.
70 Branscomb, B. H. (Prof. of NT, Durham, USA), *The Gospel of Mark* (Moffat NT Commentary), London, 1937.
71 Braun, H. (Emeritus Prof. of Theology, Mainz), 'Der Sinn der NT Christologie', *Z ThK*, 54 (1957), 341–77.
72 Id., *Gesammelte Studien zum NT und seiner Umwelt*, 2nd edn., Tübingen, 1967; includes articles on 'Understanding the NT' (283–98) and on the Canon (310–24).
73 Id., *Jesus*, Stuttgart, 1969.
74 Brockington, Rev L. H., *A Critical Introduction to the Apocrypha*, London, 1961.
75 Brooks, W. E. (Sacred Heart Univ., Bridgeport, Connecticut), article on Epistle to the Hebrews, *JBL*, 89 (1970), 205–14.
76 Bruce, F. F. (Prof. of Biblical Criticism, Manchester), *1 and 2 Cor.* (NCB), London, 1971.
77 Id., 'The Book of Zechariah and the Passion Narrative', *BJRL*, 43 (1960–1), 336–53.
78 Bultmann, R. (Prof. of Theology, Marburg, retired 1951), article on 'Das Petrusbekenntnis', *ZNW*, 19 (1919–20), 165–74.
79 Id., *Primitive Christianity in its Contemporary Setting*, trans. R. H. Fuller, London, 1956.
80 Id., *Exegetische Probleme des zweiten Korintherbriefes*, Darmstadt, 1963.
81 Id., article on 'Jesus and Paul' in *Faith and Understanding*, ed. R. W. Funk,

trans. L. P. Smith, NY, 1969, vol. 1, 220–46

82 Id., *Theologie des NT*, 6th edn., Tübingen, 1968.

83 Id., *Die Geschichte der synoptischen Tradition*, 8th edn., Göttingen, 1970 (with a supplement ed. Theissen and Vielhauer, 1971).

84 Id., 'NT and Mythology', in *Kerygma and Myth*, ed. H. W. Bartsch, trans. R. H. Fuller, London, 1972, vol. 2, 1–44.

85 Burger, C., *Jesus als Davidssohn*, Göttingen, 1970.

86 Burkill, T. A. (Prof. of Christian Thought, Cornell), *Mysterious Revelation*, Ithaca (NY), 1963.

87 Id., 'St. Mark's Philosophy of the Passion', *Nov Test*, 2 (1958), 245–71.

88 Id., 'The Condemnation of Jesus: a Critique of Sherwin-White's Thesis', *Nov Test*, 12 (1970), 321–42.

89 Id., *New Light on the Earliest Gospel*, Cornell Univ. Press, 1972.

90 Bury, J. B. (Prof. of Modern History, Cambridge, d. 1920), *The History of the Later Roman Empire*, vol. 1, London, 1923.

91 Buttrick, G. A. (et al., eds.), *The Interpreter's Dictionary of the Bible*, 4 vols., NY, 1962.

92 Cadbury, H. J. (Prof. of Divinity, Harvard, retired 1954), *The Beginnings of Christianity*, Pt. 1, vol. 2, London, 1923.

93 Id., 'Mixed Motives in the Gospels', *Proceedings of the American Philosophical Society*, 95 (1951), 117–24.

94 Caird, G. B. (Principal of Mansfield College, Oxford), *Principalities and Powers*, Oxford, 1956 (reprinted 1967).

95 Carlston, Dr C. E. (Iowa City), 'The Law in Mt. and Mk.', *NTS*, 15 (1968–9), 75–96.

96 Carmichael, J., *The Death of Jesus*, London, 1963.

97 Charles, Archdeacon R. H. (d. 1931), *The Assumption of Moses*, London, 1897.

98 Id., *The Testaments of the Twelve Patriarchs*, London, 1908.

99 Id., (et al., ed.), *The Apocrypha and Pseudepigrapha of the OT in English*, 2 vols., Oxford, 1913 (reprinted 1968).

100 Christ, F., *Jesus Sophia*, Zürich, 1970.

101 Clark, K. W., 'Worship in the Jerusalem Temple after AD 70,' *NTS*, 6 (1959–60), 269–80.

102 Cohn, H. (Justice of Supreme Court of Israel), *The Trial and Death of Jesus*, London, 1972.

103 Conzelmann, H. (Prof. of NT, Göttingen), article 'Jesus Christus' in RGG.

104 Id., 'On the Analysis of the Confessional Formula in 1 Cor. 15:3–5', *Int*, 20 (1966), 15–25.

105 Id., *Die Mitte der Zeit*, 5th edn., Tübingen, 1964.

106 Id., *An Outline of the Theology of the NT*, trans. J. Bowden, NY, 1969.

107 Id., *Geschichte des Urchristentums*, 2nd edn., Göttingen, 1971.

108 Craddock, F. B. (Assoc. Prof. of NT, Enid, Oklahoma), 'The Poverty of Christ', *Int*, 22 (1968), 158–70.

109 Id., *The Pre-Existence of Christ in the NT*, Nashville and NY, 1968.

110 Creed, J. M., *The Gospel According to St. Luke*, London, 1930 (reprinted 1965).

111 Cross, F. L. (ed., Prof. of Divinity, Oxford), *The Oxford Dictionary of the Christian Church*, London, 1971.

112 Crouch, J. E. (Lecturer in NT, Enid, Oklahoma), *The Colossian Haustafel*, Göttingen, 1972.

113 Cullmann, O. (Prof. of Theology, Basle), *Earliest Christian Confessions*, trans. Reid, London, 1949.

114 Id., *Early Christian Worship*, trans. Todd and Torrance, London, 1953.

115 Id., *The Early Church, Essays*, ed. A. J. B. Higgins, London, 1956.

116 Id., *Peter*, trans. (from 2nd edn.) F. V. Filson, London, 1962.

117 Cumont, F. (Belgian orientalist, d. 1947), article 'Attis in Pauly-Wissova', *Realencyclopädie der klassischen Altertumswissenschaft.*
118 Id., *Lux Perpetua*, Paris, 1949.
119 Davidson, R. (Lecturer in OT, Edinburgh) and Leaney, A. R. C. (Prof. of NT, Nottingham), *The Pelican Guide to Modern Theology:* vol. 3, *Biblical Criticism*, Penguin Books, 1970.
120 Davies, Rev Dr D. P. (Lecturer in Theology, Univ. of Wales), review of JEC in *Trivium*, 7 (1972).
121 Davies, Rev W. D. (Prof. of Biblical Theology, NY), *The Setting of the Sermon on the Mount*, Cambridge, 1964.
122 Id., *Christian Origins and Judaism*, London, 1962.
123 Id., *Paul and Rabbinic Judaism*, 3rd edn., London, 1970.
124 Dawson, W. R., 'Amenophis the Son of Hapu', *Aegyptus*, 7 (1926), 113–38.
125 Dibelius, M. (Prof. of Theology, Heidelberg, d. 1947), *Die Formgeschichte des Evangeliums*, 2nd edn., Tübingen, 1933.
126 Id., *The Pastoral Epistles*, revised edn. by H. Conzelmann, trans. P. Buttolph, Philadelphia, 1972.
127 Dinkler, E. (Prof. of NT, Heidelberg), 'Die Petrus-Rom Frage I', *Theologische Rundschau, Neue Folge*, 25 (1959), 189–230.
128 Id., (ed.), *Zeit und Geschichte*, Festschrift for Bultmann's eightieth birthday, Tübingen, 1964; with articles by G. Bornkamm (171–91), G. Klein (193–216), Eva Krafft (217–33) and H. Thyen (97–125).
129 Dix, G., *Jew and Greek*, NY, 1953.
130 Dodd, C. H. (Prof. of Divinity, Cambridge, d. 1973), *The Authority of the Bible*, revised edn., Fontana Books, 1960.
131 Id., *The Johannine Epistles*, London, 1946 (Moffat NT commentary).
132 Id., *The Parables of the Kingdom*, Fontana Books, 1961.
133 Id., *Historical Tradition in the Fourth Gospel*, CUP, 1963.
134 Id., *The Interpretation of the Fourth Gospel*, CUP, 1970.
135 Id., *The Founder of Christianity*, London, 1971.
136 Downing, Rev F. G., *The Church and Jesus*, London, 1968.
137 Drower, Lady E. S., *The Secret Adam. A Study of Nasoraean Gnosis*, Oxford, 1960.
138 Dungan, D. L., *The Sayings of Jesus in the Churches of Paul*, Oxford, 1971.
139 Dunn, J. (Lecturer in Theology, Nottingham), review of JEC in *The Church of England Newspaper*, 2 July, 1971.
140 Dupont-Sommer, A. (Prof. at Sorbonne), *The Essene Writings from Qumran*, trans. G. Vermes, Oxford, 1961.
141 Edwards, R. A. (Assoc. Prof. of Religion, Greenville, USA), *The Sign of Jonah*, London, 1971.
142 Id., 'An Approach to a Theology of Q', *Journal of Religion*, 51 (1971), 247–69.
143 Eisler, R. (d. 1949), *The Messiah Jesus and John the Baptist*, Eng. edn. by A. H. Krappe, London, 1931.
144 Ellis, Rev E. E. (Prof. of NT, New Brunswick), *The Gospel of Luke* (NCB), London, 1966.
145 Eltester, W. (ed.), *Judentum, Urchristentum, Kirche*, Festschrift for J. Jeremias, 2nd edn., Berlin, 1964; with articles by K. H. Rengstorf (106–29), E. Schweizer (90–3) and K. Stendahl (94–105).
146 Id., (ed.), *Jesus in Nazareth*, Berlin, 1972; with articles by E. Grässer (1–37) and R. C. Tannehill (51–75).
147 Engnell, I., *Studies in Divine Kingship in the Ancient Near East*, 2nd edn., Oxford, 1967.
148 Enslin, Morton S. (Emeritus Prof. of NT, Crozer Theol. Seminary), 'How the Story Grew – Judas in Fact and Fiction', Festschrift for F. W. Gingrich, ed.

212

Eugene H. Barth and R. E. Cocroft, Leiden, 1972, 123—41.

149 Eusebius (Bishop of Caesarea, d. AD 337), *Ecclesiastical History*, with a trans. by Lake, Loeb Classical Library, vol. 1, 1959 and vol. 2, 1957.

150 Evans, Rev C. F. (Prof. of NT, London), *The Beginning of the Gospel*, London, 1968.

151 Id., *Resurrection and the NT*, London, 1970.

152 Farmer, Rev W. R. (Prof. of NT, Southern Methodist Univ., USA), *The Synoptic Problem*, NY and London, 1964.

153 Fawcett, T. (Head of Divinity Dept., Chester College of Education), *Hebrew Myth and Christian Gospel*, London, 1973.

154 Feneberg, R., *Christliche Passafeier und Abendmahl*, Munich, 1971.

155 Ferguson, J. (Prof. at the Open Univ.), *The Religions of the Roman Empire*, London, 1970.

156 Filson, Rev F. V. (Emeritus Prof. of NT, Chicago), *A Study of Hebrews*, London, 1967.

157 Finley, M. I. (Fellow of Jesus College, Cambridge), 'Christian Beginnings', in his *Aspects of Antiquity*, London, 1968, 177—96.

158 Firmicus, Maternus Julius (d. ca. AD 360), *De errore profanarum religionum.*

159 Flesseman, E. van Leer, article on the Canon in *ZThK*, 61 (1964), 404—20.

160 Förster, W. (Emeritus Prof. of NT, Münster), *Palestinian Judaism in NT Times*, trans. G. E. Harris, Edinburgh and London, 1964.

161 Frankfort, H. (Director of Warburg Institute, London, d. 1954), *Kingship and the Gods*, Chicago, 1948.

162 Id., *The Problem of Similarity in Ancient Near Eastern Religions*, Oxford, 1951.

163 Freed, E. D., 'Variations in the Language and Thought of John', *ZNW*, 55 (1964), 167—97.

164 Frend, W. H. C. (Prof. of Eccles. History, Glasgow), *Martyrdom and Persecution in the Early Church*, Oxford, 1965.

165 Friedrich, G. (et al., eds.), *Das NT Deutsch*, 11 vols. of text and commentary, Göttingen, 1967—71.

166 Fuller, R. H. (Prof. of NT, Evanston, Illinois), *The Foundations of NT Christology*, London, 1965.

167 Id., *The Formation of the Resurrection Narratives*, London, 1972.

168 Gärtner, B. (Bishop of Gothenburg), *Iscariot*, trans. V. I. Gruhn, Philadelphia, 1971.

169 Galling, K. (et al., eds.), *Die Religion in Geschichte und Gegenwart* (cited as RGG), 3rd edn., 7 vols. Tübingen, 1957—65.

170 Gardner-Smith, Rev P. (formerly Dean of Jesus' College, Cambridge), review of JEC in *Journal of Theological Studies New Series*, 24 (1973), 561—5.

171 Georgi, D. (Prof. of NT, Berkeley), *Gegner des Paulus im zweiten Korintherbrief*, Neukirchen-Vluyn, 1964.

172 Id., *Die Geschichte der Kollekte des Paulus für Jerusalem*, Hamburg, 1965.

173 Gibbon, E., *The Decline and Fall of the Roman Empire*, Everyman edn. in 6 vols., London, 1960.

174 Glover, T. R., *The Conflict of Religions in the Early Roman Empire*, 9th edn., London, 1920.

175 Goldstein, M. (Rabbi), *Jesus in the Jewish Tradition*, NY, 1950.

176 Grässer, E. (Prof. of NT, Bochum), *Das Problem der Parusieverzögerung*, 2nd edn., Berlin, 1960.

177 Id., 'Der historische Jesus im Hebräerbrief', *ZNW*, 56 (1965), 63—91.

178 Grant, F. C. (Emeritus Prof. of Biblical Theology, NY), *The Gospels, Their Origin and Growth*, London, 1957.

179 Id., art. 'Matthew' in no. 91 above.

180 Id., *Roman Hellenism and the NT*, Edinburgh and London, 1962.

181 Id., and Rowley, H. H. (eds.), *Dictionary of the Bible*, 2nd edn., Edinburgh, 1963 (first edn. was by J. Hastings, 1909).
182 Grant, R. M. (Prof. of NT, Chicago), *A Historical Introduction of the NT*, London, 1963.
183 Grayston, K. (Prof. of NT, Bristol), review of JEC in *Methodist Recorder*, 16 December, 1971.
184 Gurney, O. R. (Prof. of Assyriology, Oxford), 'Tammuz Reconsidered', *Journal of Semitic Studies*, 7 (1962), 147–60.
185 Guy, H. A. (Divinity teacher, Southampton), *The Origin of Mk.*, London, 1954.
186 Haag, H. (Prof. of Theology, Tübingen), *Bibellexikon*, 2nd edn., Tübingen, 1968.
187 Haenchen, E. (Emeritus Prof. of Theology, Münster), *Die Apostelgeschichte*, Göttingen, 1957.
188 Id., 6th edn. of no. 187 above, Göttingen, 1968. A translation of this valuable work is now available (Oxford, 1971).
189 Id., 'Die Komposition von Mk. 8:27–9:1', *Nov Test*, 6 (1963), 81–109.
190 Id., *Gott und Mensch*, Tübingen, 1965: includes articles on 'Johannine Problems' (78–113) and Gnosticism (265–98).
191 Id., *Der Weg Jesu*, 2nd edn., Berlin, 1968.
192 Hahn, F. (Prof. of NT, Mainz), *Christologische Hoheitstitel*, Göttingen, 1963.
193 Hamerton-Kelly, R. G. (Prof. of NT, Chicago), *Pre-Existence, Wisdom, and the Son of Man*, Cambridge, 1973.
194 Hammond, N. G. L. and Scullard, H. H. (eds.), *The Oxford Classical Dictionary*, 2nd edn., Oxford, 1972.
195 Hanson, A. T. (ed., Prof. of Theology, Hull), *Vindications*, London, 1966.
196 Id., *The Pastoral Letters*, Cambridge, 1966.
197 Id., *Studies in the Pastoral Epistles*, London, 1968.
198 Hare, D. R. A. (Asst. Prof. of NT, Pittsburgh), *The Theme of Jewish Persecution in Mt.*, CUP, 1967.
199 Harrison, P. N., *Polycarp's Two Epistles*, Cambridge, 1936.
200 Id., *Paulines and Pastorals*, London, 1964.
201 Harvey, A. E. (St. Augustine's College, Canterbury), *The NEB Companion to the NT*, Oxford and Cambridge, 1970.
202 Hasler, V., *Amen*, Zürich and Stuttgart, 1969.
203 Hengel, M. (Prof. of NT, Erlangen), *Die Zeloten*, Leiden, 1961.
204 Id., *Was Jesus a Revolutionist?*, trans. W. Klassen, Philadelphia, 1971.
205 Higgins, A. J. B. (Prof. of Theology, Univ. of Wales), *The Lord's Supper in the NT*, London, 1952.
206 Id., *Jesus and the Son of Man*, London, 1964.
207 Hill, D. (Lecturer in Bibl. History, Sheffield), *The Gospel of Matthew* (NCB), London, 1972.
208 Hooke, S. H. (ed., Prof. of OT, London, d. 1968), *Myth and Ritual*, OUP, 1933.
209 Hooker, Dr Morna D. (Lecturer in Theology, London), *Jesus and the Servant*, London, 1959.
210 Id., *The Son of Man in Mk.*, London, 1967.
211 Hoskyns, Rev Canon E. (d. 1937) and Davey, Rev F. N., *The Riddle of the NT*, London, 1957.
212 Houlden, J. L. (Principal of Cuddesdon Theological College), *A Commentary on the Johannine Epistles* (Black's NT Commentaries), London, 1973.
213 Hull, J. M., *Hellenistic Magic and the Synoptic Tradition*, London, 1974.
214 Hummel, R., *Die Auseinandersetzung zwischen Kirche und Judentum im Matthäusevangelium*, 2nd edn., Munich, 1966.
215 Hurwitz, S., *Die Gestalt des sterbenden Messias*, Zürich and Stuttgart, 1958.
216 Hurry, J. B., *Imhotep*, OUP, 1928.
217 Irenaeus (Bishop of Lyons, d. AD 200), *Against Heresies*, trans. J. Keeble, London, 1872.

218 Jackson, F. J. Foakes and Lake, Kirsopp (eds.), *The Beginnings of Christianity, Pt. 1, The Acts of the Apostles, vol. 1, Prolegomena 1, The Jewish, Gentile and Christian Backgrounds*, London, 1920.
219 Jacobsen, T. (Prof. of Assyriology, Chicago), *Toward the Image of Tammuz*, ed. W. L. Moran, Cambridge (Mass.), 1970.
220 Jacoby, F., *Die Fragmente der griechischen Historiker*, 2(B), Leiden, 1962 (text no. 256, and commentary, in a separate vol.).
221 James, Rev E. O. (Prof. of History and Philosophy of Religion, London, d. 1972) *Myth and Ritual in the Ancient Near East*, London, 1958.
222 James, W. (Psychologist, d. 1910), *The Varieties of Religious Experience* (first published 1902), Dolphin Books, NY, no date.
223 Jensen, A. E. (Prof. of Anthropology, Frankfurt), *Myth and Culture Among Primitive Peoples*, trans. Choldin and Weissleder, Chicago and London, 1963.
224 Jeremias, J. (Prof. of Theology, Göttingen), *Jesus als Weltvollender*, Gütersloh, 1930.
225 Ibid., 'Kennzeichen der ipsissima vox Jesu', in *Synoptische Studien*, Festschrift für A. Wikenhauser, Munich, 1954, 86–93.
226 Id., *The Eucharistic Words of Jesus*, trans. N. Perrin, London, 1966.
227 Id., article 'Moses' in no. 250 below.
228 Id., *NT Theology. Pt. 1. The Proclamation of Jesus*, trans. J. Bowden, London, 1971.
229 Johnson, M. D., *The Purpose of the Biblical Genealogies*, Cambridge, 1969.
230 Johnson, S. E. (Ecumenical Institute, Jerusalem), *Jesus in His Own Times*, London, 1958.
231 Id., *Mark* (Black's NT Commentaries), London, 1960.
232 Josephus, F. (d. ca. AD 100), *The Jewish War*, in *Works*, trans. W. Whiston, London, no date.
233 Id., *Antiquities of the Jews*, in *Works* (as above).
234 Id., *Against Apion*, in *Works* (as above).
235 Justin (martyred ca. AD 165), *The First Apology*, in *Ante-Nicene Christian Library*, ed. A. Roberts (et al.), vol. 2, Edinburgh, 1867.
236 Id., *Dialogue with Trypho the Jew*, ed. Williams, London, 1930.
237 Käsemann, E. (Prof. of NT, Tübingen), 'Die Legitimität des Apostels', *ZNW*, 41 (1942), 33–71.
238 Id., *Exegetische Versuche und Besinnungen*, 3rd edn., 2 vols., Göttingen, 1964: with articles on the historical Jesus, vol. 1, 187–214 and vol. 2, 31–68.
239 Id., 'Sentences of Holy Law in the NT' and 'The Beginnings of Christian Theology', in *NT Questions of Today*, trans. J. W. Montague, London, 1969, 66–81 and 82–107.
240 Id., *Perspectives on Paul*, trans. M. Kohl, London, 1971.
241 Id., 'The Problem of a NT Theology', *NTS*, 19 (1973), 235–45.
242 Kahl, J. (Protestant Pastor, left the Church 1967), *The Misery of Christianity*, trans. N. D. Smith, Penguin Books, 1971.
243 Kallas, J. (Assoc. Prof. of Theology, California), *The Significance of the Synoptic Miracles*, London, 1961.
244 Id., 'Rom. 13:1–7: An Interpolation', *NTS*, 11 (1965), 365–74.
245 Keck, Rev L. E. (Prof. of NT, Vanderbilt), *A Future for the Historical Jesus*, London, 1972.
246 Kelly, Rev Canon J. N. D. (Principal of St. Edmund Hall, Oxford), *Early Christian Creeds*, London, 1956.
247 Id., *A Commentary on the Pastoral Epistles*, London, 1963.
248 Kennard, J. S., 'Was Capernaum the Home of Jesus? *JBL*, 65 (1946), 131–41.
249 Kilpatrick, Rev G. D. (Prof. of Exegesis of Scripture, Oxford), *Origins of the Gospel of Matthew*, Oxford, 1946.
250 Kittel, G. (ed., Prof. of NT, Tübingen), *Theologisches Wörterbuch zum NT*, 8

vols., Stuttgart, 1964–72; trans. ed. G. W. Bromiley, London, 1964–72.
251 Klausner, J. (Emeritus Prof. of Hebrew Literature, Jerusalem), *Jesus of Nazareth*, trans, H. Danby, London, 1925.
252 Id., *The Messianic Idea in Israel*, trans. Stinespring, London, 1957.
253 Klein, G. (Prof. of NT, Münster), review of no. 187 above in *Zeitschrift für Kirchengeschichte*, 68 (1957), 362–71.
254 Id., articles on Gal. 2:6–9 and on Lk. 12:54–6 in *ZThK*, 57 (1960), 275–95 and 61 (1964), 373–90.
255 Id., *Die Zwölf Apostel*, Göttingen, 1961.
256 Id., 'Die Verleugnung des Petrus', *ZThK*, 58 (1961), 285–328.
257 Knigge, H. D., 'The Meaning of Mark', *Int*, 22 (1968), 53–70.
258 Knox, J. (Emeritus Prof. of NT, Texas), *Chapters in a Life of Paul*, London, 1954.
259 Knox, W. L., *Some Hellenistic Elements in Primitive Christianity*, London, 1944.
260 Köster, H. (Prof. of NT, Harvard), 'Geschichte und Kultus', *ZThK*, 54 (1957), 56–69.
261 Id., *Synoptische Überlieferung bei den apostolischen Vätern*, Berlin, 1957.
262 Id., 'The Purpose of the Polemic of a Pauline Fragment', *NTS*, 8 (1961–2), 317–32.
263 Id., 'Outside the Camp', *HTR*, 55 (1962), 299–315.
264 Id., 'The Origin and Nature of Diversification in the History of Early Christianity', and 'One Jesus and four Primitive Gospels', *HTR*, 58 (1965), 279–318 and 61 (1968), 203–47. Both articles are reprinted in no. 340 below.
265 Kramer, W., *Christ, Lord, Son of God*, trans. B. Hardy, London, 1966.
266 Kümmel, W. G. (Prof. of NT, Marburg), article on 1 Thess. in *Neotestamentica et Patristica*, Festschrift for O. Cullmann, Leiden, 1962, 213–27.
267 Id., 'Jesus und Paulus', *NTS*, 10 (1963–4), 163–81.
268 Id., *Introduction to the NT*, trans. A. J. Mattill Jr., London, 1966.
269 Lake, Kirsopp (Prof. of History, Harvard, d. 1946), 'Cephas and Peter', *HTR*, 14 (1921), 95–7.
270 Lambrechts, L., 'La "résurrection" d'Adonis', *Annuaire de l'institut de philologie et d'histoire orientales et slaves*, 13 (1953), 207–40.
271 Leaney, A. R. C., *The Letters of Peter and Jude*, Cambridge, 1967.
272 Lee, G. M. review of JEC in *Theology*, 75 (1972), 45–6.
273 Leisegang, H., *Die Gnosis*, 4th edn., Stuttgart, 1955.
274 Leivestad, R., 'Exit the Apocalyptic Son of Man', *NTS*, 18 (1972), 243–67.
275 Levin, Dr S. S., *Jesus Alias Christ*, NY, 1969.
276 Lightfoot, R. H. (Prof. of NT, Oxford, d. 1953), *The Gospel Message of St. Mark*, Oxford, 1950.
277 Lindars, Fr. B., *NT Apologetic*, London, 1961.
278 Lloyd, R., 'Cross and Psychosis', *Faith and Freedom*, 24 (1970–71), 3–40.
279 Lohmeyer, E. (killed by the authorities in E. Germany, 1946), *Galiläa und Jerusalem*, Göttingen, 1936.
280 Lohse, E. (Prof. of Theology, Göttingen), *Märtyrer und Gottesknecht*, Göttingen, 1955.
281 Id., *Die Umwelt des NT*, Göttingen, 1971.
282 Longenecker, R. N. (Prof. of NT, Deerfield, USA), *The Christology of Early Jewish Christianity*, London, 1970.
283 Lührmann, D., *Die Redaktion der Logienquelle*, Neukirchen, 1969.
284 Luz, U., 'Das Geheimnismotiv und die markinische Christologie', *ZNW*, 56 (1965), 9-30.
285 Maccoby, H., *Revolution in Judaea, Jesus and the Jewish Resistance*, London, 1973.
286 Marshall, Dr I. H., 'Palestinian and Hellenistic Christianity', *NTS*, 19 (1973), 275–87.

216

287 Martin, R. P. (Professor of NT, California), *Carmen Christi, Phil. 2:5–11,* CUP, 1967.

288 Id., *Mark: Evangelist and Theologian,* Exeter, 1972.

289 Id., review of JEC in *Christian Graduate,* 25 (1972), 9.

290 Marxsen, W. (Prof. of Theology, Münster), *Der Evangelist Markus,* Göttingen, 1956.

291 McArthur, H. (ed.), *In Search of the Historical Jesus,* London, 1970.

292 McNeile, Rev A. H. (d. 1933), *The Gospel According to St. Matthew,* London, 1915 (reprinted 1952).

293 Mead, G. R. S. (d. 1933), *Did Jesus Live 100 BC?,* London, 1903.

294 Medawar, P. B. (Prof. at Medical Research Centre), 'Darwin's Illness', in *The Art of the Soluble,* London, 1967, 61–7.

295 Meeks, W. A., *The Prophet-King,* Leiden, 1967.

296 Merrill, E. T. (Prof. of Latin, Chicago, d. 1936), *Essays in Early Christian History,* London, 1924.

297 Merz, A., *Der Messias oder Taeb der Samaritaner,* Giessen, 1909.

298 Metzger, B. M. (Prof. of NT, Princeton), article on Mystery Religions and Early Christianity in *HTR,* 48 (1955), 1–20.

299 Id., article on 1 Cor. 15:4 in *Journal of Theological Studies, New Series,* 8 (1957), 118–23.

300 Meye, Dr R. P., *Jesus and the Twelve,* Grand Rapids, 1968.

301 Milburn, R. L. P., 'The Persecution of Domitian', *Church Quarterly Review,* 139 (1945), 154–64.

302 Momigliano, A. (ed., Prof. of Ancient History, London), *The Conflict Between Paganism and Christianity in the Fourth Century,* Oxford, 1963, with articles by H. Bloch (193–218) and A. H. M. Jones (17–37).

303 Montefiore, C. G. (d. 1938). *The Synoptic Gospels,* 2 vols., 2nd edn., London, 1927.

304 Morgenstern, J., *Some Significant Antecedents of Christianity,* Leiden, 1966.

305 Moulton, J. H. and Milligan, G., *The Vocabulary of the Greek Testament,* London, 1930 (reprinted 1972).

306 Muilenburg, J., 'The Son of Man', *JBL,* 79 (1960), 197–209.

307 Mylonas, G. E. (Archaeologist), *Eleusis and the Eleusinian Mysteries,* Princeton, NJ, 1961.

308 Neil, W. (Warden of Hugh Stewart Hall, Nottingham), *The Acts of the Apostles* (NCB), London, 1973.

309 Nestle, W., 'Die Haupteinwände des antiken Denkens gegen das Christentum', *Archiv für Religionswissenschaft,* 37 (1941–2), 51–100.

310 Nicol, W., *The Semeia in the Fourth Gospel,* Leiden, 1972.

311 Nilsson, M. P., *Greek Piety,* trans. H. J. Rose, Oxford, 1948.

312 Id., *The Dionysiac Mysteries of the Hellenistic and Roman Age,* Lund, 1957.

313 Nineham, Rev D. E. (Warden of Keble College, Oxford), 'The Jesus of History', in *Historicity and Chronology in the NT,* London, 1965, 1–18.

314 Id., *The Gospel of Mark* (The Pelican NT Commentaries), 1972.

315 Norden, E., *Agnostos Theos,* Berlin, 1913.

316 Oesterley, W. O. E., 'The Cult of Sabazios', in *The Labyrinth,* ed. S. H. Hooke, London, 1935, 115–58.

317 O'Neill, J. C. (Prof. of NT, Cambridge), 'The Silence of Jesus', *NTS,* 15 (1968–9), 153–67.

318 Origen (d. ca. AD 254), *Contra Celsum,* trans. with introduction and notes by H. Chadwick, CUP, 1965.

319 Pedersen, J. (Danish Semitic Scholar), *Israel. Its Life and Culture,* Copenhagen and London, 1926.

320 Perrin, N. (Prof. of NT, Chicago), *Rediscovering the Teaching of Jesus,* London, 1967.

321 Id., 'The Use of (para)didonai . . . in the NT', in *Der Ruf Jesu und die*

Antwort der Gemeinde, Festschrift for J. Jeremias, ed. E. Lohse, Göttingen, 1970, 204–12.

322 Pettazzoni, R. (ed.), *Sacral Kingship,* Contributions to the Central Theme of the Eighth International Congress for the History of Religions (Rome, April, 1955), Leiden, 1959; with papers by E. O. James (63–70) and Margaret Murray (595–608).

323 Petzke, G., *Die Traditionen über Apollonius von Tyana und das NT,* Leiden, 1970.

324 Pines, S. (Prof. at Jerusalem), *An Arabic Version of the Testimonium Flavianum and its Implications,* Jerusalem, 1971.

325 Plutarch (d. ca. AD 120), *De Iside et Osiride,* ed. J. Gwyn Griffiths, Univ. of Wales Press, 1970.

326 Popkes, W., *Christus Traditus,* Zürich and Stuttgart, 1967.

327 Purser, L. C., article 'Apotheosis', in *A Dictionary of Greek and Roman Antiquities,* ed. W. Smith (et al.), London, 1890.

328 Rahner, Fr. H. (Prof. of Church History, Innsbruck), 'The Christian Mystery and the Pagan Mysteries', in *The Mysteries* (Papers from the Eranos Yearbooks), ed. J. Campbell, NY, 1955, 337–401.

329 Rawlinson, Rt Rev A. E. J. (d. 1960), *The Gospel According to St. Mark,* Westminster Commentary, 5th edn., London, 1942.

330 Richardson, A. (Dean of York), *The Political Christ,* London, 1973.

331 Riddle, D. W., 'The Cephas–Peter Problem', *JBL,* 59 (1940), 169–80.

332 Ristow, H. and Matthiae, K. (eds.), *Der historische Jesus und der kerygmatische Christus,* 2nd edn., Berlin, 1962; with articles by E. Heitsch (62–86), J. Jeremias (12–25), W. Michaelis (317–30), W. Nagel (543–53) and R. Schnackenburg (439–54).

333 Roberts, C. H., *An Unpublished Fragment of the Fourth Gospel,* Manchester, 1935.

334 Robertson, J. M., *Jesus and Judas,* London, 1927.

335 Robinson, J. A. T. (Dean of Trinity College, Cambridge), *The Body. A Study in Pauline Theology,* London, 1952.

336 Id., *Honest to God*, London, 1963.

337 Id., criticism of JEC on television, 23 March, 1971.

338 Id., *The Human Face of God*, London, 1973.

339 Robinson, J. M. (Prof. of NT, Claremont), 'Basic Shifts in German Theology', *Int,* 16 (1962), 76–97.

340 Id., and Köster, H., *Trajectories Through Early Christianity*, Philadelphia, 1971 (includes no. 264 above).

341 Rowley, Rev H. H. (Prof. of Hebrew, Manchester, d. 1969), *The Servant of the Lord and Other Essays,* 2nd edn., Oxford, 1965.

342 Rylands, L. G. (d. 1942), *Did Jesus Ever Live?,* 2nd edn., London, 1936.

343 Sanders, J. T. (Assoc. Prof. of Religious Studies, Oregon), 'Paul's "Autobiographical" Statements in Gal.', *JBL,* 85 (1966), 335–43.

344 Id., *NT Christological Hymns*, CUP, 1971.

345 Sandmel, S. (Prof. of Bibl. Studies, Jewish Institute of Religion), *We Jews and Jesus,* London, 1965.

346 Schenke, H. M., article on Coloss. in *ZThK,* 61 (1964), 391–403.

347 Schille, G., 'Das Leiden des Herrn', *ZThK,* 52 (1955), 161–205.

348 Schmiedel, P. W. (Prof. of NT, Zürich, d. 1935), articles (a) Acts (b) Gospels (c) Lysanias and Theudas, in *Encyclopaedia Biblica,* ed. Cheyne and Black, London, 1903.

349 Schmithals, W. (Prof. of NT, Marburg), articles on 'Die Häretiker in Galatien' and on 'Paulus und der historische Jesus', *ZNW,* 47 (1956), 25–67 and 53 (1962), 145–60.

350 Id., *Paulus und die Gnostiker*, Hamburg-Bergstedt, 1965.

351 Id., *Paul and James*, trans. D. Barton, London, 1965.

352 Id., *The Office of Apostle in the Early Church*, trans. J. E. Steely, NY, 1969.
353 Id., *Die Gnosis in Korinth*, 3rd revised edn., Göttingen, 1969.
354 Schneemelcher, W., edn. of E. Hennecke, *NT Apocrypha*, trans. R. McL. Wilson et al., 2 vols., London, 1963–5.
355 Schoeps, H. J. (Prof. of History of Religion, Erlangen), *Paulus,* Tübingen, 1959.
356 Schottroff, L., *Der Glaubende und die feidliche Welt*, Neukirchen-Vluyn, 1970.
357 Scholem, G., *The Messianic Idea in Judaism,* London, 1971.
358 Schramm, Dr T., *Der Markus-Stoff bei Lukas,* CUP, 1971.
359 Schreiber, J. (Prof. of Bibl. Theology, Bochum), 'Die Christologie des Markusevangeliums', *ZThK*, 58 (1961), 154–83.
360 Schürer, E., *The History of the Jewish People in the Age of Jesus Christ,* a new English version ed. M. Black et al. vol. 1, Edinburgh, 1973.
361 Schulz, S. (Prof. of NT, Zürich), *Die Stunde der Botschaft,* Hamburg and Zürich, 2nd edn., 1970.
362 Schweitzer, A., *Geschichte der Leben-Jesu Forschung,* Tübingen, 1906.
363 Schweizer, E. (Prof. of NT, Zürich), *Erniedrigung und Erhöhung,* Zürich, 1955.
364 Id., 'Zur Herkunft der Präexistenzvorstellung bei Paulus', *Evangelische Theologie*, 19 (1959), 65–70.
365 Id., 'Mark's Contribution to the Quest of the Historical Jesus', *NTS*, 10 (1963–4), 421–32.
366 Id., *Das Evangelium nach Markus*, vol. 1 of no. 165 above, Göttingen, 1968.
367 Id., *Jesus,* trans. D. E. Green, London, 1971.
368 Scobie, Rev C. H. H., *John the Baptist,* London, 1964.
369 Selwyn, Very Rev E. G. (d. 1959), *1 Peter,* London, 1946.
370 Sherwin-White, A. N. (Reader in Ancient History, Oxford), *Roman Law and Roman Society in the NT,* OUP, 1963.
371 Id., 'The Trial of Christ', in *Historicity and Chronology in the NT*, London, 1965, 97–116.
372 Simon, U. (Prof. of Religious Studies, London), review of JEC in *German Life and Letters,* 26 (1972), 60–1.
373 Sjöberg, E., *Der Menschensohn im äthiopischen Henochbuch*, Lund, 1946.
374 Smith, Morton, 'Aretalogies, Divine Men, the Gospels, and Jesus', *JBL,* 90 (1971), 174–99.
375 Id., review of no. 324 above in *JBL*, 91 (1972), 441–2.
376 Sparks, H. F. D. (Prof. of Interpretation of Scripture, Oxford), *A Synopsis of the Gospels,* London, 1964.
377 Stauffer, E. (Prof. of NT, Erlangen), *Jerusalem und Rom im Zeitalter Christi,* Bern, 1957.
378 Steinseifer, B., 'Der Ort der Erscheinungen des Auferstandenen', *ZNW,* 62 (1971), 232–65.
379 Stockwood, Rt Rev Dr M. (Bishop of Southwark), review of JEC in *Books and Bookmen,* June, 1971, 52–3.
380 Strecker, G., 'Die Leidens-und Auferstehungsvoraussagen im Markusevangelium', *ZThK*, 44 (1967), 16–39.
381 Suggs, M. J., *Wisdom, Christology and Law in Mt.,* Cambridge (Mass.), 1970.
382 Tannehill, R. C., *Dying and Rising with Christ. A Study in Pauline Theology,* Berlin, 1967.
383 Taylor, Rev Dr V. (d. 1968), *Jesus and His Sacrifice,* London, 1937.
384 Id., *The Gospel According to St. Mark*, 2nd edn., London, 1966.
385 Teeple, H. M., *The Mosaic Eschatological Prophet*, Philadelphia, 1957.
386 Id., articles on 'The Son of Man Christology' and 'The Oral Tradition that Never Existed', in *JBL,* 84 (1965), 213–50 and 89 (1970), 56–68.
387 Thomas, J., *Le Mouvement Baptiste en Palestine et Syrie,* Gembloux, 1935.
388 Tilborg, S. van, *The Jewish Leaders in Mt.,* Leiden, 1972.
389 Tödt, H. E. (Prof. of NT, Heidelberg), *The Son of Man in the Synoptic Tradition,* trans. D. Barton, London, 1965.

390 Tokarew, S. A., *Religion in der Geschichte der Völke*, translated from the Russian, Berlin, 1968.
391 Toynbee, A. (ed.), *The Crucible of Christianity*, London, 1969, with articles by D. Flusser (215–34) and M. J. Vermaseren (253–60).
392 Toynbee, J., and Perkins, J. W., *The Shrine of St. Peter*, London, 1956.
393 Trilling, W., *Fragen zur Geschichtlichkeit Jesu*, 3rd edn., Düsseldorf, 1969.
394 Trocmé, E. (Prof. of NT, Strassburg), *La Formation de l'évangile selon Marc*, Paris, 1963.
395 Id., 'L'Explusion des marchands du temple', *NTS*, 15 (1968–9), 1–22.
396 Id., *Jesus and His Contemporaries*, trans. R. A. Wilson, London, 1973.
397 Vermaseren, M. J. (Prof. of Hellenistic Religion, Utrecht), *The Legend of Attis in Greek and Roman Art*, Leiden, 1966.
398 Vermes, G. (Reader in Jewish Studies, Oxford), *Jesus the Jew*, London, 1973.
399 Vielhauer, P. (Prof. of NT, Bonn), article 'Johannes der Täufer', in RGG.
400 Id., *Aufsätze zum NT*, Munich, 1965; includes 'Gottesreich und Menschensohn' (55–91), 'Das Benediktus des Zacharias' (28–46), and a criticism of F. Hahn's book, no. 192 above (141–198).
401 Wagner, G., *Das religionsgeschichtliche Problem von Römer 6:1–11*, Zürich and Stuttgart, 1962.
402 Walker, R., *Die Heilsgeschichte im ersten Evangelium*, Göttingen, 1967.
403 Walker, W. O., Jr., 'Postcrucifixion Appearances and Christian Origins', *JBL*, 88 (1969), 157–65.
404 Wellhausen, J., *Einleitung in die drei ersten Evangelien*, Berlin, 1905.
405 Wells, G. A., *The Jesus of the Early Christians* (abbreviated as JEC), London, 1971.
406 Id., 'The Myth of the Mushroom', *Humanist*, 86 (1971), 49–51.
407 Wetter, G. P., *Der Sohn Gottes*, Göttingen, 1916.
408 Wilson, R. McL., *Gnosis and the NT*, Oxford, 1968.
409 Windisch, H. (d. 1935), article on non-Christian testimonies to Jesus, *Theologische Rundschau, Neue Folge*, 1 (1929), 266–88.
410 Wink, W., *John the Baptist in the Gospel Tradition*, Cambridge, 1968.
411 Winter, P. (Czecho-Slovak lawyer, d. 1969), *On the Trial of Jesus*, Berlin, 1961.
412 Id., 'Tacitus and Pliny: The Early Christians', *Journal of Historical Studies*, 1 (1967), 31–40.
413 Witt, Dr R. E., *Isis in the Graeco-Roman World*, London, 1971.
414 Id., review of JEC, in *Journal of Hellenic Studies*, 92 (1972), 223–5.
415 Yamauchi, E. M. (Prof. of History, Ohio), 'Tammuz and the Bible', *JBL*, 84 (1965), 283–94.
416 Id., *The Stones and the Scriptures*, London, 1973.
417 Id., *Pre-Christian Gnosticism. A Survey of the Proposed Evidences*, London, 1973.
418 Young, F. W., 'Jesus the Prophet: a Re-examination', *JBL*, 68 (1949), 285–99.
419 Zahrnt, Dr H. (Theological editor of a German newspaper), *The Historical Jesus*, trans. J. Bowden, London, 1963.

Index of New Testament References

222

227

General Index

Some authors listed below are referred to in the text of this book only by the number allotted to them in the List of References (above, p. 208ff).

Babylon and Rome, 83, 94
Babylonians, religion of, 94, 183, 202
Bacon, B. W., 95, 159
Baird, W., 208
Bammel, E., 11, 198f
Baptism
    and Jesus, whether enjoined by him,
        19, 49, 185
        relation to his death and
            resurrection, 49, 50
    and regeneration, 50, 181
    and salvation, 49, 156f, 184, 203
    see also Jesus
Barabbas, 64, 166, 168, 171
Barclay, W., 1, 7, 12, 22, 24
Bar Cochba, 59, 142
Barnabas
    epistle of, 68-9, 118, 122, 133
    St., 128-9
Barnard, L. W., 42-3
Barrett, C. K., 11, 141
Bartimaeus, 117, 119
Bartsch, H. W., 67
Baruch, Syriac apocalypse of, 68, 195
Bauer, W., 145, 194
Beach, C., 62
Beare, F. W., 42, 44, 68, 77, 80, 136,
    162, 202
Bearman, H. V., 165
Beliefs, practical and other, 177-9, 193f
    see also Religion
Bell, H. I., 181, 190
Benjamin, Testament of, 197
Berger, K., 76
Best, E., 44, 46, 68
Bethany, 123, 134
Bethlehem, 5, 117, 119, 143-5, 147
Betz, H. D., 67, 109f
Bevan, E. R., 190, 209
Bishops, *see* Episcopacy
Bithynia, Roman province, 14, 42, 44
Black, M., 74, 146-7
Blank, J., 99
Blasphemy, 67, 89, 96, 142, 154, 165,
    175
Blinzler, J., 51, 172
Bloch, H., 201
Blood
    drinking of, 27
    and remission of sins, 46, 49, 158,
        197
    see also Sacrifice
Boers, H., 4
Bonnard, P., 95
Boobyer, G. H., 103
Boring, M. E., 66f, 149

Bornkamm, G., 12, 18, 29, 68, 74, 99,
    125, 142
Borsch, F. H., 210
Bouquet, A. C., 14f
Bousset, W., 4, 96
Bowden, J., 210
Box, G. H., 196
Brandon, S. G. F., 20-2, 57, 60, 64, 66, 79,
    94, 100, 166ff, 178, 181, 184f,
    196, 201-3
Branscomb, B. H., 95
Braun, H., 5, 26, 59, 66, 68
Brethren of the Lord, 21
    see also James
Brooks, W. E., 54
Brotherhoods, religious, 21, 23, 181, 193
    see also Societies
Bruce, F. F., 51, 66
Buddha, 189
Budge, E. A. W., 205
Bull, Mithra and, 185
Bultmann, R., 1, 7, 9, 26, 28-9, 93, 97,
    138, 150, 159, 192
Burger, C., 110, 118-20, 143
Burkill, T. A., 64, 69, 134, 138f, 157
Bury, J. B., 201

Cadbury, H. J., 88, 159
Caird, G. B., 4
Caligula, Emperor, 61, 81
Canon, NT, 40, 77
Capernaum, 72, 103, 149f
Carlston, C. E., 19, 107, 121, 131
Carmichael, J., 170-3
Catchword connections, 71, 80f, 84, 87
Celibacy in NT, 19
Celsus, 15, 16, 100, 181, 190, 202
Census decreed by Augustus, 147
Cephas
    appearance of risen Jesus to, 30, 32,
        37, 124
    faction at Corinth named after, 21
    leader at Jerusalem, 124
    Paul's criticism of, 21, 120
    see also Peter
Cerinthus, 48, 50
Chadwick, H., 16
Charles, R. H., 200, 203
Cheyne, T. K., 132
Christ
    hymns to, 37-9, 58, 101, 120
    title of, 14, 46, 52, 59, 110, 114, 175
Christ, F., 211
Christian, name of, 43, 62, 83

Drower, E. S., 191
Dungan, D. L., 66
Dunn, J., 23, 66
Dupont-Sommer, A., 121

Earth as goddess, 183, 202
Easter, 2, 56, 125, 188
Ecclesia, 74
    see also Regulations
Ecclesiasticus, see Sirach
Editing in NT, see Evangelists
Edwards, R. A., 39, 121
Egyptians, gospel of, 93
Eisler, R., 172
Elders, see Presbyter
Eleusinian Mysteries, 183, 202
Elijah, 52, 69, 104, 153-4, 156, 159, 162
Ellis, E. E., 88, 96, 153
Emperor, cult of, 14, 46, 62, 83, 94f, 190, 202
Encyclopaedia Biblica, 88, 96, 132, 148
Engels, F., 15
Engnell, I., 202
Enoch
    book of, 113, 116, 194, 196
    book of the Secrets of, 194
    Similitudes of 111, 121, 145, 198
Enslin, M. S., 132f, 139, 142
Enthusiasm, religious, 67, 99, 125f
Ephesians, NT epistle to, 17, 43, 45, 66
Ephesus, 127, 155, 183
Epictetus, 181, 202
Epiphanius, St., Bishop of Constantia, 146
Episcopacy, 44-5, 55
Eschatology
    in OT and Apocrypha, 111
    in NT, 48, 85, 148, 153, 174
    see also Judgement, Last Days, Parousia, Tribulation
Essenes, 121, 152, 195f
Ethics, see Morals
Eucharist
    pre-Christian, 185
    pre-Pauline 26, 37, 186
    see also Last Supper, Lord's Supper
Eusebius, Bishop of Caesarea, 11, 13, 59, 94
Evangelists
    as collectors, 70f, 77, 166f, 176
    deference to Jesus, 73f, 93
    as editors, 72f, 76, 82, 85, 87-9, 102, 107, 131, 139, 140-1, 148, 150f, 157f, 161, 168
Evans, C. F., 31, 94, 123, 157
Exegesis, Jewish, 39

Exodus
    book of, 50, 66
    from Egypt, 68, 188f
Exorcism, 147
    see also Demons
Explanation, requirements of, 2, 175, 205-6
Eye-witnesses of events recorded in NT, 50f, 68, 76, 78, 89f, 118, 168
Ezekiel, 165
Ezra, apocalypse of, 19, 68, 111, 113, 121, 145, 195, 197

Faith, importance of, 43, 45, 52, 63, 104, 150f
Farmer, W. R., 93-4
Fawcett, T., 5-6
Feneberg, R., 26, 188
Fig tree, cursed by Jesus, 16, 123, 158
Filson, F., 68
Finley, M. I., 12
Firmicus Maternus Julius, rhetorician, 177
Flesh
    of Jesus, 46, 48-9, 52, 54, 58, 69, 136, 159, 189
    Paul on, 58, 98
    and resurrection, 19, 159
Flusser, D., 197
Form-criticism, 70ff, 77, 81, 139, 167, 176
Frankfort, H., 181, 202
Fratres arvales, 21
Frazer, J. G., 178
Fraud, not to be imputed to early Christian writers, 40, 60, 140, 158, 162
Freed, E. D., 202
Frend, W. H. C., 68, 86
Fuller, R. H., 31, 33, 55, 182f

Galilee
    Jesus' ministry in, 71-2, 109, 116, 144, 151-3, 158-9
    Jesus' resurrection appearances in, 32, 67, 135f, 144
    see also Nazareth
Gallio, 65-6
Gamaliel II, Rabbi, 16, 92
Gardner-Smith, P., 43
Gärtner, B., 142
Genesis, book of, 54, 60
Gentiles, Christian mission to, 37, 78, 106, 108-9, 144
Georgi, D., 37

leader of Jerusalem Christians, 3, 11, 35, 65, 123-4, 141
son of Zebedee, 22, 78, 122, 136, 141
James, E. O., 178, 202
James, W., 24
Jamnia, 108
Jannaeus, Alexander, 198
Jensen, A. F., 180
Jeremiah, 27, 164
Jeremias, J., 2, 25-6, 28, 69, 74-6, 95, 164
Jericho, 69
Jerome, St., 49
Jerusalem
    Christians of, 22, 31, 34-6, 120, 123, 125, 127, 129f, 162
        their Christology, 21, 100, 165
    Council of, 65
    destruction of, AD 70, 17, 22, 79, 85, 88
        see also Temple
    Jesus' entry into, 87, 117-9, 123, 135-6, 168, 174
    Jesus' words on, 87f
    in Lk.–Acts, 32, 34, 128, 144
    the New, 129
    Pompey's capture of, 63 BC, 196
Jesse, 18
Jesus
    appearances after resurrection, 21, 26, 30-3, 37, 67
        see also Cephas, Galilee, Resurrection
    arrest, 25-6, 53, 92, 132-3, 137, 139, 165, 171
    ascension, 33, 110, 125
    baptism, 49, 52, 58, 103, 125, 128, 151, 156f, 185
    belief in, merit of, 37, 52, 150f
    betrayal, *see* Judas Iscariot
    biography, order of events of, *see* Mark
    birth and infancy, 4, 7-9, 15, 20, 97, 139, 143, 147, 151f, 155f, 159f
    blood, 26f, 49-51
        see also Blood
    brethren, 21f, 148, 150, 159
        see also James
    character, 1, 66, 100, 132, 159
    dates of supposed life, 1, 7, 18
        see also Crucifixion
    denial, *see* Peter
    descent into hell, 57
    disciples
        call of, 71, 93
        failure to understand him, 27, 102, 170
        see also Messianic secret

discourses, 29, 53, 79, 93, 192
    see also Catchword connections
family hostile to, 21, 148-9
stereotyped formulas concerning, 37-40
genealogies, 119
historicity
    importance of, 9, 206
    to be settled by rational enquiry, 3, 175
home, *see* Capernaum, Nazareth
on the Jewish law, 106-8, 129ff, 142
meekness, 22, 58, 66
miracles
    as authenticating him, 101
    origin of traditions concerning, 58, 99, 100
name, 52, 68
obedience, 38, 53-4, 66
obscurity, 58-9, 65, 97, 120, 149
sayings of the risen ascribed to the earthly, 28-9, 74, 76, 105, 114
    see also Regulations
second coming, *see* Parousia
sinlessness, 46, 48f, 53
suffering, 23, 25, 48, 51-2, 55, 58, 62, 66, 102, 115, 136, 148f, 152, 186, 189, 197
teaching
    as evidence of authority, 102, 108, 132, 149f
    not original, 1, 108
    not among earliest Christian traditions, 19, 45, 52, 58, 72
temptation, 53, 104
titles, 18, 195
transfiguration, 45, 67-8, 78
trial, 20, 53, 89, 92, 137, 145, 164f, 174f
see also Crucifixion, Fig tree, Flesh, Jerusalem, Last days, Last Supper, Logia, Messianic secret, Old Testament, Passion, Pre-existence, Resurrection, Sepulchre, Sermon on Mount, Temple
Jewish law, *see* Law
Jewish War (AD 66-70), 60, 79, 82, 92, 107, 170
Job, 52, 148
John
    apocalypse of, *see* Revelation
    the Baptist
        disciples of, 152, 154f, 156, 160, 173-4
        as Elijah, 153-4, 156, 159
        in gospels, 107, 145, 151ff, 160, 170

235

Lord's Supper, 25-7
   see also Last Supper
Love of neighbour, 46, 48, 108-9
Lucian, 15, 183, 203
Lührmann, D., 216
Luke, gospel of
   author, 22, 77, 93
   Christology, 109ff, 173
   date, 84, 88, 93
   sources, 89f, 95
   tendencies, 151, 168
   see also Acts of the Apostles
Luther, 2
Luz, U., 216
Lysander, 190

McArthur, H., 1
Maccabees, books of, 82, 95, 197, 203
Maccoby, H., 161-3, 166
McNeile, A. H., 84, 95
Magi, 107, 143
Malachi, book of, 153, 159, 164
Malchus, 91
Mandaeans, 191-2
Marcion, 127, 159, 190
Mark, gospel of
   author, 77
   Christology, 62, 64, 101ff, 137, 187
   date, 3, 15, 17, 73, 78ff, 94, 157, 165
   doublets, 78f
   geography in, 71, 78, 133, 144f
     see also Galilee
   gentile orientation of, 28, 74, 78, 80,
     144
   order of events in, 71, 81, 93, 138
     see also Pericopes
   place of origin, 79, 94
   sources, 77, 79, 176
Marshall, I. H., 37
Martin, R. P., 12-13, 22
Martyrdom, early Christian, 42, 44, 73, 137
   see also Persecution
Marxists on Jesus, 12, 15
Marxsen, W., 76
Mary, mother of Jesus, 7-8, 58, 110,
   147-8, 150, 152, 159f
Matthew, gospel of
   author, 77
   Christology, 68, 105ff, 125f
   date, 84ff
   use of OT, 106, 143
Mead, G. R. S., 199
Medawar, P. B., 16
Meekness, why stressed in gospels, 181f
Meeks, W. A., 66
Melito, St., Bishop of Sardis, 41-2

Menander, 190
Merrill, E. T., 14, 41-2, 44, 63, 68
Merz, A., 69
Messiah
   claimants of the office, 11, 89, 153
   death of, 34, 113, 170, 195, 197
   development of ideas concerning, 61,
     111ff, 143, 145, 188f, 192f, 197
   meaning of the word, 111
   suffering of, 38, 196f, 200
   titles of, 59, 146, 152, 156
   see also Aaron, Anointed, David,
     Elijah, Joseph, Joshua, Miracles,
     Moses, Resurrection, Samaritans,
     Son of man, Zealots
Messianic secret, 102-3, 119, 134, 142,
   145, 158, 168, 187
Metzger, B. M., 25, 31, 185
Meye, R. P., 126
Michaelis, W., 18
Milburn, R. L. P., 68
Millennium, 113
Miracles
   important in early Christian
     communities, 56, 101
   expected in Messianic times, 19, 66,
     99, 101
Missionaries, early Christian, 70f, 73, 82,
   100, 106, 110, 150, 169
Misunderstanding, important in development
   of religious ideas, 81
   see also Reinterpretation
Mithra, 15, 66, 185f
Moehring, H. R., 4
Mohammed, 2, 189, 206
Monotheism, Jewish and early Christian,
   181, 194f, 203
Montefiore, C. G., 87
Moore, G. F., 112f
Morals and religion, 9, 43, 181, 202
Morgan, R., 209
Morgenstern, J., 204
Moses as prototype of Messiah, 52, 66,
   68f, 153
Mountains, religious significance, 67
Muilenburg, J., 116
Murray, Margaret, 202
Mylonas, G. E., 202
Mystery Religions, 23-4, 67, 99, 162, 194,
   196, 202-3, 205
Mysticism
   characteristics of, 24, 180
   in early Christianity, 23-4, 37, 66, 95,
     148, 173
Myth, nature of, 6-9, 60, 177
   see also Beliefs

Nabat, 21
Nag Hammadi, 71
Nagel, W., 26
Nazarene, 16, 145-8, 157, 159
Nazareth, 3, 5, 18, 143ff, 157-8
Nazirite, 146-7, 157
Nazorean, 159
Neil, W., 4
Nero Emperor, 14, 41, 43
Nestle, W., 15
Nicodemus, 16, 122
Nicol, W., 217
Nilsson, M. P., 217
Nineham, D. E., 9, 30, 56, 68, 71f, 104, 137, 159, 164
Norden, E., 30

Oesterley, W. O. E., 194
Old Testament
    its prophecies of Jesus, 7, 29, 50, 61, 118, 132, 149, 164, 168-9, 182
    read at Christian worship, 118
    see also Scripture
Olives, Mount of, 80-1, 85, 135-6, 172
O'Neill, J. C., 11, 113
Origen, 16, 100
Osiris, 15, 66-7, 177, 181, 183-4, 196, 202-3, 205
Oxyrhynchus, logia of, 71, 150

Panthera, 15, 16
Papias, Bishop of Hierapolis, 77, 94, 139f
Parousia of Jesus, 94, 186
    elimination of, 90
    Paul on, 28-9
    postponement of, 68, 83-4, 87-9, 95-6, 153
    relation to his resurrection, 34, 115
    and Son of man logia, 106, 114-5
Paschal lamb, Jesus as, 50, 189
Passion of Jesus
    gospels on, 65, 110, 133ff
    as his 'obedience' to God, 38, 53
    Paul on, 19-20, 53, 187, 197
Passover, 13, 132-3, 134-5, 188-9
Pastoral epistles, 18, 45f, 56, 58, 61-3, 65, 67, 127
Paul
    Acts on, 17, 127-9
    assimilation of earlier Christian tradition, 37ff
    on 'boasting', 98, 100, 120
    conversion, 17, 34f
    and Jerusalem, 17, 21, 35f, 65, 128

on Jesus' biography, 18ff, 56, 97-8, 100, 109, 149, 163, 173, 197
on Jesus' character, 23, 66
on the Jewish law, 19, 35, 37, 66, 78, 98, 142
letters ascribed to
    authenticity, 17-18, 45
    whether composite, 17
    dates, 17-18, 45
    relation to gospels, 18ff
mysticism, 23-4
as persecutor, 34f, 67, 127, 141
as Pharisee, 66, 127, 142
on revelation, 29, 36, 127
speeches in Acts, 127-8
use of OT, 19, 29, 52
on wisdom, 38, 98
on women, 29, 67
    See also Damascus, Flesh, Gospel, Passion
Pedersen, J., 104
Pentateuch, 2
Pentecost, 182
Pericopes of gospels, 51, 70, 72, 133, 135
Perkins, J. W., 68
Perrin, N., 3, 25, 39
Persecution of early Christians
    by Jews, 73, 86, 91f, 106, 109, 127, 130, 142
    by Romans, 41-3, 45f, 55, 62, 68, 82, 106
    references to in Mk., 62, 76, 82-3, 136-7, 154
    elsewhere in NT, 43, 45f, 61, 73, 169, 189
Peter
    in Acts, 123, 174
    appearance of risen Jesus to, 32, 67
    denial of Jesus, 125, 133, 136-7, 139, 142, 189
    epistles of, 43-6, 51, 68, 77
    gospel of, 34, 68, 139
    one of the three intimates of Jesus, 78, 122, 136
    relation to Mk., 77, 94
    as the rock, 124-5
    speeches in Acts, 125, 127-8
    see also Cephas
Pettazzoni, R., 218
Petzke, G., 203
Pharaohs, 184, 190
Pharisees
    Jesus on, 74, 182
    in Mt., 85-7, 107-8, 121
    persecution of, 198
    position after AD 70, 108

and resurrection, 66
Philip the Evangelist, 110, 130
Philip, tetrarch, *see* Herod
Philo, 54, 60. 66, 194
Philostratus, 203
Phlegon, 13
Pilate, P., 3, 10, 13, 43, 45, 51, 70, 84, 104, 138, 167-9
    character, 60
    and Galileans, 171-2
    prefect, not procurator, 14
    silence of Paul concerning, 15, 19
    in post-Pauline NT epistles, 18, 45-6, 61, 101
    in other second-century literature, 58
    see also Barabbas, Crucifixion
Pillar passages, 148, 157
Pines, S., 10
Pleroma, 38, 195
Pliny, 14, 42, 44, 83
Plutarch, 66-7, 183, 185
Poimandres, 203
Polybius, 155
Polycarp, St., Bishop of Smyrna, 43, 45, 69, 78, 84, 92
Pompey, 185
Pontus-Bithynia, Roman province, 42
Popkes, W., 25f
Porphyry, 15
Preachers, early Christian, 70-2, 77, 84, 93, 138, 158
Pre-existence
    of Jesus, 18, 38, 52, 66, 92, 100, 103, 109, 110, 117, 156
    of Wisdom, *see* Wisdom
Presbyter, office of, 44, 63, 123, 127
Prophets
    early Christian, 28, 30, 66, 74, 76, 105, 114, 121, 149, 150, 152, 201
    false, 49, 101
    Jewish, 13, 28, 52, 69, 81, 100, 112, 151, 190
Proto-Luke, 20, 89
Proverbs, 105
Psalms, 53, 102, 111, 117f, 132, 135-6, 159, 182, 201
Pseudonymous works, 40, 68
Psycho-analysts on Jesus, 12, 15f
Purser, L. C., 190

Q, as hypothetical source, 39, 84, 87, 89, 90, 92-3, 95, 104-5, 110, 114, 116, 120-1, 129, 154
Quartodecimans, 188
Qumran, 29, 39, 121, 160, 173, 194
    see also Dead Sea Scrolls

Rabbinical literature, 12, 113, 159
    see also Talmud
Rahner, H., 24
Ramsay, W. M., 203
Rawlinson, A. E. J., 137
Reciprocity, ethical, 9, 181
Redeemers, non-Christian, 5, 191
    see also Saviour Gods
Regulations of Christian communities, ascribed to Jesus, 28, 73-4
Reimarus, H. S., 2
Reinterpretation of old documents and rites, 5, 49, 108, 111, 158, 178f, 182
    see also Misunderstanding, Ritual
Religion
    as basis of morality, 9, 23
    as consolation, 9, 180
    personal and tribal, 181
Rengstorf, K. H., 95
Resurrection
    on third day, 30f, 67, 115, 165
    of dead, 28, 31f, 66, 98
    and flesh, 19
    of pagan gods, 4, 162, 180f, 183-4, 195, 202
    of Messiah, 34, 113, 196
    of Jesus
        his appearances after, 21, 26, 30, 37, 67, 124, 144
        development of ideas concerning, 33f, 56, 128, 195
        form-critics' view of, 72
    see also Galilee, Sepulchre
Revelation, book of, 46, 82f, 129, 142
Richardson, A., 170
Riddle, D. W., 218
Rist, M., 68
Ritual
    reinterpretation of ancient, 178f
    relation to myth, 179
Roberts, C. H., 91
Robertson, J. M., 138, 142
Robinson, James M., 105
Robinson, John A. T., 6-9, 68, 206
Roland, 139
Rome, 41, 43-4, 58, 60, 79, 183
    see also Babylon
Rowley, H. H., 200, 203f
Russell, B., 131
Rylands, L. G., 169

Sabazius, 194
Sabbath, 36, 51, 93, 106, 108, 121, 149, 151
Sacraments, *see* Baptism, Eucharist